Why the Vote Wasn't
Enough for Selma

WHY THE VOTE WASN'T ENOUGH FOR SELMA

KARLYN FORNER

DUKE UNIVERSITY PRESS *Durham and London* 2017

© 2017 Duke University Press
All rights reserved
Printed in the United States of America
on acid-free paper ∞
Designed by Amy Ruth Buchanan and
Dan Ruccia. Typeset in Miller
by Westchester Book Group
Library of Congress Cataloging-in-
Publication Data
Names: Forner, Karlyn, [date] author.
Title: Why the vote wasn't enough for
Selma / Karlyn Forner.
Description: Durham : Duke
University Press, 2017. | Includes
bibliographical references and index.
| Description based on print version
record and CIP data provided by
publisher; resource not viewed.
Identifiers: LCCN 2017009233 (print)
LCCN 2017012717 (ebook)
ISBN 9780822372233 (ebook)
ISBN 9780822370000 (hardcover: alk.
paper)
ISBN 9780822370055 (pbk. : alk.
paper)
Subjects: LCSH: Selma (Ala.)—
History—20th century. |
African Americans—Suffrage—
Alabama—Selma—History—
20th century. | Selma (Ala.)—Race
relations—History—20th century.
Classification: LCC F334.S4 (ebook) |
LCC F334.S4 F67 2017 (print) | DDC
305.8009761/45—dc23
LC record available at https://lccn.loc
.gov/2017009233

Cover art: Woman carrying a sign
reading "No Committee Decides
Whether Our Votes Be Counted!
We Decide!!" during a protest in front
of the Dallas County courthouse.
Photograph by Jim Peppler. Courtesy
of Alabama Department of Archives
and History, Montgomery, Alabama.

CONTENTS

ILLUSTRATIONS

ABBREVIATIONS

AAA	Agricultural Adjustment Administration
ACES	Alabama Cooperative Extension Service
ADECRSA	Alabama Department of Education, Correspondence of the Rural School Agent
AFL	American Federation of Labor
AGG	Alabama Governor (Graves) Administrative Files
AME	African Methodist Episcopal
ANSC	Alabama New South Coalition
ASCD	Alabama State Council of Defense, Administrative Files
BBACC	Black Belt Arts and Cultural Center
BEST	Best Education Support Team
CWA	Civil Works Administration
DCIA	Dallas County Improvement Association
DCVL	Dallas County Voters League
EIS	Environmental Impact Statement
EOB	Economic Opportunity Board
GWC Homes	George Washington Carver Homes
JOBS	Job Opportunity for Basic Skills
LDF	Legal Defense Fund (Selma)
MOMS	Mothers of Many
NAACP	National Association for the Advancement of Colored People
NLRB	National Labor Relations Board
NRA	National Recovery Administration

NVRMI	National Voting Rights Museum and Institute
ODMA	Old Depot Museum Archives
OEO	Office of Economic Opportunity
PEST	Public Education Support Team
PWA	Public Works Administration
RFC	Reconstruction Finance Corporation
SCLC	Southern Christian Leadership Conference
SCU	Sharecroppers Union
SHAPE	Self-Help against Poverty for Everyone
SJ	*Selma Journal*
SMT	*Selma Morning Times*
SNAP	Supplemental Nutrition Assistance Program
SNCC	Student Nonviolent Coordinating Committee
ST	*Selma Times*
STJ	*Selma Times-Journal*
SUC	Selma University Catalogues
SWAFCA	Southwest Alabama Farmer's Cooperative Association
UNIA	Universal Negro Improvement Association
USDA	U.S. Department of Agriculture
USO	United Service Organizations
WPA	Works Progress Administration

ACKNOWLEDGMENTS

Kathryn Tucker Windham, one of Selma's renowned storytellers, used to tell people she was twice blessed. The line came from a poem by Jan Struther: "She was twice blessed. She was happy; She knew it." In writing this history, I have been twice blessed. Countless people have helped me along the way, offering guidance, a home-cooked meal, a thoughtful rewrite, a memory, or a willing ear to listen to yet one more story about Selma. This book would not be without their outpouring of love and support.

I fell in love with Selma over a decade ago, as a second-year student at the University of Wisconsin–Madison who went south on a civil rights bus trip. It was the "I Was There" wall at the National Voting Rights Museum and Institute on Water Avenue that first got me. As I walked through the museum's front door, to the left was a wall plastered with hundreds of Post-it notes. On these two-by-two-inch pieces of paper, participants in the voting rights campaign of 1965 had written one sentence about their contribution: "I cooked food for the marchers," "I marched from Selma to Montgomery," and even "I was a state trooper on Bloody Sunday." Later that day, Joanne Bland, the museum's director, guided our tour bus around Selma, narrating the street corners and buildings with her own stories of the movement. The week I spent organizing the museum's archives and learning about the unnamed people who made the movement happen changed the direction of my life.

I owe my beginnings as a historian to a warm and brilliant community of scholars at the University of Wisconsin–Madison. On that first trip to Selma, Steve Kantrowitz let me tag along with him and Danielle McGuire on a research trip to the reading room of the Alabama Department of Archives and History. Going through the boxes of yellowed correspondence, listening to the two of them piece together the Recy Taylor case, I felt as though I was in the presence of genius. At that moment I decided I wanted to be a historian. Steve, Christina Greene, Craig Werner, and Tim Tyson revolutionized my world, giving me a bottom-up framework with which to understand history and teaching me how to do solid research. Far beyond that, they showed me how being a scholar meant cultivating community both inside and outside of the classroom. The graduate students in the Department of Afro-American Studies, especially Charles Hughes, were an essential part of this education. Even though I was only an undergraduate, getting to witness the Harmony Bar Writers Collective in action made a lasting impression.

The unique brand of encouragement I received from Tim Tyson requires special recognition. On at least two occasions—first at the University of Wisconsin and then at Duke—I followed Tim's advice and ended up on crusades that were simultaneously the most stupid and intelligent things I have ever done. I now know that Tim's suggestions are not to be followed without due reckoning, but I am a stronger, more confident person for where they have taken me.

One of Tim's suggestions was that I move down south for a while and become a waitress. This was supposed to help me decide whether I really wanted to be a historian. Well, I didn't become a waitress, but I did pack up my little Geo Prizm and move to Selma after graduation. Thank the almighty that Joanne Bland was there to take me in. I walked into the back office of the National Voting Rights Museum one late spring day and confidently announced I was there to volunteer. All my thanks—and those of my parents—would never be enough to cover the generosity and kindness Ms. Anne extended to my earnest and naive twenty-one-year-old self. Since I come from the Upper Midwest, courtesy titles have never come naturally to me, except for Ms. Anne. She's a giant of a person whose devotion, care, and straightforwardness I aspire to match. The many others who moved in and out of the museum—Faya Rose (Sanders) Toure, Afriye We-Kandodis, Sam Walker, and James Bevel, among others—gave me an unparalleled education. Moving to Selma was like baptism by fire, and that half of a year working in the non-air-conditioned upstairs archives of the museum and living in Selma gave me daily lessons in William Faulkner's assertion that "the past is never dead. It isn't even past."

When I arrived at Duke University two years later to continue my journey toward Selma, I discovered that my people at the University of Wisconsin, the ones who had taught me so much about community, had learned many of those lessons themselves in Durham, North Carolina. When I first met my adviser—the eternally optimistic and unstoppable Bill Chafe—it felt as though I had come home. Bill has been my biggest advocate and cheerleader. He was the guardian of my best interests through graduate school, smoothing what could have been a jagged path. After six years and at least a hundred South African breakfasts together, Bill became more like family than an adviser. Twice blessed also applies to my good fortune at having not one but two advisers. Tim Tyson may be one of the world's greatest suppliers of vision, which he has done for me both as an undergraduate and as a graduate student. His warm spirit and insight have expanded what I considered within the realm of possibility.

I am forever indebted to the women on my committee, Adriane Lentz-Smith and Karin Shapiro. (For the record, my committee—Bill, Tim, Adriane, and Karin—is actually the best committee ever.) Both Adriane and Karin can admirably be described as covering all of the ground they stand on. I consider them my life coaches and will always be in awe of their fierce intellect. They are also dear friends. Adriane supplied sage advice and pop culture references in the midst of panic. She helped me see the forest when I felt hemmed in by trees and has pointed my writing in the right direction on numerous occasions. Karin, as she does with all her students, took on my research and writing as if it were her own. She invited me in as a semipermanent member of her senior thesis writing group, which was really a three-year workshop in writing, revising, and teaching. I have never met anyone who cares about and invests so much in their students, and my comrades and fellow Karin Shapiro admirers would agree. Rose Filler and Ryan Brown helped me find direction and sanity early on, and later, Jacob Tobia and Mary Tung offered thoughtful and practical suggestions. I could not have asked for better companions.

The community I found at Duke was vast. Among them, Bob Korstad and Charlie Thompson taught me much about how to be genuine in academic life. My faithful Dissertation Writing Month (DiWriMo) comrades—Dominique Dery, Darren Mueller, Matt Somoroff, and Paige Welch—made delightful company in our collective efforts to slog through yet another five pages of the chapters we were writing. Before that, my cohort in the Department of History helped me weather the early days of graduate school, especially Paige, Vanessa Freije, and Michael Stauch. I also appreciate the friendship of those who were ahead of me, Max Krochmal and Courtney Wait, Mitch Fraas, and Julia Gaffield, among many others.

Duke brought an abundance of amazing people into my life, but at the very top of that list is Darren Mueller. Much of my sanity—in graduate school, life, and otherwise—was thanks to our breakfasts at Elmo's and lunches at Q-Shack. The three years that we shared a kitchen wall showed me that living next door to one of your best friends is a godsend and a great time. Darren introduced me to my future partner, as well as to my adopted cohort in the music department, a phenomenal bunch of people whose ability to dance should not be underestimated.

For all of the people who helped me become the historian I am, this book would not exist without Selma and the people who live there. The story I tell in the following pages is probably not the one that many people in Selma would want told. Whichever way you look at it, the political and economic history of Dallas County doesn't offer much in the way of prosperity, harmony, and success. The fact is that the Alabama Black Belt has been left behind, again and again and again, in so many ways. But that sad story is not a reflection on the many wonderful people I met in Selma. These warm and generous people overwhelmed me with their kindness. They helped me find places to stay, gave me the telephone numbers of folks I needed to talk to, invited me to sit in their pews on Sunday morning, and brought me into their lives.

Nearest to my heart is the splendid staff at the Selma Public Library; they make magic happen every day. Every time I walked through the doors, there was always a smiling face saying hello and asking how I was doing; they were ready to chat about anything from microfilm and mystery novels to granola bars and faith. Director Becky Nichols carefully tends this oasis, greeting every single person as if she was waiting especially for them. She was my sounding board, listening to what I had unearthed and comparing it to her own wealth of knowledge and personal experience. Local history librarian Anne Knight did the same. I looked forward to her regular appearance in the microfilm room to make sure I knew some of the best details of Selma's history. While their intellectual generosity sustained my work, Friday afternoon sessions at the "Faith Table" with Becky and Jan Parker, the inspiring, eternally optimistic children's librarian and book club leader, sustained my soul. This loving group welcomed me into their homes and hearts, and I count them as dear friends. My thanks also go to the rest of the library staff, including Crystal Drye, Denunta Dial, Joanie Looney, Mary Morrow, and Stephen Posey.

Another special thanks goes to the people at St. Paul's Episcopal Church, who adopted me even though I wasn't an Episcopalian. From Wednesday morning breakfasts to Christmas tree hunting, the St. Paul's folks were my community. David and Betsy Powell, Harry and Molly Gamble, Bill and Bunny Gamble, Urban and Kay Friday, Ed and Sandy Green, and far too many others for me to name kept me tied into the happenings of Selma. Nancy Bennett guided me along my way and always made sure I knew that I had a place to stay when I came "home" to Selma. The Rev. Joe Knight was my biggest advocate, right behind his wife, Anne, who was my guide at the library. Beyond being living encyclopedias of Selma's history, Joe and Anne continue to be some of my favorite people to spend an evening with. To the many other people in Selma who warmly accepted me, even though I was only the next in a long line of graduate students writing about their history, know that I consider myself twice blessed because of you.

When I finished graduate school, I started working as project manager for the Student Nonviolent Coordinating Committee (SNCC) Digital Gateway Project. Although I had my historian credentials in hand, the last part of my education has come through this unprecedented, inspiring, and crazy collaboration of movement veterans, historians, archivists, and students. The SNCC folks, especially Charlie Cobb, Judy Richardson, Courtland Cox, and Maria Varela, made me feel inspired by and accountable to the history, a much-needed injection of hope after six years of graduate school. Kaley Deal, Todd Christensen, and the members of the project team supplied three years of comradeship in collaborative writing, strategizing, and jokes about movement history that wouldn't be funny to anyone else. Kaley, Emilye Crosby, Hasan Jeffries, John Gartrell, Naomi Nelson, and Wesley Hogan gave valuable support in the far-reaching undertaking of "herding cats," as Judy would say. But, most directly related to this book, working on this project has been like a three-year master class in storytelling with SNCC veteran and journalist Charlie Cobb. Charlie taught me how to tell a story.

A special thanks to the people at Duke University Press who made this book a reality, especially Gisela Fosado, Lisa Bintrim, Amy Buchanan, and Dan Ruccia. It's been an amazing opportunity.

Then there are those who supported me well before I had ever heard of Selma or came to write this book. Kim Eisenreich, Lynette Faber, Laura (Omann) Kerttula, Kerry Plath, Melissa Schorn, Mandy (Johnson)

Steffens, Nicole (Zieglmeier) Willis, and Kayla Wenker have been keeping me grounded for the last two decades. They are the most solid and phenomenal group of friends, and their unwavering presence reminds me of who I am and where I come from. Two other unexpected, lifelong friends—Terri Evans and Jean Mackey—came from my time working at the Champlin Park High School library, and they helped me become an adult with a strong dose of hilarity.

I want to express the deepest of thanks to my parents, Mike Forner and Ann Forner, for having faith in me. I will forever owe you for standing by me when I, in my confident twenty-one-year-old wisdom, stubbornly insisted on moving to the Alabama Black Belt. I regret that the only time you came to visit Selma was during that 103-degree week in August and that I can now never convince you to return. I could not have made this journey without your constant support. Know that I admire you both greatly and am the luckiest to have such fine parents. Thanks also to my siblings, Becki (Forner) Baker and Chad Forner, for reminding me that caring so much about history is weird. And thanks to my grandparents, Ray and Lois Forner, who were always checking to see whether I had started talking southern yet.

And, last, to my husband, Tim Hambourger, I could not have done this without you. Few others would spend afternoons driving down back roads deep in the rural areas of the Alabama Black Belt or taking road trips across the South with a microfilm reader wedged in the backseat. You have listened to more Selma stories than anyone should have to. You have brainstormed with me through my ruts. You have put up with bad jokes about naming our baby Selma (which we didn't). I could not have done any of this without you. Here is to a long and saner life ahead.

Map 1 Alabama Black Belt

Map 2 Dallas County

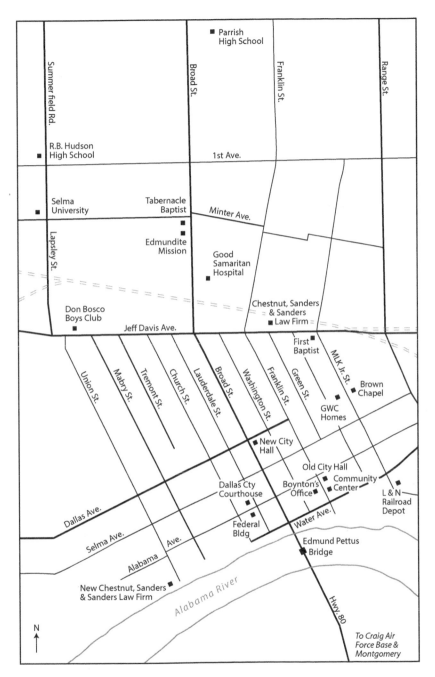

N

Map 3 Selma

Introduction

The hard wooden pews of Brown Chapel African Methodist Episcopal (AME) Church teemed with people on March 4, 2007, as the crowd waited for Barack Obama to ascend the pulpit. It was early in the presidential campaign of 2008, and the African American senator from Illinois was facing New York senator and former first lady Hillary Clinton in a fight for the Democratic nomination. President Bill Clinton and his wife had earned much respect from black Americans during his years in office, and Senator Obama's success hung on his ability to convince black voters that he was a worthier candidate than his formidable opponent. He chose Selma, Alabama, as the place to make that claim.

Rewind the scene forty years to January 2, 1965. The throng inside Brown Chapel looked hauntingly similar. Martin Luther King Jr., standing above a sanctuary jammed with local black residents, described Selma as a symbol of bitter resistance to civil rights in the Deep South. On that dark winter night, he named the city the new national battleground for voting rights, and African American residents of the Black Belt tightened the laces of their marching shoes in agreement. Two months later, shocking footage of white state troopers beating peaceful black marchers interrupted nightly television broadcasts. "Bloody Sunday," as the horrific event became known, catapulted Selma and black demands for the ballot into the national spotlight. The Voting Rights Act of 1965 became law that August, finally guaranteeing all Americans the right to vote. The legislation was christened in Washington, but it had been born in the streets of Selma.

On the forty-second anniversary of Bloody Sunday, Obama endeavored to link his candidacy to the civil rights movement. Speaking from the same pulpit where King had spoken, he declared himself one of the Joshua generation—a biblical reference signaling the cohort of doers and creators who follow in the footsteps of the visionary Moses generation. He proclaimed, "I'm here because somebody marched. I'm here because y'all sacrificed for me. I stand on the shoulders of giants." There in Selma, Obama sank his roots into the victorious legacy of the civil rights movement and positioned himself as the candidate who would continue its fight against injustice and oppression.[1]

Decades before Obama mounted that pulpit, Selma had been consecrated as a pivotal milestone in the grand arc of U.S. history. In the collective memory of the nation, Selma represents the triumphal moment of black nonviolent protest and the fulfillment of the promises of American democracy.[2] But the city Obama visited, first as a senator in 2007 and then again eight years later as the nation's first black president, bore little resemblance to this shining image.

As one drives westward from Montgomery, the four-lane Highway 80 is the freeway of the Black Belt, picking up the path of Interstate 85 after it comes to an end in Alabama's capital city. The fifty-mile journey cuts through the gentle hills of Lowndes County, revealing lazily grazing cattle in fields that once sprouted cotton. Abandoned gas stations with barred windows, rusted industrial buildings, and empty, gutted houses on what used to be Craig Air Force Base dot the final miles to Selma. From the crest of the Edmund Pettus Bridge, high above the Alabama River, the downtown comes into view. The vacant Tepper's building—once a thriving department store—towers over the surrounding businesses on Broad Street. The clothing stores and wholesale businesses that had made Selma the trading center of the western Black Belt closed up shop decades ago. Most of the bustle in downtown now centers around the intersection of Alabama Avenue and Broad Street, where the public library is one of the most integrated institutions in town. Across the street, the Downtowner, a classic meat-and-three restaurant, serves sweet tea and a catfish special on

Fridays, while the nearby Carter Drug Company still delivers prescriptions packaged in signature green bottles to the front doors of Selma's residents.[3]

To the north and east of downtown—in the historically blacker and poorer sections of the city—boarded-up buildings and abandoned houses mix with weary-looking homes whose porches have started to lose their struggle against gravity. Payday loan stores testify to how hard it is for poor people to scrape by, week after week. Meanwhile, the high school cashiers working the checkout lines at the Winn-Dixie grocery store are experts at Supplemental Nutrition Assistance Program (SNAP) cards, the payment method for the federal food assistance program. Walmart is the best shopping option in town nowadays; the Dollar General or one of the other discount stores lining Highway 14 would be the next possibility. Employment is hard to come by, and good-paying jobs are even rarer. Meanwhile, the public schools, with the exception of one elementary school on the wealthier and whiter western side of town, are almost entirely black, while nearly every white child attends the private John T. Morgan Academy or Meadowview Christian School. The Selma Country Club, showcase of wealth and segregation during the twentieth century, still does not admit black members.

The Selma that Obama paid homage to visibly and unmistakably told a story at odds with the triumphal legacy of voting rights. The black mayor sitting in office and the other African Americans serving in local government were a testament to just how much voting rights had transformed Alabama politics. Black residents could trace the paved city streets, higher graduation rates, early childhood education programs, and indoor plumbing to their gradual inclusion into the city in the years after the movement. But the numbing unemployment, gutted houses, and SNAP cards attested to barriers left unbroken by the passage of the Voting Rights Act of 1965. In the symbolic birthplace of the voting rights movement, those very rights had failed to bring economic opportunities and justice for African Americans.

This is a story of how and why the celebrated political legacy of Selma appears worlds apart from the dismal economic realities of the Alabama Black Belt. The question at its center: why was the right to vote not enough to bring economic justice to African Americans in the Black Belt? The answer requires, most important, an understanding of Selma as a place, not just a moment in time. When Selma became a symbol of the voting rights movement, everything before and after those brief months in 1965 vanished as quickly as spilled lemonade on hot Alabama asphalt in August.

Making Selma a narrow story of voting rights erases how white supremacy and agricultural and industrial development operated hand in hand throughout the entire twentieth century to keep African Americans from the full citizenship they had fought for, one comprising political rights as well as economic opportunities. The story that follows begins in 1901, the year the newly passed Alabama constitution took the ballot away from black citizens, and ends in 2000, when Selma's residents elected their first black mayor. It traces political and economic changes in Dallas County and the wider Alabama Black Belt, changes that were both national and regional developments as well as intensely local stories shaped by white citizens' concerted attempts to maintain a status quo that, above all, preserved their power.

The fight that generations of African Americans waged for full citizenship and justice in Selma unfolded alongside a century-long transformation in the agricultural economy of the Black Belt. African Americans' demands for economic opportunity, self-sufficiency, quality education, and political representation reflected and responded to drastic changes in the economic realities that structured daily life.[4] The civil rights movement came into its own at exactly the moment that cattle usurped cotton's reign over fields across the Alabama Black Belt, a takeover that sounded the death knell for the meager livings black tenant farmers had eked out on the land. The triumphal story of Selma, the one that emerged in the aftermath of the movement in 1965, rings true only if one focuses singularly on voting rights and ignores African Americans' parallel demands for economic opportunity and justice.

Placing the black freedom struggle and economic transformation side by side makes clear how voting rights could not counteract the vanishing of small farms and the arrival of low-wage jobs—and too few of them, at that—that replaced farmwork in the years after World War II. Meanwhile, local white officials fought tooth and nail to maintain political control in the wake of the civil rights movement. Their calculated intransigence effectively staved off meaningful participation by black residents in the economic and political life of Selma. The rise of the Sunbelt South and globalization further siphoned resources away from the struggling Black Belt in favor of the educated, skilled, and urban.[5] Voting rights—or even black political power—could not remedy decades of unequal investment in black communities by local, state, and federal governments.

A hundred-year vantage point explains why the movement for voting rights, one that shook the rural Black Belt and nation alike, failed to achieve the opportunity and justice local black residents had envisioned. The close-up lens of a local study reveals how local and national politics and enormous economic shifts played out in the lives of those who called the Alabama Black Belt home. Each of those people has stories that could fill pages of their own. What follows lays out the world within which they made their lives.

The Constitution of 1901

Nothing symbolized how much the Civil War had transformed the order of daily life in Dallas County more than the promising political career of Jeremiah Haralson, the former slave of a young Selma attorney. Haralson had been born into bondage near Columbus, Georgia, and sold twice before traveling the well-worn path to the Alabama Black Belt in 1859 at the age of thirteen. Founded in 1818, Dallas County was an area of fertile farmland a thousand miles square that tripled in population during its first two decades. The slave-trading season started on September 1 and continued through April 1 each year. Traders brought thousands of enslaved men and women from other parts of the South to be sold at the three-story wooden auction house in Selma. There, the crowd of well-off white men in the sitting room surveyed their potential purchases before buying slaves to labor in their cotton fields. More cotton came from Dallas County's soil in the antebellum period than from anywhere else in Alabama, which made its white planters some of the most powerful men in the state. By the time the Selma attorney purchased Haralson, 1,280 slaveholders in Dallas County owned 25,760 black men, women, and children.[1]

When the Civil War ended, Haralson decided to make good on his new freedom in Selma.[2] He taught himself to read and built a reputation off of his sharp tongue and quick wit. The famed abolitionist Frederick Douglass once declared that Haralson had "humor enough in him to supply a half dozen circus clowns."[3] During the years of Reconstruction, the federal government actively protected black southerners' civil rights, those guaranteed by the Fourteenth and Fifteenth Amendments. This enforcement helped Haralson achieve his first political victory: votes cast by newly freed men elected him to the Alabama House of Representatives in 1870. Then in 1872 he won a place in the state senate.[4]

But Haralson's political flair and flamboyant personality sometimes landed him in trouble. His opponents accused him of taking bribes and stealing bales of cotton. After he championed a bill pushing for "equal and impartial enjoyment of any accommodation" in transportation, public parks, and schools, an Alabama newspaper labeled him as "feared more than any other colored man in the legislature in Alabama."[5] This likely had something to do with Haralson's penchant for goading white Democrats about their racial anxieties. He once joked that he would not give a white woman a second glance—unless, of course, she happened to be rich. Haralson's fiery personality helped him win election to the U.S. House of Representatives in 1874, the crowning achievement of his political career.[6]

During Reconstruction, newly enfranchised African American voters elected black Republican and independent representatives, like Haralson, to state legislatures and county courthouses across the Black Belt. For white Democrats accustomed to controlling local politics, a black judge issuing decisions from the county courthouse seemed akin to anarchy. White planters and merchants viewed the southern ascendancy of the Republican Party as illegitimate, contrived by outsiders on northern terms. The brazen and self-confident manner of someone like Haralson only confirmed their suspicions. As the *Chicago Daily Tribune* suggested, white Democrats would have preferred "to see the Devil himself in Congress rather than Haralson."[7]

But while black politics set the terms of the post-emancipation period, white supremacy determined its tenor. Amid cries of "Negro domination," the Black Belt's prominent white men pledged to redeem Alabama from black rule and return the Democratic Party to power. By 1877 the federal government had forsaken its attempts to protect black southerners, and white Democrats turned to policing the ballot boxes as a means to regain power.[8] Split votes, electoral fraud, and threats were the shoals on which Haralson's career ended. From 1876 onward, white Democrats tampered with polling inspectors and vote counts, effectively preventing the black legislator from winning any future campaigns for reelection. The all-too-common practices of intimidation, fraudulent tallies, and outright violence caused thousands of black citizens to forfeit their ballots. When Haralson contested his loss to his opponent, the former white sheriff of Dallas County, in 1878, an armed mob chased him down between Montgomery and Selma and ordered him to leave the state.[9]

Black Belt Democrats could not rest easy in their political offices, however, as long as the African American majority back home retained the right to vote. During the 1890s, political alliances between poor whites and black Republicans threatened the rule of the Democratic Party and its rallying cry of white supremacy.[10] Half of Alabama's counties voted Populist during the 1890s, and only rampant ballot tampering in the Black Belt prevented Populist leader Reuben Kolb from gaining the governorship in 1892 and 1894.[11] Similar battles unfolded across the South.

Southern Democrats, beginning in Mississippi in 1890, responded to this threat by calling constitutional conventions where they used stricter qualifications to purge undesirable elements from the voter rolls. A litany of restrictions—poll taxes, property requirements, grandfather clauses, and good-character tests—barred thousands of black and poor white citizens from southern ballot boxes. The state-sponsored racial segregation of the Jim Crow era grew from these legislative gatherings. The turn of the century marked a new era of repression for black southerners.[12]

In April 1901 Alabamians went to the polls to decide whether the state should follow in the footsteps of other southern states. Leading up to the vote, the Dallas County Democratic Executive Committee argued that a vote in favor of the constitutional convention was a white man's only option.[13] Large numbers of black citizens also cast their ballots at the courthouse that day. It seems unlikely that they would have supported a convention aimed so publicly at their own disfranchisement, but the returns nonetheless came back overwhelmingly in favor. A slate of six local white Democrats—Benjamin Craig, Henry F. Reese, John Burns, Watkins Vaughan, P. Henry Pitts, and L. W. Grant—traveled to Montgomery to represent Dallas County in the convention.[14]

Throughout the thick, stifling Alabama summer, delegates gathered in Montgomery to remove black men from politics once and for all. Three months of fiery convention debates revealed the delegates' abiding but often clashing regional loyalties. Black Belt politicians enjoyed extraordinary political influence in the state, and they arrived committed to purging the black majorities in their home counties from the voting rolls. Joining them were the Birmingham industrialists, bankers, and railroad elites, known as the Big Mules, who were concerned with the threat poor white voters posed to their political reign. During the 1890s, farmers in the foothills of the Appalachians and the eastern wiregrass region had challenged white Democratic rule by throwing their support behind the Farmers' Alliance and the Populist Party. Delegates from those regions aligned against the allied Black Belt and business delegates, who, under the banner of white supremacy, could not openly advocate barring white men from the vote.[15]

After days of fierce and contentious debate, the proposed terms of suffrage included everything from long residency requirements and poll taxes to property ownership and literacy tests.[16] Black Belt delegates left no question about their racial motivations during the proceedings. "I do not propose to put my people under the hand of Negro rule because it [poll tax] might disfranchise one or two bastards in the white counties of Alabama," Dallas County attorney Henry F. Reese declared. "When you pay $1.50 for a poll tax, in Dallas County, I believe you disfranchise ten Negroes." In his estimation, losing a few poor white voters because of the poll tax was a worthwhile sacrifice to stave off black political domination. Reese also reminded delegates that local Black Belt officials "have been the bulwark of the safety of this government." "We have actually been charged with engaging in fraudulent practices in the matter of elections," he went on, "but there has never been a man . . . that has ever refused to accept the benefits of whatever little irregularities that might have occurred."[17] Populist-leaning delegates stood little chance against the combined power of the Black Belt planters and the Big Mules. The new constitution, adopted in early September, contained suffrage requirements strict enough to quell any remaining threats to white elite Democratic control.[18]

Dallas County Democrats drummed up support in mass meetings and political gatherings outside street-corner shops in the weeks before the November ratification vote.[19] Scores of African American men went to the polls that day as well, rejecting their own disfranchisement in what appeared to be the very last vote of their lives. But the editors of the *Selma Morning Times* were not concerned and predicted Dallas County's inevitable endorsement of the constitution.[20] It helped that vote tallying lay in the dependable hands of the county officials, all of whom were white Democrats and half of whom had represented the Black Belt during the convention.

The final count returned a landslide in favor of the constitution: 8,125 votes for and 235 against.[21] Similar returns came from across the Black

Belt, but Dallas County returned the largest majority for ratification.[22] That white voters made up only 20 percent of registered voters made no difference.[23] Even if every registered white man voted for ratification, 5,601 black men would have had to cast their ballot for their own disfranchisement. The arithmetic was shaky, but Black Belt counties vehemently rejected accusations of fraud in the election's aftermath. Whether they were honest or not made no difference, and the new constitution passed by a slim margin produced by enormous Black Belt majorities.[24] Governor William Jelks proclaimed that the new constitution of 1901 would go into effect on Thanksgiving Day, and white Democrats rejoiced.[25]

Even though the political death knell had sounded for black voters, the gritty work of purging the voting rolls lingered. Black men were not willing to give up their political voice so easily. In February 1902, 587 black voters along with 1,405 whites made their first poll tax payments. Each poll tax paid by black citizens marked a protest against Alabama's new political order. The county board of registrars then stood as the second line of defense against "the corrupt negro vote."[26] The new constitution gave the three county registrars almost limitless discretion, free from "any penalty for misuse of that power," in deciding which voters were qualified and which were not.[27] Selma's newspapers praised the good sense of Dallas County registrars as potential black voters met rejection. But with so much at stake, the white elite remained vigilant. When one unacceptable black voter qualified for lifetime registration, the *Selma Morning Times* issued a scathing reminder to the registrars. "The eyes of the state are upon you," the editors warned. "As Dallas goes so goes the Black Belt. Think, Think, Think." By the end of July, only 61 African Americans remained on the voting rolls in Dallas County compared to 2,230 white men.[28]

White Democrats felt little remorse. "Dallas county people have done a great many things politically that they were sorry to be compelled to do," noted the *Selma Morning Times*, "but they would repeat them without compunction ad finitum [*sic*] if it was necessary to maintain white supremacy in the state."[29] Three decades earlier, black representative Haralson had seen which way the winds were blowing. "The Democratic party, if they got power," he warned, "would inaugurate slavery in a new form; not such as it was, but by depriving us of our right to vote. . . . The gentlemen who used to own us would represent us."[30] Haralson's predictions proved hauntingly accurate. By the beginning of the twentieth century, a new legally backed age of white supremacy had dawned in the Alabama Black Belt.

CHAPTER

1

≡

The World That Cotton Made

1901–1916

Selma was a small but bustling town, perched high on the banks of the Alabama River. The wide, murky waters meandered west from the state capital of Montgomery through the Black Belt and Dallas County before making their way down to the Gulf city of Mobile. Home to 8,713 residents in 1900, Selma was the county seat and the hub of Black Belt agriculture. It was, according to the *Selma Morning Times*, "a cotton town." The white, fleecy bolls ran the local economy, and cotton's annual cycle forged an inseparable relationship between the wider county and the city.[1]

At the turn of the century, cotton supplied the direct or indirect livelihood of almost all of Dallas County's 54,657 residents: black tenants produced the year's crop; white landlords, wholesalers, and merchants made their business in its trade; and black servants and draymen and white industrial workers labored for the wages it supplied. Neither agriculture nor demographics had changed much in the forty years since the Civil War. In 1900, 83 percent of Dallas Countians were black, and most were bound to the cotton fields under tenant contracts.[2]

White supremacy—the interlocking system of political, economic, and social control that protected white privilege—had long governed life in rural Dallas County. White landlords, wholesalers, and merchants dictated the terms, under which black men and women worked the fields for nearly nothing. Racial customs, enforced with violence when necessary, kept black tenants in their place. Along with cotton's ongoing dominion, the rise of Jim Crow, with its state-sanctioned legal segregation and disfranchisement, marked a new era for white supremacy at the start of the twentieth century. These developments further cemented the grossly unequal economic relationship between black and white Dallas Countians.

African Americans responded to the barrage of attacks by mobilizing their own resources. Building off of traditions of landownership, education, and self-sufficiency, black residents forged a semiautonomous world within the dictates of Jim Crow segregation. Selma University, the educational institution of the Alabama Colored Baptists, helped create a strong black middle class made up of doctors, educators, undertakers, business owners, and tradespeople. Churches, fraternal lodges, and benevolent societies offered support to black men and women, and small corner groceries and shops bound neighbors together. As their legal and political rights shrank, African Americans turned inward to protect their communities and foster black economic and social independence in whatever ways they could.

A Cotton Town

"The hopes of a whole year are tied up in a cotton crop, and when the first boll bursts open and its white silken fibre is exposed to the morning sun, a whole section is awakened into life," proclaimed the *Selma Morning Times*. It was August 1903, and the newspaper was anticipating the opening of the year's cotton season.[3] Water Avenue, the main street of Selma, was where the buying and selling of cotton and goods took place. Despite its proximity to the Alabama River, clouds of dust still billowed behind streetcars and mule-drawn wagons, and stray cotton lint perpetually hung in the air. Wholesale establishments, commission houses, and cotton warehouses lined both sides of the bustling street. Nine wholesale grocery establishments, including R. H. and W. C. Agee Company, V. B. Atkins and Company, and C. W. Hooper and Company, garnered recognition throughout the Black Belt. Salesmen from the wholesale companies traveled through the surrounding counties, selling goods to the hundreds of crossroad clapboard stores and plantation commissaries dotting the countryside.

1.1 Horse-drawn carts drive up and down a dusty Water Avenue in Selma, 1904.
Courtesy of Alabama Department of Archives and History, Montgomery, Alabama.

Potholed dirt roads and limited transportation made the country stores the main source of goods for rural customers, and, with the help of whole-sale merchants, they stocked everything from ribbons and coffee to kerosene oil.[4] The trade area of Selma's wholesalers extended throughout the entire Black Belt, sixteen counties in a hundred-mile radius.[5]

Wholesale merchants had cotton to thank for both their profits and their influence. In addition to selling goods, wholesalers doubled as commission merchants and cotton buyers. Landowners needed the annual profits of cotton to buy supplies and necessities and extend credit to their tenants, and wholesale merchants brought the complementary roles of cotton buying and grocery selling under one roof.[6]

Sharecropping had first emerged after the Civil War. Along with com-pletely upending the South's defining institution, four years of war had devastated the region's towns and farmlands.[7] Landowners still needed the now-freed people to grow cotton, so they contracted with black tenants to live on and work their land each season. Landowners then turned to merchants for credit, a necessity in the cash-strapped region. Advancing merchants or plantation commissaries would furnish tenants with seeds and supplies to make the crop. Settlement came at harvest time each fall. Tenants turned over the bales from their summer's work to the advancing

1.2 Men stand around cotton bales in front of the Erhart Cotton Warehouse on Water Avenue in Selma, 1904. Courtesy of Alabama Department of Archives and History, Montgomery, Alabama.

merchant or landlord, who then, in turn, brought the cotton to a cotton buyer or to the wholesale house with which they carried credit.[8] Selma's wholesale establishments were known to charge 15 percent to advance credit and goods to merchants and plantation commissaries. People lived on borrowed money all year long, and the only payday in Dallas County came when the cotton was ready in the fall.[9]

As the cotton gins across the county cranked into gear each September, Selma's streets sprang to life. Droves of cotton-laden wagons crowded the warehouses and compresses.[10] Wholesale merchandising establishments worked late into the night. At M. Meyer and Company, clerks finalized purchases of cotton from farmers who had traveled long distances, while laborers unloaded the crop from the wagon and replaced it with provisions bought for the next year.[11] A short distance away, the Dallas Compress Company packed the bales into smaller parcels, which were then stored in warehouses, like Erhart's, before being sold to buyers at the Selma Cotton Exchange.[12]

Directly south of Water Avenue, the wharfs on the Alabama River overflowed with cotton bales. A storefront on the southern side of Selma's main

1.3 Black laborers load goods onto a steamboat on the Alabama River in Selma, with cotton bales piled nearby, ca. 1900. Photograph by Peter Brannon. Courtesy of Alabama Department of Archives and History, Montgomery, Alabama.

street gave wholesale merchants direct access to the wharf from the back of their establishments.[13] There, black draymen loaded thousands of bales onto steamers like the *Nettie Quill* and the *Helen Burke*, which departed for Mobile. Then the bales were loaded onto other ships bound for cotton mills in the East.[14] The remaining bales shipped out of town on the railroads; the main depot was located just east of the wharf.[15]

While business on Water Avenue hummed with the dealings of cotton, the retail shops on Broad Street boomed off of the resulting income. Jewish families, whose fathers and grandfathers had come south selling goods as peddlers, ran many of Selma's most illustrious department stores.[16] Simon Eagle had opened Eagle's Department Store in 1885 and began selling New York fashion to Black Belt citizens. The store was especially popular one March when Mr. Eagle decided to get rid of his out-of-season surplus by tossing straw hats off of the second-floor balcony. His three sons followed their father into the business, and the high-class clothing store grew to occupy over half a block on Alabama Avenue.[17]

Shoppers could also buy choice fabric and the finest, New York–made, ready-to-wear clothes at Isidore Kayser and Company, Rothschild's, and the Liepold Brothers. J. C. Adler's Furniture Company furnished Selma's fine homes, while Mr. Adler also shaped public opinion through his editorship of the *Selma Morning Times*. The Jewish-owned Schuster Hardware and Bloch Brothers Hardware sold tools and farm implements to farmers who had come to town for business on Water Avenue. Meanwhile, Benish and Meyer Tobacco, Thalheimer Liquor, and the American Candy Company traded in pleasures, not necessities.[18] Each fall, Selma's business quieted as Jewish-owned stores closed to observe the holidays of Yom Kippur and Rosh Hashanah.[19] As an integral part of Selma's prosperity, Jewish merchants and their families lived alongside, socialized with, and married into white Protestant families.[20]

The sheer volume of religious institutions bordering downtown must have assured out-of-town visitors that Selma's white citizens were indeed on the heavenly path. The First Presbyterian Church could be seen from downtown, with its redbrick bell tower rising above the dust clouds billowing down Broad Street. A half block to the west, on the corner of Dallas Avenue, the Baptists worshipped in their newly erected Gothic-style sanctuary. St. Paul's Episcopal Church shared a block of Lauderdale Avenue with the First Baptist Church, even if the congregations shared little else. The Methodists, just one more block west on Dallas Avenue, were also worshipping in a new building. Their turreted redbrick sanctuary came into being after the old Church Street Methodist Church's steeple had unceremoniously fallen through the roof.[21] Just to the north of First Presbyterian, the stained-glass Star of David at Temple Mishkan Israel marked the home of Selma's Jewish community. Together, these downtown sanctuaries were where the most prominent white families worshipped.

An array of social and civic clubs kept Selma's upper and middle classes well connected. Men debated matters of the day and listened to speakers in groups like the Elks, the Exchange Club, the Rotary Club, and the Kiwanis Club.[22] While Jewish businessmen were part of all of Selma's notable organizations, they also took their leisure at the Harmony Club, a Jewish social club located on the upper floors of a three-story building with arched windows on Water Avenue. Abe Eagle, one of the three sons in charge of Eagle's Department Store, would unwind from a day's work with a game of cards at the Harmony. His daughter, June Eagle Cohn, remembered her mother dialing up the Harmony to instruct her father, "Abe, come home to supper!"[23] While their husbands discussed business and politics, the wives gathered in social clubs like the Selma Study Club, the Ossian Club, and the Council of Jewish Women, improving their minds and organizing civic projects.[24]

Dealings in cotton made Selma the economic hub of the western Black Belt, and that, in turn, supported a sizable professional class of bankers, lawyers, and doctors. At the start of the twentieth century, the People's Bank and Trust Company, the City National Bank of Selma, and Selma National Bank served the financial needs of area residents and businesses. The three bank presidents often appeared on the rosters of local business campaigns, and they maintained especially close relationships with the wholesale merchants.[25] Selma was also the medical center of the west-central Black Belt, home to numerous hospitals and private medical practices. These institutions over time consolidated into the Vaughan Memorial Hospital and the Alabama Baptist Hospital for white patients, while the Burwell Infirmary and the Good Samaritan Hospital served African Americans.[26] A cadre of Selma attorneys represented the citizens' legal interests at the Dallas County courthouse. The surnames Craig, Keith, Mallory, and Vaughan carried through generations of Selma attorneys, who often operated as father-and-son law offices.[27]

In the spring of 1901, a stray match ignited a bale of cotton around midday at the Babcock Cotton Warehouse. "Bankers, merchants, mechanics, and firemen," reported the *Selma Morning Times*, all grabbed buckets of water and "worked like demons" to prevent the flames from spreading through downtown. Over nine hundred bales of cotton worth thousands of dollars went up in smoke. The volunteer firefighting force revealed the townspeople's common interest. Businesspeople, professionals, railroad workers, and farmers alike understood that Selma's fortune grew directly from Black Belt soil and cotton's value.[28] The local Chamber of Commerce bragged that the city drew an annual revenue of almost $8 million from the cotton crop. "Can any other city of its size show so fine a revenue from a single crop?," it asked.[29]

But not all of Selma's white citizens lived in the world of New York fashion, society, and Greek Revival mansions.[30] The Louisville and Nashville, the Southern, and the Western Railway companies all ran tracks through the Black Belt's main cotton town, and smoky engines chugged cotton bales into Selma from the surrounding hinterlands before shipping them out again to large industrial centers. Wholesale merchants owned property next to the main railroad lines and built private side tracks to funnel carloads of goods directly into their warehouses.[31] Machinists, blacksmiths, and engineers employed at local railroad shops kept the trains running, and their wages of three dollars per day helped support Selma's businesses. One Southern Railway Company payday in 1901 put $30,000 into the hands of its employees. Skilled railroad positions, reserved for white workers, provided a solid but not extravagant living for railroad families. Most lived in modest wood frame houses in East Selma.[32] Agriculture-based industries like the Buckeye Cotton Oil Company, People's Cotton Oil Company, and Dallas Compress Company sustained other working-class families on the eastern side of the city, along with wood and coal companies, the ice company, and local sawmills.[33]

The poorest of Selma's white residents worked in the Cawthon and Estelle cotton mills on the outskirts of town. The white mill workers often came from surrounding rural areas or from out of state. Fieldwork guaranteed a hard life with little money, and the textile mills offered cash wages to struggling families.[34] Workers at the Estelle Cotton Mill lived in one of the fifty-four company shotgun houses or duplexes in the mill village on the west side of Valley Creek. They shopped at the company store, sent their children to the company-sponsored school, and attended church at the village's Methodist-Episcopal Church. Across town, workers at the Cawthon Mill lived in similar company houses on St. Phillips, Mechanic, and Range Streets. Children, like sixteen-year-old Grace Cooper and her thirteen-year-old cousin Shellie, served in the ranks of the companies' workforce. They tended spindles and looms at the mill in East Selma along with their mothers, while both of their fathers worked as flagmen for the Southern Railway.[35]

Selma's textile industry offered little in job security. The Cawthons, a local family, controlled both of the city's textile mills in 1902, but hard times led to repeated changes in ownership. The mills shut down during the depression in 1908. When the newspaper sent a reporter to investigate conditions, they found "inmates" of the mill village lacking heat and other basic necessities. The company commissary and nearby shops had cut off workers' credit, and many were forced to move. Over the next twenty years, the mills went through a series of name changes—Sunset Mill, Valley Creek Mill, Selma Manufacturing Company, and the California Cotton Mill—with each new owner. Only steadily deteriorating housing, low pay, and no security remained consistent for the workers.[36]

Outside of town, the fields that fueled Selma's cotton empire and bustling department stores stretched for miles across Dallas County and out into the Black Belt. All aspects of cotton's growth depended on rural black families, and in 1900 Dallas County plantations looked much like their antebellum predecessors. African Americans operated almost 89 percent of Dallas County's 7,141 farms. Ninety-four percent of black farmers operated under some form of tenant contract; only 390 black families held any ownership in their land.[37]

South of the Alabama River and east of Selma, J. A. Minter, a fourth-generation planter, owned eleven thousand acres of fertile farmland. The family had moved from North Carolina around 1819, when Alabama gained statehood, and had been working the land ever since. Minter had over 160 African American tenants growing cotton on his property when he decided to build his own gin in 1901. Like many Dallas County landowners, he preferred black laborers over poorer whites. While white tenants would expect the same privileges as white people in the Black Belt, he explained, African Americans would not question the little that tenant life offered.[38] It was this "good and cheap labor" of black citizens that created and sustained Selma's white elite. The cotton grown by black tenants filled the coffers of Dallas County landlords, wholesalers, and merchants, and the profits then trickled through Selma in business dealings and wages. As the *Selma Morning Times* straightforwardly explained, "These lands would be worth nothing if the Negroes were moved off of them."[39]

Washington Smith, the president of the Bank of Selma, owned a large Dallas County plantation near Bogue Chitto, about fifteen miles due west of Selma. He also owned a redbrick Greek Revival mansion with four towering columns in town, where he resided with his family. During the Civil War, the Smiths became local heroes when they allegedly hid the bank's gold in one of those hollowed-out columns, never to be found by Union troops.[40] When her husband died in 1869, Mrs. Smith continued to oversee the workings of the Bogue Chitto plantation. The sheer wealth of white planters and merchants in the rural areas gave them immense personal and economic power over black tenants. After sending out a man to inspect the tenants' crops and gather the names of their advancing merchants, Mrs. Smith would instruct her tenants to bring their cotton either to her attorneys in Selma or to nearby advancing merchants in Orrville to take care of their rent notes. A shrewd, prickly woman with a keen eye for profit, Mrs. Smith closely managed how the cotton grown on her land was handled, and tenants had no say over how their debts were settled at the end of a season.[41]

In the country stores and cotton fields of rural Dallas County, and along its dirt roads, the fiefdoms of the large plantations set the rules of conduct for black residents. Tight relationships between white landowners, advancing merchants, and overseers, like those on Mrs. Smith's Bogue Chitto plantation, helped ensure that black tenants remained in their prescribed place.[42] Local government and law enforcement allowed white landowners wide latitude to reign over their property and tenants as they wished. Additionally, Alabama law allowed for plantation owners and other employers to pay the fines of a person convicted of a minor crime in exchange for their labor. It was yet another way that black laborers, already targeted by law enforcement, were bound into the service of white landowners. When agents for the Louisville and Nashville railroad came recruiting outside of Selma, they discovered that planters held a "sort of claim or mortgage on the [N]egro community." Faced with debt peonage and threats, tenants had few options.[43]

Traveling across Dallas County highlighted the gap between black and white residents' lives. Roads traversed the county's 993 square miles, tying landowners in the county to Selma's merchants and markets. A traveler on a maintained road would pass by Greek Revival plantation houses owned by white landowners, through Dallas County's small communities—Safford, Orrville, Carlowville, Burnsville, Summerfield, and Plantersville—and on to downtown department stores, the hospital, and schools like Dallas Academy. Roads traced the pathways of white life.

But these roads stopped at the plantation's gate, and worn paths were the conduits of rural black lives. Dusty trails that turned thick with mud in Alabama's torrential rain ran from back behind the main house to the tenants' quarters. Any visitor to the back quarters needed to pass by the watchful eyes of the white property owner. These paths ran from one rickety clapboard cabin with a dangerously leaning chimney to the next. Some of the sharecropper shacks at the dawn of the twentieth century had started as slave quarters. The web of dusty trails connected shacks to the plantation commissary, the nearby school and church, and the cabins of neighbors and the midwife.[44]

African Americans did not enter into tenant contracts because they wanted to; they did so because there was no other option. At least two-thirds of the black men in Dallas County over the age of twenty-one could not read. This left them no hope of challenging the terms of a written agreement or a landlord's faulty or self-serving accounting.[45] Constant debt and willful neglect on the part of landlords forced black residents into poverty. Diets of cornbread, condensed milk, strong coffee, and salt pork "over and over again, without variation, [were] hardly conducive to health" and made hookworm, pellagra, and tuberculosis common.[46]

1.4 African American woman and child in front of a cabin in Dallas County, ca. 1900. Courtesy of Alabama Department of Archives and History, Montgomery, Alabama.

Landownership remained an impossible goal for most black families. Calculating debt at the end of a season depended on the variable goodwill of plantation owners or advancing merchants. Year after year, at settling time white landlords told tenants that they had not produced enough that season to cover their debts.[47] Black sharecroppers, like Ned Cobb in Tallapoosa County in the eastern section of the Black Belt, had no recourse. One year, the owner of the land that Cobb was working died. His debt was transferred to the new owner at 90 percent, but the new owner forced him to pay the full amount. "I had the brains to see how that transaction was runnin' over me," Cobb explained, "but I had no voice on account of my color."[48] No matter how many bales of cotton they produced, the rigged accounting practices of the Alabama Black Belt ensured that black farmers

1.5 African American man with cotton bales in Dallas County, ca. 1900. Courtesy of Alabama Department of Archives and History, Montgomery, Alabama.

ended a season with hardly a cent in their pocket, year after year.[49] "Never did a state of serfdom more truly exist in Russia than in some parts of Alabama," a black weekly newspaper in Montgomery concluded.[50]

Still, many upstanding white citizens saw themselves as the guardians of black residents. "In taking away his privilege of suffrage . . . the negro has become the ward of the white man, and we conduct such wardship with honor, justice, and fairness," the *Selma Morning Times* explained.[51] But Glenn Sisk, a Black Belt native and historian, observed that the mores of slavery and Reconstruction continued to shape the attitudes of white people toward black residents. Daily interactions seemed "placid enough," he explained, "as long as there was no disturbance or challenge of the white man's supremacy." When a black person violated this norm, that act "released the delicate tensions, [and] explosions of mob violence often resulted."[52]

This played out one Sunday evening in the spring of 1901. Ten and a half miles outside of Selma on the Benton road, Deputy Sheriff Joseph Edwards ventured into a black settlement on Mrs. J. D. Jordan's land. He had gone to confront John Dawson, a black farm laborer in his mid-twenties, about some unknown matter. When the house's residents refused him entrance, the deputy fired two shots into the door and shoved the full force of his weight against it. In the Alabama Black Belt, like all over the South, loaded shotguns lay waiting in corners and over mantles in black homes. They put meat on meager tables but also gave cover when necessary.[53] A return shot from the inside of the house entered Edwards's heart, killing him instantly. Dawson fled the scene, well aware that his life depended on it.[54]

Selma's white citizens erupted over this "most dastardly crime."[55] A mob of furious white men invaded the settlement on Mrs. Jordan's land in the middle of the next night. At Angela Dawson's house, they tore the covers off of the sleeping occupants and began recklessly firing their weapons. One black man died in the rampage. A seventeen-year-old boy exiting his father's house after being awoken by the gunfire became the mob's next victim. They left his body lying by the side of the road, to be discovered early the next morning. Only on the afternoon of the following day did Sheriff Blackwell send out a posse of men to attempt to restore order. By that time, the hundred or so black residents of the settlement had fled to Selma or were hiding in the surrounding woods, fearing for their lives.[56] Only Dawson's capture by the sheriff and subsequent imprisonment in Mobile cooled white citizens' mob-inclined sentiments.[57]

A number of Selma's most civically minded citizens publicly denounced both Dawson's crime and mob violence. Such out-of-control fury reflected poorly on the county and "the civilization of its people."[58] But vocal objections did nothing to change the ever-present threat of violence that African Americans lived with. "Keeping the Negro in his place," Sisk explained, was one of the primary social objectives of white residents of the Black Belt, and violence was an essential tool in that effort.[59]

Jim Crow Segregation

Life in the Black Belt had always been about as segregated as the chocolate and white swirls of a marble cake, frosted and sitting on the kitchen table. Black and white folks had long mixed with each other on farms, in country stores, in downtown businesses, in bars, and as neighbors. Here, the personalized rules of racial etiquette kept the social order running smoothly.

African Americans knew to take off their hats, step aside, bow their heads, and say "Yes, ma'am" and "Yessir" to white citizens or face the consequences. But the twentieth century ushered in a new era, one marked by a more hard-line racial segregation. Southern states had already adopted new state constitutions to purge black voters from the rolls. Next, the freshly triumphant Democrats turned their attention toward transforming informal practices of racial separation into legally sanctioned segregation. When the Supreme Court deemed racial segregation constitutional in its *Plessy v. Ferguson* decision in 1896, it signaled to southern Democrats that the Constitution was on their side.[60]

Jim Crow came into being on city streets and sidewalks. There, segregation laws helped anonymously and uniformly enforce the racial order among strangers, instead of the personalized interactions that governed the tightly knit countryside.[61] Within a decade, southern states legislated separate train cars, schools, parks, hospitals, and waiting rooms for "white" and "colored." These codes cemented into southerners' subconscious that whites had preference in all arenas of daily life.[62] But establishing Jim Crow in a region long governed by informal customs was tricky, and the city of Selma put a good deal of effort into figuring out how to separate the intertwined lives of its black and white residents.

In April 1902, delegates of the Alabama American Federation of Labor (AFL)—twenty-three white and twelve black—gathered at Selma's Sylvan Hall for their annual convention. Business ground to a halt when the hall owner insisted that black delegates be barred from the meeting site. "While being a white man and opposed to social equality with the Negro," the AFL president reportedly declared, "he would not consent to see the colored laborer discriminated against." Fellow members seconded a resolution affirming that accredited delegates should not be excluded from the convention. A committee set out to find an alternative meeting location, and the superintendent of Selma's street railway saved the day, offering two special cars at Riverview Pavilion for the AFL's use.[63] The AFL members proceeded to elect officers for the coming year, a slate that included two black Selmians. The convention took a turn for the worse when two delegates ended up in a shooting match, but the AFL assured Selma's citizens that long-standing personal difficulties—not "the Negro question"—had caused the ruckus.[64] Delegates closed out the convention by commending Selma for its friendly attitude toward labor and congratulating the newspaper on its accurate reports of the proceedings.[65] Clearly, the rigid details of segregation had yet to be hammered out in Selma.

Butcher stalls proved yet another problem spot in enforcing racial separation. After conducting an inspection, Dr. W. W. Harper had concluded that the places where meat was slaughtered in the city were "filthy and in horrible condition—all of them." So the city council established a city slaughterhouse, where, in exchange for a license to sell meat, butchers agreed to follow certain health safeguards.[66] But Selma's newly built market house had only eight stalls, all of which were leased to white butchers in 1905. Two black butchers, Milas Martin and W. H. Edwards, had operated stalls in the old market house. When they objected to no longer being able to do business, Judge Mabry issued Martin a butcher's license, who then opened a separate market stall in East Selma. The next December, when the city's butchers met to secure their stalls for the upcoming year, Martin bid $50.50 for the stall of a white butcher. Racial preferences did not allow for a black man to outbid a white man, so the city solved the problem by erecting another market stall in East Selma where Martin and Edwards could operate.[67] It was a tempered display of racial fairness. Segregation did not need to put black men out of business, but it did need to protect the interests of white men.

The daily routines of Jim Crow slowly coalesced in Selma. Only four years after Selma's streetcar company accommodated the integrated AFL gathering, it began running separate white and colored electric cars on the Union Street line on Saturday nights.[68] By the next year, "the Jim Crow crusade . . . had become rather frenzied," the newspaper reported. It alleged that both black and white riders found interracial transit disagreeable and prone to conflict. In response to a petition, the Selma Street Railway Company began offering extra segregated cars on select lines a few months later.[69] Yet the rise of segregation laws did not split the geography of the city into black and white. Behind the enormous Greek Revival mansions in western Selma, black families lived in shacks and small cottages in backyards and off of alleyways, and a neighborhood of black homeowners was found a few blocks west, near Valley Creek. In East Selma, black and white working-class families lived next to each other in identical creaky clapboard houses.[70]

But some racial boundaries remained unbreachable. When some black women opened prostitution houses next to white establishments in the Tenderloin District, Victor Atkins, the mayor and a wholesale grocer, took action against "the disgraceful scenes" happening there. He gave them one week to relocate and threatened to fine them for vagrancy every twenty-four hours "until the resorts of this kind are separated."[71] Public interactions between black and white citizens caused no problems as long as black residents paid proper deference to the customs of white supremacy.

Black women soliciting sexual encounters next door to already-taboo white brothels broke the rules of propriety.

Jim Crow did the additional work of binding the white working class to their more prosperous neighbors across town. Although Selma's textile and railroad workers may have barely scraped by in the mill villages and East Selma's rundown houses, white supremacy at least offered them personal superiority and preference over their black neighbors. They did not always behave as their social betters wished, however. On Saturday nights, city bars were crowded with young mill men rowdily enjoying their paychecks and their liquor.[72] In the Black Belt of Alabama, where almost every man, black or white, was packing a pistol somewhere on his person, these nighttime escapades often ended in violence. In May 1902 a sixty-year-old black man was driving his buggy near the Estelle Cotton Mill when four white factory workers forced him to stop. After he failed to remove his hat fast enough, the white roughs pulled him from his seat, shot him multiple times, and tossed him into Valley Creek.[73] He died the next day. Compelled by codes of paternalism, white officials and businessmen deplored the murder of a black man by these "ruffians." The city police arrested three of the four men, whom the *Morning Times* described as "drunken rowdies, bent upon picking a fuss at any hazard . . . with the thirst of blood in their heart, crazed by mean whiskey."[74] The grand jury had two of the men committed without bail, indicating that there were limits to the bonds of race.[75]

The top echelon of Dallas County's white professionals, businessmen, and planters considered themselves best equipped to direct politics and business for the good of all citizens. Many sported buttons reading "Greater Selma" on their lapels, so as to inspire conversations in which the wearer could "sing the praises of the city in which he lives." These men were economically successful, civically involved, and confident that it was their responsibility to determine and take care of the best interests of all.[76] But poorer white residents didn't always agree. In the wake of the new constitution, the Dallas County Democratic Party ran into an unexpected dilemma when some white men refused to pay their poll tax. When deputized members of the executive committee went searching for those on the unpaid list, they headed to the local machine shops, cotton mills, and oil mills.[77] Around two hundred white men had still not paid by the day poll taxes were due. Living in East Selma gave working-class whites an education in how the city fathers cared more about their votes than they did about their well-being. A city dump neighbored the mill village homes, giving off awful smells and swarms of flies in the sweltering Alabama summers. Meanwhile, streetcar lines didn't run to East Selma, even though the Union Street line extended into the black neighborhoods in the northern part of town.[78] Undoubtedly, some poorer whites did not have $1.50 to spare for the poll tax. Others, however, likely refused to pay, fully aware that the white elites cared more about their votes than about giving working men a leg up.

Black Selma

Sometime after the Civil War, John Henry Tipton left the Tipton plantation in the southern part of Dallas County where he had been enslaved, and headed in the direction of Selma, hoping for a better life. After crossing the Alabama River in a boat carrying molasses, he left another part of slavery's legacy behind, changing his last name to Williams. He got his start working on the boats on the river, but when he had saved up enough money, he bought a hack—a horse-drawn buggy—and started charging money for rides. Soon Williams had thirteen hacks transporting Selma's citizens across the city, a regular taxi service. One of Selma's white funeral home directors took an interest in the obviously enterprising Williams, urging him to go into the mortuary business. In 1905 Williams opened the J. H. Williams and Sons funeral services at 1025 Franklin Street, in the heart of Selma's black business district downtown.[79] Like Williams, black residents in Dallas County worked to make something of their own in the years after the Civil War. They built schools and churches, opened corner grocery stores and other businesses, organized fraternal lodges and savings clubs, and bought land. Even as white supremacy constrained their possibilities, they did their best to make the freedom they dreamed of into a reality.[80]

By the turn of the century, Selma was the educational center of the western Black Belt. Black families that could scrape up the money sent their children to one of the city's four segregated schools—one public and three religious—of which Selma University was the shining star. The African American State Baptist Convention had founded the institution in 1878 as a theological seminary, and each year Selma University attracted nearly three hundred pupils to its thirty-six-acre campus on Lapsely Street. Its operating funds came from the donations of black Baptists across Alabama, and the institution prided itself on its independence. According to the school catalog, Selma University represented "the desires and efforts of a people struggling to lift up themselves." School resources were divided between teacher and ministerial training, a college program, and its preparatory department. Grammar students learned reading, writing, and arithmetic, while advanced students studied everything from history and bookkeeping to Latin, Greek, and chemistry, along with more practical trades.[81] Selma University's commitment to classical education was unusual at the turn of the century. The industrial, agricultural, and trade-based education promoted by Booker T. Washington at Tuskegee Institute in the eastern Alabama Black Belt won the most enduring and substantial support from white southerners. But Selma University got its money from black Alabamians, not white philanthropists, allowing the institution freedom to teach both intellectual and practical subjects.

A few blocks south of Selma University, Knox Academy taught grammar and high school students in a three-story brick building to the north of Jefferson Davis Avenue. An affiliate of the northern-based Reformed Presbyterian Church, the school prepared its students to make the most of Jim Crow's limited opportunities. Boys learned blacksmithing and carpentry, and women cooking and sewing. But high school students could also take classes on literature, economics, physics, and Latin, and the Knox Academy Band made rousing appearances at most major festivities of Selma's black community.[82] Across town, the Alabama AME Church operated Payne University, and nearby, on Lawrence Street, Clark School offered public education for the city's black children under the direction of Selma University graduate Richard Byron (R. B.) Hudson.[83]

Hudson was one of Selma University's star students. His parents accumulated land and a home in town in the neighboring Perry County after the Civil War, and his father served as a city councilman in Uniontown during Reconstruction. They sent young Hudson, born into freedom in 1866, to school at Selma University, where his meteoric rise became a legend. By the time he was finishing his college studies, the university had given him a position as a student teacher. In 1890 Hudson opened Selma's first public school for African Americans.[84]

Like many of Selma's black middle class, Hudson owned a home on Lapsley Street. His neighbors included Selma University; the Rev. D. V. Jemison, the pastor of Tabernacle Baptist Church and president of the prestigious National Baptist Convention; and R. T. Pollard, the president of Selma University.[85] Many of the city's black professionals had Selma University to thank for their success. By 1906 forty-six graduates made their homes in Selma and seven more in Dallas County, working as pastors, teachers, doctors, pharmacists, mail carriers, and insurance agents.[86]

In addition to being the principal of Clark School, Hudson owned a coal and wood yard off of the railroad tracks. The fuel Hudson's company supplied to black and white customers gave him financial security and bought him respect among Selma's white elites. Hudson was also interested in the financial prosperity of his entire race. In 1890 a former Selma University professor had started the black-run Alabama Penny Savings Bank in Birmingham for the purpose of cultivating thrift, economic solidarity, and racial uplift for African Americans.[87] Within ten years, the Alabama Colored Baptist State Convention had transferred all funds in its control from the white-owned First National Bank of Selma to the successful Alabama Penny Savings Bank. "Because all convention money came from blacks and since there was a skillfully-operated and successful bank of their own race, funds should be placed in that institution," read the resolution.[88] Hudson helped open a branch of the Alabama Penny Savings Bank in Selma. Located on Franklin Street, in the downtown's black business district, the bank stood as a testament to how, in the midst of Jim Crow, black Alabamians actively built the economic base of their community.[89]

Selma was full of black professionals. Another prestigious Selma University graduate, Dr. Lincoln L. (L. L.) Burwell, went on to study medicine at Leonard Medical School, later Shaw University, in Raleigh, North Carolina. He returned to Selma and opened Burwell Infirmary in 1907 to serve black patients who were refused treatment at local white hospitals. When local white pharmacists refused to fill Dr. Burwell's prescriptions, he enrolled in Howard University's pharmacy program and opened his own drugstore.[90] To the east of Selma's powerful wholesale grocer establishments, the family of Calvin L. Osborn had been running Interlink Cotton Gin since 1886, one of the few black-run gins in the entire country.[91] Likewise, Williams's taxi service grew into a reputable funeral home and ambulance service for Selma's African American residents from its beginnings in 1905.[92]

Grocery stores, barbershops, and cookhouses run by enterprising black residents stood on the street corners of Selma's black neighborhoods. Here, laborers, ministers, domestic workers, laundresses, and railroad men could buy the everyday items they needed without having to confront the racial codes of downtown. Children grew up romping within the relatively protected boundaries of self-contained neighborhoods and under the watchful eyes of neighbors.[93] Stopping at the Hunter Grocery Company or Simon Bowie's grocery store on the way home from a weekly church meeting at First Baptist also kept money invested in the black community. Economic independence brought a modicum of security for black southerners in a world of white supremacy.[94]

The jobs open to black Selmians did not offer much, however. Black adults mostly made their living as cooks, waitresses, laundresses, seamstresses, draymen, and laborers.[95] The wages were low, and rent for a shoddy cabin could cost from four to eight dollars a month. When black bowling alley workers attempted to strike for two dollars a week instead of one, the management replaced them that very same night.[96] For black women, doing domestic work in white homes also came with the threat of sexual assault, although many did what they could to protect themselves.[97] "An incipient strike is going on nearly all the time except in the winter when food is scarce among the Negroes," one newspaper reported.[98]

Black Dallas Countians formed savings clubs and benevolent societies to help themselves and their communities in the face of difficulty. One of these was the Independent Benevolent Society, No. 28, which met fifteen miles outside of town near Cahaba. Its members paid one dollar to join and twenty-five cents in monthly dues. That money went to support members in their time of need. If someone was sick and couldn't work, the society supplied them with fifty cents per week, and when Sister Bama Evans passed away, it covered her thirty-five-dollar burial cost.[99] In these small meetings with trusted friends, members could safely discuss racially charged issues away from white employers or landlords.[100]

Churches sustained black residents in ways that their meager incomes could not. The first semi-independent black Baptist congregation had formed in 1845 when white members of the First Baptist Church allowed their slaves and free African Americans to worship in the church's basement. In 1866 the congregation broke off to form the St. Phillips Street Baptist Church. What led to this event was a matter of some speculation. One story held that black Baptists left their former sanctuary with a generous financial gift from the white members. The other recalled the white pastor staving off an alleged black takeover with a pistol in the church entrance. Regardless of their genesis, the St. Phillips Street Baptist Church, which later changed its name to First Baptist Church, prospered so greatly that sections of its congregation broke off to form the equally formidable Second Baptist, Green Street Baptist, and Tabernacle Baptist Churches.[101]

African American churches provided a space for black worshippers to participate in church governing bodies, missionary societies, and state and national conventions. Excluded from political participation, black citizens could still exercise their civic duties within the independent institution of the church. J. L. Chestnut, who would later become Selma's first black attorney, remembered his grandfather and other active churchmen "engaged in pitched power struggles . . . similar to the ones white men carried on over who would be sheriff or probate judge."[102] This happened across Selma's black churches, from the Baptists to Brown Chapel AME, from Methodist churches to the Reformed Presbyterians.

Black churches also bolstered the spirit and gumption of black residents in the face of white supremacy. In 1922 Tabernacle Baptist Church began building a new sanctuary on the corner of Broad Street and Minter Avenue. One day, a church member went down to the courthouse to take care of administrative details. When the county authorities reviewed the plans, they forbid the church from having its front door be located directly on Selma's main artery. "We can't have a Nigger church on Broad Street," they allegedly stated. Not wanting to cause trouble, the contractor followed directions and built the white-columned entrance for regular use on the side street, Minter Avenue. But he erected another, identical white-columned entrance facing Broad Street—this one for show. Tabernacle's two entrances scoffed at Jim Crow segregation. The opinions and aspirations of black Selmians still mattered in their own churches, and they knew it.[103]

The Boll Weevil

All aspects of life in Selma, Dallas County, and the Alabama Black Belt—from the wholesale grocers on Broad Street to the corner stores in East Selma, from the leading white congregants at First Baptist Church to the leading black devotees at Tabernacle, from mill workers to Selma University students—came back to cotton. As established as it was, the arrival of a small but unstoppable insect challenged as never before the world that cotton made. The boll weevil first infiltrated the cotton fields of eastern Texas from Mexico in 1903. Spreading slowly northeastward, the small insects feasted on the immature buds and flowers and decimated entire crops before harvest time. As life in Selma so clearly illustrated, cotton was both the economic lifeblood and the foundation of a social order, and the threat of the boll weevil loomed like a hurricane over fleecy white fields. Selma newspapers apprehensively traced the insect's trajectory from Texas to Louisiana in 1906, to Mississippi in 1907, and to nearby Clarke County, Alabama, in 1911.[104]

While the ravaging insect lowered cotton yields, it spawned a secondary revolution in the federal government's relationship with rural farmers. The U.S. Department of Agriculture (USDA) and agricultural colleges saw the widespread fear of the boll weevil as an opportunity to challenge the region's overreliance on cotton and its hesitation to adopt modern, scientific farming methods.[105] Federally funded agricultural education had started before the Civil War. Back in 1862, the Morrill Land-Grant Act had given states public land on which to build agricultural colleges, and in 1887 the Hatch Act created agricultural experiment stations at the land-grant institutions to promote research. These institutions implemented and refined the latest techniques in scientific agriculture, while the agricultural extension programs paid educators—called agents—to bring new methods to black and white farmers across the state. In Alabama, the Alabama Polytechnic Institute (later Auburn University) was the headquarters for agricultural work among whites, while the nearby Tuskegee Institute served the separate black division.[106]

The looming threat of the boll weevil sent southern farmers searching for assistance, and the agricultural colleges capitalized on this plea.[107] Extension agents spread throughout weevil-threatened territory, encouraging farmers to diversify their crops and practice soil conservation methods as a way to slow the boll weevil. New agricultural legislation helped the agents in their work. In 1906 the USDA made demonstration agents federal employees, and the state of Alabama allotted funds in 1909 to support and expand agricultural demonstration work. This culminated with the Smith-Lever Act in 1914, which established a national extension system that distributed funds through land-grant colleges in each state.[108]

Thus, the citizens of Dallas County turned to the Alabama Agricultural Extension Service in a desperate attempt to stop the boll weevil. In 1910—three years before the pest crossed into the county—farmers and merchants raised $1,000 to secure a USDA demonstration agent "for the purpose of fighting the boll weevil."[109] Their efforts brought John Blake, a young, gregarious agriculturalist, to Dallas County as the county agent. He remained in that position for the next thirty years. Blake set about instructing white farmers and black tenants alike to diversify their crops and take precautions. A group of the county's largest farmers and prominent businessmen traveled west with him in the summer of 1912 to survey the weevil's destruction. They returned trumpeting better farming methods as their only means of survival.[110]

On July 11, 1913, Blake confirmed that the long-feared weevils had finally crossed into Dallas County, on the south side near the community of Richmond.[111] The weevil's arrival made Blake one of the most sought-out men in the county. Two years later, he described his work as "on a broader and much larger scale than ever before." Fear of the boll weevil had turned the ears of previously uninterested farmers to his advice.[112] Over the next decade, cotton yields dropped precipitously in Alabama, sometimes reaching as low as half the production per acre compared to before the weevil.[113]

But even though growing cotton became more difficult, the weevil did not end the Alabama Black Belt's dependence on its best cash crop. Selma's Chamber of Commerce admitted in 1913 that the panic surrounding the invasion, and its "consequent loss of labor and confidence, has been more serious than the actual ravages of the pest." The Extension Service did not try to stop farmers from growing the crop. Instead, it encouraged them to grow less cotton and more food crops and to do so intelligently.[114] In 1914 Dallas County produced 64,230 bales of cotton; three years later, that number was 14,230.[115] The seemingly large drop reflected a turn to grain and pasture lands, the scarcity of credit, and labor shortages as much as it did the boll weevil's impact. As a University of Alabama student born and raised in Dallas County noted, "The period from 1895 to 1914 is notable for its bold but fruitless effort to dethrone King Cotton."[116]

It was the black tenant farmers who bore the heaviest burden of the boll weevil. Locked into unfavorable contracts, they had no choice but to keep growing the cotton that landowners demanded. Meanwhile, advancing merchants and planters took fewer chances extending loans, which forced black families from the land. They were the casualties in cotton's continued dominance.[117]

In many ways, the new century had dawned in Dallas County much like any other day. Cotton still shaped the ins and outs of daily life for black and white residents of the Alabama Black Belt. Selma's prosperity depended on those who worked the fields, and black farmers, bound under tenant contracts, supplied this need. Even the boll weevil could not break the region's reliance on its favorite cash crop. Cotton was its economic scaffolding.

Cotton also shaped the social and political order of the Black Belt, and while the hard labor of its black majority was welcome, their political participation was not. When the new constitution removed black Alabamians from the voting rolls in 1901, white Democrats reclaimed their unbridled political and economic power. But black residents had been garnering their resources since before emancipation, and in the face of disenfranchisement, segregation, and violence, they turned inward, investing in the separate institutions—like Selma University, Tabernacle Baptist Church, and Burwell Infirmary—that already sustained the black community. These community resources, internally maintained, gave black Selma a modicum of security against the volatile racial order of the Alabama Black Belt.

World War I and
Making the World Safe
for Democracy

When shots rang out in Europe in August 1914, Charles J. (C. J.) Adams was working as a clerk on a railway mail car in Selma. He had been employed by the postal service for eight years, and it was one of the best jobs a black man could have. A paycheck signed by Uncle Sam came with financial independence from the dictates of local white employers, and traveling on speeding trains, snatching bags of letters dangling from the mail cranes at stations, took black clerks far from their hometowns. But the reverberations of war echoed all the way down into the Alabama Black Belt, and Adams, like all other Americans, could not imagine how a fight on the other side of the Atlantic Ocean would transform his life. By the war's end, the postal clerk would return to Selma as a first lieutenant in the U.S. Army, having served in both France and the Philippine Islands.[1]

In 1914 the United States' role in the Great War remained uncertain. Facing a country deeply divided over everything from progressive reforms and governmental regulation to corporate power and immigration, President Woodrow Wilson avidly attempted to avoid the controversies that war would inevitably ignite. But in the spring of 1917, the discovery of a

German telegram urging Mexico to join in the war against the United States inflamed the American public. On April 2 Wilson called Congress into a special session to ask for a formal declaration of war.[2] He painted the impending engagement as a battle for democracy: "the right of those to . . . have a voice in their own government."[3] Under the slogan of making the world safe for democracy, Wilson attempted to win the hearts and minds of the country's many and diverse citizens.[4]

Preparing the United States for war was an extraordinary logistical undertaking. Never before had the country had such a need to train and equip an army, produce food and war supplies, and mobilize the support of its citizens. Under the direction of the president and his cadre of progressive supporters, hundreds of new federal agencies emerged to address the many demands of mobilization. The Council of National Defense, the War Industries Board, the National War Labor Board, and the Selective Service became household names as government agencies began overseeing war production, food rations and production, finance, propaganda, and more.[5]

War mobilization reached far into the lives of Dallas County's residents, upsetting daily routines and customs. Beginning in the summer of 1917, the newly instituted draft called on white and black men alike to fulfill their patriotic obligations by serving in the U.S. military.[6] White southerners did not, even for an instant, envision young black men like postal clerk C. J. Adams serving as equals to white soldiers. But excluding African Americans from the draft would mean that white youth would have to fill the South's enlistment quota themselves. "The effect," the *Selma Times* explained, "would [be] to leave the Negroes at home and call to the colors practically every available white boy of military age."[7] Facing unfavorable demographics and the federal government, white Dallas County leaders had little choice but to relent. When the first registration day in early June came to a close, the local war rolls included two black registrants for every white one.[8]

After nearly a decade of relative independence on the railroad, Adams had no intention of being drafted into one of the army's segregated labor battalions. Instead, he volunteered for military service, joining over twelve hundred of the brightest, most educated black men in the country on their way to the first training camp for African American officers at Fort Des Moines. While the United States may have needed black soldiers to fight, white supremacists made sure that Jim Crow went with them. Those who trained at Fort Des Moines tolerated segregation as the price for officer status. Black Americans had long understood enlistment as a means to claim full citizenship. "By their valor and achievements," black soldiers would "prove to the world the Negro's claim to freedom, justice, protection, and the full rights of citizenship," one black-run newspaper avowed.[9] Men like Adams and his fellow trainees were at the front line of this battle. After five months of training, two Selma natives, Adams and William H. Dinkins, the son of the president of Selma University, received their commissions as first lieutenants in the U.S. Army.[10]

Those of Alabama's black men who were drafted into service also found themselves heading to the Midwest for training.[11] On April 2, 1918, the first batch of 160 black servicemen left Selma to train at Camp Dodge, Iowa. Black citizens cheered their boys off with a four-day fanfare. The Knox Academy Band played at the farewell reception on Friday, then there was a Saturday mass meeting and a religious service on Sunday, finished off with a Monday morning patriotic procession from the courthouse to the train station led by Mayor Louis Benish and the entire draft board.[12] As a crowd of five thousand people sent off their enlistees with bouquets of flowers, Bibles, and patriotic cheers, some pronounced it "the greatest patriotic demonstration ever [witnessed] in the history of the county."[13]

A war fought under the banner of democracy—a principle with no color lines—created problems not only for the South but for the entire nation. Black Americans used Wilson's call to make the world safe for democracy to draw attention to unequal conditions back home. Mobilization became a means for black Americans to prove their worthiness for full citizenship.[14] J. Edward McCall, a black editor in Montgomery, championed these sentiments across the Black Belt in his wartime paper, the *Emancipator*. Black Selmians could buy their copies from the black-owned Reid Drug Company or Burwell's Pharmacy and read about how their support for the war would show that "the Negro is a loyal American citizen, and should be guaranteed all the rights of American citizenship and protection." By participating in the war effort, African Americans demonstrated both their patriotism and their capability to meet the responsibilities of citizenship.[15]

Dallas County citizens, white and black, kept the patriotic fires burning at home as their sons and brothers trained for war. While the local council of defense directed Liberty bond and war savings stamp drives and thrift campaigns, a separate branch led by Selma's middle-class black leaders, like R. B. Hudson and Dr. L. L. Burwell, encouraged African American support.[16] Black citizens threw themselves wholeheartedly into the war effort.[17] A white reporter, after attending a patriotic mass meeting held in Brown Chapel, wrote that the event served "to disabuse the minds of all that [black citizens] have thought other than the most deep seated loyalty to the government and their homeland."[18] African Americans also dutifully purchased war savings stamps and Liberty bonds to help finance the war. "Show your patriotism and escape the bondage of German chains by subscribing to American Liberty Bonds," urged an ad in the *Emancipator.* Weaving together the war, full citizenship, and the newspaper's mission, it put in a plug to "also shake off the visible and invisible fetters that bind you by subscribing to The Emancipator."[19] Three miles outside of Selma, black residents in the Kent West community raised an astounding $1,530 at a "rousing" war savings stamp meeting. Even for the most cash-strapped, democracy abroad and at home was a worthy cause.[20]

It was no coincidence that the National Association for the Advancement of Colored People (NAACP) became the flagship organization championing the rights of black Americans alongside the war for democracy abroad. Established in 1909, the NAACP used the courts to challenge racial discrimination and establish full rights for black citizens. The organization gained sway during the war years as African Americans across the country responded to its call for social and political equality for blacks. As the *Emancipator* saw it, the NAACP sought to "make 11,000,000 Americans physically free from peonage, mentally free from ignorance, politically free from disfranchisement, and socially free from insult." Branches spread throughout the country—there were already sixty-eight by 1916—in a fight against segregation and white supremacy.[21] Growing from local conditions in specific communities, these branches personalized the organization's work.

In December 1918 eighty-one black Selmians gathered to organize the city's first NAACP branch. One year later, the chapter had more than tripled in size, reaching 308 members.[22] "Now is the time for all patriots and race lovers to rally around some organization for civic betterment," NAACP member and *Emancipator* reporter Joseph Sams urged.[23] Black citizens' support for the war and demands for full citizenship were clearly one and the same. Only six months after the founding of the local branch, member Rev. J. A. Martin traveled to Cleveland, Ohio, to speak at the NAACP's tenth-anniversary conference. He spoke about how the Great War had changed daily life in Dallas County. Before the war, a call would go out for "the citizens of this county" to meet at the courthouse, but when black men appeared, the authorities told them they were not welcome. After the passage of the draft law, the same notice—"all citizens will meet at the courthouse"— now also included black men. But Martin viewed this slight improvement as only the first step. The "problems in the South," he declared, would be settled only when "they will give us recognition of our citizenship and the ballot."[24]

Adams, the Selma railroad mail clerk turned first lieutenant, agreed with Martin. After serving in the segregated 366th infantry division in France, he returned home determined to exercise his full rights as an American citizen. He went to the Dallas County courthouse to register to vote, but despite his military service, paid taxes, and property ownership, the county registrar rejected his application. Independent and assured black men weren't supposed to be voting; that was the point of Alabama's constitution of 1901. Adams refused to passively accept his rejection, but he could not convince any of Selma's white lawyers to take his case. With nowhere else to turn, he appealed to the New York office of the NAACP for assistance. They suggested trying to find a lawyer in a larger city like Birmingham and gave him the address of Mr. J. S. Chandler, the secretary of Selma's NAACP chapter. The white registrar in Selma did not realize when he rejected Adams's voter registration application that he had just created a formidable opponent. Within the next few years, Adams took over the operation of the local NAACP branch, as well as organizing the Dallas County Voters League, an organization that, fifty years later, would make Selma the center of a national movement for voting rights.[25]

CHAPTER

2

"Our Country First, Then Selma"

1917–1929

At the end of 1919, the Selma Chamber of Commerce elected the young and promising wholesale grocer G. Frank Cothran as its president. Cothran was a member of one of the city's oldest families—a family that locals would say had "dug the river"—but a relative newcomer to the dry goods and grocery business. He had opened Cothran Grocery Company in the heyday of Water Avenue, when trading in cotton meant making it big. By the war's end, Cothran had "won his spurs in business circles by his own efforts," at least according to the *Selma Journal*. Lauded as a "live wire" and "a man who believes in doing things," the new Chamber of Commerce president promised to do all in his power to bring greater prosperity to Selma.[1]

Like Cothran, Dallas County's civic leaders came out of the war dreaming of progress, what they called "upbuilding," for their agricultural hamlet.[2] Mobilization had disrupted the routines of daily life for residents at the same time as it altered the agricultural landscape of Dallas County. The boll weevil had first turned farmers' and merchants' ears toward scientific agriculture as preached by the Extension Service, but the enormous food demands of war created fertile ground for these seeds to blossom.

In the name of patriotism, farmers turned away from cotton and toward foodstuffs, cattle, and poultry. The Extension Service and its new associate, the Farm Bureau, gained extraordinary influence in local affairs during the 1920s as better farming methods came to symbolize progress. These organizations, in partnership with the Chamber of Commerce, promoted scientific agriculture and cooperation among farmers and merchants all in the name of upbuilding Dallas County.

But white citizens quickly discovered that progress was unattainable without the black men and women who grew their crops, worked in their stores, and cooked their dinners. While the Chamber of Commerce and county officials did not support black political rights, many believed in helping African Americans lead industrious lives within the confines of white supremacy. The newly elected chamber president passed along secondhand suits to and bought new shoes for Lewellen Phillips, the black man who took care of his horses and drays, and he helped secure the down payment on a family home for Phillips.[3] White citizens' attempts to include black residents in upbuilding followed the logic of this southern paternalism.

During the war, black residents had fueled panic across the labor-dependent Black Belt as they packed into train cars headed to southern industrial towns or further north to war jobs in Detroit, Chicago, and Cleveland, seeking a better life. Their actions pushed white civic leaders to support agricultural education for African Americans in hopes of keeping them in the Black Belt's fields and making them better farmers. The black agricultural agents who became fixtures in the 1920s gave black residents new advocates. While white-led campaigns to improve sanitation, build better roads, and promote cooperation all nominally included black residents, none of them addressed the underlying problems of poverty and second-class citizenship. Black Dallas Countians, however, seized these limited opportunities to further their dreams of landownership, economic security, education, and independence.

When the United Stated declared war in 1917, it entered into a partnership with Allied nations already ravaged by three years of heavy fighting. While U.S. servicemen trained for combat on European battlefields, food became a crucial way for Americans at home to show their support. The U.S. Food Administration was responsible for promoting food production and conservation on the home front. To do so, the agency appealed to Americans' sense of self-sacrifice and patriotism.[4] "Put your knife and fork to work for the freedom of the [world]," an advertisement in the *Emancipator* urged.[5] Daily papers throughout the Black Belt urged residents to conserve food, observe meatless and wheatless days each week, join poultry clubs, and raise gardens for the good of the cause.[6] Food became the means by which average Americans could fulfill their war duty. Corn bread and chicken became badges of loyalty in the kitchen.

In agriculturally dominated Dallas County, producing food became the measure of patriotism. The war "is a fight . . . between the farmer of the United States on the one hand and the gaunt wolf of the Kaiser, famine, on the other hand," the *Selma Journal* explained to its readers. "The whole world is on the verge of starvation."[7] Wholesale grocer and cotton buyer W. C. Agee headed the local defense council, and he directed farmers in local wartime agricultural priorities—food crops first, then cotton, and, last, livestock. "Every farm and farmer should produce more food and feed stuff than for [our] own requirements, which shows patriotism and assures food for us and our Allies," he wrote to the defense council members.[8] The program of diversification that had begun with the boll weevil's arrival gained an aura of patriotism during the war as farmers worked to do their part, producing food instead of cotton.

Black Migration during the War

Agricultural success in the Black Belt had always depended on the labor of black tenants, and now so did white citizens' patriotic obligation. But, for the first time, a significant number of African Americans found reason to abandon the fields of the Black Belt, causing panic among Selma's white farmers. In the summer of 1916, massive flooding of the Alabama and Cahaba Rivers destroyed hundreds of acres of crops. The high waters left thousands of African American tenants without cotton or cash.[9] When the Rev. Edward W. Gamble of St. Paul's Episcopal Church and county agent John Blake headed downriver by boat to disburse rations, they encountered numerous needy black residents with plans to travel elsewhere to look for work.[10] One black resident in neighboring Perry County remembered that "it rained all the year. Every time you would look up, you could see folks that the plantations had turned out."[11] Some initial reports applauded the departures as a first step toward breaking Dallas County's dependence on its one-crop system of cotton.[12]

But as the military draft began sending more and more of Dallas County's men to war, the supply of able-bodied farm laborers fell. By the end of 1917, local newspapers began reporting on "the labor crisis." Producing food for the war effort could not be done without agricultural workers tending the fields. "The labor [famine] is working at cross purposes to the conservation campaign," one article declared.[13] Prominent citizens did what they could to remedy the situation. The local council of defense sent a letter to the Selma businessman who headed up the Alabama State Council of Defense, arguing that farmers needed to be passed over in the draft.[14] Meanwhile, the Selma Chamber of Commerce appealed directly to the secretary of war to exempt the city from government recruiting of war-industry workers.[15]

Enlistment was not the only reason Dallas County farmers were worried. The war increased the need for industrial labor at the same time as the country closed its doors to the thousands of European immigrants who had been keeping American factories running. War industries began recruiting black labor from the South to fill these positions. Facing less than ideal prospects at home, African Americans began boarding northbound trains in a tremendous exodus. The *Chicago Defender*, a black newspaper widely read and circulated across black America, became the mouthpiece of this "Great Migration."[16] One of the first reports came from Selma in February 1916. Over the months prior, hundreds of black citizens had been quietly leaving the Black Belt on trains departing from Selma. White residents were doing what they could to stop the stream, the *Defender* reported, but "the discrimination and race prejudice continues as strong as ever."[17] A seventeen-year-old reader who attended Knox Academy in Selma even wrote to the newspaper for help. She listed her skills—dish washing, laundry, nursing, and grocery or dry goods work—and asked the *Defender* to find her a job and a sponsor for her train ticket.[18] Many of the outward bound headed toward southern industrial centers like Birmingham before turning further north. Between August 1916 and June 1917, 12,037 railroad tickets from Selma to the Birmingham district were purchased, mostly by African Americans.[19]

The white citizens of Dallas County were blind to the conditions compelling black residents to leave. They accused roving labor agents of enticing black workers away with big promises of industrial jobs in the North. During the first two months of 1917, Selma's law enforcement officers arrested at least eight men suspected of being labor agents. For four of these men, their troubles started when their car broke down outside of Benton, twelve miles east of Selma. Their indecipherable license plates aroused the suspicion of the police, and they were later taken into custody at the hotel where they were staying. The men allegedly had long lists of names of "Negroes living in Selma and Dallas County," which warranted their extended lockup.[20] Local law enforcement imprisoned other accused labor agents on the grounds that they were not able to account for their previous day's movements and that "their activities among the Negroes aroused suspicion."[21] White leaders blamed these outside agitators for the alarming departure of the black labor force. The blatant intimidation and arrests won Dallas County a reputation of being especially "unwelcome territory for the labor agent."[22] Meanwhile, the Southern Railway vowed to stop furnishing trains in another effort to "discourage the Negro exodus from the South in every legitimate manner."[23]

The conflict between the steady departure of black laborers and white patriotic obligation climaxed in 1918. Prominent white citizens called a meeting at the courthouse that May to discuss the "serious situation of labor" confronting Dallas County.[24] Then, in August, the city of Selma passed a vagrancy ordinance criminalizing "any person, male or female, who wanders or strolls about in idleness, or lives in idleness, . . . having no income producing property sufficient for his support."[25] This was not the first time Black Belt officials had turned to vagrancy laws. After the Civil War, similar ordinances were used to fine and imprison freedpeople, forcing them to work for the county to pay off their debt.[26] This time, in the name of patriotism and war mobilization, the Selma City Council turned to such charges to round up idlers and compel them to work in the fields.

On the night of August 27, 1918, a group of Selma's white citizens organized the Dallas County Self Preservation Loyalty League to support the new vagrancy ordinance. The league sought to ensure that all able men between sixteen and sixty were "engaged in some kind of work required for the successful carrying out of the war with our enemies." Under the banner of patriotism, the organization proclaimed that it would take no part in "politics, religious, or labor controversy." However, the inclusion of "self preservation" in the new organization's title suggested that the vagrancy laws would also personally benefit white citizens, in addition to Uncle Sam.[27] City residents were required to carry loyalty cards with them at all times, which gave proof of gainful employment six days a week. Failure to produce the loyalty card "may at times cause some inconvenience."[28] The underlying racial motive of the vagrancy ordinances was apparent when the Selma Times reported that all of those prosecuted under the laws were black.[29] Prominent white residents clearly saw agriculture, access to black labor, and patriotic duty as interrelated and subject to their control.

Only the end of the war that November stopped local labor regulations from taking full effect.[30] In the final count, at least 1,246 African American residents had chosen to leave Dallas County between 1910 and 1920, and more departed from the rest of the Black Belt. But even though the county's black majority dropped from 81.4 percent to 77 percent, it was the only Black Belt county that had gained in population in the census of 1920. During the same period, cotton dropped from 78 percent of Dallas County's crop value to 53 percent. Wartime food production and the rise of the Extension Service were as much a part of that change as the much-discussed labor shortage and the boll weevil.[31] Wartime mobilization had forced white Alabamians in the Black Belt to recognize African Americans as necessary contributors to the war effort, whether as food producers or soldiers. This didn't create great changes in black tenant farmers' lives, but it did suggest that the federal government could be a potential ally in the future, if only for incremental progress.[32]

Reforming the Black Belt

During the early twentieth century, progressive reformers across the nation pushed for fundamental changes in how the government took care of its citizens. The progressive agenda—one set on nothing less than social transformation—included everything from limiting big business and improving sanitation to relieving poverty and securing women's suffrage.[33] White Alabamians, however, shared a deep skepticism about the benefits of government intervention in their lives, and the scope of progressive activism in the state was narrow, concentrated on limited political reforms such as regulating the railroads. At its heart, white Alabamians' dogged unwillingness to channel funds toward black Alabamians had much to do with their distaste for social reforms.[34]

World War I broke down some of Alabama's resistance to government assistance for social improvements. Draft boards had rejected a shocking 86 percent of Alabamians during the war for failing health requirements and intelligence exams, as well as receiving exemptions for family or economic considerations. The dismal rate cut deep into Alabama's pride, rallying some support for measures to improve health and education. Elected in 1918 on a platform of progressive reforms, the administration of Governor Thomas Kilby instituted Alabama's first departments of health and child welfare and doubled education spending.[35]

Disease was a major concern of civic leaders in Selma, a problem they mainly blamed on black citizens. "It is a mystery to us why more of them do not die, living in the cramped, unsanitary houses that they occupy," the *Selma Morning Times* commented.[36] Colonel W. W. Quarles, the son-in-law of banker Washington Smith, expounded on what many civic leaders saw as the problem: "It is no exaggeration to say that ninety-nine percent of our servants are blacks, and that ninety-nine percent of all our household work is performed by black servants, many of whom are walking, reeking hives of the terrible bugs to [bring] all the susceptible inmates of our homes slow and certain death."[37] However, a smallpox outbreak among white mill workers at the Valley Creek Cotton Mill belied the view that disease was only an issue on one side of the color line.[38]

In 1920 the Dallas County Health Unit opened an office downtown with the mission "to advise the public how to live and to improve sanitation and control disease epidemics" and began vaccinating schoolchildren against smallpox.[39] Meanwhile, citizens declared war against mosquitoes; they drained standing water and swamps and cut weeds in dogged faith that they could eliminate the disease-bearing pests.[40] But, like most social reforms, public health efforts didn't extend to all neighborhoods in the city.[41] Residents of East Selma—home to the railroad men, working-class whites, and African Americans—protested the selective application of sanitation regulations. Nothing was done about the foul-smelling open ditch that cut through East Selma neighborhoods, the one where the Selma Creamery dumped its by-products, and property owners sent a representative to the city council demanding to know why the city had failed to provide proper sewerage on their side of town.[42]

Even fewer traces of Alabama's progressive campaigns reached rural African Americans in the Black Belt. Despite wartime shifts toward food production, the day-to-day lives of black tenant farmers remained much the same. The county had over seven thousand farms in 1920, and 89 percent of them were operated by African Americans. Ninety-one percent of black farmers were tenants, and they lived in a circumscribed world controlled by white landowners and merchants.[43] One of these places was the Minter plantation across the Alabama River, east of Selma, on which J. A. Minter had hundreds of tenant farmers working thousands of acres. In 1919 Minter proposed a new law to the Alabama Legislature banning traveling salesmen from selling to tenants without the written consent of the plantation landlord. It wasn't enough for large owners like Minter to control black tenants' labor; they also wanted to control the people and ideas their tenants interacted with.[44] Governed by provincialism and white supremacy, the state of Alabama put little into providing opportunities for its black residents.

The same applied to public education. During Reconstruction, the task of establishing schools fell under the provenance of individual southern states, and public schools for African Americans were never a priority.[45] In Alabama a bill passed in 1890 mandated that state educational funding be allotted to counties on a per student basis. The funds, however, were funneled through a local board, which then distributed the money among white and black schools in a manner they deemed "just and equitable." Already ruffled over providing tax money for black education, white school boards channeled most of that funding into white schoolrooms.[46] Making matters worse, the constitution of 1901 then capped state, county, and municipal taxes and limited the power of counties and municipalities to go into debt. This institutionalized a situation in which property taxes did not adequately fund local schools.[47]

Regardless of how dismal their straits, African Americans saw education as an essential tool to claiming their freedom after emancipation; in hopes of forging a better future for their children, they added their own resources to the meager amounts provided. They had to proceed with care. In the Alabama Black Belt, attempts by black residents to own land, educate their children, vote, or form organizations garnered the suspicion of local white citizens. In this climate of wariness, industrial education—emphasizing practical, trade-based skills—found fertile ground.[48]

Booker T. Washington's Tuskegee Institute stood close by as a shining example of how industrial education for African Americans and white supremacy could coexist in the Black Belt. Washington urged his students to rely on their labor and make the most of their circumstances. Tuskegee's students trained in home economics, agriculture, brick masonry, and other trades, building dormitories and classrooms and working the institute's land as they learned.[49] Washington's influence spread as his pupils returned to their homes, many in the rural Black Belt, and opened their own industrial training schools. Just south of the Dallas County border in Wilcox County, former pupil William Edwards started Snow Hill Institute in 1893. He sought "to make education practical rather than theoretical," training students in the skills their lives required. R. O. Simpson, the white owner of the plantation where Edwards was born, deeded the school its first seven acres of land. Then, in 1904, a Snow Hill student, Emmanuel M. Brown, opened the Street Manual Training School in his home community of Richmond in Dallas County. Brown's students "spend no time on psychology, economics, sociology, or logic," Edwards explained. "Their time is taken up trying to raise crops, to manage a small farm, to cook, and to sew."[50]

White residents viewed industrial education as a way to make black residents more industrious that did not challenge the economic structure of white supremacy; African Americans, however, could not have seen it more differently. Edwards laid out his intentions for the students at Snow Hill Institute in his memoir *Twenty-Five Years in the Black Belt*. He wanted to make rural black residents into leaders who would "teach them how to live economically, to pay their debts, to buy land, to build better homes, better schools, better churches, and above all, how to lead pure and upright lives and [be] helpful citizens in the community in which they live."[51] White landlords supported industrial education, confident they were creating more productive tenants, but Edwards's students had their sights set on being independent landowners and community leaders.

National philanthropic organizations played a central role in supporting the educational efforts of rural African Americans. The Rosenwald Fund—run by Sears, Roebuck and Company magnate Julius Rosenwald—built thousands of public school buildings for black children throughout the South in the 1920s and 1930s. Local communities had to meet two stipulations to secure a Rosenwald school: black residents needed to give their support through either funds or donations of labor, and the county needed to agree to incorporate the school into its public school system.[52]

Fifteen miles west of Selma, black residents in the Orrville area set out in the spring of 1921 to build a Rosenwald school for their children. In addition to pooling their own financial resources, they needed the blessing of Darby M. Callaway, the white superintendent of Dallas County schools. Callaway corresponded with J. S. Lambert, the Alabama state agent for rural colored schools, throughout that spring and summer, settling funding and construction details of what would become Keith School. Complications plagued the endeavor. When funds were unavailable for building a one-teacher school, black residents consolidated their efforts and supplied five acres of land for a four-room building.[53] Then Lambert rejected the first building plan because it lacked a manual training room, "a very important adjunct to a colored school building of any type."[54] By fall constant delays in securing funding, both at Keith and another Rosenwald school, pushed the white superintendent to frustration: "We are not treating right those niggers," he wrote in one letter.[55] The Keith School finally opened its doors in 1922. The total contributions of Orrville's black residents surpassed those of the state and the Rosenwald Fund: $1,700 compared to $1,300 in public funds and $1,000 from Rosenwald. Coming from the pockets of tenant farmers and a few independent landowners, $1,700 represented an enormous commitment to ensuring an education for their children. By 1929 ten Rosenwald schools were in operation in Dallas County.[56]

Where there was a Rosenwald school, there was often a Jeanes teacher nearby. The Anna T. Jeanes Foundation, begun by a Quaker woman from Pennsylvania, hired black women to teach industrial education to rural African American children across the South. Dallas County's Jeanes teachers worked out of Selma University, starting before World War I, and complemented the school's aim of developing students' "head, heart, and hand."[57] In the early 1920s, the teachers focused on "the fundamentals of industrial work," including cooking and sewing for girls and manual training for boys. They also conducted outreach work in rural communities, organizing mothers' clubs and school improvement associations and raising funds to build new schoolhouses.[58] In the summer of 1918 alone, the Jeanes supervisor organized thirty clubs in the county and held eighteen public canning demonstrations.[59] When the Extension Service took over home demonstration work, Jeanes teachers concentrated their efforts on primary instruction in rural schools and literacy work.[60]

Jeanes teachers had their work cut out for them. Mrs. A. B. Wilson, the local Jeanes teacher, spent much of her time trying to supply rural schools with teachers; a month into the 1920–1921 school year, she had secured instructors for 103 of the 125 black schools in Dallas County.[61] With so many schools spread out across the county's nine hundred square miles, Jeanes teachers could cover only limited ground. Lambert, the rural school agent, warned Mrs. Wilson's successor against being "too scopy" in her efforts; he urged her to focus on doing a few things well and to avoid doing "everything half-way."[62] Despite these challenges, Jeanes teachers became what one Selma resident called "a little black superintendent."[63]

Black residents made the most of the limited resources available to them. The sums of money tenant farmers could raise to erect a local school illustrated the depth of their determination. Industrial education offered a means for black communities to buy land, educate their children, and establish a modicum of independence in a world stacked against them. White landlords in the Black Belt mistakenly thought they were creating more industrious and contented workers. As agricultural education and the Extension Service in the Black Belt expanded, it only gave black residents more tools to build community institutions and organize themselves within but also against Jim Crow.

The Extension Service and the Farm Bureau

John Blake was one of Dallas County's most well-known citizens. A midsized man, equipped with a small notebook and wearing a suit coat and stiff felt fedora, he had come to Selma in 1911 as Dallas County's first county agent, the local representative of the Alabama Extension Service. Fear of the boll weevil had first prompted white landowners to look for help, but in the years after the war, the Extension Service played an ever-growing role in organizing and educating Dallas County's residents. Blake spent most of his time standing in fields consulting with farmers or keeping up with a county agent's daily grind of correspondence and administrative work from his office in the courthouse. He concentrated his efforts among large white farmers, matching the racial climate of the Black Belt. They gave him their hearty cooperation, and by 1915 he estimated that he had either directly or indirectly influenced every white farmer with regard to growing cotton under weevil conditions. Scientific agriculture was his gospel. This included crop rotation and diversification, soil conservation, fertilizer use, and implementation of better farming methods, and his gregarious personality and penchant for talking "an awful lot" certainly helped his popularity.[64]

But no matter how successful the county agent was in selling white farmers on scientific agriculture, the fact remained, as he admitted himself, that "ninety-five percent of the soil is cultivated by negro tenants."[65] There was no avoiding the central fact of white supremacy in the Black Belt—bountiful crops and high-yielding farmland hung on the labor of African American farmers. So, in 1916, Dallas County hired its first black county agent, T. H. Toodle, to bring extension work to black farmers.

Toodle faced insurmountable odds from the beginning. In the credit-based, landlord-controlled system of tenant farming, African American farmers had little say over their supplies or methods. As he met with black farmers in the rural areas of Dallas County, Toodle found that nearly all of them had stopped using fertilizer since the boll weevil. "They were in the habit of buying on credit," he explained. "Now the credit has been withdrawn that prevents the use of fertilizer."[66] Without fertilizer, the Black Belt soil, depleted after decades of continual cotton production, delivered smaller and smaller yields, and black tenant farmers were short on cash and options.[67] Black county agents could promote scientific agriculture all they liked, but until the strictures of credit, spent soil, and Jim Crow's rules of order changed, success was far off.

2.1 John Blake (right) inspects a field of vetch with H. B. Stringer in 1926. Courtesy of the Auburn University Libraries, Auburn, Alabama.

2.2 African American farm laborers make hay on Charles Potter's Dallas County farm, August 1925. Courtesy of the Auburn University Libraries, Auburn, Alabama.

But black agents did become catalysts for bringing isolated rural people together in community clubs and larger organizations. In 1921 two hundred farmers joined county agent Toodle, local teachers, Jeanes Foundation supervisors, Tuskegee representatives, and students for a farmers conference at Selma University. During the event, Selma's black middle class mixed with black farmers from the Extension Service. Sessions covered everything from the proper use of fertilizer to the components of good citizenship. A dozen women, led by Mrs. R. T. Pollard, the wife of Selma University's president, demonstrated food-conservation methods, chair caning, and ways to make soap from scraps, pine needle baskets, house slippers, and brooms.[68] Toodle and his successor, C. D. Menafee, did what they could to support black agricultural work, but they also built a network of community clubs and brought rural and city residents together.[69] By 1925 black county agents were an important presence in Dallas County.

In fact, the entire Extension Service had grown in importance since John Blake and the boll weevil first arrived in Dallas County. Through weekly newspaper features, crop demonstrations on farms, and visits with farmers, Blake and his agricultural methods enjoyed widespread popularity among white landowners. Support for better farming methods permeated the consciousness of planters and merchants alike. By 1920 not only were large landowners planting good cotton seeds, but merchants began furnishing the same seeds to African Americans. "Dallas County will produce as much cotton per acre this year as she did before the weevil came," Blake reported. "Dry weather helped, but good seed and improved methods of cultivation did much."[70]

In 1921 Blake reported to his superiors at the Alabama Polytechnic Institute that he was forming a local chapter of the Farm Bureau.[71] From its local, county-level beginnings in 1911, this farmers' association had spread and grown into the national American Farm Bureau Federation ten years later. While the Extension Service focused on agricultural education, the Farm Bureau worked to support farmers' business interests and secure favorable agricultural legislation.[72] The two agencies grew in tandem after the Smith-Lever Act passed in 1914. County agents, based on their work educating and organizing local farmers, became the logical representatives to coordinate marketing and distribution for the Farm Bureau.[73]

By the spring of 1923, two hundred white farmers had joined Dallas County's local chapter of the Farm Bureau.[74] The organization promised

2.3 Dallas County farmer A. G. Deshervinan ships his turkeys in boxcars with the help of black laborers, November 1927. Courtesy of the Auburn University Libraries, Auburn, Alabama.

to adopt new farming methods to increase productivity, reduce operating costs and marketing losses, and secure more money for crop producers.[75] Cooperation for the sake of farmers' interests was the Farm Bureau's bottom line. From its central office in the courthouse, members sent out questionnaires inquiring how much of popular cover crops (such as vetch and crimson clover) farmers needed, who wanted to purchase pecan trees, and how many calves members would have to market come fall. Using this information, the local bureau then purchased supplies and marketed farmers' products collectively, securing savings and higher profits for individual farmers.[76] Hogs, turkeys, chickens, eggs, and other locally grown produce were all a part of the cooperative selling plan. Favorable reports on the bureau's programs and popularity regularly appeared in the *Selma Times-Journal.*[77]

After three years of work, Blake resoundingly declared, "Nothing has ever come into the County that has done more for the farmer and the County Agent than the Farm Bureau." In his report to the Alabama Polytechnic Institute, he wrote, "This organization has given me a great deal of assistance in my work. I have been in this County for thirteen years as agent. I do not think that I exaggerate when I say that with its help and co-operation I have been able to do more real constructive work in the past three years than I have in the other ten."[78]

While the county agent worked with the men in the fields, his female counterpart, the home demonstration agent, taught women how to improve their homes and better care for their families.[79] Helen Kennedy first began organizing home demonstration clubs among Dallas County's white girls in 1920, and her successor, Annette Tyndall, expanded that work to adults.[80] Each club was made up of a dozen or so members from a rural community, and their activities ranged from clothing projects and baking demonstrations to nutrition lectures and garden work. Farm women also sold the vegetables, eggs, and poultry from their husbands' diversified farming operations at Dallas County's Curb Market. Three times a week, farm women brought in produce from their gardens and baked goods to sell to women in town. The liberal support of city club women and the Chamber of Commerce made the market a resounding success.[81] As with the county agents, home demonstration work extended to African American women when black agent Lucille Davis arrived in 1925.[82] Thanks to the widespread influence of the Extension Service and Farm Bureau, a good many Dallas Countians knew about scientific agriculture, better rural living, and cooperative organizing.

Upbuilding

In 1922 white civic leaders reckoned that the time had come for visitors and citizens alike to understand just how much they believed in their city. An electric sign installed on Broad Street seemed like the perfect symbol of this sentiment. Shining over the heads of bustling crowds of shoppers, it was to read, "Our Country First, Then Selma." A feverish obsession of upbuilding pulsed through Selma and Dallas County during the 1920s. Combining progressive reform and economic advancement, city leaders spared little in their campaign to make Selma the cleanest, most industrious, and most harmonious city in the Black Belt, if not the entire state of Alabama. The Chamber of Commerce, women's clubs, the Rotary and Kiwanis Clubs, the Farm Bureau, and others united behind a vision of economic prosperity, modernization, and cooperation.[83]

But, like the campaigns for better sanitation and farming methods, they needed Dallas County's black majority to succeed. It was on the grounds of upbuilding that leading white citizens tentatively, but paternalistically, reached out to African Americans. In January 1925 a small group of white citizens and "leading Negroes"—educators, ministers, and professionals—gathered at the courthouse. They formed a committee to "minimize differences and to exalt those influences and agencies that are dedicated to community upbuilding with every unit sharing in the resulting benefits."[84] One of its first orders of business was "the cramped, unfit and unsanitary quarters" of black families. As one committee member pointed out, "the health of a community is no stronger than its weakest link."[85]

The Rev. Edward W. Gamble, the rector at St. Paul's Episcopal Church, emerged as the committee's most vocal advocate. An independent and assured man, Gamble walked his own path in Selma, scrapping many of the conventions of white supremacy along the way.[86] In a luncheon speech to the powerful Rotary Club, Gamble urged white citizens to take action to improve the conditions of black residents. He pleaded for "greater opportunity, more protection, and more of the comforts of life for the colored people."[87] His advocacy was not typical of white Selmians or even representative of members of the interracial committee. At the committee's next meeting, only white civic club leaders were apparently in attendance, and they discussed problems of the black citizens among themselves. Harmony and a pleasant appearance seemed to be more important than including African Americans as equals.[88] Other than turning up a supporter in the Rev. Gamble, the interracial committee did little to improve the daily lives of black residents.[89]

Civic leaders also sought to recruit new industries to the area in their efforts to build a greater Selma. Even though agriculture fueled the economic engines of Dallas County, a combination of hometown pride, boosterism, and a commitment to progress compelled city leaders to seek out new business. In hopes of attracting industry, cities across the South turned to tax exemptions; promises of cheap, nonunionized labor; industrial bonds; and local citizen financing. Together, Selma's city council and Chamber of Commerce kept pace. In 1923 the council voted unanimously to offer a ten-year tax exemption to all new textile mills or expansions within the city limits, hoping to entice industries.[90] Four years later, Harmon Hunt Frazier, the secretary of the Chamber of Commerce, and F. T. Raiford, the editor of the *Selma Times-Journal,* traveled to Chicago to meet with several business firms.[91] Shortly afterward, a large knitting mill expressed interest in Selma if the city could cover some of the relocation costs. Wealthy Selmians raised $300,000 in the name of progress, but prodigious fund-raising was still not a guarantee. When the mill chose not to relocate, civic leaders were disappointed.[92] They had no doubt that Selma was, as the Alabama Power Company advertised, an "ideal city for manufacturers."[93]

But for all of the excitement around industrial development, Selma's reign as the financial center, transportation hub, and bustling marketplace of the Black Belt still depended on agriculture. "Surely there is no need to emphasize the argument that the more closely the city interweaves its interests with the agricultural development of its surrounding area," the *Selma Times-Journal* argued, "the more certainly will both urban and rural fortunes thrive."[94] Frank Cothran and the other wholesale grocers on Water Avenue noticed how their business boomed when the local Extension Service and Farm Bureau prospered. Cooperation among farmers, merchants, bankers, and professionals seemed like a natural component of up-building, and the Selma Chamber of Commerce wanted to be a part of the action. In 1924 the chamber wholeheartedly endorsed the Farm Bureau's campaign to promote diversified farming and more food crops. Being better versed in business than in agriculture did not stop the chamber from sending a letter to every "planter and tiller of the soil in this country" praising the bureau's "magnificent agricultural program" and urging farmers to plant corn and legumes, livestock and hay, and make a living at home.[95]

One year later, representatives from the Farm Bureau and Chamber of Commerce met jointly to "work out a definite farm program for Dallas County," and Selma businessmen contributed $10,000 to agricultural development.[96] "Only a few years ago, this would have been considered foolish by the Selma Chamber of Commerce, and for that matter by the farmers," Blake reported. "Today it is realized as good business and money well spent. I consider however the wonderful spirit of co-operation existing between the business man and the farmer of our county of much greater importance than the money spent."[97]

As white farmers and merchants alike became promoters of cooperation and better farming methods, they began to pay more attention to demographics. Any program for agricultural development in the Black Belt needed to include black farmers, a fact that the Farm Bureau and Chamber of Commerce knew well. "For there is the weak link, not only in Selma's progress, but in the county as a whole," they declared.[98] To address this problem, they turned to the Negro Extension Service.

Black extension work had started before the war, but it grew to new heights with the enthusiastic support of white county agents, the Farm Bureau, and the Chamber of Commerce. Following the first joint Farm Bureau and Chamber of Commerce meeting in 1925, Mayor T. J. Rowell

2.4 John Blake supervises as a black farm laborer plows under a field of vetch in the spring of 1926. Courtesy of the Auburn University Libraries, Auburn, Alabama.

spoke to the annual conference of black farmers at Selma University. He assured attendees that Selma businessmen were deeply interested in the well-being of black farmers. Sounding more like a county agent than Selma's mayor, Rowell urged black farmers to create balanced, self-supporting farms, increase production, improve quality, and market their products more effectively.[99] The chamber threw its money behind its talk about cooperation and agreed to pay half of the salaries of a black extension agent and home demonstration agent for the county.[100]

Soon, the white Extension Service began paying attention to agricultural education for black tenants, and in March 1925 Blake brought Tuskegee Institute's Movable School to Dallas County.[101] What had begun as a simple wagon equipped with farm implements had expanded into the motorized Booker T. Washington Agricultural School on Wheels. Manned by Alabama's first black demonstration agent, T. M. Campbell, the truck traveled to rural areas to give farming demonstrations to black farmers who could not get to Tuskegee themselves. It would set up at a rural location for two or three days, include the local school and church in the program, and give demonstrations in better farming, housekeeping, and hygiene to black residents.[102] The Selma Chamber of Commerce assured apprehensive landowners that the program would not upset "local conditions and that no section or locality or farm [would] be included in these plans where objection might be offered."[103] During its three weeks in the county, the school drew crowds of rural blacks; 987 at one session that ran through the day and into the evening on the south side of the Alabama River, 750 in Marion Junction, and sizable attendances at Burnsville, Summerfield, and Plantersville.[104] Raiford, the editor of the *Selma Times-Journal*, sent a letter to Campbell afterward praising the school's excellent record: "The school did not ruffle the feelings of a single person in this county that I have heard of. We want it to come again; we will do more on a second trip than at the first."[105]

This white support for black extension work was unprecedented. Black county agent C. D. Menafee published his program for black farmers in the *Selma Times-Journal*, urging tenants to move into their homes for the next year with enough time to make fall and winter preparations and purchase fertilizer early.[106] The annual Negro Farmers Conference at Selma University began awarding cash prizes donated by the Chamber of Commerce to the black farmers with the highest yields and best methods.[107] Menafee worked to bring improved farming methods to rural African Americans and create marketing opportunities for their products. He pioneered a partnership with the Childers Packing Company and arranged for a large group of black farmers to supply vegetable crops for canning. Menafee's job was far from easy, especially given that white landowners dictated the conditions and reaped the benefits of his work. In the spring of 1928, he was driving back to Selma after spending the day in the Carlowville neighborhood rallying black farmers around a new dairy operation. Near J. B. Hain's cotton gin and store, his heart gave out on him. He died on the roadside near Sardis on the south side of the Alabama River.[108] Plantation owners and Chamber of Commerce members alike praised Menafee's work and promptly started searching for another Negro county agent. Death could not stand in the way of upbuilding.

Backlash

Despite the white civic leaders' best efforts, not all Dallas County citizens agreed with the campaign of progress. In the aftermath of the war, lynchings of black soldiers and race riots made regular headlines as black citizens tried to hang onto their wartime gains. Chapters of the Ku Klux Klan—a purely southern organization in the late nineteenth century—appeared across the country, vowing to fight anything un-American, ranging from racial unrest and bolshevism to anarchy, Catholics, and Jews.[109]

The first sign of the Klan in Selma came in 1919. An advertisement published in the local paper urged all "one hundred percent Americans" to join a newly organized chapter of the invisible empire.[110] By 1923 Selma's leading citizens—Cothran, Blake, Gamble, Mayor Rowell, and other merchants and professionals—took action against the growing threat. In a statement in the *Selma Times-Journal*, the signers stood by the Klan of their forefathers, "justified by the upheaval in the South during those stirring times [and] organized to do a necessary work of force and violence." But there was no need for that now. "The Klan can serve no necessary purpose in this City," the signers declared, "and may lead to untold harm in upsetting the relations of good will now existing among neighbors and friends and in disrupting the unity of spirit and effort that is such a transcendent factor in upbuilding this and other communities."[111]

The Klan's anti-Jewish sentiment also made many Selma citizens uneasy. Jewish members of Temple Mishkan Israel were some of Selma's most respected residents, operating Broad Street department stores, doing charity work, and participating in society. Although Selma's Jewish residents were socially all but indistinguishable from their Christian neighbors, their signatures were noticeably absent from the public statement, a testament to their caution regardless of social inclusion.[112] Shortly thereafter, the city council dealt the Secret Order a blow by passing an ordinance prohibiting mask wearing. Those in violation faced drastic fines and imprisonment.[113]

But the local Klan grew. In September 1924 an estimated three thousand to five thousand people gathered at the Just Right Swimming Pool on the Orrville road to participate in the order's naturalization exercises. At the event, as much a social gathering as a secret initiation, the ladies of the Co-operative Home did a brisk business selling cold drinks and refreshments to the crowd.[114] But the Klan was far from only a social organization. In December of that year, a Selma resident sent a letter to the U.S. district attorney detailing some of the local chapter's less savory activities. At the organization's weekly Thursday night meetings in the Gillman Building, various offenders were brought in and Klan members would "handle them very ruff [*sic*]." The letter writer accused the organization of "running Negroes away." White landowner Harry Smith came to a meeting to protest the loss of his tenant, Shannon W., who fled after Klan intimidation, but Smith's intervention accomplished little. Forcing offenders to leave town or taking them to the woods and flogging them were reportedly the organization's favored methods.[115]

These doings of the Klan certainly did not make headlines in a city obsessed with its public image. A front-page editorial published by a Klan representative stated that all citizens "living an upright and honest life" had nothing to fear from the organization.[116] In fact, those listed as members by the writer of the letter to the district attorney were themselves solid contributors to Selma's business community; two were dentists, one was president of the Keeble-McDaniel Clothing Company, others managed at Tissier Hardware, and another operated Lamar and Shanks. The respectable image the Klan tried to muster undoubtedly did not fool African Americans; violence and economic intimidation were part and parcel of white supremacy in Alabama's Black Belt.[117]

In this climate of racial terror, the racial uplift and black nationalist organization of Marcus Garvey, the Universal Negro Improvement Association (UNIA), also found fertile ground. The UNIA was committed to securing economic independence, self-determination, and self-sufficiency for black people across the world. At its peak in the mid-1920s, the organization had thousands of divisions stretching from the United States to Africa.[118] The tenets of Garveyism resonated in particular with the experiences of black residents in the rural South, and hundreds of chapters sprang up in Deep South states, including one in Selma.

The supporters of UNIA believed in protecting their families and controlling their own communities in a hostile environment.[119] Circulation of the *Negro World*, the mouthpiece of the UNIA, helped motivate and sustain these isolated rural chapters. Another UNIA chapter was in Neenah, in neighboring Wilcox County, not far from William Edwards's Snow Hill Institute. The social and economic independence trumpeted by rural Garveyites closely paralleled Tuskegee Institute's efforts to help African Americans establish economic self-sufficiency.[120] Both industrial education and economic independence had deep roots in rural black communities in Dallas County. Likewise, rural UNIA members practiced self-defense and kept their shotguns loaded for that purpose. No records or membership lists survived from Selma's chapter of the UNIA. However, its very existence suggested that black residents were searching for a way to confront the violent racial order and protect themselves against it. While leading white citizens focused on upbuilding during the 1920s, black Dallas County residents pursued education and economic self-sufficiency as a buffer against the injustices of white supremacy.

In the closing years of the 1920s, prominent white Selmians had every reason to expect the prosperity of the past decade to continue. Farmers had adopted better farming methods, allowing them to coax more products from the cotton-worn soil. The Extension Service and Farm Bureau had achieved an unprecedented level of organization among farming people. Avid support by the Chamber of Commerce had helped to unite the interests of farmers and businesspeople, and white civic leaders' commitment to upbuilding had caused them to reach out in limited ways to African American residents. World War I had not ended their second-class citizenship, as African Americans had hoped. Yet the economic opportunities of World War I opened up northern jobs and gave black residents a place to escape southern segregation. For those who stayed, the expansion of industrial education and the Extension Service provided new tools, which black communities used to build stronger schools and strive toward landownership and economic independence.

The Great Depression

Rising floodwaters in March 1929 marked a new era of hard times in the Alabama Black Belt. The Cahaba River and nearby creeks spilled over their banks, covering croplands across Dallas County. Landowners on the Furniss, Kirkpatrick, and Houston plantations to the west of Selma removed the black tenants on their land to safety, but the deluge left countless others stranded.[1] The Rev. Edward W. Gamble of St. Paul's Episcopal Church set out in the lifeboat *Montgomery* to deliver Red Cross relief to the desperate. He found that some large planters were not only refusing to feed their tenants but also denying them access to outside aid. One told Gamble that with so much need among the displaced black tenants labor would come cheap in the coming year.[2] The Red Cross spent the next two months distributing seeds, food, clothing, and furniture to those "many hungry Negroes."[3] Already struggling, rural black residents absorbed the first shocks of what would soon grow into widespread desperation.

Local newspapers headlined the plunging stock market on Wall Street that October, but business on Water Avenue and Broad Street gave no indication of the brewing storm. It wasn't until Christmastime that the first signs of the pending crisis started to show. In mid-December Gamble asked the *Selma Times-Journal* to draw attention to the growing problem of unemployment among white and black citizens.[4] The local Charity Association took up the work of providing for needy white citizens and passed responsibility for poor African Americans on to the chief of police, Norman Stanfill, who helped distribute tons of coal to the many seeking assistance.[5] When Gamble presented a list of forty-two white people who had come to him searching for work, the Chamber of Commerce took action. Already urging residents to "buy Selma products," local businessmen challenged employers to hire more laborers at the start of 1930.[6]

Signs of the economic downturn accumulated slowly over the course of the spring and summer. In February the Bank of Orrville closed because of uncollectable debt.[7] A temporary shutdown at the Alabama Cotton Mill plant in August, caused by a drop in demand for cotton products, put its employees out of work.[8] As the number of struggling and jobless grew, local aid organizations pooled their resources. Private charity instead of government aid had long governed the rural South's approach to the welfare of its citizens, and Selmians turned to these customs to face the recent bout of hard times.[9] In October 1930 the Red Cross, Salvation Army, United Charities, American Legion, the city of Selma, and the Dallas County Board of Revenue came together to form the Selma Relief Association.[10] The association began by supplying six dollars a month to fifty families, mainly for groceries, but winter and rising fuel costs loomed on the horizon. Selma's financially sound citizens reached into their pockets to pay for this aid.[11] "We know that this depression has effected [sic] many," wrote Isidore Kayser, the head of one of Selma's finest department stores, "but send to us what you can to help us in this work."[12]

The deepening depression hit black families the hardest, but relief organizations directed only paltry aid their way. In November 1930 Mrs. Joe Rosenberg, the wife of one of Selma's Jewish merchants, chose to take matters into her own hands. Tapping into her own savings, she opened a soup kitchen in the basement of Tabernacle Baptist Church, the yellow-brick church with two entrances, one on Broad Street and one on Minter Avenue. There she fed unemployed black men and their families a daily bowl of vegetable soup made with beef stock, a slice of white bread, and a piece of corn bread, all at no cost. Mrs. Rosenberg explained that while white unemployed families benefited from organized social services, no such aid was available to black residents.[13] Her initiative showcased the depth of responsibility some white citizens felt to help the needy. Mrs. Rosenberg closed her soup kitchen four months and 7,382 meals later when the Red Cross and relief organizations began extending aid.[14]

The Rev. Gamble's office in St. Paul's parish house was the other place African American residents could find help. Starting in 1931, black families could go to the church to receive one dollar's worth of groceries per week as rations of meat, meal, and peas.[15] Selma University registrar P. L. Lindsey directed the Colored Relief Association, which helped raise funds and supplemented the limited assistance provided by the Selma Relief Association.[16] By February the local charity lists bulged with the names of 132 white and 900 black families. Gamble appeared in front of the city council to plead for additional support. Selma, he argued, was "the mother who alone is responsible for the welfare of her own children." But the small amount of money the city put toward relief, combined with private donations, did not match the tremendous need.[17]

Warm weather and bountiful summer gardens helped relieve some of the cold and hunger, but by August 1931 relief organizations were already preparing for another harsh winter. The Dallas County Red Cross chapter urged farmers and gardeners to "conserve every ounce of food and to prepare to take care of themselves through the winter."[18] Meanwhile, the Chamber of Commerce geared up for a citywide fund-raising drive, appointing citizens to speak to ministers, congregations, and luncheon clubs. "The obligation rests upon Selma citizens to feed and care for every indigent person within our gates," Chairman Morris Bloch explained, "and that obligation is going to be met by the public-spirited people of the community."[19] Not all white Dallas County residents shared in this conviction. Some landowners drew scorn from the more publicly charitable citizens when they confiscated all of their tenants' foodstuffs as rent payment in late October 1931 and forced them to apply for the limited relief available in Selma.[20]

While poorer families suffered, Selma's department stores, wholesale groceries, and banks continued to prosper. Money made in the booming 1920s helped cushion well-off white residents from the harshest realities of the Depression. In the spring of 1931, Carter Drug Company hosted a grand opening for its new $5,000 soda fountain, which it claimed was "one of the three best soda dispensaries in the southeast."[21] Wealthy Selmians had enough resources to enjoy luxuries like a cold Coca-Cola and dancing at the new pavilion at Kopecky's place on Old Orrville Road.[22] A new Kress store opened, and shortly afterward Tissier Hardware store underwent renovation and expanded.[23]

Inter3.1 June Eagle's father co-owned Eagle's Department Store, shown here in 1935. Photograph by Walker Evans. Courtesy of the New York Public Library.

June Eagle grew up in a large apartment at Arsenal Place just west of downtown Selma. Her father owned Eagle's Department Store and Boston Bargain, and the income from the store sheltered his ten-year-old daughter from any suffering during the Depression. She spent the summers riding up to Kenan's Mill on bicycles and swimming at the Selma Country Club with friends. Miller Childers, whose father owned Childers's clothing store, also never went without the necessities of life. During the depths of the Depression, white transients would knock on the back door, asking whether they could rake the yard in exchange for a meal. Childers was used to black men doing this, but the break in racial custom signaled a new degree of hardship.[24] Max Hagedorn, a member of Temple Mishkan Israel, acknowledged that while prosperous families lost money, it was nothing like the hard times that impoverished residents were facing. He urged the Jewish community "to give in this campaign as they have never given before. . . . This is a community responsibility."[25]

Despite pockets of wealth, the deepening crisis stretched local resources thin. In October 1931 the city council passed a one-cent gasoline tax, an action that highlighted the severity of the situation. White Dallas Countians and their ancestors before them had fiercely opposed both taxes and government meddling. But voluntary subscriptions could no longer support so much charity work, and council members saw the "distasteful" tax as the most feasible way for Selma to meet "the obligation of taking care of the down and out people within her gates."[26]

By January, however, the sheer masses applying for aid at the racially segregated relief offices required even more fund-raising. Impoverished rural residents coming to Selma for help found themselves turned away: "It is not possible for the city to shoulder the county's bread and meat problem," the *Selma Times-Journal* conceded.[27] Black churches tried to help, opening their doors on chilly winter nights to give African Americans without coal a warm place to sleep, but these gestures proved only a drop in the bucket.[28]

Eventually, individual charity and local government aid stretched to the breaking point. The 1931–1932 school year came to a close with a warning that only enough funds existed to support a four- or five-month school term the following year: "There are no sources of public revenue that can be tapped."[29] The Red Cross reported in July that it had distributed relief to an astounding 843 families in the past year.[30] By the fall of 1932, local representatives began considering applying for a federal loan from President Herbert Hoover's Reconstruction Finance Corporation (RFC).[31] F. T. Raiford of the *Selma Times-Journal* summed up the feelings of many white citizens when he argued that the responsibility of relief was "a community matter."[32] But the resources of the community had run dry.[33]

In November 1932 white Selmians cast their ballots for Franklin Delano Roosevelt in the midst of the local crisis.[34] The Rev. Gamble reported that the situation among black residents was desperate: many had no food, clothes, or shoes and "no means of alleviating their own distress."[35] The board of revenue rejected Gamble's request for an additional $1,500 in aid because it had no funds available.[36] Dallas County's unemployment list had five thousand people on it, with three times as many black as white names. Then, in the new year, the Red Cross cut off its charity work outside of the city limits because the limited funding could not stretch to all of the county residents who needed help.[37] County commissioner J. A. Minter, whose family had been operating its plantation in Tyler since 1819, assured the county government that "hundreds of negroes are in no worse condition than last year, and will be in the same conditions next year." However, the relief office turned away dozens of persons.[38] "Dallas County Relief Problem Now Pressing," declared the *Selma Times-Journal* in January 1933, noting that "most of the persons applying for aid Monday were white."[39]

The Depression had sapped local resources. When the city and county governments applied for a loan from the federal government's RFC, they had nowhere else left to turn.[40] In a last move of desperation, the city council resorted to creating its own scrip currency in February 1933 to loosen the credit freeze paralyzing businesses. Nearly heroic attempts to muster local resources had done nothing to stop three spiraling years of worsening economic conditions. It pushed white Selmians to the conclusion "that something is wrong with our money system."[41] In these desperate circumstances, white and black citizens were willing to put their faith in a new way and a new deal.

CHAPTER

3

≡

Plowing Under

1932–1940

On a spring day in 1929, Amelia Platts sat on a train heading west through the freshly plowed fields of Lowndes County. She was accompanied by the head agent of the Negro Division of the Alabama Extension Service and was on her way to Dallas County to begin her job as the African American home demonstration agent. Her traveling companion joked that she had better get ready to jump out when they got to Selma because the city was so small that the train would not even stop at the station. He may have been kidding about the train but not about how isolated and out of the way her end destination was. Samuel William (S. W.) Boynton, the Negro county agent and her new colleague, met Platts at the train station. He had taken over when C. D. Menafee died of a heart attack a year earlier and was hard at work trying to help black farmers feed their families, bring in some profit, and throw off the shackles of tenant farming. As he drove Platts to the house of Dommie Gaines, one of Selma's few black registered voters, where she'd be staying, neither of them knew how their work would eventually upset the social order of the entire Black Belt.[1]

The Depression hit in full force soon after their arrival and made times worse for black farmers. As local governments and relief efforts faltered, Americans began demanding unprecedented action from the U.S. government. President Franklin Delano Roosevelt came into office with a broad plan for recovery; his New Deal for the American people fundamentally altered the federal government's relationship to its citizens.[2] New federal agencies pumped much-needed money into Dallas County's economy during the 1930s, paying for everything from agricultural supports and public works projects to employment programs and labor benefits. And local officials eagerly pursued it all.

But money from the federal government came with strings attached, forcing Dallas County's white civic leaders to loosen their grip on local control. While New Deal agricultural programs paid landowners to plow up their cotton crops, they also guaranteed that otherwise-disfranchised black tenants had a right to vote in new farm referenda. Roosevelt's meager inclusion of African Americans undermined southern practices of white supremacy, and people like Boynton and Platts saw the federal government as a new potential ally in their quest for fair treatment, better opportunities, and justice. Bypassing local authorities, Dallas County's black extension agents brought the needs of black residents directly to New Deal agencies. The new two-story African American community center they built in downtown Selma stood as a testament to their efforts. But white Dallas Countians had their limits. When black sharecroppers struck for dollar-a-day wages, law enforcement and landlords unleashed an onslaught of violence to crush their efforts.

The New Deal fundamentally altered the landscape of Dallas County. The plowing under of crops marked the beginning of the end of cotton's long reign. White landowners no longer had to depend on the labor of black tenant farmers, and the new pastureland where cotton once stood paved the way for cattle raising. Boynton took to warning black farmers that the only way they would stay on the land was to buy it or become a white-faced cow. Together, Boynton and Platts led the way in promoting economic independence for Dallas County's black residents, as well as calling on the federal government for aid. This didn't immediately bring down the social order of the Black Belt, but the slight shift in the balance of power created small changes and gains that later organizing would build on. Once white citizens realized how the New Deal was encroaching on the fiercely guarded boundaries of white supremacy and their economic dominance, their previously enthusiastic support withered like corn in an Alabama cotton field.

The New Deal

In March 1933 President Roosevelt ordered a nationwide banking holiday, the first action in his program for economic recovery. Thanks to the depth of local wealth, Selma's banks had remained stable throughout the early years of the Depression, but they and the rest of the nation's financial institutions temporarily shut their doors while the federal government instituted new security measures. When the Selma National Bank, City National Bank, People's Bank and Trust Company, and Selma Savings Bank reopened, business surged under the new regulations. A "more buoyant tone" permeated the business district, reported the *Selma Times-Journal*, and after no runs on the bank materialized, the municipal government quietly relieved the special deputy officers it had hired.[3]

The recovery agencies of the New Deal debuted over the following months, bringing relief programs with them. The RFC, a holdover from the Hoover administration, provided the first direct relief in Dallas County.[4] In late February 1933, the local office began hiring the needy to do roadwork. Within the first two weeks of operation, the RFC employed 728 men out of the 2,455 applicants from Dallas County.[5] Margaret Shupe, the executive secretary of the Red Cross, transitioned from local to federal relief work, becoming a case worker with the RFC. She began recruiting young men to work in forestry camps, which eventually became part of the Civilian Conservation Corps, and she remained a consistent face over the next few years even as the names of the federal programs changed.[6] By the time summer arrived, the president's early efforts had won resounding endorsements from Selma's staple institutions. Although the farm and industrial recovery plans had yet to be unveiled, the county board of revenue, the city council, the Farm Bureau, the Selma Cotton Exchange, and the American Legionnaires all pledged their support.[7]

In a place like the Black Belt, any economic recovery hung on agriculture. So when Secretary of Agriculture Henry Wallace revealed the details of the federal government's farm plan in June 1933, they took landowners aback.[8] The newly created Agricultural Adjustment Administration (AAA) proposed plowing under millions of acres of cotton in an ambitious attempt to decrease supply and raise prices. In return for withdrawing their acres from cotton production, the federal government offered cash payments to planters. In Dallas County the program was projected to take thirty thousand to thirty-five thousand acres out of production. It might have been unorthodox, but cash was a lucrative selling point. The county's largest landowners called the AAA a "lifesaver" as they eagerly signed on.[9]

Instead of building a bureaucracy from the ground up, the AAA relied on already-existing farm organizations to implement its program. The responsibility for drumming up support and reducing cotton acreage in Dallas County fell to county agent John Blake and the local Farm Bureau. Informational meetings assured attendees that the new agricultural program would not interfere with their control over black tenants. Any money for tenant-worked land that was taken out of production would go directly into the landlord's pocket. The AAA's use of already-existing local structures only furthered the power of those in control. Over the next few weeks, local committees pounded the dirt roads, inspecting acreage and signing up landlords and tenants.[10] On the last day of July, Blake gave the orders to destroy the cotton crops. The thirty thousand acres plowed under were projected to bring $250,000 into the county.[11]

While the AAA demolished fields of summer cotton, merchants and labor groups met in Selma to work out the details of the new National Industrial Recovery Act. Enlisting the voluntary cooperation of businesses, the new industry-wide codes regulated prices, implemented set work hours and wage standards, and assured bargaining rights for workers.[12] Blue-and-white National Recovery Administration (NRA) posters began appearing in Selma store windows after a mass meeting at the courthouse in early August. "Local employers are cooperating 100 per cent in the blanket wage and hour agreements of the NRA," the *Selma Times-Journal* reported, praising the signs.[13] The Buckeye Cotton Company added forty-five new employees on a third shift after it switched employees to eight-hour days and five-day workweeks. Workers began earning the same pay for forty hours a week that they had been receiving for seventy-two.[14] The new NRA protections for workers prompted a surge of local labor organizing. Selma's textile workers, carpenters, paperhangers, and retail clerks all met to charter union locals and discuss higher wages.[15] Four-minute speakers took to the churches to explain how the NRA would bring the economy back, and black and white women set out on foot to solicit universal cooperation.[16] An NRA official praised Selma for its exemplary compliance.[17]

New Deal programs also attempted to put the millions of unemployed citizens back to work. In November 1933 the Civil Works Administration (CWA) replaced the RFC's temporary relief program. The Dallas County CWA office coordinated local public work projects for the purpose of placing the unemployed in reliable, well-paying jobs.[18] The federal program paid

3.1 Sidewalk scene in downtown Selma, 1935. Photograph by Walker Evens. Courtesy of the New York Public Library.

laborers thirty cents per hour for a thirty-hour workweek, as well as providing 30 percent of the material costs to municipalities.[19] The local employment office received thousands of applications from men and women formerly on the relief rolls seeking work in sewer repair, park landscaping, and building and roadwork.[20] Two weeks into the program, "Saturday night crowds on Broad Street and jostling groups on Alabama and Washington and in the vicinity of the food stores and markets" were a testament to the new CWA payroll in Selma.[21]

Unequal in Practice

The first years of the New Deal forged a new relationship between the federal government and American citizens and extended assistance to people who had been consistently bypassed in local relief efforts. Still, the president's promise of economic recovery did not apply equally to black and white citizens. A long history of one-party politics and disfranchisement gave southern politicians unequaled seniority and influence in Congress, and the New Deal's success depended on the cooperation of southern congressmen. As a result, the politics of white supremacy pervaded many relief agencies. And with local boards coordinating programs like the AAA and CWA, racial discrimination was part of the daily operation of New Deal programs in the South.[22]

The administration of AAA programs in the Alabama Black Belt made this imbalance clear. While the largest landowners profited mightily from the reduction in cotton acreage, black tenants and sharecroppers on the land absorbed the bitter aftereffects of federal handouts to the rich. The AAA, on paper, required landowners to distribute the cash they received from plowing under cotton among the tenants who worked the land. Yet by the first fall, reports of pocketed money and displaced sharecroppers trickled back to Secretary of Agriculture Wallace.[23] Making cash payments to tenants for not planting cotton was unthinkable in the Black Belt's social order. Dallas County received a quarter of a million dollars from the first cotton plowup; almost none of this went to black tenants.

That December, rural African Americans streamed into Selma after landlords forced them off the land.[24] The U.S. agricultural census of 1935 confirmed the trend. White operators had worked 133,047 acres of land in 1930, but that number had ballooned to 224,293 acres by 1935. In the span of five years, over 70,000 additional acres of land were put into farm production, while the land that black farmers worked fell by nearly 20,000 acres.[25] With the local Farm Bureau administering federal agricultural programs, black farmers had little recourse against noncomplying white landlords.[26] On top of this, the Alabama CWA disqualified tenant farmers from employment relief, charging that many owned property and "enjoyed ample means to make a livelihood."[27]

But while the AAA consolidated white landowners' economic hold, it challenged the South's political order by insisting that black farmers had the right to vote in farm elections. In Dallas County 7,100 "land-owners, tenants, share-croppers, or those who have any rights involved in the growing of cotton" were eligible to vote in the referendum on cotton controls in December 1934.[28] Hundreds of thousands of AAA dollars hung on—at the very least, nominally—supporting black voting. "This AAA voting is giving [African Americans] ideas that they can become regular voters," the Dallas County sheriff observed. "I think it's dangerous." Federal aid came with potentially revolutionary side effects and suggested to black farmers that they might have an ally in the federal government, a place they could turn to when local officials refused to comply.[29]

The racial effects of New Deal programs appeared in Selma in other ways. The business community's honeymoon with the NRA codes ended as quickly as it had started. The NRA mandated that black workers be paid a minimum wage far higher than what local custom dictated, and the Chamber of Commerce threw its weight behind what it hoped would become a "south-wide movement" encouraging federal authorities to consider "the peculiar labor conditions in the southern states." Under the guise of saving the jobs of "Negro porters, delivery boys and others employed around places of business," Selma employers argued that they could not afford the federally prescribed wages for black employees. Either wages needed to be lowered, or employees would need to be let go.[30]

Local white NRA officials decided to take the problem into their own hands. In August 1933 F. J. Ames, owner of the Selma Manufacturing Company and a representative of the NRA, sent a proposal to a group of black ministers. He asked the Ministerial Alliance to endorse paying black workers lower wages than the NRA codes mandated. A committee of white delegates was leaving for Washington immediately to present the plan, Ames explained, continuing, "I earnestly request that you approve this plan so that the committee . . . may feel that they have the entire support of the leaders of the colored race in Selma."[31] Rev. E. D. Hughes, the Ministerial Alliance's president and pastor of Brown Chapel AME Church, bravely hand-delivered the group's response to Ames: "We have read Mr. Roosevelt's code. We have carefully read all phrases and have no suggestions to offer. Thank you very much for your special interest manifested in our group."[32]

Two days later, two deputy sheriffs appeared at Hughes's door and demanded his presence at the courthouse. He was met by a group of about thirty of the city's leading white citizens, included Norman Stanfill, the chief of police; H. Hunt Frazier, the secretary of the Chamber of Commerce; and E. C. Melvin, the president of Selma National Bank. "We have found that you are not the type of citizen that exactly fits into a community like Selma and Dallas County," the spokesman informed Hughes. "Therefore we have decided that 24 hours from this minute, which is now 3:25 P.M., are long enough for you to get your business together and get out of town."[33]

Hughes did not leave quickly enough. Two days later, five carloads of armed officers came to his house and chased down the man who was taking Hughes's car to a filling station. By the time they returned for Hughes, he had been tipped off and was barreling north at sixty miles per hour in a friend's car. One, then two, then three cars appeared behind them. At a curve with steep ravines on both sides, the friend slowed the car down to twenty-five miles per hour, and Hughes threw himself out into a thick cloud of dust. The mob continued on after the speeding car. Hughes stayed in the ditch, hidden under bushes, until nightfall. He then managed to hitch a ride to Montgomery, never to set foot in Selma again.[34]

The national NAACP appealed Hughes's case to the NRA in Washington, D.C., only to receive a polite response stating that this was a case of "infractions of local laws," and the official could not see what steps the administration might take. "I confess I am deeply puzzled by your letter," NAACP president Walter White responded, "in which you state that the national recovery administration is helpless and can do nothing in the case at Selma, Ala."[35] There was little question that the federal government was no more than a tepid ally, at best.

Issues of race and labor continued to flare up in Dallas County. In July 1934 sixty black relief-roll workers refused to get on the trucks to do county roadwork when they learned that they would be paid only one dollar a day for ten hours of work. They had been promised thirty cents per hour for a thirty-hour workweek. The superintendent of work turned their names over to the county administrator, who approached the state headquarters with the situation. Its solution was "to strike names of the malcontents from the relief roll of the county and to withhold the regular relief checks." The superintendent was instructed to hire nonrelief workers until the disappearance of relief checks helped the striking workers see their error.[36]

Organized-labor threats elicited the same passionate reactions as did challenges to the local racial order. In 1934, 250 textile workers at the California Cotton Mill in Selma voted to join in a nationwide strike. The mill, however, threatened to shut down before workers could walk out. The Chamber of Commerce also intervened. "Selma has never had a strike," member Harry Maring stated, "and this fact has been one of the city's real talking points, as it indicates the good conditions which exist here between all groups."[37] Early the next Tuesday morning, company management posted a closing notice at the mill. Textile workers still walked out before the regular 6:00 p.m. closing time, but the mill's preemptive shutdown squelched any union action.

In July 1937 the National Labor Relations Board (NLRB) revisited the mill's closing at hearings at Selma's federal courthouse. The Textile Workers Organizing Committee, looking to represent workers in the reopened and renamed Sunset Mill, accused the mill of shutting down on account of labor organizing activities. It also charged that when the mill began work again, it discriminated against union-friendly workers, selectively hiring former employees or new hands.[38] Company officials recorded no comments, but it was no secret that local businessmen stood firmly against unions. In the NLRB-supervised election at the Sunset Mill one week later, both white and black employees cast their ballots.[39] This time the Textile Workers Organizing Committee lost the election by 5 votes out of a total of 277.[40] Having the right to organize did not stop fierce antiunion opposition.

Dallas County's wealthy and powerful reaped big benefits from the New Deal. The Farm Bureau, controlled by large landowners, dictated who received the largesse from the new agricultural programs. Unsurprisingly, black tenants got little. Likewise, white business and civic leaders controlled public work programs and swiftly minimized any challenges to the status quo, such as when they ran Rev. Hughes out of town. But the federal government's limited promises were still disruptive. African Americans refusing discriminatory wages and workers threatening to unionize required action. The New Deal did not unravel the South's long history of white supremacy, but it did give support and hope to those poor and black southerners seeking to overturn a system that kept them on the bottom.[41]

Black Farmers and the Extension Service

County agent S. W. Boynton and home demonstration agent Amelia Platts knew almost every black person living in the rural areas of Dallas County and a good number of those living in Selma as well. They had already been working to bring government programs to African Americans when the New Deal began. The AAA, NRA, and other agencies might have been administered by local white boards, but Dallas County's black extension agents made sure their people took the fullest advantage of the federal government's new, if lukewarm, aid to African Americans. Boynton and Platts seized the chance to connect the people they served with the maximum possible aid they could squeeze out of the New Deal programs.

In May 1928 Boynton began what would become a twenty-year tenure as Dallas County's black farm agent. He had grown up in Griffin, Georgia, the oldest son of an independent and successful farmer, and trained at Tuskegee Institute under the renowned agriculturalist George Washington Carver. When T. M. Campbell, the head of Tuskegee's Movable School, introduced twenty-six-year-old Boynton to John Blake, Boynton had already served for two years as a county agent in Lamar County, Georgia. The Dallas County

3.2 S. W. Boynton inspects the compost pile of L. K. Page of the Old Town Community on a farm tour, 1933. Courtesy of the Auburn University Libraries, Auburn, Alabama.

Farm Bureau and black farmers' clubs approved Boynton's hire, and the new county agent got to work, connecting black vegetable farmers with the Childers Packing Company and establishing dairy routes across the county.[42]

A year later, Platts joined Boynton as the black home demonstration agent.[43] When she was growing up, her father had operated a wood yard in Savannah, Georgia, and built a two-story house for his family; he and his wife had raised their ten children to be leaders. Platts received a degree in home economics from Tuskegee Institute and taught at a Rosenwald school before beginning her work as Dallas County's home demonstration agent. The first day she went into the country, Boynton gave her some advice about talking to farm people. "Always be kind and don't say anything that will make them think your education is so far above theirs," he told her. "They may be unlearned, but they are intelligent and can teach you a whole lot you don't know."[44]

Working in the rural areas of Dallas County, Boynton and Platts saw upfront the harshness of daily life for African Americans. "I had read in school that Abraham Lincoln signed the Emancipation Proclamation in 1863," Platts explained years later. "I believed in this until I went to Dallas County, Alabama." They met families who worked all year producing cotton and never broke even when they settled their debts with the landlord each fall.

They found children who attended school only from November to March so that they could work in the fields. They heard story after story of violence. The wrongs they encountered traveling the back roads of Dallas County convinced Boynton and Platts that only landownership and political rights could end the oppression of rural people. It became their life's work.[45]

With over a hundred thickly settled black communities in Dallas County in the 1930s, the county agents first faced the daunting task of connecting with rural residents. Much of their work depended on community clubs formed to teach rural people better ways of living. By 1932 at least twenty-four home demonstration clubs were operating across the county, from Safford to Plantersville and Bogue Chitto to Minter.[46] The club officers met once a month at the county agents' office in Selma as the Club Leaders Association. At these meetings, club leaders kept up-to-date with the latest demonstration methods and met other leaders from across the county. Back home, they led local club work when the agents could not be there.[47]

In May 1930 Platts brought the county nurse to Bogue Chitto, fifteen miles west of Selma, to give typhoid inoculations. Bogue Chitto was a community of black landowners whose residents had inherited land their grandparents had bought after the Civil War. Many had worked the land as slaves when it had been the Quarles plantation.[48] During Reconstruction nearly every man in Bogue Chitto was a registered voter and exercised that right until it was taken from them by force. Owning land gave the residents independence, and they knew how to protect their own. Local lore had it that the Klan came calling one night, looking for a Bogue Chitto man who had refused to doff his hat to a white man and say "Yessir." They were met by a spray of bullets and did not come back.[49]

Over nine hundred Bogue Chitto residents gathered at the clinic grounds that spring day for inoculations. Platts taught club songs and talked about club work to those who were interested.[50] She found Bogue Chitto citizens "receptive, and willing to follow the guidelines to better the community." "This club is one of the live-wires of the County," Platts wrote in her annual report a few months later, "and the work being done is far above [that of] the average club." When Dallas County black agents began holding voter registration classes a decade later, Bogue Chitto was one of the first communities to open its doors.[51] The same was true of black landowning communities across the Black Belt. Gee's Bend in neighboring Wilcox County and White Hall in Lowndes County, communities that had bought land under New Deal programs, were also at the epicenter of movement activity in the 1960s.[52]

3.3 Mrs. Jamerson, a club leader in the Tyler Community, displays her canned goods in 1928. The home demonstration agent called her a leader "who can can." Courtesy of the Auburn University Libraries, Auburn, Alabama.

Platts and Boynton urged farmers to adopt live-at-home programs, which involved planting big-enough gardens and raising enough livestock and poultry to supply the family with almost everything it needed. They found that black city dwellers were inclined toward the Extension Service's practices of self-sufficiency as well.[53] Many families kept small gardens and harvested pecans from trees in their yards, and some, like Mabel Blevins, raised cows and chickens in their backyards. Blevins, whose husband worked for the post office, did not have an outside job but sold her milk and butter to black neighbors as a source of income. She also opened her house to black visitors, as all of the city's hotels were for whites only.[54] In addition to working in processing plants and as domestic workers, Selma's black citizens also eked out a living through bootlegging. J. L. Chestnut grew up on a block where four of his neighbors sold corn whiskey.[55]

Each February, schools closed, and black city and county residents amassed at Selma University for the annual Negro Farmers Conference and Ham Show. Attendees watched demonstrations, viewed exhibitions, and learned how to make what they needed at home.[56] The ham show was Boynton's idea. He had been encouraging black farmers to raise hogs as a means to earn extra income and put meat on the dinner table, and the Farmers Conference of 1930 showcased five thousand pounds of ham. Feeding one's own family and depending on themselves—a staple message of black extension agents—offered African Americans a thin shield against the local customs of white supremacy. Other presentations—"How I Can Succeed in Dairying," "Successful Gardening," "Poultry Raising," and "Home Improvements"—taught black farmers ways to be more self-sufficient.[57] Conference attendees "have decided that the only way back to prosperity is to make an independent living," Platts reported.[58] Selma University's president, William H. Dinkins, also supported cooperation and economic independence within the black community. "Such co-operation would be the means of giving us a fuller share in the determination of the course of events," he wrote.[59] If white supremacy denied African Americans political rights, economic independence was another means to subvert the order of Jim Crow.

With Boynton's assistance, black farmers also organized their own seg-regated unit of the Farm Bureau in the early 1930s. The black unit did not meet with the white unit, but "they have the privilege of making all their purchases and selling their produce through the main Farm Bureau," Boynton explained. Pooling interests let black members collectively buy their fertilizer, seeds, and feed at lower costs, as well as market their hogs,

3.4 S. W. Boynton training 4-H club boys how to judge poultry in 1933. Courtesy of the Auburn University Libraries, Auburn Alabama.

poultry, sheep, and cotton for higher profits. All government loans were routed through the local Farm Bureau, so black farmers needed to be included if they hoped to survive.[60] After Roosevelt's election, Boynton and the Negro Farm Bureau brought word of the new agricultural relief programs and farm loans to black farmers.[61] The Negro Farm Bureau's representatives traveled to Chicago in 1935 to attend the organization's national convention, where they listened to President Roosevelt and Secretary of Agriculture Wallace speak on the farm program. A delegation of white farmers from Dallas County also attended but separately.[62] The following year, over a hundred black extension members journeyed to Tuskegee to hear Wallace speak about the soil conservation plan.[63]

In June 1936 Dallas County's two black extension agents got married. Amelia Platts and S. W. Boynton's common work in the rural areas of Dallas County had brought them together, but marriage meant that the new Mrs. Boynton had to resign her position as a home demonstration agent, which was open only to single women. Lucy Upshaw arrived a month later to assume the duties of the demonstration agent.[64] The Boyntons opened a life insurance office on Franklin Street, in the black business district downtown. Although Amelia Boynton no longer headed up rural organizing, she explained that "the friendships I had made in those early years endured, and my office became a listening post for the affairs of the black community." Her daily work extended far beyond the insurance business. Black residents walked through the office doors seeking help of all kinds, whether it was information, notary services, insurance, employment, tax advice, or farm advice.[65]

Voter registration had always been a priority of S. W. Boynton. When his future wife turned twenty-one years old, he brought her to the courthouse to register to vote. Platts's mother had been a devoted women's suffragist, bringing her daughter along in the horse and buggy as she brought people to register to vote. Witnessing the dependency of the people they worked with only reinforced for the Boyntons the importance of the vote. "My husband and I decided that we were going to help people register," she explained. As county agents, they began holding meetings in rural churches and homes to teach people to fill out the registration forms.[66]

Events in the mid-1930s gave new life to the Boyntons' voter registration efforts. In 1936 the Reformed Presbyterian Church was forced to end its sixty-five-year relationship with Knox Academy when the Pittsburgh-based church ran out of money. Knox Academy was a pillar of Selma's black community, and a group of black citizens, the Selma Civic League, assumed the management and financing of the school to keep it from closing.[67] The group was a subsidiary of the newly reinstated Dallas County Voters League (DCVL). C. J. Adams, a World War I veteran and railroad clerk, had first organized the league in the late 1920s to encourage African Americans to become registered voters. His efforts, however, did not make much headway in Selma's repressive racial climate.

But the potential closing of Knox Academy in 1936 rekindled DCVL. There were few black registered voters in Selma, and even fewer were willing to get involved in politics, so the first meeting was small. C. J. Adams, S. W. and Amelia Boynton, Henry Boyd, P. L. Lindsey, Dommie Gaines, and A. G. Carroll made up the roster. They sent a petition to the board of education requesting a high school with twelve grades and a new building for the public Clark School. "This was perhaps the first petition ever sent to the city fathers by organized blacks," Amelia Boynton recalled. The white board members ignored it.[68] But in June 1937 the city school board did decide to take over and incorporate Knox Academy into the public school system.[69] Then in October 1940, thanks to funding from the New Deal's Works Progress Administration, Knox opened an eleventh grade for black students.[70] Organizing around the public schools had brought new life to DCVL. Over the next two decades, Adams and the Boyntons determinedly continued building DCVL as their base for black political organizing.

Sharecroppers Union

While the Boyntons worked to help people get a leg up during the Depression, the desperate situation of tenants also gave birth to another organization in the Alabama Black Belt. During the bleak years of the mid-1930s, the Sharecroppers Union (SCU), organized by Alabama's Communist Party, spread throughout the region. Its goals were "union, justice, and better life" for sharecroppers, tenant farmers, and small landowners.[71] In Tallapoosa County on the northeastern edge of the Black Belt, thirty black sharecroppers organized the union's first local in 1931. The black men and women who joined the SCU could not necessarily recite Communist ideology nor locate the Soviet Union on a map, but members like Ned Cobb understood that it was an organization for poor people. As he saw it, the union "was workin' to bring us out of bad places where we stood at that time and been standing since the colored people had remembrance."[72]

In Tallapoosa County SCU members began meeting in secret. The literature they distributed called for sharecroppers to have the right to market their own crops, be paid a dollar a day in cash, grow their own food, and have a nine-month school year for their children. White landlords did not take the SCU's challenge to their authority lightly. White law enforcement officials, vigilantes, and black union members exchanged a volley of deadly gunfire over the course of several days near Camp Hill, Alabama. The body of one union member was dumped on the steps of the Dadeville courthouse, and dozens more black farmers were arrested.[73] Southern whites knew full well what was at stake in the demands of poor black tenant farmers and rose quickly to protect their interests.

By 1934 sharecropper strikes had spread westward across the Black Belt into Dallas County and neighboring Lowndes County. The New Deal's Agricultural Adjustment Act and Bankhead Cotton Control Act helped fuel the flames of discontent. Paid to not plant cotton, white landowners did not need their tenants' labor in the same way as before and had extra money to buy farm machinery. Tenants found themselves booted from the land or converted into easily exploitable wage hands. The spread of SCU locals stemmed directly from the displacement and abuses caused by federal programs.[74]

The battles of the SCU came to a head in Dallas County in May 1935. Black tenants, who sometimes received as little as thirty-five cents for a ten-hour workday, struck for dollar-a-day wages. White landlords and law enforcement officials mounted a violent campaign to neutralize the threat.[75] From the very beginning of the strike, white landlords bloodied black share-croppers or ran them out of their homes, and the sheriff arrested eighteen sharecroppers. Saul Davis, a union leader, was one of those placed in jail. Two days after his arrest, white law enforcement officials delivered him into the waiting arms of a white mob allegedly made up of American Legion-naires.[76] The terror only worsened when International Labor Defense repre-sentatives connected with the Communist Party came to Selma to investigate the violence. On May 12 Sheriff Reynolds arrested Henry Johnson and Ber-nard Owen in a private home and held them for over twenty-four hours for interrogation. The sheriff then released them at gunpoint into the hands of a band of seven men in three cars. One of the cars was the green Plymouth driven by the sheriff. The mob drove Owen and Johnson fifteen miles out-side of Selma, stripped off their clothes, and tied their hands around the trunk of a tree. They then beat them with horsewhips and ropes until blood dripped down their sides. After muttering threats of lynching, one vigilante lit a piece of paper and held the flame to one of the men's wounds.

Other black workers and investigators suffered similar fates. Ed Arnold was taken from his job, placed in jail, and released into the hands of the mob three nights later.[77] Willie John Foster, a black worker from Birmingham, came to Selma to investigate the earlier arrests. After being arrested while walking down Selma's main street, the desk sergeant at the jail released him to what an International Labor Defense organizer called "the landlord-police terror gang."[78] A week later, he still could not be found.[79] At the end of June, the body of a black man, presumed to be Foster, was found off of Summerfield Road, reportedly buried by the police, who had threatened the black neighbors into silence.[80] Robert Wood, the district secretary of International Labor Defense, pleaded with Alabama governor Bibb Graves to intervene and end the violence. "Not only the United States Constitu-tion, but all state and community laws," he wrote, "are being violated in this reign of terror directed against working people by united forces of police and landlords."[81] The onslaught against the SCU extended into neighbor-ing Lowndes and Perry Counties over the summer. While the Communist Party's newspaper, the *Daily Worker*, reported that some landlords raised wages to seventy-five cents a day to stop the strike from spreading, the strike of Dallas County's sharecroppers brought little gain at a deadly price.[82]

The swift and violent reaction of white officials and landowners illustrated what was at stake. The social order of the Black Belt—which protected the wealth and authority of white citizens—was built on cheap, dependent, unorganized black labor and backed by terror and violence. The SCU strike threatened the racial and economic foundations of Dallas County, and it evoked an immediate response from white citizens seeking to protect their interests. As the *Daily Worker* observed, "Landlords from the outlying plantations own the Selma shops. The Selma cops are employed to preserve the peace—for the landlords."[83] The SCU strike laid bare whites' desperate need to maintain power by any means necessary, whether lynching, beating, or murder.[84]

The terror may have quieted the activities of the SCU, but it did not kill the determination of its rural black members. "The landlords are crazier than ever," one SCU member in Selma explained, but "they can't stop the organizin' noway."[85] In July 1936 forty SCU members from across the Black Belt gathered in New Orleans and issued a call to action.[86] The delegates affirmed black sharecroppers' right to organize for better working conditions and wages free from the vigilante terror that had left so many members dead.[87] They urged "all workers to utilize their legal right to armed self-defense when they are attacked by thugs and mobs to protect their lives and homes."[88] They demanded equal pay for equal work for women; higher wages for cooks, domestic workers, and washerwomen; and free medical care for new and expecting mothers. The SCU attacked the poll tax for strengthening the power of the landlords and industrialists and discouraging law enforcement officials from providing equal justice. They also reprimanded the AAA for worsening the conditions of tenant farmers.[89]

But resolutions did little to change the repressive conditions that black sharecroppers faced at home. Two years after the dollar-a-day strikes in Dallas County, the mail carrier on an Orrville route opened a bundle of SCU publications addressed to Butler Molette. Molette was a thirty-seven-year-old union member and farmer who had never been to school and could not read or write, although his wife could. After the postal employee began threatening Molette's life, the family fled to Birmingham.[90] "If President Roosevelt is going to carry out the mandate the people of this country gave him on election day, if law and order is to be established in the cotton country," one SCU member wrote, "the constituted government authorities will act at once to see that lives are protected and the right to organize is established."[91] That call fell on deaf ears. Black tenants appealed to Roosevelt to challenge the provincial and repressive culture of the rural South, but the

New Deal gave little to black sharecroppers in its early days. The federal government's tepid inclusion of African Americans in AAA voting and wage codes did suggest a new potential ally for black Dallas County residents, but it was a promise yet unfulfilled.[92]

From Relief to Public Works

In 1936 the American people once again put their confidence in President Roosevelt. In his second term of office, the tenor of the New Deal shifted, from providing immediate relief to building and strengthening the nation's communities for the long term. A growing block of black voters, southern liberals, unionists, and northern radicals, dissatisfied with the conservatism of the early New Deal, championed more progressive, further-reaching reform. Concern about the stunted economic landscape of the South and the rise of fascism in Europe also fueled this push for change.[93] Roosevelt's second term marked a shift toward promoting large-scale public works projects and addressing the needs of the rural poor.[94] As the federal government became a somewhat more dependable ally, African Americans put their hopes in the New Deal and federal aid to help challenge the local boundaries of white supremacy.

The nationwide rampant unemployment of the early 1930s had caused Americans to rethink their ideas about the role of the federal government in citizens' daily lives. More than at any other time in the nation's history, American citizens began to see unemployment as a structural problem of the economy, not an individual failure. This prompted a new faith in the government's ability to address such issues, as well as hope for the saving grace of public works. The Public Works Administration (PWA) and the Works Progress Administration (WPA) of the New Deal were on the front lines of pushing public works projects as a means of building lasting change.

During its tenure, the PWA built a national infrastructure, funding the construction of bridges, dams, schools, hospitals, and public buildings throughout the country. The agency worked to stimulate the economy by creating a demand for building materials while putting money into workers' pockets. The federal government solicited project proposals from individual cities, which gave municipalities the ability to choose the projects of greatest benefit to their communities. Financing for projects took the form of a combination grant-loan package. The PWA agreed to fund 30 percent of the project cost by a grant and provide low-interest loans to communities to cover the remaining balance.[95]

Roosevelt appointed Secretary of the Interior Harold Ickes as administrator of the PWA. Each project was required to meet standards for engineering soundness, legal authority, and financial capability. Ickes's careful scrutiny meant PWA projects moved slowly but were mostly free of corruption.[96] The PWA's enabling legislation made no mention of discrimination standards, but Ickes mandated that projects hire African Americans in proportion to the census of 1930. He used the same proportional standard to funnel federal funds to black-sponsored projects. While local administration of PWA projects thwarted many of Ickes's efforts, the PWA spent an unprecedented amount of federal funds on African Americans as compared to other public or private agencies.[97]

Selma's white civic leaders had always had big dreams for their city, but it was the city's black residents who took the first steps in pursuing public works funding. Rural African Americans from the county regularly traveled to Selma to do their shopping and socialize. While downtown businesses appreciated their black customers' dollars, none of the merchants provided a sitting area or restroom for them. S. W. and Amelia Boynton came up with the idea of bypassing the obstinate local white officials and securing federal funding to build a black community center. In January 1936 they held a kickoff meeting, initiating a campaign among black Dallas Countians to raise money to cover the labor costs of the building. White Selmians, however, were about as enthusiastic at the prospect of federal aid coming directly to local black residents as they were about setting fire to a cotton warehouse, and the campaign met obstacles at every turn.[98]

So the Boyntons turned to the Rev. Edward W. Gamble, their most reliable white advocate, to front their project and appeal to the PWA for funding. After raising $3,000 among black residents, the group successfully secured a $17,000 direct grant from the PWA. Unlike other federal projects, the grant did not require the city government to match the funds. It only asked the all-white city council to provide a plot of land valued at $2,500. Black residents in Dallas County had already raised part of the money for the land, meaning that the proposed project would cost the city only $1,500.[99] It was as cheap a price tag for a brand-new building that anyone could hope for, but where to put it was the problem. When the city council announced a potential location on Lawrence Street, white property owners protested so vigorously that the council rescinded its proposition and resumed searching for another location.[100] "At meeting after meeting with city officials," Amelia Boynton explained, "we would present requests and each time some of the members would block it." Months after its start, municipal inaction had stalled all progress on the black community center.[101]

It took a string of unexpected happenings in late 1937 to break the stalemate. It began when the president of the city council, Milton Wood, passed away that November. Then, a month later, another council member, Otto Erhart, died unexpectedly. It was unfortunate to lose two members of the city council at once but not unheard of in municipal affairs. However, while Erhart's funeral arrangements were still being finalized, Sidney Katzenberg, a coal merchant and the council member representing the third ward, died of a heart attack, and only a few hours later Councilman W. C. Hall was seriously injured when he was hit by a car. These ill-fated councilmen had been among the staunchest opponents of the community center. After the string of municipal tragedies, the Boyntons found the remaining council members finally willing to support the project. "Heaven knows whether or not this was indirectly an answer to prayer," Amelia Boynton recalled, "but anyway, the city council decided not to stand in the way but to buy a piece of property and permit the government project to proceed. Our dream came true."[102]

In January 1938 work finally began on the community center. The plot of land was on Franklin Street, just down from the train station and in the downtown's black business district. Local black contractor George Wilson designed the two-story yellow-brick building, which included restrooms, showers, an auditorium, and the offices of the Negro Extension Service and Farm Bureau. Securing funds for lighting and obtaining furniture caused further delays, but in January 1940, four full years after the Boyntons began raising funds for the building, the community center finally opened its doors to black residents.[103]

Unlike the black community center, public works projects sponsored by the city council received enthusiastic support and speedy follow-through. Mayor Lucien P. Burns and county commissioner G. C. Blanton traveled to Washington, D.C., in October 1936 to lobby for PWA funding for a new city hall and jail.[104] They secured grant money that month, and the ground breaking took place only three months later at the Alabama Street lot, which happened to be right next to the lot that would become the community center.[105] The building costs totaled $180,000. The PWA provided $81,000 in an outright grant for the construction, and the Selma city government issued notes and bonds to cover the remaining balance.[106] By the end of 1937, city business was under way in the hallways and offices of the new municipal building. Funding from the PWA also built Selma a new white high school, replacing the aging and overcrowded Tremont Street High School. The PWA offered the city a $145,125 grant in August 1938 with the stipulation that construction begin within eight weeks.[107] Work on the building started right on schedule, and after the Thanksgiving break in 1939, Selma's white high school students began attending classes in the brand-new Albert G. Parrish High School. From proposal to completion, the project had taken less than a year and a half.[108]

In November 1937 the city of Selma received more good news when Alabama governor Bibb Graves announced a plan to build a new bridge over the Alabama River. Funded by state and federal money, the bridge seemed to leading citizens like a guarantee of a promising economic future. Securing a location, appraising the property, and working out other details took time, and flooding and unforeseen delays slowed construction. But in May 1940 the arching Edmund Pettus Bridge—named for the revered hometown Confederate general and U.S. senator—was complete. Selma spared nothing for the opening extravaganza; speeches by former and present governors, barbecues, historical tours, music by the Selma high school band, and a ball were all part of the festivities. The demand for *The Cavalcade of Selma, a Historical Pageant* was so great that it held two performances on the day of the bridge opening.[109]

The Edmund Pettus Bridge, connecting Selma to the highways of Alabama and the nation, stood as a grand symbol of how federal and state funding had chipped away at Selma's insularity. Money pouring into Selma during the New Deal changed the landscape of the city in concrete and lasting ways. Promises of funds, agricultural support, and buildings moved leading white citizens to reluctantly relinquish some of their local control, even when that infringed on customs of white supremacy. While city officials attempted to regulate the federal dollars entering Selma, black residents still benefited. In addition to the PWA funding for the community center, the WPA operated a daycare center for African American children a block away from the Boyntons' house on Lapsley Street and paid for adult education classes. "When the federal government created the PWA and then the WPA," Amelia Boynton remembered, "people were kept from starving and the doors opened for young children to get proper food."[110] This aid also suggested to black residents that there was another place to turn, outside of the Alabama Black Belt, for relief and assistance—and, later, political and economic justice.

By the late 1930s, the acute desperation of the Depression was fading into the past, thanks to President Roosevelt's relief programs. The New

Deal offered Dallas County farmers sizable sums of money each year to not plant cotton on their land. It brought relief aid, jobs, and regular paychecks to thousands of out-of-work citizens. Public works projects not only employed local residents but planted forests on overworked land, repaired sewage systems and roads, cleaned up parks, and built a better school for white children, as well as new city offices. When Dallas County's head of the AAA resigned in 1941, he estimated that he had distributed over $4 million in local aid since his start in 1933.[111] Despite the millions of dollars that had poured into the county, the closing years of the decade marked a turning point in white residents' opinions about the president and his economic recovery programs. The scale tipped when federal aid began posing larger threats to the local racial order. In the late 1930s, the federal government's increasing interest in aiding tenant farmers, equalizing wages, and supporting unions caused white Dallas County residents to rethink their priorities.

In July 1937 outrage exploded in the Black Belt over the proposed Black-Connery Bill. The local newspaper labeled it "the end of the honeymoon of the New Deal and the farmer."[112] The bill, which became the Fair Labor Standards Act of 1938, called for minimum-wage and maximum-hour standards across the nation.[113] White landowners in Dallas County opposed the bill, which would force them to pay black farm laborers higher wages. It was "the greatest peril to confront [the South's] economic interests since the imposition of carpet-bagger rule in reconstruction days," the *Selma Times-Journal* accused.[114] Speakers at the Kiwanis Club and the Farm Bureau condemned the bill and its "threat to the personal liberties of the farmer."[115]

Landowners had no intention of increasing black farm laborers' pay. In August 1938 the WPA offered to provide additional employment for farm families with cash incomes of less than $300. The county commissioners declared that they were "not interested" in taking part in the plan.[116] With approximately six thousand eligible people in the county, local farm organizations feared the effects that such a program would have on farm labor.[117] The plan passed only after a delegation from the Selma Retail Merchants argued that it was "economically essential at this time that new cash sources be made available for this section where cotton is the basis of most incomes."[118]

Mumblings of discontent with New Deal regulations swelled into accusations of federal meddling by the end of the decade. When the president, citing his National Emergency Council's report, labeled the South the country's "number one economic problem" in July 1938, it only confirmed white southerners' growing suspicions about the New Deal.[119] Confronted with a farm labor shortage in 1940, white Dallas County farmers unleashed a torrent of criticism against President Roosevelt's relief efforts. They blamed the shortage on the federal government's intervention. "The situation is one which was inevitable from the time that government started directing the destinies of the citizenry," the local newspaper declared. "The combination of crop restriction measures and ready relief money has rapidly drained the rural areas of [the] workers necessary to till and cultivate our rich black soil."[120] Accusing WPA relief programs of tempting black laborers away with easy alternatives, Dallas County's white landowners and citizens demanded that the federal government extricate itself from the "agricultural meddling of the past seven years."[121]

In her report in 1935, Mrs. Luella C. Hanna, the Negro women's extension agent for the state of Alabama, acknowledged that the New Deal had not brought prosperity to black farmers in the way they had hoped. But, she wrote, "it has loosened the chain of economic slavery somewhat and set the slave on the path which leads to the road of prosperity." After experiencing the "good fruit" of the New Deal agricultural programs, Hanna saw that "the black slave is left (as he was [for] nearly three-quarters of a century) with meager benefits, disturbed and lonely." She argued that it would be up to the black extension agents and their live-at-home program to put black farmers "well on the road to prosperity."[122] The values of independence, economic self-sufficiency, education, and landownership ran deep in rural black communities, and in Dallas County, S. W. and Amelia Boynton worked hard to mobilize these and other resources to win economic and political justice for African Americans.

The brief honeymoon that white Dallas County citizens had with the New Deal came to an end much along the lines of what Mrs. Hanna had laid out. The New Deal had put large sums of money straight into the pockets of white landowners and businessmen, and local control kept practices of white supremacy firmly entrenched. But it also fundamentally challenged the status quo by including African Americans in AAA voting, wage codes, and other federal funding. Although this modicum of fairness left much to be desired, black residents saw their new and direct relationship with the federal government as a way to circumvent local white authority. As black residents successfully used the federal government to challenge the boundaries of white supremacy, white citizens rejected President Roosevelt's aid as it began to look like reform rather than restoration of the status quo.

Craig Air Force Base

May 1940 was a good month for Selma and Dallas County. Following a weekend of festivities celebrating the opening of the Edmund Pettus Bridge, Alabama congressman and Selma native Sam Hobbs revealed that he was trying to secure an air base for Selma as part of the growing national defense program.[1] After a long-distance telephone call from Washington, D.C., in late June, Mayor Lucien P. Burns announced that the U.S. Army had chosen Selma as a site for an Air Corps Pursuit Training School. The base would be located four and a half miles south of town off of Highway 80 and was to host three hundred officers and eight hundred enlisted men.[2] Within a week, the base had already tripled in size from the originally projected 640 acres to 1,700 acres. Local officials negotiated settlements with large white landowners—Dr. W. W. Harper and J. B. Hain—and smaller black owners—A. Parnell, Joe Yelder, Simon Durant, and Percy Brown—to accommodate the expansion.[3] They then agreed to lease the acreage to the federal government for ninety-nine years at a cost of one dollar per year.[4] The Federal Housing Authority committed to building a two hundred–home complex adjacent to the new base to house the incoming officers and their families.[5]

While the New Deal helped pull the United States out of the Depression, a burgeoning conflict in Europe loomed on the international front. The global economic crisis of the 1930s gave rise to the aggressive dictatorships of imperial Japan, Nazi Germany, Fascist Italy, and the Communist USSR. In September 1939 Germany, under the command of Adolf Hitler, invaded Poland. The outbreak of war pushed the United States away from its position of neutrality, and the country embarked on a massive defense buildup. New military bases, like the one in Selma, coupled with wartime production, created an industrial boom, increasing demand for labor and raw materials.[6]

Beyond the prestige of being part of the national defense effort, the arrival of the base—given the name Craig Air Force Base after a local lieutenant who had been killed in a bomber crash in San Diego, California—brought the promise of prosperity for Dallas County. "From its very inception the pursuit school will constitute the equivalent of two or three major industries," the *Selma Times-Journal* explained. "[It] will release a huge annual payroll into channels of trade and bring about an immediate impetus in growth of the community."[7] The new air base not only created jobs in construction and civil service for local residents but also promised to increase traffic for area businesses and tradespeople. During the negotiating process, Congressman Hobbs secured assurances from the War Department that local contractors and local materials would receive preference throughout construction.[8]

The initial erection of the base required a workforce of 1,196 people.[9] A huge array of tasks needed to be completed before it could be operational: $2.3 million worth of projects including grading, grubbing, draining, and sodding the field; constructing forty-three buildings, including barracks, a mess hall, a firehouse, medical facilities, storage warehouses, repair shops, a parachute warehouse, and three airplane hangers; and building base roads.[10] With the federal government as their new customer, local businesses thrived. The airfield's arrival marked the end of a decade of depression in Dallas County.

In addition to construction materials and supplies, the air base needed a ready pool of workers to run operations. A vocational training program, funded by a national defense appropriation and run by the Selma public schools, launched classes to train local people in relevant trades.[11] Race, as usual, dictated which trades Selma residents could learn. In the recently vacated high school building on Tremont Street, white workers took classes in carpentry, electrical work, plumbing, painting, and roofing. Meanwhile, black workers learned bricklaying, plastering, and concrete work at Knox Academy.[12] By the time Craig's Advanced Flying School opened in the spring of 1941, newly skilled local workers filled civil service jobs as aircraft sheet-metal workers, electricians, welders, mechanics, and leather workers.[13] Mrs. Louise Rice of the Dallas County Welfare Board reported a 257-person drop in welfare cases, "the effect of defense employment," she explained.[14]

Besides new jobs and booming business, the air training school changed up the social routines of Dallas County citizens. The buses and taxis of the new Selma Bus Lines, Inc., traversed the city, delivering civilians and soldiers to and from the airfield.[15] Within four months, these lines began serving area schools as well. Two buses left Carter Drug Company on Broad Street each morning at 7:40 a.m., one covering West Selma and one covering East Selma, before dropping white children off at school.[16] Recreation and entertainment opportunities became a priority as young soldiers started arriving at the base. Paul Grist, the general secretary of the YMCA, headed up the recreational work at the local branch of the United Service Organization (USO), which was housed in the old YMCA building on Broad Street.[17] Local civic leaders encouraged housewives to invite soldiers to their homes for dinner and to "keep the jar full of cookies" for when soldiers came to visit.[18]

Selma's young women also enjoyed the new airmen who circulated through town. The city hosted a parade to celebrate the arrival of the first class of cadets. Jean Martin, who was a senior at Parrish High School during Craig's first year, remembered the soldiers appearing over the crest of the Edmund Pettus Bridge. "I swear, everyone had a convertible. . . . They all had their hair cut short, and [were] bronze, brown, tan, from flying," she recalled. "And they came over the bridge; we thought they were the most gorgeous. It was just like a movie." Martin's best friend, June Eagle, met her future husband, Seymour Cohn, when the young enlistee came to a service at Temple Mishkan Israel one night.[19] Over the years, the airfield supplied many of Selma's young women with husbands.

The first thirty-nine cadets of Craig's Advanced Flying School received their wings on the stage of the Wilby Theatre downtown in May 1941.[20] Other signs of the pending war were beginning to appear in Selma. Since the previous summer, convoys of military men and equipment had been passing through town. They often camped overnight at Rowell Field, where the Cloverleafs, Selma's minor-league baseball team, played.[21] The Selective Service Act authorized the United States' first peacetime draft, and in October 1940 young men between the ages of twenty-one and thirty-five lined up outside of Selma's polling centers to register.[22] By the end of the month, 224 Dallas County men, black and white, had received their call-up, and inductees shipped out for training over the next year.[23] The re-institution of the local defense council marked mobilization on the home front.[24] C. W. Hooper was elected as the council's permanent chairman, following in the footsteps of his father, Lloyd Hooper, who had served as Alabama's state chairman of defense during World War I.[25]

When Japanese planes bombed Pearl Harbor on December 7, 1941, Selma and the nation were prepared for war. The economic prosperity that Craig Air Force Base brought to Dallas County was an example of what World War II would do for the nation. The airfield gave the federal government a stronger physical and financial presence in Dallas County than ever before. But no one complained, as the employment, job training, services, and business that Craig brought pulled its host community out of a long depression.[26]

CHAPTER

4

Becoming White-Faced Cows

1941–1952

J. L. Chestnut Sr. had grown up on his father's forty-acre farm in Beloit, nine miles west of Selma, where independence and self-reliance were necessary survival skills for a black landowning family. He learned how to butcher in the 1930s while working at the meat market of Green Suttles, who also owned the Selma Stock Yard. In the racial customs of the time, Chestnut made eight dollars a week serving only black customers while the white butcher earned fifteen. From the day his son, J. L. Chestnut Jr., was born in 1931, the elder Chestnut instilled in him the central lesson about life and white people: "Best to do your own thing and, as much as possible, steer clear of them." By 1936 J. L. Chestnut Sr. had begun operating a corner grocery store together with his brother, the Chestnut Brothers Market and Grocery, in the black section of Selma, half a block away from their home on Mabry Street.[1]

As a high school student, J. L. Chestnut Jr. listened as returning World War II veterans denounced the daily injustices he witnessed in black Selma. The war had given rise to a radically different political terrain, in addition to ending a decade of economic depression. Under the banner of democracy, the federal government called on the patriotic support of all Americans. That included black citizens, and this—just as it had twenty years earlier—shook the ramparts of the South's racial order. In Dallas County African Americans dutifully enlisted as soldiers, mobilized on the home front, and grew food for the war effort. S. W. Boynton and C. J. Adams, Selma's local race men, drummed up support, using the war effort as part of their campaign for a fair share and full citizenship. Across the country, African Americans fought the Double V campaign, a two-part battle for victory against fascism abroad and racism at home.[2]

By the end of the war, cotton's reign over the Alabama Black Belt was also nearing its end. New Deal crop restrictions and soil conservation programs had made pasturage and cattle profitable. During the war years, J. L. Chestnut Jr.'s uncles ran a thriving dairy farm on the land where they had grown up, grazing milk cows in fields that had once grown cotton. Cattle needed bigger farms, and during the 1940s, herds of white-faced Hereford cows replaced thousands of black tenants in former cotton fields across the Black Belt. Then the war's end ushered in a golden age of mechanization. Cows and cotton pickers didn't need tenants, who steadily left for elsewhere. As the traditional plantation faded into the past, so, too, did the economic organization that had evolved with it, and Dallas County's civic and political leaders began looking toward a more industrialized future for the region.

In Washington, D.C., an emerging liberal coalition within the Democratic Party mounted new attacks on segregation, and white southerners rallied in defense. White civic leaders in Selma broke ground on a new black high school one year after J. L. Chestnut Jr. graduated from Knox Academy, where plaster from the long-condemned third floor fell down on the heads of students. It was a last-ditch attempt to claim that separate but equal was, in fact, equal. But black Selmians weren't fooled. They continued building their own community—from black-owned parks to credit unions—and crafting independent resources that would sustain black Selma however the racial order of the Black Belt might swing.[3]

Wartime Mobilization

In October 1940, two weeks before draft registration began, twenty Dallas County men boarded a truck at the Dixie Chevrolet Company and drove to the U.S. Army recruiting office in Montgomery. They were going to volunteer. Seventeen of them were African American.[4] Over the following weeks, black citizens responded to Uncle Sam's appeal and came out to register for the draft. Dallas County's draft board decided it was wise to let any and all African Americans register at Selma University, likely hoping to avoid racial conflicts at other locations.[5] The university's president, William H. Dinkins, was himself a veteran of World War I, one of the select black officers who along with C. J. Adams had trained at Fort Des Moines in Iowa. He spoke to a contingent of new black enlistees preparing to leave for training. He encouraged them to take advantage of opportunities "to serve, to learn and to earn" and assured them that they would return to civil life better equipped to help themselves and their people.[6]

Patriotic service didn't mean an escape from segregation for African Americans. Local black enlistees often headed to Fort McClellan near Anniston, Alabama, for training.[7] Once there, they trained for combat with black GIs from across the country in the segregated Ninety-Second Infantry Division.[8] The military frequently relegated African Americans to menial service jobs. A navy-sponsored drive in Dallas County urged black men to volunteer for its messmen branch. The *Selma Times-Journal* thought it was a superb opportunity, praising how black men "cook and serve food and receive splendid training which may benefit them in civilian life should they choose work in hotels or dining cars."[9] African Americans encountered the all-too-familiar racial discrimination, this time perpetuated by the War Department.[10]

When President Franklin Delano Roosevelt gave his annual address to Congress in 1941, he spoke of the "four essential human freedoms" necessary to protect democracy worldwide—freedom of speech and worship and freedom from want and fear. "Freedom means the supremacy of human rights everywhere," he declared.[11] But between the president's professed principles and African American experiences lay a chasm, and A. Phillip Randolph, head of the influential Brotherhood of Sleeping Car Porters union, set out to hold the president accountable to his words. Randolph suggested that African Americans march fifty thousand strong to Washington, D.C., to demand an end to segregation in defense industries and the armed services. With a target date of July 1, 1941, he began organizing a massive march on Washington through grassroots units across the country. Government officials watched the planned march with growing trepidation, nervous about the impact of thousands of black Americans descending on the capital city. Only six days before the march, the president yielded to the pressure. He issued Executive Order 8802, which banned discrimination in "defense industries or government" and created the Fair

Employment Practices Committee to investigate allegations of racial discrimination. With the president's concession, Randolph canceled the march on Washington.[12]

But victories for African Americans in the nation's capital faced a long, tumultuous road before they reached black residents in Dallas County. In the summer of 1942, Alabama governor Frank Dixon refused to sign a contract with the War Production Board that would have allowed state prisons to manufacture cloth for the army. He cited the federal government's ban on discrimination in wartime production as his reason, calling it an effort "to break down the principle of segregation." "I will not permit the employees of the State to be placed in a position where they must abandon the principles of segregation or lose their jobs," he declared. Leading white citizens in Dallas County applauded the governor's stand and invited him to be the guest of honor at a local barbecue the following week.[13]

World War I had forced the federal government to create an infrastructure for wartime mobilization with no precedent or experience. This time, when fighting erupted on European soil again, the wheels of the American war machinery spun into motion. New military bases, many concentrated in the South, like Craig Air Force Base, complemented those already in operation and collectively trained thousands of new enlistees from the national draft. On the home front, campaigns geared toward frugality—saving, recycling, home production, conserving, and rationing—defined the war's presence.[14]

War mobilization unfolded in Dallas County much as it had twenty years earlier. The Dallas County Defense Council worked side by side with the local chapter of the American Red Cross, coordinating war work, raising money through war bonds and savings stamps, and drumming up patriotic support. Scrap-metal drives collected scarce materials for defense industries. In Selma housewives could donate their aluminum to the defense program at a depository outside of Abe Eagle's Boston Bargain store.[15] Bond drives, patriotic rallies, and rotating soldiers at Craig Air Force Base gave the war a physical presence on Selma's streets.

While white soldiers could relax at the downtown USO, Jim Crow prevented black enlisted men from even setting foot inside its door. Selma's black leaders, many of whom were as invested in the war efforts as their white counterparts, rallied to support their soldiers stationed at Craig Air Force Base. The Selma Colored Civic League, whose membership overlapped with the Dallas County Voters League (DCVL) and the Negro Extension Service and Farm Bureau, solicited donations to give black soldiers a place where they could unwind.[16] On Christmas day in 1942, the newly completed black community center hosted an eighteen-piece orchestra and invited black GIs to come and dance until midnight.[17] C. J. Adams, a World War I lieutenant and the president of DCVL, helped turn the community center's second floor into a proper black USO, which opened in May 1943. Duke Ellington, Earl Hines, Nat King Cole, Fats Domino, and other touring performers and their bands made regular appearances there, playing swinging shows that echoed out into Franklin Street.[18]

Adams and county agent S. W. Boynton took charge of organizing the local war effort, alongside their fight for full citizenship and economic security for black residents. Boynton, having gained a reliable reputation in agricultural work, coordinated the black division of the U.S. bonds drives at the request of the white defense council.[19] Adams, meanwhile, mailed out thousands of bond rally posters to ministers and leaders as Boynton's right-hand man. As Adams explained, purchasing war bonds was not only black citizens' patriotic duty but also an "opportunity to render a service to democracy."[20] That Dallas County's two leading race men threw their support behind the war was revealing. Black residents knew full well that supporting a war against fascism abroad challenged white supremacy at home.

Agriculture during the War

While fighter planes and ammunition poured off assembly lines in industrial centers, the patriotic duty of producing food for the troops fell to the Alabama Black Belt. "Dallas Will Help to Feed the World," the *Selma Times-Journal* trumpeted in the early days of the local Food for Freedom campaign.[21] As in World War I, the federal government called on farmers to produce vegetables, eggs, livestock, oil, and grain for the war effort and to grow enough at home to feed themselves and their neighbors. Farm speakers were frequent visitors at Selma's wartime assemblies, as when the president of the Alabama Farm Bureau, Walter Randolph, spoke to a town meeting at Rowell Field. Black citizens were welcome, too, but only in the special section of the grandstand that the city council had reserved for them.[22] Growing food for the war effort, however, had no color lines. "Our program for Negro farmers is the same as that for white farmers," the Negro Extension Service's weekly radio broadcast announced, "the production of more food and feed to win the war and win the peace."[23]

As the gears of wartime mobilization cranked into action, county and home demonstration agents found themselves dispensing patriotic counsel in addition to agricultural advice.[24] The relationships they had built during years of traveling back roads and the fact that their paychecks came directly from the federal government made them an obvious liaison to rural Americans. In 1942 the U.S. government enlisted the Extension Service to organize a neighborhood leadership system in every county and community in the nation.[25]

By that time, Dallas County's black agents were already hard at work on food production and conservation programs. A full eleven months before the bombing of Pearl Harbor, S. W. Boynton and Lucy Upshaw had gathered citizens at the community center to discuss "the part negro citizens may take in the National Defense Program."[26] The wartime neighborhood leaders' organization paralleled the agricultural and home demonstration clubs that S. W. and Amelia Boynton had first organized in the early 1930s. Every rural community already had a club with local leaders, who relayed information from the extension agents. During the war, club leaders simply added patriotic duties on top of the agricultural program. S. W. Boynton praised these groups for "doing much to touch every family in the county in the way of keeping them well informed." These community leaders promoted food production, collected salvage material, sold and bought war bonds, and raised funds for the Red Cross. "It has been through these organizations," Boynton reported, "that our people have worked to carry on the splendid war program."[27] A state official estimated that black extension agents carried out "at least 90% of the War Emergency Programs in which the rural population was expected to participate."[28]

It helped that the defense program's focus on food production and self-sufficiency complemented the existing priorities of Alabama's black county agents. For Boynton, scientific agricultural methods of raising food and livestock had always been a means for black farmers to secure more money, greater independence, and the possibility of landownership. War work amplified these goals in the name of patriotism, and black extension participants understood that mobilizing for freedom abroad and working for personal freedom at home were two sides of the same struggle. Boynton encouraged black farmers to raise livestock, sell milk, preserve food at home, and sell the surplus as a means to buy "clothing, home and farm equipment, farms and homes, and war bonds."[29] Mr. and Mrs. U. G. Anderson, landowners in the Bogue Chitto community, owned six milk cows and shipped their milk daily to the cheese plant in Safford on the western edge of the county. This work gave them $90 of additional income per month, or $1,080 per year. In 1944 the new Selma canning plant added "another source of income to the county," providing a local market for farmers to sell their snap beans, okra, and sweet potatoes. Growing food to sell and use at home immediately benefited farmers.[30]

Rural women partnered with their husbands to make their farms and homes self-sufficient. Demonstration agent Lucy Upshaw crisscrossed the county, instructing women in poultry raising, gardening, food preservation, home dairying, and clothing projects. Young members of 4-H clubs also contributed, learning agricultural methods in service of the war. Upshaw encouraged rural boys and girls to take up poultry projects "so that their families could be assured of enough meat and eggs to fulfill their dietary needs first, then sell the surplus."[31] When some of these 4-H members appeared on a radio broadcast from Tuskegee, the announcer declared, "Dallas County 4-H girls are right on the firing line, backing up their parents who're fighting on the home front."[32]

Despite black contributions to the war effort, the racial order of the Alabama Black Belt remained firmly in place. Recreational opportunities for black residents were virtually nonexistent. So when segregation stood in their way, black Dallas County residents turned to themselves. As they had done with the community center, rural club leaders decided to pool their own resources to buy land for a recreational area and 4-H camp for black residents. Unsurprisingly, S. W. Boynton and Adams took the lead. They found a 110-acre plot six miles west of Selma that had a fish pond and tall thickets of pine trees. "The farm people began to raise money by selling fish, candy, and anything else saleable, and giving programs in churches to raise money," Amelia Boynton explained. The networks were the same ones—churches, mutual aid societies, community clubs, and organizations—that rural club leaders turned to for war mobilization.[33]

By 1941 the Negro Farm Bureau and the Home Demonstration Council put $1,000 down on the land. They named it Joyland. "The farm and home clubs and 4-H clubs did a very fine job in helping purchase the land," S. W. Boynton reported, but "one of the finest [pieces] of work done in connection to raising the [last] $2,000.00 was the part the Chesterfield Club played in sponsoring the project." This group of Selma's middle-class black men brought in entertainers for fund-raising events, as well making their own personal contributions. Adams chaired these efforts and, according to S. W. Boynton, "worked hard in raising the funds that cleared up this mortgage." It took almost three years to come up with the remaining $2,000, but by August 1944 they had done it.[34]

On August 23, a bus left the community center at 1 p.m., stopped again at the Reid Drug Company, and then delivered its passengers to Joyland. Under the shady pine trees, people from rural clubs, societies, and Sunday schools mixed with Chesterfield Club members and others in Selma's black middle class, eating barbecue and drinking lemonade. The crowd of almost a thousand celebrated their mutual accomplishment by grandiosely setting fire to the paid-in-full mortgage. In recognition of their significant fundraising efforts, Dorothy Kahn, a member of the Sardis 4-H club, and Jerelean Dennis, from Richmond's, "were given the honor of helping burn the mortgage." Having something that belonged to black people was a reason to celebrate.[35]

Farming wasn't easy during the war years. Military service and jobs in wartime industries drained young men from the countryside, creating a severe shortage of labor. "Lack of labor caused our crops to suffer this year," Mildred Brown, a club member from the King's Landing community, explained. "Some of the men left to work on defense jobs in Selma, Mobile, and Birmingham. Some were drafted." S. W. Boynton agreed. "All young men on our farms are just about gone—many into the army, and others to cities for better employment," he admitted on a Tuskegee radio program. To compensate for this absence, farm women stepped in, taking on larger portions of farmwork in addition to managing their homes. Mrs. Brown reported that "the women folks have tried to carry on our work of gardening, poultry raising, and food preservation, along with it the extra work on the farm. This has meant hard work and plenty of it."[36]

White landowners watched nervously as the laborers of Dallas County left for military service and defense work. It was "undoubtedly true that the defense industrial boom is responsible in part for the drain upon farm labor," the *Selma Times-Journal* noted, but "the basic conditions go deeper than that."[37] Federal crop reduction programs had brought prosperity to large landowners and lessened their need for tenant labor. Between 1940 and 1945, the number of farms operating in Dallas County dropped from 5,713 to 4,857. Black operators, the majority of whom were tenant farmers, made up almost 94 percent of those who had left the countryside.[38]

But during World War II, white farmers found that too many laborers had left for jobs elsewhere. They blamed relief programs for providing rural African Americans with, in the words of the *Selma Times-Journal*, the "comparatively soft living made possible by wages far above their actual ability to produce." Laborers would never again be satisfied with the low wages of agricultural work compared to "industry, the wage-hour law and the WPA for labor."[39] When the farmworker shortage took on pressing proportions before the fall harvest, the president of the Dallas County Farm Bureau appealed directly to President Roosevelt. He argued that rural workers employed on non-defense-related WPA projects were a serious problem and needed to be released for "the essential occupation of gathering crops which might do a great deal to decide the outcome of world conflict."[40]

By May 1942 the city council decided to reinstate Selma's old vagrancy laws, mandating that all able-bodied men and women be employed or face vagrancy charges. Mayor Lucien P. Burns declared that "plenty of jobs can be found now," and after meeting with WPA officials and white farmers, he announced a new agricultural wage scale: seventy-five cents a day for women and one dollar a day for men.[41] As in World War I, prominent white citizens invoked patriotic duty as their primary motivation, yet they used harsh penalties to force black citizens to work for almost nothing. The local newspapers rallied to rid the city of idlers, adopting the slogan "work, fight, or git."[42] Area draft boards did their part by grouping all farmers as 2-c and 3-c and granting deferments to farmers who sold their food-crop surplus for the war effort.[43] This practice continued until March 1944, when the Selective Service declared that the army, not agriculture, had priority in drafting eighteen- to twenty-six-year-old men.[44] But even with the shortages, white Dallas Countians still voted to turn down the use of German prisoners of war as harvest hands. They cited feeding costs and inexperience as reasons, but the bottom line was that the Black Belt's racialized system of agriculture preferred black citizens over white enemies as laborers.[45]

By 1944 the war's end was on the horizon. Landowners in Dallas County paused to take a long, hard look at their agricultural priorities and discovered that, from a postwar perspective, the labor shortage looked more like a blessing than a curse. Between 1930 and 1960, a virtual agricultural revolution had taken place in the Alabama Black Belt. Massive cotton plantations had ruled the Alabama Black Belt when they bolstered the personal wealth and power of large landowners and wholesale merchants.[46] But the Depression, black migration north, and new federal agricultural programs had drastically changed the equation. New Deal agricultural programs that paid landowners to remove cotton acreage from production radically restructured the traditional ways of southern agriculture. Black tenant farmers found themselves without fields and homes as white landowners took tenant-operated lands out of production and pocketed the payments. As black labor became increasingly unnecessary, white landlords turned toward wage work and day-labor agreements. This gave them the freedom to hire workers temporarily without providing black families even the meager acres, cabins, and supplies that had come with tenant arrangements.[47] As a result, the number of tenant-operated farms plummeted. In 1930 tenants operated 6,230 Dallas County farms; in 1940 they operated 4,743; by 1945 the number had dropped to 3,763; and by 1950 tenants worked only 3,178 farms. In twenty years, more than three thousand tenant farmers had abandoned or were forced off of their farms, and the rate of tenancy in Dallas County dropped from 87.8 percent to 70.5 percent.[48]

Cattle in the Cotton Fields

Removing cotton fields from production did not mean that the land lay idle. During the New Deal, the federal government embraced soil conservation programs as a way to prevent overproduction and replenish the land. Suddenly, planting pasture grasses—perfect for livestock raising—looked more lucrative than tending fields of cotton, and white-faced Hereford cattle made their entrance into the former cotton kingdom.[49] It was in 1940, at the cusp of Dallas County's transition to cattle, that longtime county agent John Blake retired. He received showers of praise for his steady encouragement of diversification, home production, and pasturelands over the years. "John Blake gave Dallas a head start over other sections of the state in dairying and then livestock production," reported the *Selma Times-Journal*. "His chief reward has been witnessing the creation of a new agricultural empire on the lush lime land of the Black Belt."[50]

The cattle industry in Dallas County flourished in conjunction with other local assets. In the northwestern corner of the county, near Marion Junction, the Black Belt Experiment Station oversaw an extensive agricultural research program. Run by the Extension Service at the Alabama Polytechnic Institute, the station had opened in 1931 for the purpose of developing agricultural methods compatible with the Black Belt's prairieland. Since the nineteenth century, farmers had fought to keep johnsongrass, a tall perennial plant, from taking over cotton fields. But diversification and the turn to cattle caused farmers to reevaluate the grasses already growing from the soil.[51] The Black Belt Experiment Station developed methods of pasturage suitable for prairie soil, such as use of johnsongrass. "Farmers around here thought the people at the research station had gone crazy when they started putting fertilizer on grass," county agent Lawrence Alsobrook later

4.1 Crowds gather for the annual field meeting at the Black Belt Experiment Station in Marion Junction, ca. 1930s. Courtesy of Alabama Department of Archives and History, Montgomery, Alabama.

admitted. But new insights about pasturage gave beef cattle a boost in the region.[52]

Cattle producers also benefited from a local market for their livestock. In 1929 Green Suttles, himself a large landowner, opened the Selma Stock Yard, creating a viable local market for cattle. A decade later, the Zeigler Company built a meatpacking plant next door to the stockyard, which expanded beef producers' sales opportunities and helped meet wartime food demands.[53] The cattle boom overtook the county so quickly that in 1942 the *Selma Times-Journal* felt confident asserting that "the livestock industry blossomed so magically that it soon challenged and ousted King Cotton as the leading money source of this section."[54]

4.2 New Selma Stock Yard facility, ca. 1940s. Photograph by Lance Johnson. Courtesy of Alabama Department of Archives and History, Montgomery, Alabama.

Suttles was at the forefront of this revolution, and changes in his own farming operation highlighted the transition from cotton to cattle in the mid-twentieth century. Suttles's original farm had over a thousand acres of land, planted primarily in cotton. As the Selma Stock Yard grew, Suttles shifted his operation toward cattle; the complementary setup let him purchase calves and hold them on his property to wait for better prices. Then, in 1952, Suttles purchased a three thousand–acre property that had forty-nine black families living on it, raising cotton and corn on shares. During the first year, Suttles cleared the land by bulldozer, built fences, and prepared the property for livestock production. He changed the tenants living there from shares to a cash-rent basis. Ten families left after the first year, and others continued to trickle away thereafter. By 1960 Suttles's farm had forty-three hundred acres with only forty acres in cotton. Of the seventy-some tenant families who used to make their living on the land, only four remained; they worked under cash-rent contracts and, as one observer described, "just barely eke[d] out a living."[55] Purchasing thoroughbred cattle required financial resources that few but the largest landowners, like Suttles, possessed. Thus, the abundant capital and large landholdings that defined Dallas County's cotton plantations also facilitated the transition to cattle.[56]

Although handicapped by lack of financing and limited landownership, some black farm owners managed to move from cotton into the more profitable livestock industry. John Mitchell, a black farmer from the Beloit community, to the west of Selma, owned a hundred acres of land—"clear of debt"—on which his sixty-six cattle and purebred Hereford bull grazed. He visited the Black Belt Experiment Station upon starting out to learn more about pastures and oats. Mitchell then sold his beef cattle at the Selma Stock Yard when they held their regular sales. "I'm convinced that livestock is the salvation of the farmers in this section," Mitchell explained on the Negro Extension Service's radio broadcast. "Since I've been raising cattle I've made more cash money from the sale of my cows each year than I have from cotton."[57]

Dairy cattle also offered smaller black farmers a means to supplement their incomes without the many acres needed to graze beef cattle. Unable to meet the stringent regulations governing top-grade milk, all of Dallas County's black farmers produced Grade B milk, which was used for cheese making. Milk routes covered the county; trucks picked up the farmers' full cans of milk in the morning, delivered them to the cheese plant or condensery, and then returned the empty cans in the evening. Being in the milk business gave black farmers a check every two weeks, year-round.[58]

Three of J. L. Chestnut Jr.'s uncles, Preston, Mallory, and Frank Jr., ran an especially successful cattle business on their eight hundred–acre farm in the same community as John Mitchell. Their father, Frank Chestnut Sr., had bought the first forty acres of land with the money his father—a white man who owned a boardinghouse in Marion Junction—had given him before he died. On that farm he "raised almost everything his large family—eleven children—needed," his grandson recalled.[59] By the mid-1940s, the Chestnut brothers' dairy herd had over thirty cows and brought in $300–$350 per month, enough to pay for a new dairy barn and four electric milkers. They grazed the cattle on a hundred acres of "good lush improved pasture" of oats, Caley peas, and frosted johnsongrass that supplied most of their feed. The farm also had 125 beef cattle, which brought in $2,000 annually. "We have two tractors, a combine, and two hay balers which we use for custom work with neighbors when not in use on our farm," Preston explained. "This brings in additional income." This family of astute businessmen divided the work of farm management: Preston was general manager of the farm and took care of the finances, Frank managed the beef herd and hired out machinery, and Mallory had charge of the dairy herd.[60] In addition to their farm, Frank Chestnut Jr. and J. L. Chestnut Sr. operated a grocery store and meat market near Selma University.[61]

Even though the Chestnut brothers' operation was a testament to how black farmers with some resources could prosper in the Black Belt, theirs was still a precarious position. One day, two state sales-tax agents walked into the Chestnut Brothers Market and Grocery carrying an unpaid tax bill of thousands of dollars for meat slaughtered under J. L. Chestnut Sr.'s butcher permit during the war. Green Suttles had helped him apply for the permit, and he had asked Chestnut whether a couple of white butchers could slaughter some meat using his permit as a favor. When Chestnut raised the issue of the large bill with his former employer, Suttles denied any involvement, saying that he operated a stockyard and did not sell meat for retail. The tax agents' position was that meat sold under Chestnut's permit was his responsibility, so he auctioned off the store and its contents to pay taxes that weren't his. The state confiscated his wife's teaching paychecks for the next three months. Chestnut eventually got a job scrubbing floors and emptying trash cans at Craig Air Force Base.[62]

For black tenant farmers, most of whom had far fewer resources than the Chestnuts, the arrival of the white-faced cows marked the end of their lives on the farm. Picking cotton by hand had required the same amount of labor whether grown on subdivided tenant farms or on large estates, but livestock raising required large swaths of land for pasturage and feed. Beginning in the 1930s, farms in Dallas County ballooned in size as white landowners consolidated their holdings and got rid of their tenants. By 1950 the average farm size was 122.6 acres, well above double the 48.4-acre average of twenty years earlier.[63]

With cattle already pushing black tenants from the land, the mechanization of cotton picking following the war only sped up the process. Landowners in Dallas County had dabbled in mechanization as early as the 1920s, but early tractors could not match the quality and accessibility of cheap black labor. It was not until the mid-1940s that International Harvester and other farm implement companies perfected mechanical cotton harvesting, garnering the serious interest of cotton producers.[64] The war, however, channeled any excess metal into defense through rationing, making it, as the white county agent explained, "very difficult to acquire new farm machinery."[65] Mechanization came to the Alabama Black Belt only when wartime production restrictions ended.[66] The new availability and affordability of cotton pickers directly threatened tenant farmers' tenure on the land. Mechanized pickers worked best on large plots of land, which spread the operational costs over more acres.[67] As the number of tractors on Dallas County farms increased, the number of tenant farmers went down.[68]

In his annual report for 1946, S. W. Boynton laid out how the growth of larger farms spelled doom for tenant farmers. Beef cattle required large amounts of pastureland, and farm machinery allowed cotton growers to produce on a large scale. For Boynton, these changes meant "that many of the tenant farms are being closed out."[69] J. C. Ford, the state coordinator of Negro extension work, agreed. "A disproportionate number of the families that are being crowded off the farms are negroes; not being crowded off because they are negroes," he explained, "but because they live in those areas of large plantations where tractors and the establishment of pastures and perennial hays are reducing the need for human labor." Displaced families had nowhere to turn. Many left Dallas County and the rural areas and headed to cities to find employment. But, Ford warned, "it is difficult for entire families, untrained for anything except the farm, to go to cities or towns and make their way."[70]

S. W. Boynton was forever pushing black farmers to buy land as a measure of security. "'The time will come, ladies and gentlemen,'" Amelia Boynton remembered him saying, "'when the only way you are going to stay on this white man's place is to turn into a white-faced cow. Soon your farm will be turned into pastures or rented to the government and you will be turned out to graze elsewhere.'"[71] Going beyond his duties as a county agent, Boynton worked to secure financing for black farmers who wanted to move off white people's land and buy their own. He made use of existing government programs but also called on his personal connections with A. G. Gaston, Birmingham's black millionaire, and others in Atlanta and New York who were willing to help black people trying to make something for themselves.[72]

Southern Segregation under Attack

By 1950 cotton had come to the end of its long reign in Dallas County. The fields that used to parade "cotton right up to the cabin door" now sprouted pastures with foraging white-faced Hereford cattle.[73] Cotton, however, had been more than just a crop; the puffy white bolls had forged the foundations of the economic, political, and social relationships in the Black Belt. White supremacy in the Alabama Black Belt grew from the cotton fields, and when cattle replaced black tenant farmers, the transformation shook the ramparts of Jim Crow segregation.

Through the New Deal programs, Roosevelt had put forward the proposition of economic security and human decency for all American citizens. This vision helped bring northern liberals, African Americans, and labor organizers into the burgeoning left wing of the Democratic Party. Their efforts to build an inclusive, small-*d* democratic United States collided head on with the party's southern and deeply segregationist roots. White southern Democrats had not taken it lightly when the president, citing the National Emergency Council's report, named the South "the nation's number one economic problem."[74] The New Deal's minimum-wage bills and support for union organizing had already threatened white southerners' provincial control over black labor. World War II both heightened democratic movements rooted in the New Deal and provoked a fierce backlash and the coalescing of southern Democrats.[75]

Southern voting restrictions were a key target of the liberal wing of the Democratic Party. In September 1942 Congress passed the Soldier Voting Act, which waived poll tax requirements for American soldiers. White Dallas County citizens had seen the swarms of local black GIS shipping off to war and knew the threat their votes would pose long after hostilities had ceased. Alabama congressman Sam Hobbs, a native of Selma, called the act "an attack on [the] Southern way of life and on white supremacy."[76]

Two years later, the Supreme Court overturned the all-white primary in the *Smith v. Allwright* decision, a case argued by the NAACP. White southerners had long claimed that the Democratic Party was a private organization that could restrict membership and bar African Americans from participating in primary elections. The Supreme Court's ruling dismantled an essential tool that white southerners had relied on to keep African Americans away from the ballot box.[77] Alabama legislators, accepting that the state's Democratic Party would need to be at least nominally open to black voters, responded by passing the Boswell Amendment. It mandated that prospective voters be "of good character," understand "the duties and obligations of good citizenship under a form of government," and be able to "read and write, understand and explain," any section of the U.S. Constitution. In January 1946 the Alabama Democratic Executive Committee lifted the white-only primary rules and began campaigning for the ratification of the Boswell Amendment.[78] The *Selma Times-Journal* obscured nothing, explaining that the amendment was "for the purpose of protecting white supremacy at the polls in this state."[79] Alabamians ratified the amendment, but the Supreme Court declared it unconstitutional in 1949.[80]

Meanwhile, the NAACP honed in on dismantling legal segregation and what Thurgood Marshall called "the fiction of separate but equal." The lifeblood of the NAACP was the African American membership in branches throughout the country. Beginning in the 1930s, the national organization used local discrimination suits to build a broader attack on segregation in education, transportation, housing, and voting.[81] Attorneys Charles Houston and Thurgood Marshall led the hard-fought crusade. With the whites-only primary already dismantled, the *Morgan v. Virginia* decision in 1946 overturned segregation on buses and trains that crossed state lines. Then, in 1948, *Shelley v. Kraemer* struck down racially restrictive covenants in housing. And in 1950 the NAACP won cases regarding segregation in higher education, paving the way for the monumental *Brown v. Board of Education* decision in 1954.[82] The NAACP's earliest arguments against segregated education hung on the premise that separate but equal had never been equal. So when white southerners rallied in defense, they concentrated on bringing some equality to black schools.[83]

Never before had the public schools for Dallas County's black children received so much attention. It began in October 1940 when the city school board used WPA funding to open an eleventh grade for black students at Knox Academy. The top floor of Knox's three-story building had been condemned when J. L. Chestnut Jr.'s mother was a student, and it was still boarded up when Chestnut attended in the 1940s, with plaster apt to fall down on the heads of students in second-floor classrooms. Also, the new eleventh-grade classroom was equipped with leftovers from the recently closed white Tremont Street High School, so separate but equal still didn't look equal when Chestnut compared Knox to the "nicer, newer, and larger" all-white Parrish High School.[84] In 1942 the Alabama Legislature officially extended the black school session to eight months, a vast improvement over the three- or four-month terms typical for rural schools. The Dallas County Board of Education unpleasantly learned that the state meant to withhold funds until "all colored schools of Dallas County" had "150 teaching days."[85]

White Selmians' attempt to preserve segregation ultimately built black students the first new high school building they had ever had. In February 1944 the city school board announced that it had applied for a $150,000 direct grant from the Federal Works Agency to build a two-story, twenty-classroom high school for African Americans.[86] White city leaders were especially pleased when the project acquired federal status. That meant that the only thing the city had to supply was the property for the site.[87]

Construction on the high school, located just north of Selma University on Summerfield Road, began in April 1948.[88] Meanwhile, the Dallas County Board of Education built two upper-level schools for black students: the new Shiloh Junior High, two miles outside of Sardis on the south side of the Alabama River, and a new building for Keith School, which had begun as the Rosenwald school near Orrville. The *Selma Times-Journal* praised the building campaign, claiming that "Dallas County will take enviable ranking with any in the nation as regards facilities for Negro education."[89] The money for these schools came from State Building Commission funds "designated for Negro School buildings."[90] Selma's new R. B. Hudson High School—named for the Selma University graduate and principal of Clark Elementary School—opened its doors in May 1949. Black teenagers now had a gym and an auditorium, a cafeteria, a library, science laboratories, and shops, along with new classrooms. But for all of white Selma's sudden fuss about equality, one black resident was quick to point out that the concrete floors at Hudson High were still not as good as those over at the white Parrish High.[91]

White Dallas Countians' sudden interest in black education clearly did not stem only from the goodness of their hearts. With attacks on segregation mounting, white southerners took concerted steps to bolster separate but equal. "If we are to maintain the principle of segregation, desired by both races," an editorial in the *Selma Times-Journal* explained, "we must maintain comparative educational facilities." The new R. B. Hudson High School "should constitute proof that the citizens of Selma are in earnest about meeting their just obligation under a system they consider imperative for the welfare of everyone concerned." After years of blatantly underfunding black education, southerners were finally putting their money where their mouth was in the fight for segregation.[92]

Black Institutions

Whether in new or old buildings, Selma's black teachers continued preparing their students to face the world they were born into. The racial order of the Alabama Black Belt still stood strong, and teachers, along with the wider community, instilled in their young people an understanding of citizenship, democracy, and the backwardness of segregation. John Shields, a graduate of Shaw University, had begun teaching civics at Knox Academy when it added the eleventh grade. He was an atheist, received at least part of his paycheck from the WPA, and made it known, as his student

J. L. Chestnut Jr. remembered, that if the police or Klan came to get him in his book-lined house on Broad Street, "they would have had to bring him out feet first."[93] Shields taught his civics students that segregation was in no way and by no means natural and that it was designed to exploit black people for their labor. "Many of the concepts Shields taught at Knox Academy," Chestnut later recalled, "became part of the framework through which I have looked at life ever since."[94] This type of education continued at the new R. B. Hudson High School. Louretta Wimberly learned "that because you are an American citizen, . . . you have certain inalienable rights. And they used to teach us those inalienable rights."[95] White southerners' attempts to equalize education in the 1940s and 1950s only provided more resources for black educators to challenge the underpinnings of white supremacy. Selma's black students remembered their teachers "supporting us from behind the scenes" when they rose to challenge segregation in the 1960s.[96]

Another local institution helped black Selmians weather Dallas County's racial order. In 1937 a group of white Catholic priests, the Fathers of St. Edmund, arrived in Selma and opened a mission to serve the needs of black residents. Next door to Tabernacle Baptist Church on Broad Street, they erected St. Elizabeth's Mission for the Colored. Four years later, the Sisters of St. Joseph, a group of Catholic nuns from New York, joined the Edmundites' efforts, opening the St. Elizabeth Parish School for black children. The nuns also started a nursing home for the aged and took over the operation of the Good Samaritan Hospital—locally known as "Good Sam"—in 1944, where they gave medical care to black residents, who were barred from Selma's other hospitals.

In 1947 Father Nelson Ziter, a young, newly ordained priest from Massachusetts, arrived at the Edmundite mission in Selma. Sitting outside on an August day, he noticed a group of teenage boys walking back and forth. "This all you guys got to do is just walk?," he asked. "Why don't you go play ball or go do something?" They told him that there was nowhere to go, so Father Ziter offered to let them use the parish hall at night to play Ping-Pong. That was the beginning of the Don Bosco Boys Club. Ziter renovated a building on Union Street, and soon dozens of boys were crowding into its recreation rooms, library, and snack bar. Ziter then organized basketball and baseball teams and began pushing the boys toward college, as well as finding them scholarships.[97]

Over at Good Samaritan Hospital, the Sisters of St. Joseph began training black women as nurses. Etta Smith Perkins heard that the sisters were

4.3 Members of the Don Bosco Boys Club playing Ping-Pong and boxing at their clubhouse, 1950. Courtesy of Society of Saint Edmund Archives, Saint Michael's College, Colchester, Vermont.

starting a one-year program "for black girls to go into colored nursing because we couldn't get in these other schools." So she told Sister Louis Bertrand that she was interested and became one of the eleven members of the first practical nursing class in 1950. As a child, Perkins had walked over to the Burwell Infirmary from her home near Selma University in the evenings to help take care of patients. She began what would be a lifelong career at Good Samaritan. Perkins named her first child after Sister Remegia, the nun who taught "the nursing arts—that is the care of a patient and why you do it."[98]

The Fathers of St. Edmund and the Sisters of St. Joseph gave African Americans a place to turn to that did not conform to local racial customs. After the war, the Fathers hired Edwin Moss, a local veteran and graduate of Alabama State University, to manage their daily operations. Moss's father had run the Torch Motel, one of Selma's only hotels open to African Americans. Like the Chestnut family, Moss raised his son to value how independent, black-run businesses and institutions gave the black community something of its own. In 1950 Moss partnered with the Fathers of St. Edmund to open Selma's first black-run credit union. The city's white-run banks refused to give loans to African Americans for their homes, cars, or anything else, and a credit union could help give black Selma a financial base. Black citizens in the eastern Black Belt had taken a similar approach when they opened the Tuskegee Institute Federal Credit Union in 1938. When St. Elizabeth's parish did not have enough members to support a credit union, Moss turned to the Pride of Alabama Elks Lodge—the black fraternal order of which he was exalted ruler—to charter the Elks Federal Credit Union. He assumed the position of manager and treasurer of the new institution. For the first time, black Selmians had ready access to credit. When black members found themselves unemployed and threatened with foreclosure, "we would take over the mortgages and keep them from losing their homes," Moss explained. For Moss, his position with the Fathers of St. Edmund gave him the independent salary and support he needed to bring the black financial institution to life.[99]

The Dixiecrat Revolt

On April 12, 1945, Franklin D. Roosevelt died, and Vice President Harry Truman assumed the presidency. A year earlier, southern Democrats had used their political might to unseat the former vice president, Henry Wallace, an avid New Dealer, in favor of Truman. Their pick was a moderate Democratic senator from Missouri who had supported the New Deal out of political expediency, not ideological passion. White southerners trusted Truman to moderate the strengthening liberal wing of the Democratic Party. But they failed to take into account how demographics had shifted at the party's base. While southern legislators maintained their seniority and power within Congress, the northern, urban, and liberal coalition constituted a new majority in the party after the war. Truman's success now depended as much on African Americans, organized labor, and New Deal liberals as it did on white southerners.

Henry Wallace made Truman's task more difficult when he broke from the Democrats to run for the presidency in 1948 under a third party, the Progressive Party. His platform included passing a federal civil rights bill to enforce the Fourteenth and Fifteenth Amendments and protect black citizens and reinvigorating New Deal reforms to ensure economic security for Americans citizens. Wallace took his campaign south, speaking to crowds on a nonsegregated basis.[100] Meanwhile, President Truman pushed back. On February 2, 1948, Truman sent a message to Congress calling for legislative action on civil rights. The move revealed the waning influence of white southerners in the Democratic Party. Never had civil rights risen so high on the national agenda in the twentieth century, and white south-erners exploded in outrage.[101] Ed Fields, the editor of the *Selma Times-Journal*, accused Truman of being a "machine politician," labeling his civil rights message "an open challenge to many of the South's most cherished customs and traditions." Truman had infuriated the Black Belt, he alleged, in ways "witnessed rarely since Reconstruction days."[102]

This indignation only worsened when, at the Democratic National Convention of 1948, the delegates adopted a strong civil rights plank over the blatant opposition of the party's southern wing. Southern Democrats reconvened in Birmingham shortly thereafter and organized themselves as an insurgent wing of the party, the National States' Rights Party, com-monly known as the Dixiecrats.[103] Southern Democrats held important po-sitions of influence within Congress; not willing to risk these strongholds of power, the Dixiecrats chose to wage their battle within instead of outside the party. The *Selma Times-Journal* summed up the whole ordeal as "the Truman rape of the Democratic party."[104]

Support for the Dixiecrat movement ran strong among Dallas County residents, especially the powerful cadre of white landowners, business-men, and professionals. Walter C. Givhan was the president of the Dallas County Farm Bureau and a state legislator. He operated a large plantation out in Safford on the far western edge of the county. First elected to the Alabama House of Representatives in 1930, Givhan was chair of the agri-cultural committee and used his position to watch out for the interests of the wealthiest landowners.[105] He threw his full support behind the Dixie-crat cause, declaring that he would "spend the rest of my life in jail before casting a vote for Harry S. Truman or any other candidate who supports his theories of government." From his position as president, Givhan brought Dallas County's tightly organized and influential Farm Bureau along with him.[106]

Every fall, the Dallas County Farm Bureau hosted a barbecue for its members to celebrate another year of cooperation and good business. In 1948 Givhan transformed the annual gathering into a massive rally to de-fend states' rights and segregation. Hundreds of Farm Bureau members and guests from surrounding counties flocked to listen to well-known seg-regationists from across the South. Fielding Wright, the governor of Mis-sissippi and running mate of the Dixiecrat presidential candidate, Strom Thurmond, addressed the crowd of two thousand gathered at Twilley's Lake. He warned them to "stand solid" in the general election or "endure a shameful period of social and economic exploitation."[107] The Dixiecrats' political rebellion did not pan out, and Truman won the election of 1948. But their challenge, backed by white southerners like Givhan and influential organizations like the Farm Bureau, laid the groundwork for future battles over segregation.

Recruiting Industry

White southerners' defense of segregation and states' rights unfolded alongside the South's midcentury agricultural and industrial revolution. Since the 1920s southern states had courted northern industries, largely as part of local boosterism and upbuilding efforts. Chambers of commerce used promises of cheap, nonunionized labor, tax exemptions and subsidies, and abundant natural resource to tempt industries southward.[108] A study of neighboring Wilcox County in the 1940s described the typical factories that relocated to southern plantation areas. They were run by northern managers "who like the South for its relatively cheap unorganized labor and the cooperation of local authorities in keeping out unions and recruiting labor."[109]

Selma, as the economic center of the western Black Belt, jumped into this feverish competition for industry. Craig Air Force Base had been a major economic boon to Dallas County, and local business and civic leaders worked to add new private industries to complement their public-defense luck. In 1941 a cigar manufacturer based in the East came to town to conduct interviews with local women. The secretary of the Chamber of Commerce, H. Hunt Frazier, applauded how the cigar factory would help Selma achieve a balance between agriculture and industry and provide additional employment for farm people.[110] The I. Lewis Cigar Manufacturing Company set up operations in the old Sunset Mill by Valley Creek. A former mill worker recounted how Frazier sold Lewis on Selma. He told the interested cigar executive that "the pay scale down here was $0.15 an hour and he could get plenty of help for that pay." "That was the pay scale that the Cigar Factory started the people to work at," she remembered.[111]

As the mechanization of cotton and the turn to cattle pushed people off of farms, these new labor-intensive, low-wage industries brought jobs without challenging Dallas County's economic status quo. In August 1944 the King Pharr Canning Plant began canning okra, peas, beans, spinach, and sweet potatoes at its new Selma plant. White employers put African Americans in the lowest-paid, hardest, and dirtiest jobs, as they had done in agricultural and other wage labor. The canning plant hired 165 black women to cut the okra. It promised to hire twenty to twenty-five white women for "labeling, inspecting, and other types of semi-skill duties" once operations got under way.[112] Industrial development in the Black Belt was meant to bolster the existing racial and economic order, which put black workers at the bottom. To the local politicians and the Chamber of Commerce, that made the King Pharr plant "an ideal acquisition." It provided jobs for city residents and a market for the rural ones, and did nothing to upset Selma's racial and economic status quo.[113]

The Chamber of Commerce's development program in the early 1950s worked to recruit more "suitable industries to convert more of our abundant raw materials into the finished product."[114] One of these was the new southern branch of the Independent Lock Company that opened in Selma in October 1950. This came after a successful local campaign to sell $400,000 in industrial bonds to finance the construction. In total, the Independent Lock Company promised to employ three hundred workers and bring an annual payroll of $750,000 to town.[115] Selma businessmen were confident that the new industry would be good for the economy and create no disturbances.

Dallas County's white leaders understood how economic and racial control went hand in hand.[116] State representative Givhan was a key player in the city's massive postwar industrial recruitment drive to "secure Selma's future."[117] Under Givhan's leadership, the Dallas County Farm Bureau—an organization concerned with the economic interests of large farmers—became a platform for segregationist causes. Protecting white supremacy at home also meant defending against federal intervention. The Farm Bureau stood for "the freedom of the press, freedom of speech, freedom of religion, and freedom to work and operate our own business without interference from bureaucratic bureaus," Givhan wrote to his constituents.[118] It was no secret what he meant by these freedoms. He was affirming what white southerners understood as their prerogative: to pay black workers as little as they liked and to be free of interference from labor unions and the federal government alike. With ever more frequent challenges to the South's racial order, white southerners like Givhan stood ever more firmly by this position.

In the fall of 1953, J. L. Chestnut Jr. entered law school at Howard University in Washington, D.C. It was John Shields, the civics teacher at Knox Academy, who had first suggested that Chestnut become a lawyer. "Go get yourself a law degree and fight the system. *Evil* damn system," he told him. Chestnut had tallied the daily injustices of being black in Selma, including watching his father lose his store on account of a white man. During his first semester at Howard, the aspiring lawyer from Selma spent hours in the basement of Howard's library, listening to the NAACP attorneys who gathered there to strategize for their final attack on school segregation. The death knell of segregation had sounded, even though it still ruled in practice in Alabama. J. L. Chestnut Jr. would play his own part in dismantling the racial order of the Black Belt when he returned home in 1958 as Selma's first black attorney.[119]

World War II marked a turning point for Dallas County. No longer was southern segregation secure from first national and then local challenges. War mobilization demanded the participation of all Americans, and African Americans across the nation again leveraged their patriotic service to expand the parameters of democracy. While black Americans and liberal Democrats partnered to dismantle segregation within the federal government, black residents in Dallas County strengthened their own community connections and bolstered their economic resources while supporting the war effort. Only a decade later, these efforts would grow into a frontal attack on local practices of white supremacy.

Meanwhile, the agricultural revolution rooted in the New Deal came to fruition in the Black Belt and replaced cotton fields and sharecropper shacks with pastures full of grazing white-faced cattle. No longer did cotton single-handedly dictate the daily lives of Dallas County's residents. White business leaders increasingly turned their focus toward industrial development, seeking to preserve the Black Belt's racial and economic status quo. As the Democratic Party pivoted toward civil rights, white southerners rallied to defend their own. The Dixiecrat movement fought to curtail federal intervention and bolster white supremacy, but the accelerating changes in the Black Belt made it nearly impossible to maintain the tight-fisted provincialism of early days. By the early 1950s, the stage was set for the civil rights and segregationist battles that would dominate the next decade and a half.

"I Like Ike"

Smarting from the Dixiecrat defeat in 1948, white southerners turned their attention toward the presidential election of 1952. People like Farm Bureau president and state legislator Walter Givhan were determined this time to stand firm against the liberal integrationists who seemed to be taking over. Battle plans began early in Dallas County. In 1951 Givhan arranged for Senator Harry Byrd, an ardent states' rights supporter and high-profile legislator from Virginia, to address the crowds of white farmers and segregation supporters at the Farm Bureau's annual barbecue. Dixiecrat leaders saw the Dallas County barbecue as an opportunity to bring white Democrats from across the South together. After Byrd's address, States' Righters intended to gather at a conference to draft campaign plans for the upcoming election. Givhan adamantly maintained that the Farm Bureau did not take an active role in politics, but the facts clearly suggested otherwise.[1]

The Dixiecrats' overlapping commitment to states' rights and white supremacy had deep roots in Alabama's Black Belt. The *Alabama Journal* predicted that the spirits of Selma's revered nineteenth-century senators John Tyler Morgan and Edmund Winston Pettus would smile down on the upcoming gathering. It was the senators' "loyalty to the United States Constitution's principles of state's rights and . . . guarantee against federal dictation in local affairs," claimed the editorial, that had driven their support of the "Confederacy's protest against centralized tyrannies."[2] Racial motivations lay barely under the surface of southern Democrats' allegiance to states' rights. "Grown-up white Southerners had always known that Dixie depended on localism, on their right to be left alone to manage their unique 'Negro Problem,'" southern-born historian Glenda Gilmore observed.[3]

The Dallas County Farm Bureau and the Chamber of Commerce spent all of October preparing to welcome five thousand people to town, including notable politicians and governors from half a dozen southern states.[4] Rain poured down on the morning of the barbecue, but the wet weather did not stop throngs of white citizens from packing the bleachers of Memorial Stadium. From the soggy baseball field, Senator Byrd castigated the Truman administration and called for an "immediate uprising of political virility in the South" to reclaim the Democratic Party.[5] Afterward, the crowds enjoyed seventy-seven hogs' worth of barbecue prepared by a small army of workers on pits behind right field.[6] The Dixie Democrats of Alabama reconvened at the courthouse later that afternoon for the explicitly political portion of the day. Although missing what the newspaper called "the high brass of the party," they adopted a manifesto calling for a "re-emphasis [on] local state government, restoration of the courts and Congress to their rightful place in government and a limit on federal taxation."[7]

Other white southerners turned their hopes in a different direction: General Dwight D. Eisenhower and the Republican Party. In the revered World War II hero, they saw a true leader, one whose "concept of Americanism" and "executive ability" would bring an end to the recent upheavals in Washington. As Democratic loyalists since the Civil War, the willingness of white southerners to now consider the Republican Party marked an enormous ideological shift. In the midst of the Farm Bureau's preparation for its states' rights guests in October 1951, the *Selma Times-Journal* published an open letter to Eisenhower. "Ike, the people of the United States as a whole want you for their next President," it declared. "This is especially true of the honest, patriotic, 'fighting' South. They want you for President Ike, because our great nation desperately needs a leader."[8]

The shifting political landscape of the postwar period had pushed white southerners to question which party would best protect their priorities. When Eisenhower announced his candidacy for president in January 1952, the *Selma Times-Journal* lined up behind him.[9] The local newspaper spoke for many white Dallas County residents when it affirmed that Eisenhower "would make a great President along the lines of moderation[,] and a sharp Southern reversal of allegiance would serve to teach Democratic radicals that they cannot hope to continue in power indefinitely without conceding due respect to the once Solid South."[10] Republican enthusiasm flourished in Dallas County. Eisenhower's calls for decency and limits in government appealed to white citizens, and when he urged local control for the Fair Employment Practices Committee, they deemed him a protector of states' rights. In their eyes, he was "a Democrat of the old school."[11] Even Harry Truman's announcement that he would not run for reelection did nothing to stem this change of heart.[12] In July three hundred of Dallas County's former Democratic voters pledged their support to Ike in a telegram leading up to the Republican National Convention.[13]

After Eisenhower secured the Republican nomination, a contingent of citizens organized themselves as the Dallas County Citizens for Eisenhower. The group, under the direction of attorney William B. Craig, chose not to affiliate with the national Republican Party. Instead, it focused its attention on "dissident Democrats" frustrated by "mismanagement and corruption in Washington and abuse of the South by national party leaders."[14] Attorneys Edgar A. Stewart and A. T. Reeves, along with cotton merchant Charles Hohenberg, headed up the speakers committee, while Mrs. Mortimer P. Ames and Mrs. James Kenan took charge of the women's campaign. Subcommittees of women organized transportation to the polls and babysitters so mothers could cast their vote for Eisenhower.[15] A photograph of Libba Kenan Buchanan and Pat Cammack graced the pages of the *Selma Times-Journal* after they attended an Eisenhower rally in Birmingham. Their smiles shone above a "Dallas County Likes Ike" sign stuck to the side of their car. Buchanan worked as a secretary in the local headquarters, while Cammack "did yeoman service" drumming up support.[16]

Excitement ran high in the weeks leading up to the presidential showdown between Eisenhower and Democratic candidate Adlai Stevenson. Local Eisenhower advertisements urged voters to "Put Patriotism above Party! Principles above Politics!"[17] Sample ballots circulated, instructing white Selmians how to vote a split ticket. "DO NOT mark in the circles below party emblems unless you want to 'vote her straight,'" the *Selma Times-Journal* warned. It was the first time white voters had ever needed to know how to vote anything other than Democratic.[18]

On Tuesday, November 4, Dallas County joined the Republican column for the first time since Reconstruction, and Eisenhower won a resounding national victory. A 464-vote majority secured the county for Ike and made Dallas the only county in Alabama's Fourth Congressional District to desert the Democratic ranks. Long before white southerners abandoned the Democratic Party en masse during and after the civil rights movement, Dallas County's white residents keenly understood where their loyalties lay in the new political landscape. The majority of the county's citizens, reported the *Selma Times-Journal*, "have discerned that the Republican leadership of today comes closer to upholding their political traditions than does the Democracy of northern bosses and radical minorities." It projected that other Alabama counties would fall in line, as serious thinking would "make clear the fallacy of following a stolen party label which our grandfathers would have repudiated even quicker than they seceded from the Union."[19]

In December 1952 president-elect Eisenhower wrote a thank-you letter to the *Selma Times-Journal*, expressing "my deep personal gratitude for the outstanding work you did on behalf of our campaign." He claimed that on election night "we won the right and the high privilege to embark upon the Crusade to which you and I had pledged ourselves."[20] Eisenhower failed to detail what that crusade entailed, but white Dallas County citizens understood it as a formidable defense of states' rights, limited intervention by the federal government, and the protection of segregation. White southerners entered the 1950s more confident that the federal government was again on their side.

CHAPTER

5

≡

Segregation's Last Stand

1953–1964

In the early 1950s, a white law student from Yale University arrived in Selma to study the "status of the Negro in Dallas County." Harris Wofford, who would later become a U.S. senator, had been stationed at Craig Air Force Base in the mid-1940s. He bonded with two white families from Marion Junction during his time in the air force, but he had never known African Americans as anyone other than domestic workers or farmhands—that is, until he returned five years later to ask them about their lives. Wofford also asked white officials and businesspeople to give their thoughts on local race relations. In a conversation with the white woman who was working at the Chamber of Commerce, she told him that Selma was "a nigger heaven." When Wofford repeated that assessment to an African American resident, the woman got tears in her eyes. "How could any white person think that?" she asked. "God help me from heaven, if Selma is a Negro heaven."[1] That unbridgeable chasm between the two women's perceptions would define the second half of the twentieth century in Dallas County.

The years after the war marked the beginning of an unprecedented attack on the South's white supremacist order. Southern politicians united to fight against the Democratic Party's meddling in the affairs of southern states, while white southerners closed ranks in defense of segregation. But the racial skirmishes that had taken place in Washington immediately after the war appeared on the ground in the Alabama Black Belt during the 1950s. In Dallas County African Americans drew on the relationships forged through farm, church, school, and community associations to mount an increasingly forceful attack on the bulwarks of white supremacy. Bolstered by black protest campaigns escalating across the South, black citizens demanded better jobs, respect, equal funding for education, and the right to vote. Meanwhile, white Dallas County citizens, shocked by the homegrown civil rights campaigns emerging in their own backyards, did their best to preserve and protect segregation. Thousands of white men joined the local white Citizens' Council in the aftermath of the Supreme Court's *Brown v. Board of Education* decision striking down—at least nominally—separate but equal.[2] Citizens' Council members, connected through civic clubs, the Farm Bureau, and the Chamber of Commerce, used economic intimidation to fight any and all dissidents and defend Jim Crow.

As the institutions of white supremacy came under attack, the Black Belt faced a new economic order in which industrial development superseded the waning plantation economy. As cattle took over the cotton fields, black tenant farmers found themselves without work or homes. Selma's business and political leaders turned their hopes toward attracting industries that would create jobs and bring prestige but also preserve the racial and economic status quo. The Chamber of Commerce's development strategy advertised the Black Belt's cheap labor and resources, low taxes, and antiunion climate to relocating industries. Such an approach depended on a harmonious image of Selma as a city united toward progress and free from racial and labor unrest. In a period when black residents were increasingly pushing back against the dictates of Jim Crow and local workers were striking for better wages and benefits, white political and business leaders desperately worked to control and contain visible discontent in the name of industrial development. Quieting internal and external disagreements, however, strained relationships even among white officials. From the divisions, a young white appliance salesman, Joseph T. Smitherman, emerged to usher in a new political order, forged in the fires of the African American civil rights movement.

NAACP and the Fikes Trial

In the spring of 1953, the wife of a white airman at Craig Field reported that a black man had broken into her house on First Avenue.[3] With a mask covering everything except his eyes, she claimed, he held a knife to her neck and then raped her.[4] One month later, Jean Rockwell, the daughter of Selma's mayor, Chris Heinz, awoke to find a black man with a butcher's knife standing in her bedroom. Her husband was downtown, working at his job as a pharmacist at Carter Drug Company, and her two children were asleep in their Mabry Street home while Mrs. Rockwell fought off what the *Selma Times-Journal* called a "rape attempt." She survived uninjured although she "suffered shock following the terrifying experiences."[5]

White Selma panicked. In 1944 a Swedish sociologist, Gunnar Myrdal, had observed that sex was "the principle around which the whole structure of segregation of the Negroes . . . is organized."[6] White men ruled the South's racial and sexual caste system and faced no penalty for sexually assaulting black women. However, if a black man approached a white woman, he took his life in his hands. "The much-traveled sexual backroad between the races was clearly marked 'one way,'" southern-born historian Timothy Tyson summed up.[7]

Night after night that May, Selma residents reported black prowlers lurking at their windows and in their alleyways.[8] Black businessman Preston Chestnut called his nephew J. L. Chestnut Jr., who was studying law at Howard University, with the updates. "The police were getting five or six calls a night—'There's a nigger in my house! I saw him! I saw him!'—from white women all over Selma." The police eventually arrested William Fikes, a black employee of the Pan-Am Service Station in the neighboring city of Marion, after they found him in an alleyway on the edge of the white side of Selma.[9] Law enforcement officers grilled Fikes for nearly twenty-four hours before he admitted to attacking Mayor Heinz's daughter.[10] Police captain Wilson Baker then secured Fikes's full confession for all crimes after nine hours of questioning a week later at Kilby Prison.[11] White Selma attorneys Sam Earle Hobbs and Hugh S. D. Mallory were assigned to defend Fikes against two of Alabama's most serious capital charges: rape and attempted rape.[12] The defense questioned the validity of their client's confession, his guilt, and his sanity, but the all-white jury found him guilty. To the shock and dismay of white Selmians, however, they decided to sentence Fikes to ninety-nine years of imprisonment instead of death because one member did not believe in the death penalty.[13]

Black Selmians paid close attention to the uproar and subsequent trial. Since the 1930s the small but dedicated Dallas County Voters League had been meeting in S. W. and Amelia Boynton's insurance office. Stacks of dusty farm publications and NAACP bulletins greeted members on their way to the big table in the office's backroom, where they strategized about voter registration. During his work as a farm agent, S. W. Boynton had encouraged black rural residents to buy land and vote. White residents had sung Boynton's praises when he taught better farming methods, but "as soon as he began to work to free his people from the bondage of plantation slavery, to get them to buy homes and to register and vote," Amelia Boynton recalled, "he became a menace to the white society." In 1951 S. W. Boynton resigned his position as county agent, forestalling what he saw would be his dismissal for unwelcome political activity.[14]

C. J. Adams, the president of DCVL and Selma's other most notorious race man, was also targeted for his activities. "When Adams walked into a store downtown," J. L. Chestnut Jr. remembered, "his manner was such that the white storekeepers wouldn't be laughing and smiling and calling him 'Uncle.' He was no-nonsense and white people were very uncomfortable around him." Since World War I, Adams had been helping black Dallas County residents apply for federal programs. He was arrested several times for allegedly notarizing false documents, spending a year in prison in the late 1940s. When he got out, Adams, "old, sick, [and] tired, had had enough of Selma." Chestnut, whose parents were friends with Adams, drove the World War I veteran north to spend the rest of his days with family in Detroit.[15]

In the years before the Fikes trial, the NAACP—the country's number-one civil rights organization—had been reaching out to local communities across the South. Field secretaries like Ella Baker traveled across the South building branches, recruiting rank-and-file members, hosting fund-raising drives, and finding plaintiffs for the NAACP's legal attacks on segregation.[16] S. W. Boynton had made a career of tapping into anything and everything that could help his people, and he joined with J. D. Hunter and Ernest Doyle, both veterans of World War II, to reactivate Selma's chapter of the NAACP. By 1952 the branch had 102 dues-paying members. When the Fikes trial seized the attention of Selmians, black and white, Boynton turned to the NAACP for assistance. Sunday after Sunday, he made his rounds of Selma's black church circuit, trying to raise funds to bring in two lawyers from the NAACP Legal Defense Fund for Fikes's defense.[17]

When black NAACP attorneys Peter Hall and Orzell Billingsley walked into the circuit clerk's office to request an insanity hearing for Fikes, the battle over civil rights became a local reality in Selma.[18] Never before had black lawyers tried a case in a Dallas County courtroom, and for white citizens it was as if hell had indeed frozen over. Hall and Billingsley did not intend just to fight Fikes's indictment but to take on the injustice of the system itself. The day before the trial, Chestnut found Hall drinking whiskey at the mirror-tiled bar of the Elks Club, "looking for respectable, educated black citizens to testify that they had never been called to serve on a jury."[19] During the trial, the two attorneys called over fifty upstanding black citizens as witnesses to support their argument that African Americans were systematically excluded from juries. Publicly testifying on the side of NAACP attorneys in the courthouse was about the riskiest thing a black man could do in Dallas County. Those who stood witness were longtime race men with independent incomes. Besides S. W. Boynton, they included Tom Moss and McKinley Jackson, farmers active in the Extension Service; World War I veteran Mark Thomas, who ran a grocery store and operated a cattle farm; and J. D. Hunter of the local NAACP, who earned his living as a minister and insurance agent.[20]

Hall and Billingsley won a retrial of the case, forcing the jury commission to add black names to the rolls. But when the new jury was selected, the attorneys passed over all African Americans, again producing an entirely white jury. It took the jurors less than an hour to return a guilty verdict for Fikes and, this time, a sentence of death, which the U.S. Supreme Court eventually overturned.[21] Despite the verdict, the presence of NAACP attorneys in the Dallas County courthouse marked the arrival of civil rights in Selma. Black people brought their children to the trial to "see black men who weren't bowing or Uncle Tom-ing in the presence of important white people," Chestnut explained.[22]

The Citizens' Council

Nationally, the NAACP was making headlines as the Supreme Court weighed the fate of segregation in the *Brown v. Board of Education* case. The organization had established legal precedents against segregated schooling over the course of three decades, beginning with graduate programs and slowly working its way down to elementary schools. White southerners saw the writing on the wall and began building new black schools, like Selma's R. B. Hudson High School, to inject the appearance of equality into segregated education.[23] In the lead-up to the court's ruling, Alabama senator Walter Givhan railed against any "breakdown of our traditional segregation policy." Federal outlawing of segregation, he threatened, would force white southerners to turn to racially exclusive private schools. "The people of Alabama are grimly determined to preserve our way of life, and to maintain home control of our educational program," he declared.[24] But on May 17, 1954, the court overturned the doctrine of separate but equal.

It was a day white southerners called "Black Monday," and it marked the beginning of an all-out battle to preserve the status quo.[25] Less than two months later, leading white men from Indianola, Mississippi, formed the first Citizens' Council for the purpose of preserving segregation through legal means, not violence. Their idea took off, and chapters spread like kudzu across the South.[26] The Dallas County Citizens' Council announced its existence that November, only two weeks after Alabama NAACP delegates met at Tabernacle Baptist Church for a three-day conference.[27] M. Alston Keith, an attorney and the chair of the Dallas County Democratic Executive Committee, was the council's spokesman. Distancing the new organization from the Ku Klux Klan, Keith explained to a reporter that members were not "anti-Negro" nor "vigilantes." The council instead vowed to defend segregation through the legal and effective tactic of "economic pressure," making it "difficult, if not impossible, for any Negro who advocates de-segregation to find and hold a job, get credit, or renew a mortgage."[28]

On the night of November 29, 1954, nearly twelve hundred "Black Belt farmers, merchants, bankers, professional men and public officeholders" filed into the auditorium of the Selma Junior High School for the first Citizens' Council meeting. Over six hundred white men paid the three-dollar membership fee after listening to the council's "plans for applying economic pressure to Negro advocates of integration," bringing the total to eight hundred members.[29] The council's membership list was a who's who of local power in Selma.[30] Mayor Heinz and the probate judge Bernard Reynolds cochaired the committee that selected the council officers, and Givhan served as chair of the local, and later state, council. Ed Fields, the editor of the *Selma Times-Journal*; Jim O. Risher, a wealthy cattle rancher; the circuit judge James A. Hare; and Aubrey Allen, who was in charge of agricultural loans at the City National Bank, were only a few of the upstanding men the organization attracted.[31] Selma's chapter of the Citizens' Council quickly became the arbiter of public opinion and municipal politics, as well as one of the strongest chapters in the state.

Joseph T. Smitherman was working as an appliance salesman when the Citizens' Council began. He grew up in East Selma on the wrong side of the tracks before becoming a city councilman in 1960 and then mayor in 1964. Smitherman recalled that anyone hoping to be someone in Dallas County needed to be an active member of the Citizens' Council. While Smitherman was still a salesman, a black employee of a café did something to offend the council; Smitherman was sent to instruct her employer to "get rid of the nigger." "I didn't like pressuring another merchant," Smitherman remembered, "but I did it."[32] Economic intimidation like this took place quietly, behind the scenes, as council members revised their public position. Keith explained that the organization's tactics boiled down to "nothing more than simply sitting down with the recognized Negro leaders, who have the best interests of their race at heart, talking over our mutual problems and working out a peaceable solution beneficial to both races."[33]

In June 1955 over five thousand white residents filled Memorial Stadium to hear former Georgia governor Herman Talmadge defend segregation and local self-government at an event sponsored by the Citizens' Council.[34] The astounding turnout seemed to testify to white residents' monolithic support for the council, but differences between hard-line segregationists and more moderate whites existed. Joseph Knight, a young marine who had just returned from the Korean War, sat in the audience. His mother had "dragged" him to the event, which promised to be both the political and social event of the season. Knight did not buy Talmadge's segregationist tirade. Growing up in rural Hazen, he'd had close relationships with black neighbors, even if the balance of power was not equal, and he had just returned from service in an integrated military. He fumed to his mother on the car ride home that it wasn't right. When they passed two black servicemen in Selma waiting for a bus to Craig Field, she pulled over and asked, "Do you boys need a ride?"[35]

The Knights, the Rev. Edward W. Gamble and his family, the librarian Patricia Blalock, and other white Selmians made up a contingent of moderates who did not support the doings of the Citizens' Council.[36] But as civic and business leaders gathered forces to defend segregation, the possibility of public dissent among white southerners evaporated. Kathryn Windham, a white reporter at the *Selma Times-Journal*, remembered how Selma's white moderates "were pressured and there was bitter conflict— friendships broken and economic suffering." Those who disagreed mostly stayed quiet, allowing the Citizens' Council to reign as the singular voice of white citizens.[37]

Selma's NAACP chapter and the Citizens' Council came head to head over the issue of school desegregation. In August 1955 twenty-nine black residents—emboldened by the Fikes trial and the recent Supreme Court decision—submitted a petition to the superintendent demanding that black students be admitted to Selma's white schools. "The time for delay, evasion or procrastination is past," it read, stating that the school board was "duty bound to take immediate concrete steps leading to early elimination of segregation in public schools." The only immediate concrete action that followed was retaliation. The *Selma Times-Journal*, a reliable segregationist mouthpiece in the mid-1950s, printed the names and home addresses of each and every black signatory.[38]

Within a week, the petitioners, one by one, lost their jobs and retracted their signatures. The Selma Marble Works, Cloverleaf Creamery, the Bayuk Cigar Company, Miller and Company, the Selma Country Club, Ford Construction Company, the YMCA, the Cleveland Table Company, and Selma Junior High School all fired the petitioners they employed. J. D. Hunter, the local NAACP chapter president and a signatory, called the firings "clear-cut cases of pressure being applied because of the petition." But Keith, the Citizens' Council's spokesman, claimed that the council would "take neither credit nor censure" for the developments. Instead, he praised the united response of white businesses: "[The employers] did just what we have been advocating all along."[39] In the end, only the founding NAACP chapter members Hunter and Doyle refused to withdraw their names. Doyle was told in no uncertain terms that he should reconsider. He remembered that when he did not, "the Citizens' Council blacklisted me, and I didn't make another white dollar for twenty years."[40] Hunter worked for a black insurance agency and fared better, although his access to credit disappeared. Ultimately, the school board did nothing with the petition, simply ignoring it.[41]

In the days following, black Selmians organized a boycott of Cloverleaf Creamery, which had fired one of the signers. John Smitherman, a local black grocer, reaped the benefit as milk sales soared at his grocery. One day, a white female sales representative came by to inquire about the change in sales, but Smitherman was busy and asked her to call him back. The Citizens' Council caught wind of it and interpreted the grocer's request as a pass at a white woman, a story similar to that of the Emmett Till murder case, which had been running in the newspapers. Within the hour the phone in his store rang with instructions for him to be out of town by five o'clock that afternoon.[42]

But Smitherman decided to stay, which exacerbated the situation. First, wholesale grocers boycotted his store and prevented him from purchasing goods.[43] Then someone set fire to his next-door neighbor's house. Three nights later, they corrected their error, and night riders fired shots into his Church Street home from a car. That same evening, a carload of white men snatched a black porter off of his bicycle and drove him ten miles out of town before he convinced them that he was not John Smitherman.[44] Smitherman withstood the harassment, staying in Selma until the boycott destroyed his business. Then, Smitherman and his wife packed their three children into a car in January 1956 and headed north for Detroit, just as Adams had done a few years earlier.[45]

Shifting Demographics

The Citizens' Council's use of economic intimidation quietly and effectively stifled dissent, and as the economic order of the Black Belt shifted in the years after World War II, that control and outward harmony became increasingly important to Selma's civic and business leaders. By 1959 the number of farms in Dallas County had plummeted to 2,816, well below the 7,096 that had been in operation thirty years prior. The decline came as prosperous landowners expanded their operations, buying more land to suit cattle grazing and mechanical cotton pickers. The average size of farms more than tripled, from 48.2 acres in 1930 to 169.3 acres in 1959. Farming in Dallas County no longer depended on black agricultural laborers. Even though 60 percent of farms were still operated by tenant farmers, they worked only 13.8 percent of the county's farmland. The sun was unquestionably setting on decades-old practices of cotton production.[46]

The changes in farming in the Alabama Black Belt were part and parcel of a drastic shift in demographics. Since the 1830s African Americans had made up an overwhelming majority of the population.[47] Black citizens totaled 83 percent of Dallas County residents at the turn of the century, but by 1960 that number had fallen to 57.7 percent.[48] They had left searching for better jobs and opportunities elsewhere beginning in World War I, but the Black Belt's agricultural transformation intensified the trend. S. W. Boynton's prediction—that African American farmers needed to turn into white-faced cows if they wanted to stay on the farm—had come true. Selma public schools found that the conversion of cotton farms had "forced tenants to go into the city to seek employment or move entirely out of the area."[49] These changes created an abundance of people fresh from the farm looking for a new way to survive.

With all of these people, Selma seemed to be splitting at the seams. The population had grown from 19,834 in 1940 to 28,385 in 1960.[50] In 1949 the federal Public Housing Administration approved the construction of three hundred low-rent apartments in Selma, separated into one white and one black housing project.[51] When demolition for the purpose of clearing land for the new projects began two years later, black residents found their neighborhoods targeted for slum clearance.[52] The white Valley Creek Homes on the western side of Selma was built on top of a formerly black neighborhood.[53] The new George Washington Carver (GWC) Homes—a ten-building, 216-unit complex—was to be built around Brown Chapel AME Church on the eastern side of the city. Residents on Sylvan, St. Ann, St. Phillips, and Lawrence Streets received notices that their homes were in a "slum area" and slotted for demolition. But the compensation offered by the housing authority did not match the value of their homes. "If we were people of means and money, we wouldn't mind, but to the majority of us 'our home' is our life's savings," the homeowners pleaded. "We don't have the kind of homes handed down on 'silver platters,' but the kind we burnt the night oil [for] washing, ironing, cooking, and doing odd jobs."[54] City officials ignored their pleas, and their homes were destroyed to make room for the GWC Homes, which opened the next year.[55]

The people being pushed into southern cities by agricultural changes needed work, and white civic leaders saw new industries as the solution.[56] Southern business progressives partnered with state governments to establish new industry-enticing subsidies beyond what individual cities already offered. After the war, Alabama passed legislation allowing cities to form industrial development corporations, which could then use public bond money to fund the expansion of private industry and construction of plants. Development-minded businessmen in Selma—Rex Morthland of the People's Bank and Trust Company, investment banker Catesby ap R. Jones, and former mayor Lucien P. Burns of the City National Bank—secured the city council's approval for an industrial board in April 1950. Its stated purpose was to balance "our agricultural economy with new industries by inducing manufacturing, industrial, and commercial enterprises to locate in Selma and thereby further the use of the agricultural products and natural resources in Dallas County."[57]

Unions, Civil Rights, and Resistance

The Selma Chamber of Commerce enthusiastically jumped on the industrial recruitment bandwagon, but they did so with a clear idea of the kind of industries they were looking to attract. As the plantation economy withered, political and business leaders searched for economic development that would reinforce the status quo built on the foundation of cheap black labor and white supremacy. The industries that best fit the bill were those that paid low wages to unskilled workers and opposed unions on their shop floors. As the mouthpiece of industrial development, the Chamber of Commerce trumpeted low labor costs and antiunionism as Dallas County's major selling points. A publication in 1961 detailed for prospective companies how the local wage rates for skilled workers—$1.00–$1.75 per hour for unskilled male workers, $1.25–$1.75 for semiskilled, $1.80–$2.50 for skilled—hovered very near the national minimum of $1.00 per hour. In case low labor costs weren't enough, the next page was titled, "IN SELMA UNIONS DON'T WIN ELECTIONS," followed by a chronicle of every unsuccessful union vote in the city during the preceding five years.[58]

But the chamber's best efforts did not stop all union activity in Selma. In the spring of 1955, local telephone employees and rail workers nearly brought services to a halt when they joined national strikes.[59] To keep service running, company officials hired scabs and then off-duty personnel from Craig Air Force Base as stand-in switchboard operators. Striking Southern Bell employees amassed outside the building, protesting the use of military men as strikebreakers. The potential violence was averted only when Craig's commander arrived in person to remove his off-duty servicemen.[60] Three weeks later, members from all of Selma's union locals gathered at the National Guard Armory for a mass meeting. In front of the three hundred people gathered, labor leaders castigated the South's use of "cheap labor" to attract new industries. They warned management that unions were in Selma to "stay and grow."[61]

But unions faced fierce opposition in a city where business leaders, municipal officials, and the courts were united against them. A union vote was scheduled to take place at the local Independent Lock Company (ILCO) plant in 1953. Before the vote, the Industrial Development Board urged workers to do their part in keeping labor troubles away from Selma. "Does a union really care what happens to our city?" they asked employees in a letter published in the *Selma Times-Journal.*[62] But ILCO workers paid no heed and voted in favor of representation by the International Union of Electric, Radio, and Machine Workers.[63]

Two years later, in September 1955, Local 793 went on strike at ILCO's plant on Burnsville Road. Striking workers carried signs accusing the company of treating its southern workers unfairly. Tommy Shoults, vice chairman of Local 793, charged that employees in ILCO's northern plants received nearly double the wages and more benefits than Selma's workers.[64] An integrated group of male and female strikers—half of the company's workforce—kept up a round-the-clock picket line. Such a public affront to both segregation and harmonious labor relations brought a swift reaction.[65] The *Selma Times-Journal* accused workers of being ungrateful for ILCO's new jobs and better wages—"pay comparing favorably with the average prevailing in the area"—and threatened that if disruption continued, "it will be impossible to obtain general support [for attracting new industries] in the future."[66] One week later, Judge Hare single-handedly put an end to the strike, granting a temporary injunction against Local 793 for conducting an illegal strike.[67]

The ILCO workers' timing didn't help matters. They had first voted in the union in the midst of the Fikes trial in 1953. They then went on strike in the fall of 1955 at the exact moment that the NAACP filed its school desegregation petition in Selma. In the eyes of white officials and business leaders, unions and civil rights activism were equal threats to the status quo, and bad timing further ensured Local 793's defeat.

Union activity remained muted in Selma during the rest of the 1950s. Workers voted down representation at the Bayuk Cigar Company, Ames Bag Company, and Cleveland Table Company in 1957, and then the Alabama Metallurgical Company and Coca-Cola in 1960.[68] As with the Citizens' Council's tactics of economic intimidation, unions failed partly because of pressure and threats. The manager of the Bayuk Cigar Company had a reputation of being a good-humored and fair man, but he did everything he could to thwart union organizing in the company. "He tried to be overly friendly to Negroes in order to prevent their voting for a union," a white Selma resident, Joseph Ellwanger, recalled. "After the vote was over and they did not vote for the union, he was less friendly. Considerable pressure was put upon the Negroes not to vote for a union, lest they lose their jobs." Management could exploit racial divisions in the face of union threats, using poorly paid black workers to threaten the better positions of white workers.[69] "Selma is *not* a union town. People here are just not sold on it," the assistant secretary of the Chamber of Commerce had confidently told

Harris Wofford a decade earlier. "And agitation is discouraged," he added. Clearly little had changed since then.[70]

Civil rights and union activity in Dallas County in the 1950s unfolded amid escalating civil rights activity nationwide. In nearby Montgomery, African Americans sustained a massive boycott of the segregated city buses for nearly all of 1956. After Rosa Parks's arrest, the Selma City Council passed an array of segregation ordinances regulating "the separation of white and colored persons" in taxicabs, restaurants, rooms, auditoriums, yards, ball-parks, and public parks, as well as forbidding racial mixing in everything from dominoes to golf.[71] Then, in 1957, President Dwight D. Eisenhower sent federal troops into Little Rock, Arkansas, to protect the nine black students desegregating Central High School. Instead of defending states' rights and white supremacy, the president set a precedent for federal in-tervention on behalf of civil rights. The *Selma Times-Journal* accused the president of being weak-minded and of having been swayed by "constitu-tional rapists and racial renegades" into "this new occupation by carpetbag troops." Eisenhower's picture, the newspaper declared, would no longer hang above its editorial desk.[72]

That same fall, the Ku Klux Klan celebrated a conspicuous rebirth in Dallas County. In November 1957 five six-foot-tall crosses wrapped in fuel-soaked rags were set ablaze, three on Highway 80, one near ILCO, and one at the intersection of Highway 14 and Range Street.[73] When the Klan pa-raded through Selma's neighborhoods a week later, leading white citizens dismissed the hooded order as out-of-town visitors, "not representative of the citizenship element" of Dallas County.[74] Yet a Klan rally in 1958 drew nearly a thousand cars and twenty-five hundred Klan affiliates to a field five miles north of town. Police captain Wilson Baker appeared at the rally as part of his campaign for sheriff. His appearance, although castigated later, suggested that a number of Dallas County citizens—and potential voters— stood in the crowd.[75]

Politicians and business leaders wanted nothing to do with the Klan and its violent reputation. As Wofford observed, "the whites of the Black Belt are said to be too refined to go much for the Klan."[76] Also, industrial development depended on maintaining an image of harmonious race rela-tions. But other than vocal denouncements, local white officials did little to stop the activities of the hooded order. When a fifty-car Klan parade wound through the black neighborhoods of East Selma, the chief of police, Ed Mullen, insisted that they were within their legal rights and only needed a parade ordinance if the motorcade had included a band.[77] The Klan also

5.1 Ku Klux Klan sign posted on the door of St. Elizabeth's Church, the African American Catholic parish established by the Fathers of St. Edmund, February 1950. Courtesy of Society of Saint Edmund Archives, Saint Michael's College, Colchester, Vermont.

added its welcome signs—shaped like a sawmill blade with blood dripping from its teeth—alongside the signs of civic organizations and churches that welcomed visitors when they drove into Selma.[78] In practice, the Klan's vigilantism reinforced the Citizens' Council's seemingly more palatable use of economic reprisals to protect segregation.[79]

Meanwhile, the Citizens' Council maintained its stronghold on white public opinion, boasting at least sixteen hundred members. Notable organizations, like the Kiwanis and Rotary Clubs, as well as the Farm Bureau, threw their weight behind the council's defense of segregation. The *Selma Times-Journal* noted that the speech at the Farm Bureau barbecue in 1958 was "devoted more to federal usurpation of states' rights which has resulted in the school segregation crisis than to agriculture."[80] Selma's chapter of the Citizens' Council was the strongest in the state of Alabama, and M. Alston

Keith and other Dallas County members traveled throughout the surrounding Black Belt, helping organize new chapters.[81] By the summer of 1958, the Alabama Citizens' Council had moved its headquarters to Selma and soon afterward elected Givhan, the longtime president of the Dallas County Farm Bureau, as its permanent chair.[82] At a barbecue featuring segregationist Mississippi senator James O. Eastland, the council pledged "to make personal contact with every white voter in Dallas County and ask them to join the organization."[83]

The Citizens' Council's seemingly united front did not prevent the federal government from investigating discriminatory voting practices across the South. In December 1958 Bernard Reynolds, the probate judge, received a subpoena instructing him to appear before the Civil Rights Commission in Montgomery with the county's voting records in hand.[84] This invasion by "federal civil rights carpetbaggers" prompted an elaborate campaign of resistance by county officials.[85] First, the county convened a grand jury to impound Dallas County's registrar files in a supposed investigation of illegal voter registration practices.[86] Three months later, the courthouse crowd then agreed to grant the Civil Rights Commission access to the files "but only with rigid restriction which at best will give the investigators nothing more than a peep into the records," the *Selma Times-Journal* explained.[87] By 1960 public officials saw what the future held and stopped identifying voters by race.[88]

When the Civil Rights Commission requested access to Dallas County voter records, it also subpoenaed six black residents, including S. W. and Amelia Boynton and Dr. Sullivan Jackson, to testify about voter discrimination.[89] Dr. Jackson was a dentist and a World War II veteran who lived across the street from the Boyntons near Selma University. He explained that he had tried to register two times but never received an answer from the board of registrars. "I am an American citizen. I believe I have a right to vote," Jackson testified. "I fought for my country. I believe in the principles in it, and I don't see any reason why I should have to run back and forth to register."[90] Testifying only made matters worse for Jackson. Afterward, the city cut off the dentistry work they had contracted him to do for local prisoners, and his wife lost her job as secretary at the Selma Housing Authority. Average citizens might not have known about the hearings, Mrs. Jackson reflected later, but "the power structure knew, as always."[91]

The responsibility for subduing any immediate racial or labor troubles fell on Dallas County's sheriff, Jim Clark. It was a duty he relished. Clark had grown up in Elba, in the Wiregrass Region of Alabama, and moved to

Dallas County in 1948 as a cattle farm operator near Browns. Appointed sheriff in 1955 by Governor Jim Folsom, Clark had never endeared himself to the white Selmians, who saw themselves as his social betters. They thought he was rash and uncouth and despised his alleged involvement in illegal whiskey sales and gambling.[92] But the sheriff won the support of many rural residents, and he won his reelection campaign in 1958 by accusing his opponent, police captain Wilson Baker, of being a pawn of the Selma political establishment.[93]

When it came to maintaining the status quo, however, members of the Citizens' Council, Chamber of Commerce, and local government were of one mind, and in the fall of 1958, union trouble demanded action from Sheriff Clark. Striking workers from the Birmingham and Tuscaloosa plants of the Zeigler Packing Company had formed an early morning picket line in front of Selma's Zeigler plant and roughed up a local worker trying to go to his job. Sheriff Clark and Blanchard McLeod, the circuit solicitor, mobilized special deputies to deal with the disturbances. Over the next two days, "more than 100 law enforcement officers and special deputies armed with shotguns, rifles, pistols, and clubs assembled at the plant to protect Zeigler workers and prevent formation of picket lines," the *Selma Times-Journal* reported.[94] No picketers returned, but Sheriff Clark's expeditious actions received high praise. "This is a peaceful and orderly community," the newspaper affirmed, "and it will take whatever steps are necessary to remain that way."[95]

In February 1960 four black students sat down at a lunch counter in Greensboro, North Carolina, and sparked a flood of parallel lunch counter sit-ins across the South. Facing such a threat, Sheriff Clark regularized his posse and added defense of segregation to its founding purpose of anti-unionism. In a standing-room-only meeting at the courthouse a month later, Sheriff Clark deputized three hundred men for special duty during emergencies. Solicitor McLeod instructed the possemen to "use whatever force is necessary to repel any attack made against the peace and dignity of Dallas County." "The day of passive resistance has passed," he declared.[96] The next day, fifty-two members of the mounted posse paraded through town on horseback. Jim O. Risher, a cattleman from Tyler and chair of the Citizens' Council, captained the mounted posse, while wholesale grocer W. M. Agee took over the posse on foot.[97] "When the citizens of a community are prepared to take speedy and effective action against self-seeking trouble-makers," the newspaper praised, "there is rarely cause for such action on a major scale."[98] It mattered little to the white establishment whether Sheriff Clark's posse defended against labor unions or civil rights agitation; economics and race were—and always had been—part and parcel of the same battle to preserve white supremacy and local control.

But white business leaders still worked to quiet and control disturbances in the name of harmony and progress. In 1956 the Alabama Metallurgical Corporation (Alamet) announced plans to build a multimillion-dollar plant in Selma.[99] According to the president of the Chamber of Commerce, the company's arrival marked "the beginning of a new era of industrial expansion for the entire Central Alabama area."[100] Alamet was what business leaders saw as an ideal industry. A. E. Peterman, the company's president, sent a letter to employees urging them "to keep the union out of our plant." Alamet conducted operations "in such a way that a union is not necessary for good wages, good employee benefits and good working conditions." Peterman, charging that unions would hurt both the company and workers, emphasized the unlimited potential of "working together without outside interference."[101] The Chamber of Commerce confidentially circulated the Alamet letter to all of its members. "Whenever you have an opportunity to support the philosophy advanced in Mr. Peterman's letter," the general manager of the chamber urged, "you will be rendering a valuable service to all industries in this area by positively asserting your views."[102] Influenced by the company's strong antiunion policy, Alamet employees twice voted down union affiliation in its first two years of operation.[103]

Despite the antiunion climate, members of Local 793 at ILCO walked off their jobs for a second time on October 18, 1961. Their picket signs echoed striking workers' claims six years earlier as they demanded equal benefits with ILCO's northern employees. Company officials let it be known that the strike "seriously threaten[ed]" the company's continued operation in Selma.[104] The newspaper aligned itself with ILCO. "Our only interest is to preserve this industry, and possibly to further exploit its extensive plant to the point of attracting another payroll for the betterment of our people," it explained.[105] A week later, the Chamber of Commerce intervened for the sake of "the general welfare of this community." In a full-page ad in the *Selma Times-Journal*, the chamber pleaded with striking workers to return to their jobs on Monday morning. "In the interests of fellow-citizens, . . . let Selma's leadership stand shoulder-to-shoulder with you in our efforts to protect your jobs and keep on working to bring more industry into this area, which will help to give you greater security and raise generally your plane of living."[106] Significant pressure pushed some striking workers to relent, and by midday Tuesday 50 percent of ILCO workers had returned to their jobs.

Local 793's strike collapsed eight days after it began as employees crossed the picket lines, and the company hired over a hundred new workers. When the workers who had struck for the duration tried to return to their jobs, ILCO refused to let them in.[107] As a result, 263 union members found themselves out of work. Local 793's vice president, Robert Zetwick, demanded redress and accused business leaders of intervening, falsely promising to protect workers' jobs if the strike ended. "The Chamber of Commerce said they'd help us," Zetwick proclaimed. "Well, we need their help."[108] When the chamber insisted it could not intervene, Zetwick resorted to a full-page ad in the *Selma Times-Journal*. "These people, your friends and neighbors, returned to work after Selma's leading citizens and merchants with whom they have dealt throughout most of their lives urged them to end their strike," he entreated. "They never gained the opportunity to return to their machines. THESE MEN AND WOMEN WERE LOCKED OUT BY ILCO."[109] But his appeal brought no response from the chamber or the company, and two weeks later ILCO's corporate headquarters announced that the company planned to continue operating its Selma plant.[110] Whether standing against unions or civil rights, business and industrial leaders lined up on the side of preserving the area's economic and racial status quo.

SNCC Comes to Town

While politicians and businesspeople responded to the changing economic order of the Black Belt, black Selmians made civil rights an unavoidable issue in the spring of 1963. The newspaper headlines—the Montgomery bus boycott, sit-ins in Greensboro, Freedom Rides—heralded that black Americans were serious in their demands for full citizenship. Rev. Martin Luther King Jr. had gained a reputation as the nation's number-one civil rights agitator, and his organization, the Southern Christian Leadership Conference (SCLC), focused its attention on securing national civil rights legislation. Meanwhile, the Student Nonviolent Coordinating Committee (SNCC, pronounced "snick") emerged out of the student sit-ins. By 1963 SNCC, under the guidance of Ella Baker, had moved from direct action to voter registration and community organizing. The young people who made up its ranks partnered with black residents in the rural South to attack the ramparts of white supremacy.[111]

Black residents in Dallas County had long been working toward full citizenship and economic justice. Years of segregation had fostered, by necessity, black professionals and strong black-run institutions. Selma University and R. B. Hudson High School, the Extension Service and the community center, Good Samaritan Hospital, the Elks Federal Credit Union, and Tabernacle Baptist Church all contributed to the individual and collective advancement of African Americans, setting the stage for later challenges to white supremacy.[112]

In 1963 local and national efforts merged when SNCC field secretary Bernard Lafayette arrived in Selma. Lafayette, at the age of twenty-two, was already a veteran of the movement. As a student at American Baptist Theological Seminary, he had become a disciple of nonviolent direct action and participated in the Nashville sit-ins. That led him into SNCC and from there to the Freedom Rides. He went to SNCC's Atlanta office one day, planning to be put in charge of his own southern project. "Well, there's only one other place," SNCC's executive secretary, James Forman, told him, "and that's Selma, Alabama, but we've scratched that off the map." The SNCC workers sent to scope out the city had concluded that "the white folks were too mean and the black folks were too scared." But, young and confident, Lafayette said he'd take it.[113]

When Lafayette met Amelia Boynton on his first visit to Selma in 1962, he knew he had found himself a project. Before beginning, he stopped in Montgomery to get some practical advice about how to do voter registration from Rufus Lewis, who had been organizing citizenship schools in the rural Black Belt for decades. "I didn't need to reinvent the wheel in each new location but instead build off the existing foundation," Lafayette explained. When he and his new wife, fellow SNCC activist Colia Liddell, arrived in Selma in 1963, Lafayette assigned himself as a full-time staff member of DCVL. S. W. and Amelia Boynton, J. L. Chestnut, dental hygienist Marie Foster, James Gildersleeve, and other DCVL members became the Lafayettes' earliest supporters.[114]

Back in January, Foster had started teaching citizenship classes to help people practice taking the voter tests before going to the courthouse to register. She was a fiery woman who worked for her brother, Sullivan Jackson, in his dental office directly above the Boyntons'. Only one man showed up to her first class, even after Foster had advertised in person at every major black church in Dallas County. But "she stayed with him until ten o'clock, taught him to write his name, and continued to hold the classes," J. L. Chestnut remembered. Some of her most determined and reliable participants were the people from the Browns and Bogue Chitto communities, the same people educated in cooperation and self-sufficiency by S. W. Boynton and the Extension Service.[115] When someone succeeded in registering, their names were added to the honor roll of black voters posted on the wall of the Boyntons' insurance agency.[116] By the time Lafayette arrived, the honor roll listed a total of 156 names.[117]

Beyond DCVL members, the SNCC field secretaries didn't have much luck among local adults. "The possibility of losing your job was real," Chestnut explained, "and you had to consider whether or not you could do without it."[118] In March, though, Colia Lafayette reported, "We made a 'Lucky Strike' in Selma." Cleophus Hobbs and Charles Bonner, students at R. B. Hudson High School, were pushing Hobbs's broken-down green 1954 Ford toward home one Sunday afternoon when Bernard Lafayette joined their effort. Sitting on the porch afterward, he explained what he was doing in town and invited them to go canvassing the next day at the GWC Homes. The next night, Hobbs and Bonner went to SNCC's weekly voter registration workshop in the basement of Tabernacle Baptist Church. After they spread the word to their friends, thirty-nine high school students showed up at the next meeting, where they discussed the voter test and canvassing techniques and sang freedom songs. From that point on, Hudson High students—Bonner, Hobbs, Charles Mauldin, Bettie Fikes, Willie Emma Scott, Terry Shaw, and others—became the backbone of the movement. They knocked on doors, passed out leaflets, trained in nonviolent workshops in the basement of Tabernacle or St. Elizabeth's Mission of the Fathers of St. Edmund, and plotted actions they could take against segregation.[119]

The SNCC workers found another strong base of support in the independent black farmers, the same people who had been primed by years of S. W. Boynton's gospel of landownership and voter registration. Within a week of their arrival in town, the Lafayettes knew about Bogue Chitto's reputation for staving off a Klan attack and their willingness to shoot back, and they found four residents who volunteered to canvass in the area. Another local recruit, Rev. Seborn P. Powell, was a minister in a church just south of Bogue Chitto. He pounded the dirt roads around Orrville, teaching people in St. Mary Church, Rising Star Baptist Church, Salem Baptist Church, and Providence Baptist Church how to register. At the end of July, Rev. Powell brought Fred Smith and four other people to the courthouse to try to register.[120] Besides being active in the Extension Service, Smith's family was part of the selective Farm and Home Development Program, which helped black farmers increase their farm income and practice efficient and productive farming.[121] C. D. Scott, who had succeeded S. W. Boynton as the county agent, worked closely with the farmers in the program. He noted that, in addition to working cooperatively with other families and developing leadership skills, participating farmers were "more willing to accept citizenship responsibilities."[122] So when Smith went down to the courthouse in 1963 to try to register, he was acting on the lessons of self-sufficiency, landownership, and full citizenship that he had learned in the Extension Service.

S. W. Boynton helped pave the way for SNCC, but by 1963 the years of activism and harassment had taken their toll. That spring, Boynton lay in failing health at Burwell Infirmary after a series of strokes. Bernard Lafayette often sat by his side at the nursing home, where Boynton would still urge passersby to register to vote.[123] In May 1963 Boynton died, and Lafayette used his memorial service as Selma's first mass meeting. The flyers read, "Memorial Service for Mr. Boynton, and Voter Registration." "We put the two things together because that's what he stood for," Lafayette explained.[124] On the night of May 14, 350 black residents nervously congregated at Tabernacle Baptist Church to honor Boynton and his legacy of voting rights.[125] It was a powerful symbolic end to Boynton's life of dedication to the cause of racial justice.

Inside, the crowd amened as SNCC's James Forman avowed from the pulpit, "The Constitution gives us our rights, but unless we attempt to exercise them, we lose those rights." Outside, Sheriff Clark, members of his posse, and young white men wielding wooden table legs ominously circled the premises. Finally, a white coach from Parrish High School ordered the angry white crowd to go home. "He saved a whole lot of white folks from being killed," Lafayette later admitted. "Some of the members in that church had not been trained in nonviolence and had their weapons with them." One thing black and white southerners held in common was a belief in self-defense. Shotguns and rifles rested against doorframes and across the mantles of many African American homes both in rural areas and in the city of Selma.[126] While both SNCC and SCLC relied on nonviolence as a tactic, armed protection was part of civil rights activity in Selma from the very beginning.

Throughout the summer of 1963, the mass meetings continued and grew, and the Citizens' Council convened to stifle the burgeoning action.[127] Taking out a full-page ad in the *Selma Times-Journal*, the organization urged white citizens to ask themselves, "What have I personally done to maintain segregation?"[128] Three days later, two white men attacked Bernard Lafayette outside of his house. They clubbed him in the head multiple times, giving him a bloody gash that needed stitches. It was only when Lafayette's neighbor leaped across his porch with a rifle that the men fled. That same night, in Jackson, Mississippi, a sniper shot and killed NAACP leader Medgar Evers in his driveway.[129] At the end of August, sixty-eight hundred people packed into Memorial Stadium to hear Alabama governor George Wallace speak at the Citizens' Council's annual barbecue. Wallace swore that he would "never become resigned to accept integration." During his forty-minute speech, the cheering crowds interrupted him twenty-three times.[130]

As SNCC brought more and more people to the courthouse to try to register, a group of black moderates, under the banner of the Dallas County Improvement Association (DCIA), was moved to submit their own list of grievances to city leaders. The DCIA, including people like Edwin Moss of the Fathers of St. Edmund and the Elks Federal Credit Union, first submitted their petition to the municipal government. It called for an end to "the brutal and savage" way the police treated African Americans, the hiring of black residents in jobs other than as common laborers, and the correction of "certain known unjust practices" in local businesses through the formation of a biracial committee. As the petition made clear, voting rights was only a part of black residents' fight against the racial order of the Black Belt.[131]

When Mayor Heinz refused to act, DCIA's black businessmen and ministers appealed directly to Selma's businessmen. "Let it be known that the Negro Citizens here, too, are no different [than] those all over the country who are seeking those rights and freedoms that they feel they justly deserve," the DCIA wrote in a letter to all retail merchants, "those privileges that will enable them to live with dignity and to assume those responsibilities that should be shared by all citizens." While they stressed that they, too, wanted harmonious race relations, the DCIA demanded that merchants promote black employees to sales clerks, pay all black workers "a livable wage," treat all customers with courtesy, and remove "White" and "Colored" signs from the premises.[132]

The Chamber of Commerce called an emergency meeting where they voted to ignore the letter and support local merchants' opposition to integration. Furthermore, members pledged to secure representatives from "all civic, commercial and fraternal organizations" who would meet "to support segregation policies" and formulate "future attitudes and policies."[133] They also drafted a list of rights and principles necessary to preserve the "mutual confidence, trust, and respect between the races." Whether in buying or selling property, operating a private business, or engaging in any other activities, white chamber members claimed their right to individual authority or, as they put it, "the right to select one's own associations, whatever the occasion."[134] Echoing familiar states' rights credos, Selma's business leaders affirmed that local control would and should override racial justice.

But SNCC's voter registration campaign continued to gain momentum, and classes held at the Boyntons' insurance agency, churches, and rural communities like Sardis, Orrville, Bogue Chitto, and Beloit kept a steady stream of people applying at the courthouse.[135] Then, in September, a bomb exploded at the Sixteenth Street Baptist Church in Birmingham, killing four black girls. The Hudson High students who had been working with SNCC felt that they had to do something, so they staged sit-ins at three Selma drugstores, the first direct-action protests seen in the city. At Carter's, Willie Robinson bought a tube of toothpaste from the cosmetics counter and then walked over to the fountain and asked to be served. While he was being turned down, Harmon Carter, the owner, came up from behind and slugged him across the head with an axe handle, giving him a wound that required multiple stiches.[136] Across town, Hudson High School students poured out of their classrooms in a massive walkout and congregated at Brown Chapel AME Church. The effect of the students' protest "on the local Negroes was tremendous," one SNCC worker reported.[137]

On Monday, October 7, black residents amassed at the courthouse on what SNCC deemed "Freedom Day." The Dallas County Board of Registrars accepted applications only on the first and third Mondays of each month, and SNCC wanted to get as many people as they could to try and register. Throughout the morning, the line grew until 350 people waited on the sidewalk. Sheriff Clark and his entourage of posse members patrolled the scene, "dressed in khakis or fatigues, carrying guns at their hips, clubs in their hands," SNCC observer Howard Zinn recalled. The afternoon sun blazed, and few had entered the courthouse doors. When two SNCC workers tried to bring water and baloney sandwiches to those in line, the posse and recently arrived state troopers brought one of them to the ground, shocking him with cattle prods. All of this occurred in plain sight of the federal building located directly across from the courthouse, but no one intervened as a truck carted the two men off to jail.[138] At 4:30 p.m., the courthouse closed, and the intrepid line dispersed; only forty applications had been processed by the board of registrars that day.[139]

Repercussions from Freedom Day soon followed. Charles Dunn, the owner of the Dunn Rest Home and a staunch segregationist, employed forty black women in his nursing home. Passing by the courthouse on Freedom Day, Dunn recognized two of his employees—Annie Lee Cooper and

Elnora Collins—standing in line. He fired them both within days. When Dunn attempted to photograph Collins to prevent her from getting further work, she refused. Dunn then struck her with a cattle prod, lacerating her arm. "Such treatment was too much for the other colored employees to take," Amelia Boynton explained, "so all of them walked off in protest of Mr. Dunn's cruelty."[140] By the fall of 1963, there was no question that SNCC organizing had laid the groundwork and emboldened black Dallas Countians to demand fair treatment and their right to the ballot.

White Political Conflicts

Chris Heinz had been elected Selma's mayor in 1952. He was the chosen successor of Lucien P. Burns, the mayor from 1932 to 1949, when Burns stepped down to become president of the City National Bank. Burns and the political dynasty he cultivated represented the city's most powerful men, committed to defending segregation, the status quo, and their own power. It was during Heinz's tenure in office that civil rights—in the Fikes trial and the NAACP school desegregation petition—escalated to an immediate threat.[141] The explosion of civil rights activism in Selma pushed influential white citizens, like Mayor Heinz, Citizens' Council chairman M. Alston Keith, Judge Hare, and H. Hunt Frazier of the Chamber of Commerce, to prepare for a knock-down, drag-out fight to preserve their southern way of life. Over in the governor's mansion, George Wallace was doing the same thing. Whether campaigning on "Segregation Now! Segregation Tomorrow! Segregation Forever!" or standing in the schoolhouse door, "Wallace reinvigorated white Alabama's resistance," J. L. Chestnut explained, who was watching everything unfold from his vantage point as Selma's only black attorney. The midcentury revolution in agriculture and industry only heightened the attempts of Selma's ruling class to maintain control. Outsider business threatened to disrupt this local grasp on power, and the old guard leaders of Black Belt plantation areas worked to limit its influence. "The city fathers who controlled Selma's economy and dominated the Chamber of Commerce were uninterested in industrial expansion or any type of change," Chestnut summarized. Rumors among black leaders and younger white businessmen alike accused Selma's political machine of turning away interested industries because they would have challenged the area's racial order and antiunion climate.[142]

By the 1960s younger businessmen were fed up with what they saw as Mayor Heinz's and the Chamber of Commerce's miserly and protectionist recruitment strategy for new industries.[143] In 1962 Rex Morthland and B. Frank Wilson (the president and vice president of the People's Bank), the tractor dealer Carl Morgan, the investment banker Catesby ap C. Jones, and others founded the Committee of 100. Their purpose was to create a "new industrial image of Selma."[144] Instead of looking backward like the segregationist old guard, the new contingent of Black Belt businessmen had economic motives and a farsighted view of the future in mind.[145] "The negative approach which stymied Selma for so long has finally been channeled into a positive action," chairman Otis "Red" Adam explained, "and the Committee is very optimistic about what it can accomplish."[146] Later that year, the Committee of 100 broke with the chamber during the election of directors. In an unprecedented move, they ran six alternative candidates and gave their approval to only four of the twenty chamber nominees, many of whom were tied to the county's political establishment.[147] The rogue businessmen were defeated in a fierce election, but the setback only encouraged them to regroup. When they did, they chose to take on Mayor Heinz himself in the mayoral election in 1964.[148]

The man the young businessmen lined up behind was Joseph ("Joe") T. Smitherman, an appliance salesman turned city councilman. Smitherman had been a month old when his family moved to East Selma. His father, a sawmill man, lost his job, then died not long afterward, leaving his wife to care for their three boys and three girls. Everyone in East Selma was dirt poor, and Smitherman started his life with no more material possessions than the black neighbors who lived near the family's shotgun shack house at 2518 Water Avenue. Government commodities and a small welfare check helped keep the family fed. Even though his friends' fathers had jobs on the railroad, Smitherman grew up fully aware that he was living on the wrong side of the tracks.[149]

Walter Stoudenmire, a city councilman and owner of the Selma Appliance Company, gave Smitherman one of the biggest breaks in his young life when he offered the eager, big-eared twenty-something-year-old work selling appliances.[150] Smitherman sold his way into a better life, one Frigidaire at a time, and his ambition grew. Selma's political and business elite kept a tight grasp on political control. Their families had "dug the river," they dined at the Selma Country Club, and they lived on a combination of old and new money. Coming from the other side of the tracks, Smitherman resented what the elite stood for. In the mid-1950s, he took over Stoudenmire's seat on Selma's City Council when Stoudenmire ran for council president. Councilman Smitherman immediately positioned himself as Mayor

Heinz's archnemesis. Railing against the "country club crowd" and rich attorneys, Smitherman presented himself as the man who could represent the rich and the poor, pave the city streets, and bring jobs to town.[151]

In 1964 Smitherman, at the age of thirty-four, threw his hat into the mayoral race. Because segregation wasn't a debatable issue in Selma or the state of Alabama in the 1960s—every white person was publicly for it, even if they had some doubts buried deep inside—Smitherman was unquestionably a segregationist. He was also, however, part of the business moderates willing to make small, token compromises on racial issues for the sake of economic development. Those southern businessmen, with their ears to the ground, eyed a future where towing a hard line for segregation could very well become bad for business.[152] Smitherman played himself up as the mayoral candidate for change and progress, speaking to the concerns of the Committee of 100. "For the past 30 years a favored few have dominated Selma's destiny!" one of his campaign slogans read. "Are you satisfied with Selma's progress under their control, or do you agree that after 30 years it's time for a change?" Always a brash man, the young challenger even went so far as to publicly accuse the municipal machine of intentionally keeping the area's minimum wage low.[153] In March 1964 those who believed Smitherman's platform of "paving streets, recruiting industry, and serving *all* citizens—meaning all whites," Chestnut explained, elected him mayor. His victory marked the end of the old segregationist order.[154]

By the mid-1960s, the group of young businessmen of which Smitherman was a part, willing to soften racial practices in the name of good business and economic prosperity, had successfully staged a coup in city hall and then the Chamber of Commerce. But their readiness to make small concessions could not stop the growing tide of civil rights activism across the South. The Fikes trial, the school desegregation attempt, and SNCC's voter registration efforts had made civil rights a Selma issue, and, responding to their worst fears, white Dallas Countians rallied to the defense of segregation. As the Citizens' Council used economic intimidation to silence dissent, the local political machine worked diligently to contain any and all racial and labor agitation. Change was in the air. But before Mayor Joe Smitherman could establish a new approach to business and segregation in Selma, local civil rights activity captured the attention of the entire nation.[155]

INTERLUDE

1965

In 1964 SNCC set up a literacy project at St. Elizabeth's Mission, where Father Maurice Ouellet, the only white person in Selma to publicly support local black activism, was the pastor. Project director Maria Varela instructed her staff to keep a low profile and stay away from the SNCC office downtown because literacy work couldn't get done if its staffers ended up in jail. Then, on July 2, 1964, President Lyndon Johnson signed the Civil Rights Act into law, legally ending racial discrimination in public places. On the Fourth of July, the literacy project staff members decided to stop in at the whites-only Thirsty Boy restaurant to test the law. Sheriff Jim Clark wasted no time arresting the group, illustrating that laws from Washington did not necessarily apply in Selma. When the local young people staffing Selma's SNCC office got word of the incident, they jumped into action.[1]

An hour after the Thirsty Boy arrests, a dozen black teenagers purchased tickets at the Wilby Theatre and asked manager Roger Butler if they could sit in the all-white section downstairs. Complying with directions from the theater chain's owner, Butler did not block them. So Sheriff Clark brought an end to the integration by invading the theater with his deputies and possemen. They chased black patrons out and harassed those waiting in line outside. By 6:40 p.m., Clark had ordered both the Wilby and the Walton theaters closed owing to disturbances.[2] That night, two five-foot-tall crosses burned on the northern edge of town.[3]

The Civil Rights Act of 1964 was a product of years of direct-action protests, starting with the student sit-ins and the Freedom Rides and continuing with the Southern Christian Leadership Conference's more recent campaign in Birmingham, Alabama. In the spring of 1963, SCLC had partnered with local black residents to stage a frontal attack on segregation. Bull Connor—Birmingham's unpredictable and deeply racist public safety commissioner—responded with force. Vivid images of black children ricocheting down the street after being blasted by police-directed fire hoses and being mauled by police dogs provoked a national outcry. For the first time, President John F. Kennedy publicly threw his support behind civil rights. When Kennedy was assassinated that fall, Johnson used his political might and Kennedy's legacy to push through civil rights legislation.[4]

Back in Selma, circuit judge James A. Hare used his authority to end any and all testing of the new Civil Rights Act.[5] He issued an injunction forbidding SNCC, DCVL, SCLC, the Klan, and other organizations from meeting. Then, not taking any chances, he banned the very assembling of more than two people in any public place. The judge's injunction knocked public protest in Selma out cold just a week after it started.[6]

Behind closed doors, however, the Dallas County Voters League charted their next move. Amelia Boynton and DCVL had brought SNCC to Selma with full understanding that their local struggle gained potency when they partnered with a larger civil rights organization.[7] So when Judge Hare's injunction hindered SNCC's work, Boynton turned to Martin Luther King Jr. and the recently victorious SCLC. She traveled to Birmingham to urge SCLC members to stage a full-blown campaign against political repression in Selma.[8] As SCLC's Andrew Young remembered it, "We did not choose them, they chose us."[9]

Fresh off its victory with the Civil Rights Act, SCLC set its sights on national voting rights legislation. Since 1961 SNCC had been organizing around the vote in Mississippi. By 1964 they and local people had laid the groundwork for voting rights as a national issue, moving from voter registration to the organization of a parallel political party made up of black Mississippians. At the Democratic National Convention in 1964, a sixty-eight-member delegation of the Mississippi Freedom Democratic Party challenged the seating of the all-white Mississippi Democratic Party, seeking to prove that

Inter6.1 Amelia Boynton speaking at a civil rights meeting at Brown Chapel, May 1966. Photograph by Jim Peppler. Courtesy of Alabama Department of Archives and History, Montgomery, Alabama.

black southerners wanted to vote but were prevented from doing so. Voting rights were at the forefront of the nation's consciousness, and SCLC was looking to replicate the mass protests and media attention that had worked so well in Birmingham. Selma's well-organized black community, intransigent white elites, and history of voting rights activism made it an ideal testing ground. "We wanted to raise the issue of voting to the point where we could take it outside of the Black Belt," SCLC's C. T. Vivian explained. "We were using Selma as a way to shake Alabama, so that it would be no longer a Selma issue or even an Alabama issue but a national issue."[10]

The proven strength and determination of black Dallas County citizens sold SCLC on Selma's potential. When SNCC arrived in 1963, they found the "economic, religious, political, and fraternal" organizations in Selma's black community "old" and "stabilized." The organizing work of SNCC tapped into deep community networks forged in parallel and decades-long fights for better jobs, quality education, legal justice, and self-sufficiency.[11] These demands got pushed to the background, however, as SCLC began formulating a nationally geared campaign for voting rights.

From its earlier campaigns, SCLC had learned that a successful movement needed a clear focus that captured the nation's attention. Three years earlier in Albany, Georgia, police chief Laurie Pritchett withered media coverage by methodically but quietly arresting civil rights protesters. Martin Luther King Jr.'s organization did not make the same mistake again. When police commissioner Bull Connor assailed black schoolchildren, the campaign in Birmingham made headlines across the world. The ability of SCLC to secure new voting rights legislation depended on another nationally broadcast morality play starring white segregationists brutalizing nonviolent black marchers. In the hotheadedness of Sheriff Clark and his posse, SCLC saw the potential of another Bull Connor.[12]

The Selma campaign began on January 2, 1965, the same day black citizens celebrated emancipation from slavery. Seven hundred people packed into the pews of Brown Chapel AME Church, listening while Martin Luther King Jr. called Selma "a symbol of bitter-end resistance to the civil rights movement in the Deep South." It was the first mass meeting since Judge Hare had issued the injunction six months earlier. "Today marks the beginning of a determined, organized, mobilized campaign to get the right to vote everywhere in Alabama," King boomed to the crowd. Afterward, King met with representatives of DCVL, SNCC, and SCLC to map out a blueprint for the movement. [13]

Over the next eight weeks, SCLC and SNCC staffers organized the city into wards, recruited block captains, and knocked on doors to find volunteers who would attempt to register to vote.[14] On January 18, the next Monday that the registrar's office was open, black adults marched, two by two, to the courthouse. The recently elected Mayor Joe T. Smitherman and his newly appointed public safety director, Wilson Baker, tried to head off any incidents, but the explosive Sheriff Clark claimed dominion over the courthouse. When protestors refused to move into a back alley on the second day of protests, Clark's temper rose, and he seized Amelia Boynton by her coat collar, roughly dragging her to a patrol car.[15]

That Friday afternoon, Selma's black teachers, led by DCVL member Frederick D. ("F. D.") Reese, marched from Clark Elementary School to the courthouse to try to register. Never before had a group of middle-class teachers—whose paychecks were signed by the white school board—demonstrated so visibly. When Clark roughly barred them from the courthouse steps, the headlines in national newspapers read, "Alabama Sheriff Turns Back Negro Teachers" and "Negro Teachers Protest in Selma: 105 Demonstrators Pushed Away with Nightsticks."[16] An SCLC member later told the press, "Every time it appears the movement is dying out, Sheriff Clark comes to our rescue."[17] Meanwhile, the editor of the *Selma Times-Journal* pleaded with Selma's citizens to take a stand against Clark's actions, "if this city and county are to return to the status of dignity, respectability, and decency which they have always known."[18]

With Selma's white officials working to quiet the voting rights movement, SCLC leaders expanded demonstrations into the surrounding Black Belt counties.[19] On February 18, state troopers shot a young black man when they attacked a night march in neighboring Perry County.[20] Jimmie Lee Jackson died one week later, bringing the nation's attention back to the Black Belt. From the pulpit in Brown Chapel, SCLC's James Bevel proposed symbolically marching Jackson's body from Selma to Governor Wallace in Montgomery, and those in the pews agreed. Many of them had been among the thirty-four hundred residents arrested in the preceding month of protest.[21]

On the morning of Sunday, March 7, black residents gathered in the GWC housing project surrounding Brown Chapel, ready to march to the state capital. On the opposite side of the Edmund Pettus Bridge, state troopers, Sheriff Clark, and his posse waited, some on horseback and others equipped with billy clubs and gas masks. Hosea Williams of SCLC and SNCC's John Lewis led the march, but Amelia Boynton, Marie Foster, and hundreds of local black residents who had built the movement followed behind. The line crested over the sharply arched bridge and came to a stop in front of a barrier of law enforcement officers. Major John Cloud, the commander of the state troopers, ordered the marchers to stop and disperse at the foot of the bridge. They did not, and a few minutes later, he gave the order, "Troopers, advance!"

With billy clubs swinging and tear gas filling the air, law enforcement officers and posse members advanced. Those at the front of the line crumpled unconscious from direct beatings while others stumbled frantically back toward Brown Chapel, seeking refuge, bleeding and panicked. The posse and troopers continued their rampage all the way to the GWC Homes. There, however, they met bricks and bottles, as black residents retaliated. "I was out on the bridge today because I thought it was right," a man told the crowd at Brown Chapel later that night. "But while I was on the bridge, Jim Clark came to my house and tear-gassed my eighty-year-old mother, and next time he comes to my house, I'm going to be ready." Leaders of SCLC desperately urged the traumatized and angry crowd to remain nonviolent.[22] In Dallas County, where independence and protection had always involved a gun, it was a testament to local residents' determination that there was no retaliation.

That night, footage of what became known as "Bloody Sunday" was broadcast into American living rooms. Images of white state troopers brutally beating peaceful black marchers horrified the collective conscience of the nation. When Martin Luther King called for people to come to Selma and join "our peaceful, nonviolent march for freedom," hundreds came.[23] The residents of the GWC Homes opened their homes, giving strangers places to sleep. Two thousand people marched behind King in another protest march on Tuesday, one that turned around at the bridge so as not to violate a federal injunction. Elsewhere, civil rights sympathizers marched in the thousands, demanding federal intervention, while a bipartisan coalition of lawmakers rallied for swift congressional action.[24] That night in Selma, white men outside of Selma's Silver Moon Café beat white Unitarian minister Rev. James Reeb. He died shortly thereafter.[25]

The crisis in Selma pushed President Johnson to action. "It is wrong, deadly wrong, to deny any of your fellow Americans the right to vote in this country," Johnson declared in a televised address one week later. After detailing a new voting rights bill, the president, in the language of the movement, vowed that "we shall overcome" the country's "crippling legacy of bigotry and injustice."[26] King watched the speech in Sullivan and Jean Jackson's living room on Lapsley Street, not far from the Boyntons' house and down the way from Selma University.

The march from Selma to Montgomery finally became a reality later that week after securing the approval of the federal judge Frank Johnson. Finding black landowners to volunteer their land for campsites, securing portable toilets, organizing transportation, coordinating food and water, and a thousand more tasks consumed organizers. "Assignments were divided up among staff and off they went," Jean Jackson remembered. "Calls were pouring in from everywhere."[27] Because Highway 80 was only two lanes through Lowndes County, Judge Johnson limited the march to three hundred people for that section. The task of selecting the three hundred fell to SNCC staffer Frank Soracco. In proper SNCC fashion, he made sure that the local men and women who had gone to jail and faced down Sheriff Clark received the honor of walking the entire fifty-four miles.[28]

On Sunday, March 21, over three thousand people triumphantly marched across the Edmund Pettus Bridge. Instead of billy club–wielding possemen, members of the federalized Alabama National Guard walked alongside, protecting the marchers.[29] Five days later, the exhausted but determined group of three hundred started walking from Montgomery's outskirts to the city center. As they approached the capitol building, their numbers swelled to twenty-five thousand. Not far from the spot where Confederate president Jefferson Davis had taken his oath of office, Martin Luther King spoke to the crowd. "The confrontation of good and evil compressed in the tiny community of Selma generated the massive power that turned the whole nation to a new course," he proclaimed. While he reminded the audience from where the movement had come, King urged those gathered to "march on the ballot boxes" until justice was achieved. "How long? Not long," he said in closing, "because the arc of the moral universe is long, but it bends towards justice."[30] But the arc had not bent far enough that night. In the process of shuttling marchers back to Selma from Montgomery, a carload of Klan members—including one Federal Bureau of Investigation informant—shot into a car driven by a Detroit mother and volunteer, Viola Liuzzo, killing her on the side of Highway 80.[31]

On August 7, 1965, President Johnson signed the Voting Rights Act into law. Over fifty years of carefully guarded voter restrictions in the South came to an end, and federal examiners descended on southern counties to protect the right to vote for all citizens.[32] The movement that had grown from black Dallas County citizens' fight against white supremacy succeeded in securing voting rights legislation designed to protect all Americans. The first half of 1965 forever changed Selma; however, the long and painstaking work of turning the promises of the voting rights movement into reality for African Americans' daily lives was only beginning.

CHAPTER

6

≡

Making the "Good Freedom"

1965–1976

Joanne Blackmon Bland became a freedom fighter before the age of ten. Standing with her grandmother outside of Carter Drug Company one day, Bland wanted to go in and order at the lunch counter—the same lunch counter R. B. Hudson High School students had targeted for their first sit-in. Her grandmother explained that colored children were not allowed to do that. Then, leaning over, she told Bland that when they got their freedom, she could do that too. "I became a freedom fighter that day," Bland recalled. "I understood that Grandma was going for the *good* freedom. Abraham Lincoln had given me *a* freedom, but not the *good* freedom." When the voting rights campaign swept Selma, Bland marched to the courthouse and received her first ride on a yellow school bus as it drove her, her grandmother, and other protestors to jail.[1] The Voting Rights Act of 1965 guaranteed African Americans the political tools necessary to dismantle the entrenched system of white supremacy. But this monumental achievement marked a beginning rather than an ending. Making the "good freedom" a reality quickly proved a difficult undertaking.

As the national spotlight turned away from Selma in the aftermath of the movement of 1965, black citizens in Dallas County forged on. Drawing energy from the exploding new black voter base and working within movement-inspired organizations, black residents took on local political, economic, and social injustices. The federal government became their principal but still reticent ally. For the first time since Reconstruction, the national government put its might to use, requiring white southern officials to at least consider treating African Americans as full citizens. Ballooning numbers of black voters, the end of segregated school systems, the hiring of black public employees, and racially balanced election districts were all products of federal intervention. Meanwhile, Lyndon Johnson's War on Poverty funneled millions of dollars into programs to empower poor people and eradicate poverty. It was a time of hope for black citizens, who, due to their own efforts, witnessed small changes for the better accumulate in their lives. In Dallas County, War on Poverty funding helped support a cooperative for black farmers, provided day care programs, supported employment for low-income teens and adults, and paved roads and put streetlights in long-neglected black neighborhoods.

Selma's white business and political leaders, battered by all that had transpired, fought determinedly to dictate the pace of change and repair the city's image. A new generation of more moderate businesspeople had replaced the old guard segregationists, but they, too, were interested in maintaining local control. Fierce resistance from white elites stymied federally supported advances in black employment, legal justice, and school desegregation during the 1970s. With his domineering political style, Mayor Joe Smitherman wrested control of local War on Poverty funding away from a black-led grassroots organization of poor people and installed a board of white moderates and black middle-class representatives to supervise a program that met his approval. The Chamber of Commerce continued its policy of favoring low-wage, nonunionized, and racially stratified industries. So black workers remained stuck in the worst jobs as the decades-long agricultural revolution finally foreclosed on the livelihoods of black tenants and small farmers alike. Welfare became many people's only option. After the movement, it had seemed as though Bland's "good freedom" was at hand, but white officials and businessmen only fought harder to maintain the status quo as they felt their control slipping.

6.1 Black citizens entering the federal building in downtown Selma to register to vote. Photograph by Jim Peppler. Courtesy of Alabama Department of Archives and History, Montgomery, Alabama.

After the Movement

"After the march to Montgomery, most everybody went home—except, of course, we local folk," recalled J. L. Chestnut. "We were at home."[2] While national media attention turned elsewhere—the escalating crisis in Vietnam or the uprisings setting the nation's cities on fire—Dallas County citizens began sorting out what life would look like in the aftermath. Organizers from SNCC and SCLC remained in Selma, but disagreements ran rife over where the movement should go now that voting rights had been obtained. Facing outside scrutiny, Mayor Smitherman agreed to biracial meetings with the Dallas County Voters League (DCVL), now headed by Rev. F. D. Reese. Local black leaders called for fair employment and representation in city government, integration of public facilities, courtesy titles for black citizens, and an end to police brutality. But the new mayor refused to budge. White moderates, in Chestnut's estimation, "were trying to determine how much they would have to give up to get the Yankees off their back and bring the marches to a halt." Smitherman's refusal to compromise did not stop him from insisting that black residents call off their boycott of downtown businesses, and as he put it, give their "vocal support [to] Selma's industrial development."[3]

Meanwhile, boxes of clothing and food began pouring into Brown Chapel and First Baptist, signaling the shock Americans had felt seeing the living faces of Black Belt poverty on their television sets. The work of distributing aid was taken up by SCLC and DCVL, and, before long, accusations of fraud and favoritism flew like willow flies in August. Months of marching had taken a toll on the men and women who sustained the movement.[4]

Stalwart members of DCVL had every intention of maintaining their leadership positions after the voting rights movement, which pushed them to increasingly act in their own self-interest. Rev. Reese, a Selma native, had begun teaching science at R. B. Hudson High School in 1960, the same year he became a Baptist minister. Soon after, he was elected president of the Selma Teachers Association, and later DCVL, and he used his positions to rally the support of the teachers, which ultimately cost him his job. After the voting rights movement, Reese put his leadership credentials to use to open biracial negotiations with white city officials.[5] Meanwhile, the city's obstinate refusal to address their demands compounded black residents' frustration and caused cracks in the temporary unity of the past year. Black residents from East Selma's Ward 5B rebelled against DCVL's attempt to maintain control. Fed up with their children trekking long distances to get

6.2 Rev. F. D. Reese of the Dallas County Voters League, sitting in an upholstered chair behind the pulpit during a meeting at a rural church. Photograph by Jim Peppler. Courtesy of Alabama Department of Archives and History, Montgomery, Alabama.

to Hudson High, the residents began raising funds to purchase a school bus. When DCVL's vice president, Ernest Doyle, insisted that all money needed to be channeled through DCVL's coffers, ward residents refused and split from the organization. On their own, they raised enough funds to buy the bus.[6]

While black Selmians grew wary of the power grabs of movement leaders, their sense of self-worth and empowerment thrived, a tribute to SNCC's grassroots organizing work. In East Selma, one of the city's poorest sections, residents' involvement in voting rights protests had done nothing to alleviate the piles of rubbish, standing water, muddy streets, and cracked sewage pipes that were a daily norm. In the summer of 1965, three SNCC workers partnered with East Selmians who were active in the movement and organized weekly ward meetings for residents to talk about local problems.[7] In early July, Claudia Mae Strong hosted the East Selma People's Convention in her backyard. The theme of the evening was "If we don't help ourselves, who will?"[8] Convention attendees backed registering to vote and running candidates for office as a means to paved roads, better housing, sewers, and playgrounds. Not taking any chances, however, they also vowed to take up direct-action tactics—like not paying taxes and suing the city for misappropriation of public funds—if the traditional political process failed them.[9]

While middle-class black leaders petitioned public officials, black employees demanded fair treatment and better pay on the job. At the Coca-Cola bottling company in Selma, black workers began organizing a union with the help of civil rights workers. The men demanded $1.25 an hour for a forty-hour workweek, instead of the $0.64 per hour they currently made for fifty hours. "I just don't see how a man with seven children can survive on take home pay of $29.66," Willie Fuller, one of the local strike leaders, explained.[10] But the South's long history of racially divided workforces hurt the efforts of black Coca-Cola employees. At the NLRB election in August 1965, the union lost by one vote. "I didn't want to join no nigger organization," one of the company's white workers said. Four years earlier, the situation had been exactly reversed; a group of white Coca-Cola workers had failed to form a union when the company urged the black workers to vote against it.[11] As Mayor Smitherman explained later, employers had always been able to pressure white employees by telling them, "If you can't do better, and you won't for this price, we'll get a black to do it."[12] Voting rights did little to resolve the enduring racial divisions in Selma's workplaces.[13]

Even with the promise of political rights for black citizens, the structural roots of poverty sank deep in the Alabama Black Belt, and they were not easy to dig up. In 1960, 52 percent of all Dallas County families lived in poverty, but an extraordinary 84 percent of black families eked out a living on less than $3,000 per year. Meanwhile, 43 percent of homes were classified as deteriorating or dilapidated, and more of them had television sets than flush toilets. A ninth-grade education made anyone in the county better educated than most of their neighbors, but among African Americans over half had not made it to the sixth grade.[14] For the voting rights movement to usher in meaningful change, activists increasingly believed a myriad of other issues—substandard housing, underfunded education, lack of access to cash and credit, malnutrition, poor health care, and subpar transportation—needed to be addressed. As SNCC's Courtland Cox put it, the vote was "necessary but not sufficient."[15]

This growing awareness of the structural roots of poverty also resonated in the halls of the U.S. Capitol. Extending civil rights and eradicating poverty were essential to Johnson's dreams of a Great Society. In 1964 Congress passed the Economic Opportunity Act, a far-reaching antipoverty bill. The Office of Economic Opportunity (OEO) opened that October to spearhead new War on Poverty programs. These fell into two primary categories: Title II Community Action Programs—projects developed by poor people to address local and immediate needs—and Title III programs, specifically targeted at rural poverty. Most important, the War on Poverty insisted on as much participation as possible by the poor who would be served by its programs. Coupled with the newly enforced federal civil rights protections, the OEO offered black citizens in the Alabama Black Belt a way to further their fight for political rights and economic justice.[16]

Two SCLC staff members—Rev. Harold Middlebrook and Shirley Mesher—led efforts to create an antipoverty committee of black and poor people in Dallas County. Middlebrook, a small-statured black minister, and Mesher, a fiery white woman from Seattle, had arrived in Selma in the end days of the national movement and became deeply involved in organizing around economic issues. They worked in the same building, 31½ Franklin Street, that housed the Boyntons' insurance agency and SNCC's office, and movement organizers benefited from this close contact. Amelia Boynton had used her knowledge from years of Extension Service work to connect outside activists with willing rural communities. During the summer of 1965, SCLC and SNCC workers ventured out into the county, speaking at rural churches, distributing leaflets, and trying to reach as many poor people as possible.[17]

Organizing work during the voting rights campaign in 1965 mainly stayed within the boundaries of Selma, but it was out in what locals called the "rurals" that antipoverty organizers found their best supporters. In many ways, this was a legacy of S. W. Boynton and the Negro Extension Service's mission to build economic independence and self-sufficiency among black farmers. "People in the rural [areas] are much more politically educated than the city people are," black Dallas County farmer Joe Johnson explained. "They are more aware of the political facts, and they cooperate a whole lot more."[18] Martha Prescod, a SNCC worker, encountered this when she drove with Amelia Boynton to an antipoverty meeting in the county. When Prescod asked, "Why are people poor?," one of the farmers in the crowd responded, "Because someone steals their labor." Prescod then asked why someone would steal a person's labor. "Then I received a ten-minute description of the crisscrossing of economic and political power in the county along with how these people were related to one another by blood and marriage," she recalled. "That was the last time I attempted to teach any kind of political education class in Alabama."[19]

By the fall of 1965, organizers had marshaled a coalition of poor people, independent farmers, and others who sought official designation as Dallas

County's antipoverty agency. When their attempts to include local white officials went nowhere, the group moved forward alone, holding a series of public sessions in Selma.[20] They called themselves Self-Help against Poverty for Everyone (SHAPE) and chose local African American minister Ernest Bradford as their spokesman. Earlier in the year, the mayor had submitted his own proposal for a Community Action Program, which the OEO rejected for its lack of black participation. "The white folks' poverty committee," Rev. Middlebrook explained, did not have "the Negro community or any poor whites. . . . They are all businessmen or people who are pretty well set."[21] The widening influence of SHAPE around town, however, reinvigorated Mayor Smitherman's interest.

Two days after a SHAPE gathering in late October, the mayor announced his intention to apply again for antipoverty funds. He stated that he would not give his support to any "self-appointed group . . . which attempts to go around local government to obtain antipoverty [funds]," completely ignoring SHAPE's efforts to reach out to city officials.[22] On Thursday, November 4, city officials, business leaders, SHAPE members, and DCVL activists convened at the National Guard Armory to hear the mayor's proposal. The plan proposed by SHAPE called for a black-majority board paralleling Dallas County's population and prioritizing the participation of poor people.[23] What the mayor proposed instead was a board with equal numbers of black and white members and a smaller executive board that would administer the funds.[24] Smitherman also stipulated that an eleven-man African American committee would choose all of the black representatives and that Bernard Reynolds, the white probate judge, would have final say over the proposed black members.[25]

Understandably, SHAPE balked. Five days later, 450 citizens, most of them black, crammed into Green Street Baptist Church to debate how they should respond.[26] Tension between the black middle-class leaders and Dallas County's mobilized poor filled the sanctuary. The rural and working-class people that SHAPE helped empower jeopardized the authority of Selma's traditional black leadership. As one SHAPE member explained, now a man from the rural areas "could stand up just like any preacher and voice his opinions[,] and his opinion carried just as much weight because he had discovered that he was a man." Middle-class leaders, like DCVL's Rev. Reese and Ernest Doyle, had put their efforts into negotiating with city officials, a strategy that secured some concessions but also their own personal power. That night at the church, Reese took the stage in support of the mayor's plan, while SHAPE's Rev. Bradford stood in staunch opposition. A line had been drawn between SHAPE and the black middle-class leaders of DCVL. [27]

Over the next three months, a group of black ministers joined forces with Mayor Smitherman, trying to compel SHAPE to participate in the city's plan. "Nobody is trying to shove the poor people out," Rev. J. D. Hunter reasoned. "But when I go to court I want a lawyer, and when I go to church I want a preacher." A decade earlier, Hunter had refused to remove his name from the NAACP school desegregation petition, but now he was suggesting that poor people had no place in antipoverty leadership. With black middle-class leaders in Mayor Smitherman's camp, the balance of power was stacked against SHAPE's coalition. After burning through their limited options, SHAPE grudgingly relented in January. They nominated representatives to Smitherman's board, figuring that some say was better than none at all.[28]

The OEO officials praised the new forty-eight-member community action agency for including public officials, civic organizations, civil rights leaders, and poor people. While the half-black, half-white board looked good on paper, "the key people who are active on CAP [Community Action Program] in the Negro community," Mesher explained, "are in close political coalition with the white power structure, again to the dismay and displeasure of the majority of the community." Smitherman had helped divide black citizens into those who were for and those who were against him, a pattern that would play out again and again to the benefit of his own power, at the expense of poor people, like those in SHAPE.[29]

The First Post-1965 Election

Even though SHAPE lost its fight for War on Poverty funds, it fired up a constituency of working-class people fed up with self-appointed black leaders and white control. One county over, Stokely Carmichael and SNCC workers were partnering with local activists to drum up support for an independent, black-led political party in Lowndes County. The Democratic Party in Alabama continued to be the political home of the white power brokers. Its slogan was "White Supremacy for the Right." Instead of supporting the party that had unleashed its full arsenal against civil rights, black Lowndes residents formed an independent political party aimed at winning control of the local government. The Lowndes County Freedom Organization ran a slate of working-class black residents as candidates for county offices. They chose the black panther as their symbol.[30]

6.3 Man addressing a political rally of the Dallas County Independent Free Voters Organization at the National Guard Armory in Selma, April 1966. Photograph by Jim Peppler. Courtesy of Alabama Department of Archives and History, Montgomery, Alabama.

Seven months after federal registrars got to work processing voter applications in Selma's federal courthouse, Dallas County's rolls included 10,200 black and 12,100 white registered voters.[31] In mid-March, members of SHAPE gathered to form their own independent political party, just like their neighbors in Lowndes. The primary election in the spring of 1966 was the first election for newly registered black residents, and the Dallas County Independent Free Voters Organization (DCIFVO) wanted political power. "Negroes must come together and act as one strong group if we want to change the conditions we live in," a DCIFVO handout urged. "The white people will not help us win control of our government. They will not give us candidates who will work for our welfare." They elected as their chairman Clarence Williams, a SHAPE member and shop steward at Curtis, King, and McKensey Products Company, Selma's first unionized plant with a black voting majority. Just as SHAPE knew that poor people were best equipped to come up with solutions to their own problems, DCIFVO believed that black people could address the needs of the black community best.[32]

The primary in 1966 pitted old guard segregationist Jim Clark against former public safety director and racial moderate Wilson Baker in the

6.4 Children holding Dallas County Independent Free Voters Organization posters with the slogan "Strength through Unity" at a gathering at George Washington Carver Park, April 1966. Photograph by Jim Peppler. Courtesy of Alabama Department of Archives and History, Montgomery, Alabama.

race for sheriff. Once again, the position of F. D. Reese and DCVL clashed with that of DCIFVO's poor and rural members. The DCVL threw its support behind Baker. As they saw it, black voter numbers had grown exponentially but still did not match the number of registered white voters. They worried about the possibility of a run-off election if a black candidate ran for sheriff. Meanwhile, if black voters came out for a white candidate, Reese reasoned, "then that man must have some 'caterance' to the desires of the Negro communities." Thinking back on the race, J. L. Chestnut observed that Reese and Doyle "were beginning a transformation from civil rights leaders to politicians, from outside protesters to inside manipulators."[33] In contrast, DCIFVO refused to pick between the lesser of two evils regarding white candidates and instead focused on organizing its own slate. On May 3, the day of the primary, DCIFVO nominated Samson Crum for sheriff, Addie Lilly for tax assessor, Agatha Harville and two others for the board of revenue, and others for tax collector, coroner, and the school board.[34] After the polls closed in the Democratic primary that night, Sheriff Clark and the Dallas County Executive Committee chose to throw out six boxes, citing alleged voter irregularities. The alleged "irregularities"—meaning all of the votes cast in majority black neighborhoods—would have given Baker the lead. The resulting legal case moved immediately into federal court. Within weeks, a judge ordered a recount of all of the boxes, which ensured Baker's nomination.[35]

Taking a cue from DCIFVO, Clark entered the November race as an independent candidate. Railing against the federal government and "black power" for taking over the Democratic primary, he vowed to maintain law and order in Dallas County.[36] But Clark had lost favor with the new generation of moderate, image-conscious leaders, like Mayor Smitherman, banker Rex Morthland, and newspaper editor Roswell Falkenberry. On election day, Baker squeaked into office with DCVL's support and Crum's withdrawal from the race.[37] The DCIFVO candidates, on the other hand, suffered enormous defeats. Clarence Williams, DCIFVO's chairman, partially blamed their loss on DCVL's endorsement of the entire Democratic ticket—a move that directly benefited Baker. But he refused to be defeated. "We're out to establish a democratic system in the county," Williams declared. "We intend to stand up politically, any way we can. We're going to keep on fighting."[38]

While SHAPE and DCIFVO members organized for their piece of the good freedom, white officials and leaders worked to maintain control and uphold the status quo. Civil rights protests had made it clear to southern business leaders that racial violence and hard-line segregation were now bad

6.5 Woman carrying a sign reading "No Committee Decides Whether Our Votes Be Counted! We Decide!!" during a protest in front of the Dallas County courthouse. Photograph by Jim Peppler. Courtesy of Alabama Department of Archives and History, Montgomery, Alabama.

for business.[39] This line of thinking motivated Mayor Smitherman and the Committee of 100, a new generation willing to make limited concessions in the name of progress and power.

New Industries in Selma

In the heat of the demonstrations in 1965, the Hammermill Paper Company announced it was building a $30 million plant outside of Selma, giving the Chamber of Commerce a substantial victory. It turned out that cattle were not the only thing that thrived in former cotton fields. Timber grew tall in the Black Belt, and the papermakers came looking for a ready supply of pulpwood. Economic considerations, not racial motivations, drove Hammermill's decision, but the company became the object of national disparagement for investing in a place that so flagrantly denied black people the right to vote. Meanwhile, the governor, George Wallace, rolled out the red carpet, offering Hammermill cheap land and water, a 50 percent reduction in property taxes, approval of its water disposal system, and even a new bridge across the Alabama River to alleviate traffic.[40]

Hammermill understood that good business and a good image went hand in hand. Company executives assured the public that they would implement a color-blind hiring policy and use their corporate citizenship to encourage the protection of voting rights.[41] That did not, however, stop the Selma Chamber of Commerce from voting against endorsing a mid-April statement by the Alabama Chamber of Commerce expressing mild support for integration. When the statement appeared in the *New York Times*, their absence was conspicuous. Executives from Hammermill made heated phone calls to Mayor Smitherman and other business leaders. The city council passed a resolution calling for the chamber to reverse its position. Factions within the chamber squared off in a two-hour meeting, one side arguing it should not concede and the other arguing that millions of dollars were on the line. "A dollar bill will change a lot of people's positions," Smitherman explained years later. The faction in favor of endorsing the statement won because "it was something we had to do because of economic pressure."[42]

New industries that relocated to the Black Belt still mostly fit within the area's economic and racial order rather than challenging it. By the late 1960s, agriculture had nearly completed its transformation into an occupation for only credit- and resource-rich large landowners.[43] By 1969 the average size of Dallas County's 1,204 remaining farms was 312.8 acres. Five years earlier, it had been 215.1 acres. Tenant farmers still operated

32 percent of farms, but the remaining 325 black tenants worked only 3 percent of all farmland.[44] Displaced black farmers either left the area or turned to the low-wage, nonunion jobs recruited by local economic development schemes. Textile manufacturing became one of Dallas County's major industries. In 1966 Dan River Mills opened a plant twelve miles east of Selma in neighboring Lowndes County, and then Laura Industries and U and W Manufacturing opened in Selma shortly thereafter, producing military clothing for government contracts.[45] By 1972 five apparel and textile companies employed 1,100 people, one-quarter of all manufacturing employees in Dallas County.[46] Black women, the lowest-paid segment of Selma's workforce, did the majority of textile work.

In August 1967 Laura Industries' employees walked out on strike, demanding that the company recognize the International Ladies' Garment Workers Union.[47] Even though 80 percent of employees had walked out, the president of Laura Industries called the strike illegitimate.[48] Strikers like Robert Nunn and Leona Bowden accused the company of refusing to pay injury compensation, firing people by their first name over the loudspeaker, and setting quotas so high that workers could never meet them.[49] "A civil rights law had been passed but that don't mean we have gotten our civil rights," one union organizer explained. Workers went on strike to be "treated like human beings."[50]

As the strike continued into September, black middle-class leaders lent their support. Rev. Reese urged a six hundred–strong rally at Green Street Baptist Church to march from Brown Chapel to Laura Industries.[51] Rain turned the planned Monday morning march into a protest caravan to the Bell Road Industrial Park, where picketers demonstrated outside the company.[52] Those who had supported DCIFVO in past elections were skeptical of the DCVL leaders' involvement. While Rev. Reese, Rev. P. H. Lewis, businessman Edwin Moss, and Rev. C. C. Brown tried to negotiate with downtown politicians, strike leader Robert Nunn threatened, "If Wallace doesn't give us what we want[,] we are going to burn Selma down."[53] The strikers remembered how other workers had permanently lost their jobs when trying to bring unions to Selma, and working-class African Americans had neither the financial cushion nor the willingness to let white public officials dictate the pace of change. Fed up with never-ending barriers, Laura Industries' workers were ready to use more drastic measures.

The company, however, had the resources and political support to outlast the strike. With time, strikebreakers, followed by employees who abandoned the strike, brought Laura Industries' production back up to quota.[54]

The strike failed to win any concessions. Sometime during the next two years, however, company employees did succeed in voting in the union. But in June 1969 Laura Industries closed entirely. The *Selma Times-Journal* reported that the shutdown was due to "unprofitability" and hinted that the union was to blame. After the closing, former Laura executive David Wallace along with James Utsey, owner of U and W Manufacturing Company, formed a new corporation, U and W Industries. They then purchased all of Laura Industries' physical assets and moved U and W Manufacturing Company to the old Laura Industries site. The key difference: "U and W does not have a union contract," the *Selma Times-Journal* reported.[55]

The campaign for voting rights in Selma had not brought down employment barriers. "The number of jobs that have opened here to black people are minute," SCLC's Shirley Mesher noted. Most black women kept working in households for $12 to $15 per week, and some nonunionized laborers made only thirty-six cents an hour, while farmworkers earned a dollar a day.[56] In 1974 the federal government extended minimum-wage standards to domestic workers. The white women who spoke to the *Selma Times-Journal* despaired that their own take-home salaries each week would now be reduced to barely $20.00 after they paid their maids $1.90 per hour.[57] Mesher observed that white residents might have disagreed about the proper course of action regarding civil rights, but "they're united in saying that you don't have a right to that dollar. You do not have a right to disrupt their economy."[58] This tripartite commitment to attacking unions, maintaining low wages, and controlling antipoverty funds effectively kept Dallas County's racialized and unequal economic system in place.

Antipoverty Efforts

Bringing home wages far below the poverty line, black families turned to government welfare to make ends meet.[59] But receiving assistance through programs such as Aid to Families with Dependent Children came with a litany of restrictions and regulations. In the Alabama Black Belt, white people administered welfare, and black people received it. White female welfare workers had the authority to monitor the smallest details of poor black women's lives, from their relationships and parenting to their finances. In 1966 the Selma welfare office cut off Sylvester Smith—a café waitress who made sixteen dollars a week—from Aid to Families with Dependent Children for allegedly sleeping with a man who wasn't the father of any of her four children. The man-in-the-house rule mandated that if a woman on welfare had sex with a man, then he was obligated to take on the financial responsibility for her children, regardless of his biological or legal relation to them. Smith refused to accept the local welfare office's decision. That social worker "didn't have no right to cut my kids off. Sitting down there in that air-conditioned place and saying my kids can't get aid," she exclaimed. "She never came around to my house and found anybody there."[60] Smith filed suit in federal court, and in June 1968 the Supreme Court ruled in her favor. Children could not be denied federal assistance "on the transparent fiction that they have a substitute father," the decision stated.[61]

But Smith's victory was only one against the larger problem of poverty. In many areas of the South, the federally supported Commodity Food Program distributed surplus food to poor people. The Dallas County Board of Revenue agreed to participate in the program in June 1965, only after Washington officials threatened that there was a "strong possibility" that administration of the program would be turned over to civil rights groups.[62] Then, in 1967, food stamps replaced commodity food. The new program let poor people pay ten dollars and receive twenty dollars' worth of food stamps, giving them more money to choose their own groceries. But food stamps also required cash to purchase them, and securing cash became an additional burden for those already dependent on welfare or insufficient jobs. "How in the world can you buy food stamps with something you ain't got?," Agatha Harville, an active member of SHAPE and DCIFVO, asked. "It's a deal to starve you to death." Food stamps forced black families already stretching welfare income to its limits to spend money on food that before had gone to rent, gas, and clothing.[63] Programs like Aid to Families with Dependent Children and food stamps may have kept poor people just barely afloat, but it gave them virtually no means to escape from the well-worn cycle of dependency.

After wresting control of the antipoverty board from SHAPE, Mayor Smitherman appointed Joseph Knight, an ex-marine from Hazen and a close friend, as the director of the Selma-Dallas County Economic Opportunity Board (EOB). Under Knight's direction, the EOB secured funds for programs ranging from summer work training for teens and Project Drain-O (which employed residents in public works projects) to preschool for children.[64] The Operation Mainstream program employed hundreds of low-income men in city service positions and supported four hours of classroom work per week.[65] Three neighborhood centers in the city and four in the rural areas gave poor residents access to nutrition programs, medical services, community programs, and childcare.[66] Knight called the "huge, thick, blue book" of federal programs "my bible. I studied that thing, and if there was money out there, I went for it."[67] Within five years, OEO programs had brought in nearly $6.5 million in federal funding to Dallas County.[68]

While white leaders praised the EOB's success, black people in Dallas County remained skeptical. The War on Poverty might have attempted to break down the economic structures that trapped poor people at the bottom, but, in practice, white local and state officials thwarted anything that would disrupt the status quo.[69] For example, black residents called Operation Mainstream "the Nigger in the Ditch Program." "It was just as segregated as ever," Shirley Mesher recalled. "The white fellows drive the truck and the black fellows load the garbage just like on the city garbage truck."[70] Likewise, the job training at the neighborhood centers was mainly in domestic work and day labor, and the childcare was a far cry from early childhood education. Many of the residents living around the community centers agreed that the "Selma-Dallas County Economic Opportunity Board is carrying out the wishes of the 'establishment' in maintaining the *status quo*." According to Rev. L. L. Anderson, the pastor of Tabernacle Baptist Church and a member of the antipoverty board, "the only thing our CAP [Community Action Program] Board has done is provide temporary relief-type programs whose small benefit . . . ends when the project terminates."[71]

The fight over Head Start, which began when the Atlanta OEO office rejected Dallas County's proposal in the summer of 1967, highlighted some of the problems. The regional office accused the EOB of failing to recruit enough white children for the early childhood education program.[72] Knight, in a fiery hearing in Selma's federal building, lambasted the OEO officials, who had "arrived in air-conditioned automobiles, will leave in air-conditioned airplanes, and will take their air-conditioned theories back to the air-conditioned Washington offices, leaving local citizens to try to handle the problems they leave behind." But SHAPE and DCIFVO's Clarence Williams agreed that not enough effort had been made to involve poor white people.[73] A year later, Dallas County still had no official Head Start program, even though both the EOB and SHAPE had submitted applications to administer the $250,000 program. In the meantime, SHAPE had started its own independent day care center, run exclusively based on donations, at St. Paul's AME Church in Selmont.[74] It took four more years until an official Head Start program began operating in Dallas County.[75]

Some War on Poverty funds did make it into the hands of poor people in the Alabama Black Belt, however. Through Title III programs, the OEO issued grants directly to poor-led grassroots organizations, effectively bypassing power-grabbing local and state officials and businesspeople, and by 1967 it had shifted its attention to rural poverty. In the Black Belt, the growth of large farms suited for mechanization, cattle, and timber had driven many black farmers off the land. "Without a massive crash program to help solve our problems, many of us will be driven to the Northern ghettos," SHAPE member Joe Johnson told a reporter. "We are fighting to stay on the land." Poor farmers knew how to grow crops, but they needed help with technical know-how and marketing, so Shirley Mesher, Johnson, and others began formulating plans for a vegetable-growing and marketing co-op.[76]

In July 1967 the OEO granted $399,967 to the Southwest Alabama Farmers Cooperative Association (SWAFCA).[77] The co-op had grown to almost a thousand members spanning ten Black Belt counties and had already sold its first crop of cucumbers. Johnson, a man with a fourth-grade education and one business suit, was its president. He lived on an eighty-acre farm he rented deep in the rural areas of Dallas County. There was no telephone, electricity, running water, or rugs on the floor of his house, and he had to walk three miles to the highway and hitchhike to town to get to co-op meetings. Helping poor farmers buy supplies, learn new farming techniques, and market their crops together was SWAFCA's mission. "When you have 1,500 acres of okra to sell instead of five acres, you can talk different," Johnson explained. The co-op embodied the same cooperation and self-sufficiency that the Negro Extension Service had been teaching since the 1930s. As Johnson saw it, "We want to build a new economy in Alabama."[78]

The co-op also worked to protect black farmers against discrimination on the part of landowners, suppliers, buyers, and government programs. In 1965 the Civil Rights Commission concluded that black farmers had been systematically denied access to "federally-financed agriculture programs whose very task was to raise their standard of living."[79] Johnson put it more clearly: "We don't have the soil conservation service experts testing our land. We don't have bankers lending us money. We don't have the Agriculture Dept. giving us help, loans, or information. But we're pulling together anyhow." The OEO's support of SWAFCA allowed the co-op to hire advisers and provide the technical services that local USDA officials regularly gave to white farmers.[80]

There was no question that SWAFCA produced results. Co-op members would bring their produce to substations in each county, where it was graded. From there, it would go to Selma, where it could be sold together for a higher price. In its first summer, SWAFCA sold over a million pounds of produce—cucumbers, peas, and okra—for more money than farmers would otherwise have received. By selling cooperatively, Albert Turner of SCLC and SWAFCA explained, co-op members could get ninety dollars per ton of cucumbers rather than the sixty dollars per ton they got before. In his estimation, SWAFCA was "the economic arm of the Civil Rights Movement."[81]

White officials and businessmen agreed. Federal money channeled directly to a black-led organization of poor people threatened everything about the Black Belt's economic and political order, and leading whites set out to kill SWAFCA. In March 1967 Mayor Smitherman and Probate Judge Reynolds assembled a who's who of the Black Belt's leading officials and businesspeople at the Dallas County courthouse to mobilize an "all-out fight" against the OEO's grant.[82] The powerful delegation—including representatives from two Alabama vegetable canning companies—flew to Washington a week later to present their case directly to the deputy director of the OEO.[83] When their efforts failed to reverse the OEO's decision, the fight against SWAFCA became local. Credit dried up for co-op members. State troopers stopped two semitrucks full of SWAFCA produce for traffic violations and kept them idling until they ran out of gas, causing the cucumbers to spoil in the July heat. Local politicians and the regional OEO besieged SWAFCA's central office with nonstop investigations.[84]

"I think that people sometimes have the idea that [the local economic structure] is sort of haphazardly thrown together," Mesher, who was working as an adviser for SWAFCA, explained. "It's not at all. It is very tightly knit, and very interwoven, and very carefully thought out."[85] When SWAFCA and the OEO challenged this structure, the white elite retaliated swiftly and with vengeance. This opposition squelched the co-op's attempts to become an economic engine for poor farmers in the Black Belt. Its members marketed vegetable crops for a few years, but limited funding, lack of experience, and continual harassment slowly killed the organization.[86] As SWAFCA's experience clearly revealed, the more War on Poverty funding challenged the racial and economic status quo of the Black Belt, the faster white officials worked to neutralize that threat.

School Desegregation

Besides antipoverty funding, the federal government was making its presence felt as it began enforcing school desegregation, a full ten years after the *Brown* decision. The Selma school district instituted a freedom-of-choice plan—although not by its own choice—at the beginning of the 1965–1966 school year. It allowed parents to enroll their children in any school they wished. Grades one through four were eligible the first year, grades five through eight the next year, and the high school the year after that. The masterminds of freedom-of-choice plans assumed that no white parent would willingly enroll their child in a black school, and, meanwhile, so few black students would enroll in white schools that segregation would effectively be preserved.[87] Just as the district had hoped, only nineteen black students appeared in formerly white elementary classrooms on the first day of school in the fall of 1965.[88]

While almost anyone would have been hard pressed to call Selma's public schools desegregated in 1965, the threat alone was enough to give birth to the John T. Morgan Academy, an all-white private school.[89] Citizens' Council leader M. Alston Keith and others had first started exploring the private school option five years earlier.[90] As public desegregation loomed, white southerners had turned to private academies to preserve segregation. Keith and his accomplices had exactly this in mind when they drafted the academy's articles of incorporation, which stated that "the corporation shall be and is hereby irrevocably committed to the custom and practice of separation of the white and negro races in its activities . . . as most conducive to the welfare of both races and the public interest."[91]

But the private school idea remained only an idea until desegregation arrived. John T. Morgan Academy—named for Dallas County's esteemed senator, a vehement supporter of the Confederacy—opened in an antebellum mansion on Tremont Street with 119 students in its first classes.[92] The next school year, when desegregation came to the public middle schools, Morgan's campus expanded to the Houston Park Church of Christ to accommodate the new seventh and eighth grades. In the spring of 1967, the school broke ground for a new campus on the western edge of Selma, and by the 1968–1969 school year, Morgan Academy had a fully accredited elementary school and a high school reaching the tenth grade. In the background of the photo of the fourth-grade class in Morgan's very first school yearbook, two classmates held up a Confederate flag.[93]

Meanwhile, Joanne Bland, whose first ride on a school bus had been to jail, was one of the first black teenagers to integrate Parrish High School under the freedom-of-choice plan. When her father told her she was going to be a part of the integration team, she cried. "To go to a place where you're not wanted by the students and teachers because they felt we were forced upon them made everybody unhappy," she remembered years later. "There were just eight of us, and sixteen hundred and ninety-two of them, dedicated to making our lives miserable."[94] She and her classmates remained a tiny minority at Parrish High as the freedom-of-choice plans failed, as intended, to desegregate southern schools.

Finally, the federal courts intervened. In 1969 thirty Alabama school systems—including Selma and Dallas County—received federal court orders to submit plans for "disestablishing" their dual school programs. If the Selma school board refused, then the government threatened to draw up its own plan for desegregation. It was an ultimatum that fostered compliance. Under the new plan, the white Parrish High would become Selma's singular high school, and the black Hudson High would turn into West Side Junior High, one of two middle schools. Elementary schools would be zoned by residence areas, and at least 25 percent of teachers in each school would be African American. Superintendent Joe A. Pickard stressed again and again that quality education could continue only if the majority of white students, as well as blacks, stayed in the public schools. "If the public schools greatly deteriorate," he warned at a Rotary Club meeting, "the economy is bound to follow in rapid order."[95] The *Selma Times-Journal* "without reservation, unhesitatingly," threw its full support behind the public schools too.[96]

But those white parents in East Selma—the poorest and most integrated section of town—saw that demographics were not on their side. The desegregation plan reassigned white East Selma children to majority-black local schools. One father went so far as to say that he would rather "sign them all up to go to the war in Vietnam" than send his children to their new, mostly black school. When these white parents formed the Concerned Parents of Dallas County, attorney Henry Pitts, son of the city attorney, and conservative Presbyterian minister Cecil Williamson took up their cause. The parents' group also condemned the school board. When vacancies arose, the sitting board was responsible for appointing new members. This self-perpetuating structure was a holdover from Reconstruction, originally instituted to prevent black citizens from gaining seats. The Concerned Parents accused the board of failing to fairly represent all areas of the city when it appointed new members, an objection that arose just one month after the school board appointed African Americans to fill two vacancies. While Pitts took on the school board, Williamson castigated the *Selma Times-Journal* for supporting desegregation, calling it "left-leaning" and out of touch. But their ranting failed to stop desegregation. When the school zoning remained unchanged, Williamson opened an extension branch of Meadowview Christian School, his private segregationist academy, and offered all white children in East Selma cut-rate tuition.[97]

In September 1970 Selma's desegregated schools opened without crisis. The halls of Morgan Academy and Meadowview Christian School might have been fuller that fall, but on the first Friday night of the school year, black and white fans gathered in proper Alabama fashion to inaugurate the new Selma High School football team. At Memorial Stadium—where the Farm Bureau and Citizens' Council had hosted segregationist speakers a decade earlier—the Selma High Saints trounced their Demopolis opponents. "If parents and students will wait before they impulsively condemn and desert, if they will contribute to easing some of the problems," the *Selma Times-Journal* implored, "Selma High will be the fine educational institution this city must provide for its children." Desegregation was at least the first step toward opening opportunities for all of Selma's children.[98]

Electing Black Representatives

The movement in 1965 had fixed voting rights and Selma together in the eyes of the nation, but it took over seven years before a black candidate won a seat in local office. The first major election since the Voting Rights Act had revolutionized southern voting rolls took place in 1968. Six black candidates ran for city council seats that year, while Rev. Anderson, the minister at Tabernacle Baptist Church, threw in his name for mayor.[99] African American voters gave black candidates their nearly unanimous support, but none of the candidates emerged victorious. Part of the problem was the city's at-large election scheme. Instead of having citizens vote only for the representative in their ward, all registered voters could cast ballots for representatives in all city wards. In Selma at-large elections meant that the city's fifty-two hundred registered black voters could never secure a majority against the eighty-two hundred registered white voters, even if everyone cast ballots along racial lines.[100] With black residents holding no political leverage on the city council, the white councilmen could safely ignore the demands of African American residents.

This changed in 1972 when a new state law forced a complete revamping of Selma's election procedures. The city council had a choice. It could either maintain its current ten-member body but replace at-large elections with representatives elected by district, or keep at-large elections but reduce its membership to five. Switching to district elections would practically ensure that four of the ten council members would be black, given Selma's racial demographics. On the other hand, at-large elections would likely keep the city council white, but half of the current councilmen would lose their jobs. Businessman Edwin Moss presented a petition straightfor-wardly summing up the sentiments of black Selmians: "We, the citizens of black Selma, would like to participate in the operation of our city." Mean-while, J. L. Chestnut threatened to sue the city under the Voting Rights Act if the council failed to vote in favor of districts.[101] In January 1972 the city council voted to retain its ten-member makeup, virtually guaranteeing that the first African American representatives since Reconstruction would be seated in the fall.[102]

On October 2, 1972, the Selma City Council swore in F. D. Reese, Ernest Doyle, Lorenzo Harrison, J. C. Kimbrough, and William Kemp as its first black council members. It was the middle-class black leaders from DCVL—not those from SHAPE or DCIFVO—that secured this first opportunity at po-litical representation.[103] Although black representatives held five of the ten seats, they did not have a voting majority because the council president—still elected at large—also had voting power. Carl Morgan, the owner of the Black Belt Tractor Company and a World War II veteran, was the council president.[104] When Morgan cast his votes along with the other five white council members, they overruled the black members six to five. Attempts by the new black council members to secure gains in employment and public services for Selma's black community repeatedly ran up against the oppos-ing white majority. When Reese recommended that one of J. L. Chestnut's new law partners be appointed city attorney, the mayor remarked that the Chestnut, Sanders, and Sanders law firm "was continually keeping the city in lawsuits," and the white councilmen proceeded to reappoint city attorney McLean Pitts on a six-to-five vote. Additionally, every time Reese proposed to employ black and white residents in city government in proportion to population, white members voted the resolution down.[105]

Yet Joe Smitherman was a shrewd, opportunistic, and intelligent mayor who knew full well that his political future lay in the hands of black vot-ers. African Americans made up a sizable portion of the voter rolls after 1965, and white politicians across the South started paying more attention to black demands when they needed those votes.[106] As Chestnut saw it, Smitherman approached Selma's new racial order with the mantra, "If you give just a little, you won't have to give a lot." Smitherman paved streets in Selma's black neighborhoods, employed more African Americans in government, and made sure that everyone knew he was doing it. What he didn't mention was that the money he used came straight from the fed-eral government and that he handpicked which black men served on what committee.

Smitherman was a master of public opinion and excelled at the dramatic. When black members were still a new feature on the city council, Smitherman would privately offer to pave streets in a black councilman's district but then encourage the member to propose the plan himself at a municipal hearing. The mayor would publicly attack the black member's proposal for a few weeks before loudly withdrawing his opposition. The dramatic routine boosted black councilmen's leadership credentials as they faced down the mayor, while Smitherman won support by appearing magnanimous in his change of heart. Despite the theatrics, the presence of black representatives on the council and Smitherman's fervent desire to win votes brought a notable improvement in public services for African Americans, as well as better treatment in city hall.[107]

The Chestnut, Sanders, and Sanders Law Firm

In the fall of 1971, Henry "Hank" Sanders, a young black lawyer, drove over the Edmund Pettus Bridge, turned right, and found himself in Selma's main black business district. He and his wife, Rose, had returned to Alabama after graduating from Harvard Law School and spending a year in West Africa, and they were looking to set up a practice. Something about the people going about their business that Saturday morning struck Sanders. "I instantly knew that this was where I was supposed to live and work," he recalled.[108] So Sanders went to see J. L. Chestnut, Selma's one and only black lawyer, and Chestnut offered to show him the ropes. Before long, the new attorney in town was badgering Chestnut to form a partnership with him and Rose, who had moved to Selma that spring. They could do more together, he argued, to develop civil rights lawsuits, work across the Black Belt, and serve the black community. Chestnut finally gave in. In June 1972 the three attorneys formed their new law firm while sitting in Hank's office in the Elks building. Serving the black community was their purpose. "If battling City Hall and the county courthouse over jobs and fair representation required litigation we'd have to finance ourselves," Chestnut explained, "we'd do it."

While black council members worked for change within city government, the Chestnut, Sanders, and Sanders law firm turned to the federal courts to win civil rights gains in Selma.[109] They became Mayor Smitherman's fiercest adversary. In their first year of operation alone, Chestnut, Sanders, and Sanders filed two lawsuits charging "widespread discrimination" in local city and county hiring practices and a class-action suit demanding that Dallas County be redistricted on a one-man, one-vote basis.[110] First, the law firm would threaten a lawsuit to encourage action, and then, if that fell on deaf ears, they would file in federal court.[111]

And litigation was only the beginning. Selma's black youth gained their most passionate advocate when Rose Sanders moved to town. She organized programs for preschoolers through teenagers, always celebrating black history and culture. "She ruffled feathers" in white and black Selma, Chestnut recalled, not hesitating "to call white people racist or black people sell-outs."[112] Meanwhile, Hank Sanders approached situations strategically and methodically, often working in the background to get things done. Chestnut joined Rose in speaking out and drawing attention, while maintaining his long-standing relationships with "the powers that be." Chestnut, Sanders, and Sanders became "part legal services, part legal defense fund, part civil rights organization (picketing, boycotting, marching), part youth-development agency, part political-organizing headquarters," Chestnut explained. It was on the front line of making civil rights promises into reality in the Alabama Black Belt.[113]

Cutbacks

During the late 1960s, the War on Poverty, public housing, and welfare programs funneled great quantities of federal funding into Dallas County. Smitherman was known to claim that "the only thing tainted about federal money is, tain't enough."[114] Much of this money went to city operations, paving Selma's streets, improving its sewer lines, paying for parks and recreation programs, and writing paychecks for the garbage collectors and other city employees. It was a far cry from the War on Poverty's vision of empowering the poor, but it kept the mayor popular and city services running.[115] The escalating Vietnam War and ballooning military spending, however, slowly ate away at the money flowing into domestic social programs. As the Democratic Party fragmented over the war and social movements, and the liberal agenda seemed to disintegrate, the Republican Richard Nixon rode a conservative backlash into the White House in 1968. Nixon wasted little time disassembling the OEO and cutting back federal spending. Meanwhile, the cost of war and President Johnson's failure to raise taxes created rising inflation and a loss of real income, signaling hard times ahead.[116] Even Mayor Smitherman's enthusiastic search for outside resources could not keep federal funding flowing, and by the 1970s the pools of money Dallas County relied on to improve public services were drying up.

The shock waves from President Nixon's cutbacks reached Selma in early 1973. As the president transferred the administration of federal programs to the states, the limited funding stretched to cover larger areas. Selma lost $450,000 when Operation Mainstream expanded from a city-based program to a new ten-county district in 1973. A delegation from Dallas County managed to salvage $150,000 as a direct grant after flying to Washington, but their pleading could not stop the federal government's broader phase-out.[117] This presented a major crisis in Selma. The local EOB brought in more than a million dollars to the economy each year, and its director called it "an industry vitally needed."[118] Local officials went so far as to hire Jean Sullivan—a Selma resident and Alabama's Republican committeewoman, well versed in Washington politics—as a lobbyist to bring federal programs to the city.[119] But pending federal cuts made Sullivan's a losing battle. Over the next few years, War on Poverty programs, which supported day care, community centers, elderly feeding programs, and low-income jobs, disappeared.[120]

In September 1974 the Better Communities Act gave Selma one final influx of federal funds. The city received a whopping $5,480,000, astoundingly more than what other areas of similar size received. The number was so high, the mayor explained, because Housing and Urban Development "did not want to cut off cities which were dependent heavily on federal funds." From 1968 through 1972, Selma had received an astronomical $17 million in federal funds. The Better Communities money, however, could only be used for public improvements, not salaries as the funding in years past could.[121] The shifting political climate and the tightening federal pocketbook that accompanied it posed a serious problem for Selma's future.

In the hands of white public officials, War on Poverty funding temporarily relieved poverty but did not touch its causes in the Black Belt. The poverty rate for African American families did drop from 84 percent to 60 percent between 1960 and 1970. But by 1970, the year that Selma city schools desegregated, only 19 percent of black residents had graduated from high school, and seventh grade was the median level of education completed. The experiences of SWAFCA had highlighted how difficult it was for agriculture to provide a living for black families and how racial discrimination was alive and well. Meanwhile, stagnant industrial growth and unemployment still defined the Black Belt, and by the mid-1970s the era of federal spending for social programs had come to an end.[122]

At the same time, Selma's status as the shopping center of the western Black Belt was slipping away. Residents in surrounding counties began bypassing Selma in new cars and heading for Montgomery or Birmingham on smoother highways to make their big purchases.[123] The Selma Mall, "a new vista of trade," opened on the north side of town in February 1972, seeking to entice shoppers back to the area.[124] But its opening drew more people away from the downtown. Tepper's Department Store and Sears, Roebuck and Company left behind vacant buildings on Broad Street to move to the mall, while department and variety stores like Meyers, Jackson's, Kress, and Leon's tried to run two locations.[125] Downtown lost even more of its draw when the acclaimed Hotel Albert, modeled after the Doge's Palace in Venice, was torn down in 1968 because of financial troubles, and the Wilby Theatre caught fire in 1972. A new city hall, library, and convention center—paid for by urban-renewal funds—filled the newly vacant block.[126] As customers stopped going downtown, longtime Jewish store owners closed up shop. Eagle's Department Store closed in 1973 after eighty-eight years in business, Rothschild's in 1974, and Barton's in 1976.[127]

The bonanza of industrial growth that had come with Hammermill, Dan River Mills, and other textile plants stagnated a decade later, leaving workers struggling. The Alabama Power Company spurred hope in 1972 when it announced plans to build a nuclear power plant in Dallas County, south of Orrville. Projections estimated that the two-unit plant would offer 2,875 jobs and a weekly payroll of $750,000 once it was operational, but faults discovered deep in the earth ended these dreams as quickly as they started. Alabama Power was left with hundreds of acres of land, and Dallas County got no new jobs. "This was only the first blow to the city in the 1970s," *Selma Times-Journal* reporter and later Chamber of Commerce president Jamie Wallace recalled.[128] Layoffs became a familiar occurrence out at the All-Lock plant and Hammermill.[129] Between 1971 and 1976, over seven hundred jobs disappeared from the county, and by July 1975 unemployment in Dallas County had reached 11.8 percent and was still rising.[130]

A Decade after the Voting Rights Movement

By the mid-1970s, black residents' patience had worn thin. Things had improved since 1965, but many of the gains came straight from the mandates and coffers of the federal government, not from local white officials. During school desegregation, black administrators and teachers, like Joe Yelder, the principal of Hudson High School, had been downgraded to assistant positions to their white counterparts. Instead of becoming Selma High's principal, as seniority would dictate, Yelder was put in charge of

6.6 From right to left, Rev. F. D. Reese, John Lewis, Coretta Scott King, and James Robinson participate in a reenactment march on Edmund Pettus Bridge in 1975. Courtesy of Society of Saint Edmund Archives, Saint Michael's College, Colchester, Vermont.

the majority-black Eastside Junior High. The same thing happened to Andrew and Nancy Sewell, who went from being the coach and librarian at Hudson High to being the assistant coach and assistant librarian, with white superiors, at Selma High. All the while, an overwhelmingly white, self-appointed school board governed the district. In 1975 J. L. Chestnut filed suit against the white-majority board, charging that its racial makeup was discriminatory and its self-perpetuating nature undemocratic.[131] A group of black parents expressed concern over "the hard times black principals, teachers, students and parents have suffered at the hands of this very white school board."[132] But the school board remained unresponsive. A few months later, it passed over Yelder again, appointing West Side Junior High's white principal as the new principal at Selma High. The board then hired another white principal outside of the district to fill the vacancy, instead of promoting Evans Rutledge, the black assistant principal.[133]

So black parents and members of Selma's Legal Defense Fund (LDF) set up picket lines outside of the superintendent's office on Washington Street.

They were fed up with discriminatory hiring, the white-majority board, and the way black students were concentrated in vocational classes. After a week of pressure, the school board and superintendent relented, agreeing to negotiations.[134] Five representatives from the LDF, including Rev. L. L. Anderson and Rev. F. D. Reese, met with school board members behind closed doors. However, the only visible concession in what they billed as a "mutual accord" was Rutledge's appointment as West Side Junior High's principal.[135]

By October, the LDF announced it would resume protests because of the school board's bad faith in implementing the earlier agreements. No black head coach had been appointed to a major sport; Rutledge did not have the same authority as the other principals; Selma High continued to elect dual queens and student officers; and no qualified and respected black person had been appointed to the school board.[136] Mayor Smitherman—after first calling black protesters "political opportunists"—pushed the school board to listen to the LDF's grievances. The LDF presented them in the packed city council chambers. "It is not enough to say you will give due consideration," attorney Sanders warned. "We cannot wait any longer." The school board made a small concession two weeks later, appointing Preston Chestnut, J. L. Chestnut's uncle and a respected businessman, as a member. Such action bought time, but it did not solve the problem.[137]

White citizens' continued unwillingness to include black citizens in the governing of the city and schools would come back to haunt them. Ten years after the voting rights movement of 1965, black residents were still waiting for the "good freedom" to arrive. Significant changes had taken place in Dallas County. Black residents had vigorously organized for economic justice, jobs, political representation, public services, and respect and had won some small gains. But, as Chestnut explained, "almost every step of progress for black people, required either a confrontation—a lawsuit, a boycott, a march, or the threat of them—or a federal regulation requiring black participation as a condition for receiving money. Very little happened voluntarily."[138] White leaders' shrewd and effective grasp on control kept the economic and political status quo in place. It was a strategy that helped cripple Dallas County and the Alabama Black Belt as the twentieth century came to a close.

Closing Craig Air Force Base

When Craig Air Force Base celebrated its twenty-fifth anniversary in 1965, the *Selma Times-Journal* called the $140,000 the city of Selma had spent for the land under Craig "the best money the Selma folk ever spent." Each month, $1 million in military and civilian payrolls from Craig "poured directly into the Selma trade area through Air Force funds." Even more military funds flowed into the city through operating costs and contracts to maintain base facilities. Alongside agriculture and manufacturing, Craig was Dallas County's other important industry.[1] Selma was also home to the servicemen who came through Craig's training program and their families. They moved into neighborhoods, joined churches, and sent their children to local schools—which received $100,000 of additional federal funding annually for their efforts.[2]

From its earliest days, Craig Air Force Base's fate hung on the ever-changing winds of national defense priorities. Three times before—in 1945, 1962, and 1971—a local delegation had flown to Washington, D.C., to successfully lobby for Craig amid rumors of a closing. Back home, they vigilantly monitored what Mayor Chris Heinz had called the "perfect relationship" between the base and the area's citizens.[3] When industrial air pollution forced Craig to ground training flights in the early 1970s, the *Selma Times-Journal* urged action, claiming that "the future of the Air Force facility that has contributed so markedly to our area is imperiled."[4] But not all threats could be dealt with locally. In the mid-1970s, serious military cutbacks at the end of the Vietnam War and skyrocketing energy costs resulting from the Arab oil embargo again pushed the Department of Defense to consider closing bases to reduce costs.[5]

In the winter of 1976, local officials flew to Washington one more time after another round of rumors surfaced that Craig might be shut down.[6] It was a rare purpose that black and white Selmians agreed on. Father James P. Robinson of the LDF, also a former Don Bosco Boys Club member, petitioned the Congressional Black Caucus to intervene on Craig's behalf. Robinson called the air force base a "positive influence for good in our quest for continued equality and dignity." Shutting it down would be a "tragic loss for the total citizenry in this Civil Rights bastion of the nation."[7] The Selma delegation flew home thinking that they had saved the base for another year. But on March 10, 1976, the air force announced that it was officially considering shutting down Craig Air Force Base, along with Webb Air Force Base in Howard, Texas.[8]

Closing a base involved weighing the priorities of the Department of Defense against the local economic impact.[9] The air force had six months to draft an environmental impact statement (EIS) examining the proposed shutdown's effects on the local community. Then area citizens had a chance to respond at a public hearing before the air force issued the final EIS a few months later.[10] This drawn-out process gave local communities time to mount their challenge to the proposed closure, and the day after the announcement, Mayor Joe Smitherman began rallying his troops. He approached Rex Morthland, the president of the People's Bank and Trust Company, to chair the Selma and Dallas County Craig Air Force Base Study Committee. Besides being a respected economist, Morthland knew how to negotiate in Washington and was well placed to coordinate local efforts. He appointed Edwin Moss, the moderate and respected black businessman, to one of the five committee seats, a nod to how the seriousness of the task transcended Selma's usual racial divides.[11] Their cause was a difficult one. Craig's facilities registered near the bottom in comparison with the air force's seven other undergraduate pilot-training bases. It had the lowest annual pilot production capacity, bad weather for flying, two runways instead of three, limited room to expand, and outdated structures left over from World War II.[12]

Given that Craig's assets did not give the study committee much to work with, they chose to focus on the potentially catastrophic impact of the closure. Dallas County's economy was one of the least healthy and most dependent on the base, as compared to other communities that hosted bases, and Morthland's committee hired a consulting firm based in Washington, D.C., to lay out how Craig's closure would bring economic ruin.[13] The final report laid waste to decades of high praise and grand claims by Dallas County boosters. It argued that bases should be closed only in places with full employment, adequate housing, and poverty levels low enough to allow the local economy to recover quickly. It then painted a staggeringly bleak picture of Dallas County's economic health, even with Craig Air Force Base. In 1969 almost 40 percent of the county's population lived in poverty. This was over ten points higher than in any other county with an undergraduate pilot-training base. The per capita personal income in 1974 was $3,709, compared to $4,824 for Alabama—itself the lowest state in the nation—and $5,486 for the nation. Craig's personnel made some of the highest salaries in the county—$11,679 in comparison to the $6,293 received by county employees. Undercutting years of economic-development hype, the report concluded that "efforts to increase manufacturing employment by bringing in new industries have not yet met with great success; incomes are low; and housing conditions for many families are inadequate."[14] It claimed that over ten thousand jobs in agriculture had disappeared since 1949.

All of these conditions impacted black families the most. African American families earned only 36 percent of the median income of white families, for a total of $8,494 per year. A quarter of Dallas County's housing qualified as substandard in 1970, but over 60 percent of the units that black families lived in lacked proper plumbing facilities. The report predicted that black families would be hardest hit by Craig's closure since low-income blacks were the most vulnerable to job loss. "By nearly any measure used, income levels are lowest in Dallas County and the incidence of poverty is highest," the report concluded. "The County economy clearly is the least prosperous of those with UPT [undergraduate pilot-training] bases."[15]

In the lead-up to the November hearings, Morthland urged citizens, "Now is the time for all of you to get into the act."[16] Selma's leaders hung their hopes on the public forum, believing that their concerns would be relayed to the secretary of defense. The air force had released its draft EIS in September, but it seriously understated the economic impact of Craig's closure. "It's an important day for Selma," the *Selma Times-Journal* wrote on the eve of the hearing, "and everyone must be together and of one mind. Save Craig."[17]

Even though saving Craig garnered biracial support, white officials' consistent unwillingness to accommodate black demands came back to haunt them in the days before the hearing. Six months earlier, black teenagers with the Black Belt Arts and Cultural Center, in partnership with the councilman F. D. Reese, had petitioned to rename Sylvan Street as Dr. Martin Luther King Street.[18] Reese submitted a hefty petition of support to the city council, but the white majority rejected the proposed change.[19] Then they rejected it again in July and again in October.[20] With the Craig Air Force Base hearings upon the city that fall, Reese and a group of black citizens threatened to demonstrate. The pressure helped two white councilmen have a change of heart, as they explained that "any negative reaction during public hearings could be detrimental to Craig Air Force Base's future." With some additional bargaining, Sylvan Street became Martin Luther King Street. "If you want something you have to fight for it," Reese explained, summing up what Selma's black community learned from the incident. "Apply pressure."[21]

The three low-ranking air force officers who showed up at the November hearings—not ones with a direct line to authority—were not what city officials had been expecting.[22] Over six hundred people crowded into Selma's Convention Center during the two-day hearing. Individual testimonies stressed again and again how closing the base would irreversibly impair the local quality of life and the viability of the local economy, as well as national economic goals. Father Robinson pleaded for "the marginal people," the domestic workers, cooks, and poor people who would be hardest hit.[23] The fifty-seven people who testified included Alabama governor George Wallace, many of Alabama's congressmen, local government leaders, businesspeople and private citizens. Reports commissioned by the Craig study committee confirmed these predictions of economic catastrophe, but the hearings ended before the reports were ready. It was not clear that they would have made a difference in any case.[24]

Afterward, Morthland and a five-person delegation flew to Washington to meet with air force officials. They brought their reports with them, hoping to make one last case for the devastating effects of closure.[25] However, when the final EIS report came out in late February, it did not include any of the testimony from the public hearings or the findings of the two studies. All local efforts had amounted to nothing.[26] Craig ranked as one of the lowest of the seven undergraduate pilot-training bases in operational capacity, and the air force expressed scant concern for how the surrounding community would be impacted. In a last-ditch attempt, city and county political leaders returned to the capital one more time to meet with Alabama's congressional delegation, and Governor George Wallace appealed Craig's case all the way up to newly elected president Jimmy Carter.[27] But the signs looked bad when, on March 16, the secretary of the air force, Thomas Reed, flew into Craig Air Force Base unannounced and spent an ominous hour touring the base's facilities and then flew out again.[28]

The announcement came on March 30, 1977, that Craig Air Force Base would be closed.[29] Over the coming months, civil servants, military personnel, and air force equipment made their final exit through Craig's gates, one by one and bit by bit. It was a long, gradual process. In mid-August, the last class of undergraduate pilots received their wings, and their departure left the runways and airspace silent.[30] Within a year, Craig's 2,800 military and civilian employees had dwindled to a 106-member caretaker force.[31] With them went the base's $34.5 million payroll and $3.3 million in local contracts.[32] For Selma and Dallas County, already besieged by unemployment and poverty, Craig's closing marked the beginning of another, longer round of hard times at the dawn of the 1980s.

CHAPTER

7

≡

"Last One Out of Selma,
Turn Off the Lights"

1977–1988

Without the regular injection of air force dollars, Dallas County's economy was left tottering between agriculture and small-scale manufacturing. June Cohn, who was running a travel agency with her husband, Seymour, after closing Eagle's Department Store and Boston Bargain, watched their business dry up. Five years after Craig Air Force Base closed, 77 of Dallas County's 493 retail businesses had shut their doors.[1] The hard times inaugurated by Craig's closing only got worse as the 1980s wore on. When business leaders set out to fill the void left by Craig Air Force Base, they found that Dallas County's bargaining chips did not have much value in the new Sunbelt South. Promises of tax incentives, low labor costs, and anti-unionism did not have the same draw to the technology-driven, innovative corporations flocking to southern cities. Poor education, poverty, isolation, and racially divisive politics all stopped the Alabama Black Belt from joining in the Sunbelt's prosperity. At the same time, local industries packed up in search of cheaper labor in Mexico or China. As garment factories, furniture companies, and other industries moved away, the long-standing joke, "Last one out of Selma, turn off the lights," seemed increasingly true.[2]

Ronald Reagan's arrival in the White House only made Dallas County's existing problems worse, especially for the almost 50 percent of black residents living below the poverty line.[3] Riding a conservative backlash into office, the Reagan administration pushed forward unprecedented cuts in social spending programs and used unemployment to rein in inflation, all the while cutting taxes. In the Alabama Black Belt, double-digit unemployment arrived with the new decade and stayed until its end. Austerity and stringency in Washington shattered the lives of Dallas County's many low-income residents as disappearing welfare and public services left the poorest with nowhere to turn.

The local political discord only got worse with the industrial and federal drought of the 1980s. Mayor Joe Smitherman and white politicians kept firm control of local power by accommodating black demands selectively and to their own benefit. Black people might have sat on boards, but they held no meaningful political power. In the midst of the economic crisis, the Chestnut, Sanders, and Sanders law firm mounted a head-on attack against Smitherman's iron grasp. Part civil rights organization, part law firm, they organized black youth and low-income mothers, built political support for black candidates (often one of the partners) running for office, and filed lawsuit after lawsuit in federal court challenging the legality of continued white political control. As black Dallas Countians fought to bring the political promises of the Voting Rights Act to fruition twenty years after its passage, the chasm between black and white grew deeper.

Filling Craig's Void

With the announcement of Craig's closing, Selma's civic and business leaders shifted their prodigious efforts from saving the base to future development.[4] Mayor Smitherman made sure to tell national news reporters that Selma had yet again been "sold down the river" by the federal government. But instead of contesting the air force's decision, the mayor focused on reacquiring the base's property and making plans.[5] Within two weeks, the Craig Field Airport and Industrial Authority was created to broker the transition in partnership with the federal government.[6] The city and county governing bodies elected five leading citizens to serve on the board, with Edwin Moss as the sole black representative.[7]

Meanwhile, the Chamber of Commerce revved its industrial recruitment efforts into high gear. In April a group of civic and business leaders took a research trip to Salina, Kansas, and Laredo, Texas, to see how other communities had dealt with base closures.[8] They decided to set their sights on 480 air-related industries, hoping to sell the base's flight capacities. In August 1977 the chamber brought a hundred interested company representatives to Selma, where they toured the area's three industrial sites— Craig Field, Selfield, and the Bell Road Industrial Park—on chartered Greyhound buses.[9] "We can look for the cream of the crop, good, clean industries that hire more people, that pay high wages and that are going to stay with us," Carl Morgan, the chairman of the Craig Industrial Authority, explained. He hoped that this would put Dallas County on the path to prosperity some southern cities were experiencing.[10] "No longer should we boast that we have 'cheap labor,'" the *Selma Times-Journal* implored. "Our future depends on our people—that's what industry is really after: quality people."[11]

But bold pronouncements in the face of economic disaster did not reverse Dallas County's record of antiunionism and low-paying, low-skill industries. While the air force was debating Craig's fate, 280 members of the United Steelworkers union at Bush Hog, a farm implement company in Selma, went on strike. They demanded a forty-cent per hour raise plus increases in retirement and insurance plans.[12] Under Alabama's right-to-work laws, not all employees at a plant were required to join the union local, and soon the standoff included the strikers, the company, and those nonunion members who continued working. One Tuesday morning, union workers overturned the car of an employee trying to enter the plant, leading to the arrest of six strikers. A spokesman for Bush Hog complained that roofing nails had been spread in the streets leading to the company's entrances. Meanwhile, the *Selma Times-Journal* reported shots being fired into the homes of workers both for and against the strike.[13] While company and union officials attempted to reach a settlement through a federal mediator, the strikers extended their picket lines to Selma's police headquarters. They accused the city police of unfair treatment, especially when police cars provided escorts for Bush Hog trucks leaving the plant.[14]

Stalled negotiations started up again after an explosion at the plant in March tore a two-by-five-foot hole in the wall of a main assembly building.[15] The blast happened days before the announcement of Craig's closure. The *Selma Times-Journal* urged a quick settlement before the strike and its associated violence tainted Selma's reputation for "good employer-employee relationships."[16] This reputation owed more to local companies' penchant for strikebreaking than to their willingness to negotiate, a pattern that Bush Hog confirmed. When the company refused to reinstate striking employees over strikebreakers, union workers continued striking.[17] By June, Bush Hog's production with the newly hired nonunion workers was running near normal, and in early July Local 7827 called off its strike, accepting the company's lower January settlement. When the union met the next day, one leader urged strikers to remember the city officials who refused to help them when the next election came around.[18] But long memories did not bring concessions, better wages, or jobs. Carl Jones, a twenty-one-year company veteran and former union president, insisted that Selma was "scab town, USA," vehemently antiunion despite having some of the lowest wages in the Southeast.[19]

Despite talk of good jobs in the wake of Craig's closing, the Bush Hog strike made clear how low wages and antiunionism continued to reign. Fifteen percent of Dallas County's 16,040 employed workers belonged to a union in 1977. As Jack Wright, a Hammermill employee and vice president of the United Paperworkers International Union local, saw it, local people were against unions because of fear and ignorance about how much good a union did. While five Hammermill employees doing the same work were paid five different wages before unionization, now "we're just making for good working conditions," Wright explained. "We sell an honest day's work for an honest day's pay." The difference between union and nonunion wages was "striking." Unionized workers averaged from $5.34 to $10.30 per hour, while salespersons, grocery checkers, and janitors made only $2.75 and welders and machinists $3.00 to $5.00 per hour.[20] Keeping unions out of Selma kept wages low and workers divided.

But the industrial recruitment strategy that had done so well at maintaining the racial and economic status quo of the rural South was fast becoming a liability. By the late 1970s and 1980s, the nation's economy had shifted from low-wage, low-skill jobs toward jobs requiring high-skilled, well-educated, technologically savvy workers. Much of this growth took place in the new Sunbelt South—a band of booming metropolitan areas spread across the South and West replete with defense funds and high-tech industries.[21] The Sunbelt's combination of good jobs and good education brought prosperity to cities like Raleigh, Atlanta, Huntsville, and Dallas. But that vibrant growth did not reach into the Black Belt with its overwhelmingly black population. Of the 400,000 new high-tech jobs created in the South between 1977 and 1981, 87 percent were located in metropolitan regions while only 0.4 percent were in the Black Belt.[22] The Southern Growth Policies Board called the uneven growth a "consequence of schools that have not always served all people equally, as well as economic systems built on low-wage, low-skilled employment." Highlighting the growing gap between the Sunbelt and Black Belt South, the board titled its report in 1986 *Halfway Home and a Long Way to Go.*[23]

In September 1977 chamber officials and local politicians—all white—gathered in Gulf Shores, Alabama, to plan for the area's economic development after Craig. The air force base's closure forced them to confront the new service-oriented, high-tech economy head-on. Chamber president Jim Bradley indicated that disagreements existed over the type of industries to recruit, "whether you want to bring in big or small industries, with high or low wages, with or without labor unions." He banned the media from the retreat, explaining that it would "hinder the ability of members to talk freely."[24] Decisions in Selma had long been made in meetings like the exclusive—and exclusively white—meeting at Gulf Shores, where neither black citizens nor their concerns were welcome.

But even consensus among white civic leaders did not solve the area's deeper problems. In November a seventeen-member delegation flew to California in an attempt to woo Lockheed Aircraft Service Company.[25] But despite the nearly $2 million in bonuses that Selma's leaders offered, Lockheed chose the deactivated Webb Air Force Base over Craig.[26] Its director of public relations attributed the decision to the availability of skilled workers. Lockheed had suggested in its meeting with the Selma delegation that Webb's 85 percent white, 15 percent black population was more favorable to finding high-skilled workers than Selma's fifty-fifty population. Mayor Smitherman and the probate judge Johnny Jones charged the aircraft company with discriminating against black Selmians, a position they had no hesitation taking when it served their personal interests.[27] Lockheed's decision made it clear that Dallas County's abundant but low-skilled workforce no longer offered the attraction it once had.

Industries did slowly move into the vacant Craig Field over the next decade, but none matched the funds and people of the air force. Lifetime Industries, a roofing-tile manufacturing company, became the first industrial tenant in January 1978; Jet Exteriors, Incorporated, came that November, and Beech Aircraft Corporation in December, but the development officials struggled in their recruitment efforts.[28] The roots of Dallas County's difficulties looked much like those of the rest of rural America. Over in Montgomery, nearly sixty miles away, Interstate 85 dead-ended into Interstate 65 instead of continuing westward through the Black Belt. Interstate access was almost a must if a county hoped to grab its own sliver of Sunbelt prosperity. Meanwhile, as rural residents moved away in search of jobs, resources followed. Selling Dallas County was a tall order when prospective industries could see the crumbling houses, the scarce day care centers, and the visible effects of low wages.[29]

Reaganomics

Hard times hit during the late 1970s, not just in the Alabama Black Belt, but across the country. Facing hyperinflation rooted in government deficits from the Vietnam War, Americans found that their dollar now bought a much smaller cart of groceries. They also started feeling luckier if they even had a job as the automation of industrial jobs and the steady outflow of manufacturing companies moving overseas left more and more people out of work. The Arab oil embargo, the Iranian hostage crisis, and the Soviet Union's invasion of Afghanistan made the unquestioned economic and military might of the United States seem far less certain. Meanwhile, President Richard Nixon's resignation after the Watergate scandal shattered citizens' faith in politicians and the federal government.[30] In Dallas County cutbacks in federal spending and local layoffs only added to the catastrophic effects of Craig's closing. "The effects of the long-awaited recession are starting to appear in Selma," the *Selma Times-Journal* wrote in the spring of 1980.[31] That summer, Dallas County's jobless rate hit double digits, at 10.2 percent, and did not come down again for another decade.[32]

Out of what President Jimmy Carter called the country's "crisis in confidence" emerged Ronald Reagan, the conservative former governor of California, with a new vision for America. Reagan threw in his name for the presidency in Mississippi at the Neshoba County Fair in August 1980. Twenty-six years earlier, three civil rights workers had been murdered outside of Philadelphia, the Neshoba County seat, their bodies buried in an earthen dam. Gesturing to the legacy of the Citizens' Council and white southerners' resentment of black civil rights gains, Reagan vowed to support states' rights, reduce the size of the federal government, and decrease regulation and taxes.[33] By tapping into American discontent with government and the mounting white Christian conservative backlash, Reagan captured the presidency in November 1980. In his inaugural address, Reagan laid out what would be his governing principle: "In this present crisis, government is not the solution to our problem. Government is the problem." A commitment to cutting taxes, reducing federal spending, and eliminating government regulations guided his administration's policies over the next eight years.[34]

At the time of Reagan's election, nearly half of the people living in Dallas County were already scraping by on incomes below 150 percent of the poverty level; these included an astounding 70.7 percent of black residents. Many of these families depended on federal government programs to keep their little ones fed, and Reagan's election to the White House spelled disaster for them.[35] "Up until now, we had the luxury of everybody doing good and federal funds flowing," Mayor Smitherman claimed, a bit optimistically, before summing up the new reality: "Now the federal funds ain't flowing."[36] During the spring of 1981, the local offices of the Department of Pensions and Securities and the Unemployment Compensation Agency, as well as the school superintendents, fretted about how cuts to food stamps, child nutrition programs, welfare, extended unemployment benefits, and Medicaid would play out in Dallas County.[37] Poor people were already struggling before the proposed cuts became law. Mrs. Jewel Kynard wrote to the *Selma Times-Journal* explaining the dire situation her family faced. The previous winter, her husband had been in the hospital, and the family could not afford heat, water, or electricity. "Unemployed, I had to borrow $238 to get them back on," she wrote. "Now he has been back in the hospital, still unable to work and we're behind again. He filed with Social Security but to no avail, so he's applying again."[38]

The Reagan administration assured Americans that it would maintain social programs for the "truly needy," but the list of programs on the chopping block made it doubtful that anyone actually qualified. Everything from food and nutrition, housing assistance, and school lunches to student aid and extended unemployment assistance fell into the category of unessential.[39] When the fiscal year began in October 1981, new cuts directly affected a thousand Dallas County families, with more damage projected as Congress finalized the budget. The working poor bore the harshest load when stricter standards for programs like Aid to Families with Dependent Children meant an end to their eligibility.[40]

As federal social programs withered, poor citizens began turning to church and charity organizations. "We are bracing for the blow," admitted a local Salvation Army officer one year into Reagan's presidency. "This year there are even more people below the poverty level. More people were making it before and can't this year." Churches, meanwhile, struggled to provide for the many falling through the gaping holes in government aid. In the past, tax incentives had encouraged wealthy congregants to donate. But when the Reagan administration lowered the tax bracket for the richest, those financial incentives dried up. "People now have to give for benevolent reasons, rather than financial ones," Rev. Phillip Wise of the Selma Ministerial Association explained. When even the local Department of Pensions and Securities—the government agency in charge of welfare—began routing aid seekers to individuals and businesses for help, it was obvious just how bad times had become in Dallas County.[41]

Cuts to federal programs fell hardest on the people living in uninsulated clapboard houses, who were just scraping by and had no place to turn. Making matters worse, double-digit inflation and interest rates sent the costs of daily living soaring. Even Dallas County's middle class couldn't afford the early 1980s. The best home loan to be found had a 17.5 percent interest rate, while the majority of banks offered loans at 18–20 percent.[42] The chairman of the Federal Reserve Board, Paul Volcker, kept interest rates high in an attempt to rein in inflation. His policy stabilized inflation but dragged the country into an economic recession.[43] Unemployment exploded, and poor and working-class Americans bore the brunt of the downturn. While the wealthiest Americans tightened their belts by forgoing a family vacation or putting off the purchase of a new car, those at the bottom lost their jobs and burned through all of the resources they had.[44]

Layoffs and closings ruled the day in Dallas County during the spring of 1982. The Gibson Discount Center closed, while General Battery cut back about half of its workforce.[45] As high interest rates hit farmers, demand for farm machinery plummeted. Bush Hog laid off a hundred employees in March and then shut down its entire production facilities in July.[46] A survey conducted by the Chamber of Commerce found that 376 workers had been cut by seventy-six area manufacturers in the past year.[47] Job vacancies attracted scores of people. A position with the police department received 140 applicants, and nine months later four hundred people applied for forty temporary jobs at the Piggly Wiggly grocery store.[48] By November 1982 Dallas County's unemployment rate hovered at a record high of 19.5 percent.[49]

A combination of bad crop years, high interest rates, and tight lending policies also wreaked havoc on local agriculture, causing numerous Dallas County farmers to lose their farms. John Henderson was one of them. He had bought his first acre of land in 1937 at the age of twenty but then lost his 440-acre farm at Five Points, south of Orrville, in a mortgage foreclosure sale in July 1983. Cotton had sustained him and his family up until 1976; in 1977 he borrowed $400,000 to plant his fortieth crop but failed to make a profit owing to drought and low prices. The same pattern repeated itself for the next five years, putting him out of business. Inflation pushed interest rates and product prices up at the same time as crop prices either fell or failed to match inflation. "If a farmer has farmed the last six years, he owes money," Henderson explained.[50] In 1983 the season opened with fifteen fewer farms than the year before, with most selling out in an effort to pay off farm debts. Carl Barker, the president of the Dallas County Bank, explained that most farmers had more debt than their farmland was worth.[51] As farmers sold off their machinery in auctions, the local farm dealerships suffered. By 1984 the number of farm implement dealers had dropped from seven to three.[52]

Reaganomics—the Reagan administration's program of tax cuts, reductions in government spending (except for defense), and deregulation—decimated all segments of Dallas County's economy. Federal cuts to social programs disproportionately hurt Selma's low-income black residents who were already living below the poverty line, while unemployment pulled the rug out from under the white and black working class. Meanwhile, the shifting tax burden meant that the poorest Americans paid significantly larger shares of their income in taxes at the same time as the wealthiest citizens paid less.[53] Most of the country had weathered the worst of the recession by 1983. The national unemployment rate dropped steadily from its high of 10 percent in 1983 to 5.4 percent five years later. But almost none of that recovery made it to the rural Alabama Black Belt, where the recession barreled on through the rest of the decade.[54]

While federal spending cuts pummeled Dallas County, an increasingly globalized economy chipped away at the Black Belt's hard-won industrial jobs. Sunbelt cities like Raleigh, Charlotte, Atlanta, and Dallas settled into their good fortune as technology-driven jobs and federal investment attracted educated, middle-class citizens. But that boom skipped over rural regions that had little to offer in terms of education, skills, or infrastructure.[55] The timber, apparel, and paper companies that did come to the Black Belt were as different from the Sunbelt's innovative corporations as eggs, milk, and butter were from an icing-coated, candle-topped birthday cake.[56] Raw materials did not equal the value of the finished product. Already on the losing end of economic development, the rise in foreign competition sealed the rural South's fate. By the early 1980s, companies began bypassing the rural South to locate their plants in developing countries with fewer regulations and thousands of people willing to work for almost nothing. The gospel of low-wage, antiunion labor that southern business leaders had touted since before World War II proved mighty unreliable in the new economy.[57]

In August 1985 Dan River Mills, a cotton sheeting plant located just east of the Dallas County line, announced it was closing, thanks to imports and the depressed textile economy. The decision added Dan River Mills' 250 employees to the large number of area residents already out of work. The Auburn Technical Assistance Center sent a team to Dallas County to trace what happened to the workers in the months following the plant shutdown. After nine months, only 46 percent of the 219 people interviewed had found work, on average commuting sixty-six miles—the distance to Montgomery—to their new jobs. Those who managed to find jobs were mainly white men, while white women and African Americans came back with little. Despite the dismal prospects of finding work in Dallas County, the majority of ex–mill workers—with family ties and homes in the area—remained. They made ends meet by buying less food or clothing, delaying medical care, and falling behind on installment payments.[58]

Working at Dan River Mills had never been employees' dream job. One black Baptist minister had started as a sweeper and moved up to become a tie-in operator. He called the plant "the rottenest place in the world." The company allegedly failed to regulate the heat and humidity, ignored reports about unsafe machine conditions, and refused to take injured workers to the doctor. Numerous employees referred to the supervisors as "overseers," and the minister insisted, "They drove us like ANIMALS!"[59] But with unemployment hovering at 17.6 percent, Dan River Mills' pay of $6.06 per hour—still twenty cents lower than the average textile worker's wage in the Southeast—let families get by.[60] Unemployment benefits, known locally as *pennies*, helped for a limited time, but the majority of ex-workers did not find a job before they ran out. "There's just no jobs in Selma," one white woman in her sixties told the Auburn Technical Assistance Center's interviewers. "I'm still looking, but there aren't any jobs."[61] A forty-year-old black worker found the same thing: "My pennies are running out. I would like to work and it's just not here in Selma."[62]

Shortly after Dan River Mills shut down, Beech Aircraft Corporation, one of the celebrated industries that had moved to Craig Field, announced it was closing.[63] Business owners shared their take on the local economic crisis with Auburn interviewers. Many believed that a small group of elites had prevented certain industries from coming to the area. "The local economy ain't worth ****. Our business is off 50%," one owner of a recreational equipment store indicated. "I don't think our city fathers want any industry in here that will pay anything."[64] Public employees also spoke of the desperate situation. A social service worker explained that people with good work records now confronted a labor market that had little demand for their skills. "It was as if the rules of the game had been changed, and in the middle of it all, the means to alleviate the disruption in mill workers' lives (retraining is one thing that comes to mind) were also being scaled back," the worker assessed, tying unemployment to federal spending cuts.[65]

In 1986 the Selma-Dallas County Economic Development Authority concluded that the area had lost jobs owing to "a shift in manufacturing to lesser developed countries where labor is cheap." The combination of "the basic restructuring of the national economy" and the lingering effects of Craig Air Force Base's closing "represent conditions that are almost beyond the control of the leadership of this area."[66] One of the white interviewers working with the Dan River Mills study also spoke of the desperateness of Selma's situation: "As much as it pains my conservative soul to say it, there can be little hope for economic recovery in the Selma area without implementing sweeping programs reminiscent of FDR's New Deal." Public works programs funded by federal, state, and local governments would need to provide employment for the displaced workers because, as he saw it, "even Alabama-owned businesses will not open factories [in rural areas] without being offered tax incentives." Without proactive measures, the interviewer suggested that the dark local quip—last one out of Selma, turn off the lights—might come true.[67]

Meanwhile, the Reagan administration offered no help as it continued reducing federal social programs, cutting taxes for the wealthy, and deregulating. The *Selma Times-Journal* laid out the bleak situation at the dawn of the new year in 1987. Illiteracy, poverty, lack of industry, and disappearing agricultural jobs doomed the Alabama Black Belt to remain an economic backwater. Reckoning with the seriousness of the situation, the editors, who had never been advocates of federal intervention, concluded, "Alabama's economic progress, perhaps even the federal government's record on human rights, will be measured in direct proportion to the support given the economically and socially disadvantaged of the Black Belt."[68]

But the federal government under Reagan had little interest in addressing Selma's misfortunes. Under the guise of new federalism, the administration systematically transferred social programs from the federal government to states and municipalities, a move that resonated with states' rights at the same time as it cut spending.[69] Meanwhile, massive increases in defense spending and lower taxes for the wealthy sent the budget deficit soaring. Instead of addressing the root causes of the deficit, the Reagan administration cut more programs benefiting average citizens. In December 1985 Congress voted to end federal revenue sharing, a program that had funneled hundreds of thousands of dollars into the operating budgets of local governments.[70] Mayor Smitherman admitted that this would cost Selma $780,000 a year. Education, transportation, and health care all bore the brunt of lost revenue.[71] To weather what amounted to a 9 percent reduction in the city's budget, the city council voted to raise gasoline and cigarette taxes and cut public employees.[72] President Reagan's cuts to domestic spending cost Alabama $1.9 billion in federal assistance between 1981 and 1986.[73] During his two terms in office, the bottom 60 percent of Americans saw their incomes decline, while those of the top 5 percent increased. The boom years experienced by some Americans seemed like a cruel lie for Alabama's Black Belt.[74]

Maintaining White Political Control

The economic straits of Dallas County in the 1980s aggravated existing political divisions until they were as raw and stinging as an open blister. As the twentieth anniversary of the Voting Rights Act approached, white majorities still controlled every governing board of the city and county, even though 52.6 percent of Selma's population was black, and 54.6 percent of Dallas County's population.[75] Having black council members and government employees did translate into better treatment for black citizens in both personal interactions and city services. But not holding a voting majority prevented black council members from having more say in the city's operation. The persistence of white political control throughout the 1970s had shown African Americans that if they wanted people they trusted in positions of authority—not black people who would accommodate the white powers that be—they needed a black majority. "We recognize the fact that politics here, it is a black and white thing," Clarence Williams, who had been a member of SHAPE, DCIFVO, and SWAFCA, explained. "If you want to elect black politicians, you are going to have to elect them with the black vote." But decades of disfranchisement and persistent poverty paired with frustration and disappointment contributed to low turnout among black voters, a major problem when racial demographics split nearly fifty-fifty black-white.[76] As black activists stared down mobilization concerns, at-large election districts, and the cunning intransigence of white politicians, their fight for political power laid bare the depths of division and desperation in Dallas County.

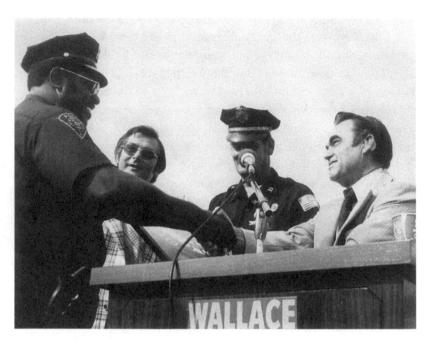

7.1 George Wallace shaking hands with an African American police officer
in Selma with Joe Smitherman standing to one side, ca. 1970s. Courtesy of
Alabama Department of Archives and History, Montgomery, Alabama.

Joe Smitherman loved his job as mayor. He loved the power and the
attention, but he also loved Selma. Although he had wrestled his way into
office as a business-minded segregationist, Smitherman keenly understood
what the Voting Rights Act meant for his political future. In a city where
African Americans made up a majority, his continued stay in his beloved
office depended on winning black votes. In many ways, Smitherman was
the hometown version of the man he admired most—Alabama's master
politician, Governor George Wallace. A dynamic, cunning, oftentimes
charming, and always politically astute man, the mayor used federal dollars to pave streets in black neighborhoods and stood on the side of school
desegregation when it became prudent. He fostered congenial relationships with black council members, like F. D. Reese, by day and stopped
in at the black Elks Club to joke and dance at night. But underneath the
mayor's outward transformation, his bottom line never changed: Smitherman would do whatever was needed to maintain his personal power and
the spotlight that went with it.

In 1979 Mayor Smitherman declared war on the Ku Klux Klan.[77] Rewind to thirteen years earlier, and he had been on a first-name basis with the head of the local chapter. When Joe Knight took over Selma's antipoverty agency, Smitherman had invited Knight to the mayor's office, introduced him to the head of the Klan, and instructed the Klan leader to leave Knight alone.[78] But times had changed. The local Klan had reappeared after a series of racially charged crimes, including allegations that a black man had attempted to rape a white woman. This time, Mayor Smitherman accused the Klan of being outside agitators. He praised Selma's good race relations and continued to publicly denounce the hooded order as they marched throughout the summer.[79] As J. L. Chestnut saw it, the local white "shakers and movers" had forged important relationships with a few token black citizens, something that helped them maintain the status quo by conceding only a little to black residents. "At the present, the arrangement is working without serious challenge," Chestnut explained, and the Klan directly threatened the "nervous, shallow 'truce' engendered and maintained by this tokenism."[80]

But black citizens had been hearing the mayor's words of goodwill for too long to put much faith in his sincerity, so they gathered at Tabernacle Baptist Church to arrange their own protection against those parading in white sheets.[81] "Blacks will protect their property and persons, and Blacks should not take up arms, and go into the streets," read the resolutions of those gathered. From there, the list went on to record deeper grievances: lack of jobs for black people or black teachers and administrators in public schools, continuing segregation within Selma High School classes, and city and county school boards that lacked meaningful African American representation.[82] Mayor Smitherman might have been willing to denounce the Klan, a position that wouldn't cost him a cent politically in the late 1970s. But political representation, jobs, and public schools directly cut into white control, and Smitherman had no intention of negotiating away his own personal power.

Nothing highlighted how far Smitherman and white council members would go to maintain control more than the ongoing fight over the city school board. In 1977, under a federal court order, the city council had assumed responsibility for appointing board members, bringing an end to its self-perpetuating nature.[83] But it was a symbolic victory at best. With a white majority on the council, black councilmen never controlled enough votes to appoint black school board members of their choosing. In 1979 black businessman Edwin Moss urged the council to fill existing vacancies with black members and offered a list of recommendations. Instead, the white majority chose to maintain the board's previous composition of seven whites and four blacks.[84] Then, in 1982, the council's white majority, against the wishes of the black council members, again voted to reappoint all three of the white board members whose terms were expiring. "This particular strategy and procedure that you all are using now is 'racist,'" the normally moderate-tempered Councilman F. D. Reese accused. "That's all it is because you are definitely concerned about the majority of the school board being white."[85] He was right. As long as a white majority controlled the city council, they made sure a white majority controlled the school board.

Selectively accommodating black demands didn't stop white politicians from exploiting racial politics when it played in their favor. When Craig Air Force Base closed, the air force left behind neighborhoods of sturdy, well-maintained military homes. In 1978 the Craig Industrial Authority, with the backing of the Chamber of Commerce, agreed to purchase the 526 units. But low-income housing was completely absent from their proposal, despite the 450-long waiting list at the Selma Housing Authority. A black group representing the interests of low-income residents had asked to participate in the planning, but their request was denied on the grounds that they did not belong to the nearly all-white Chamber of Commerce. The local Legal Services Corporation, a federally funded assistance organization, then filed a lawsuit demanding that a portion of Craig's housing be set aside for low-income residents.[86]

Lawsuits and questions of ownership brought city and federal negotiations to an acrimonious halt.[87] In January 1980, over two years later, a U.S. district court judge demanded a settlement within sixty days, and local officials saw the low-income housing issue as a means to compel the federal government to act.[88] Carl Morgan—who was serving a brief stint as mayor after Smitherman had dramatically renounced city politics and resigned for six months before deciding to run again—decided to move four poor black families into the empty houses in a takeover from the federal government.[89]

Morgan's stand failed to impress the lawyers from Legal Services as well as other black Selmians. "I believe those people are being used as pawns by the Airport Authority," Rick Ebbinghouse, the attorney heading up the efforts to secure low-income housing, told the *Selma Times-Journal*. "It's a smokescreen to avoid the issues raised by our suit."[90] By the early 1980s, Selma's white politicians had mastered the art of strategic accommodation.

By making limited concessions to civil rights demands and allowing token black representation, local officials could preserve white control, secure federal funding, and stave off accusations of discrimination.[91] The Craig housing takeover gave city officials the opportunity to exploit racial politics for their own political gain. Attorney J. L. Chestnut agreed, claiming that the only black people involved were the squatters and that white politicians had switched sides only to harass the federal government into doing what they wanted.[92]

Morgan's actions compelled the federal government to drop some of its demands for public transportation and commercial businesses in the Craig housing, a move that hurt future residents instead of helping them. Four years after Craig's closure, an agreement was finally reached that reserved 175 units for low-income residents. In practice, however, all Section 8 homes were segregated on the west side of Lackland Drive, while owner-occupied homes were to the east. When poor black residents finally began moving to Craig in the winter of 1983, they reaped few if any benefits from the years of grandstanding by white politicians.[93]

Challenging the Status Quo

Until the day that Hank and Rose Sanders moved to Selma and opened a law firm with J. L. Chestnut, Smitherman basked in his reign over local politics. Always prepared to take a stand and make a deal, the mayor slept soundly at night, knowing that practically nothing could challenge his dominion. But the Sanderses' partnership with Chestnut changed that equation. The new, black-run law firm declared outright war on racial injustice wherever they saw it. When the Chestnut, Sanders, and Sanders law firm set up shop in a small brick building on Jefferson ("Jeff") Davis Avenue, it hardly seemed like the beginning of the demise of Smitherman and white political control. The firm's power came from its advocates' overlapping spheres of organizing. As Rose Sanders built community organizations within Selma's black neighborhoods, Chestnut attacked white supremacy through legal avenues, and Hank Sanders worked to cultivate black political might, with much crossover between the partners' efforts. Smitherman wanted to maintain his own and, more generally, white control, and the Chestnut, Sanders, and Sanders law firm wanted equal representation and justice for black people. Their purposes had little in common. In the disastrous economic terrain of the 1980s, this rivalry grew into bitter enmity as white political and civic leaders fought tooth and nail to maintain control.

As the economic crisis and federal abandonment left Selma's poorest struggling, Rose Sanders threw herself into ameliorating the glaring need all around her. Soon after her arrival in the early 1970s, Sanders formed the Black Belt Arts and Cultural Center (BBACC). "All I did," she explained, "was use the arts to teach and to inspire and connect with the culture, especially with African culture and African experiences." The center's teenage members staged plays about black history and current issues like teen pregnancy, drugs, and, later, AIDS.[94] They took African dance and theater classes and sponsored the yearly African Extravaganza celebration.[95]

From BBACC grew the McRae Learning Center. When Mabel McRae retired from teaching in the Selma city schools, she turned her attention to early childhood education, and news spread that she was teaching three- to five-year-old children how to read. Sanders (whose daughter Malika was born in 1973), along with Vivian Chestnut, Lola Doss, Nancy Anderson, and Ora Gaines (Sanders's mother), decided to expand McRae's teaching methods into an early childhood education program for black children.[96] McRae Learning Center opened in June 1978, and within a decade it had grown from twenty-five to eighty children and moved to a more centralized location on Range Street. Lawyers and doctors, as well as mothers and grandparents who depended on welfare to make ends meet, sent their children to McRae. The school, as Gaines saw it, filled a void for children whose mothers were overworked and undereducated and were raising their kids on their own.[97] "At McRae, I know they will be cared for," agreed a social worker from the Department of Pensions and Securities. "They help the children tremendously by giving them socialization skills as well as baths, clothing, hot meals, and love. And for the children who come from homes where there are no parenting skills, McRae provides care and concern."[98]

From the McRae Learning Center grew Mothers of Many (MOMS), a program for low-income working mothers. It was "one of the most effective things we did," Sanders explained later.[99] The program equipped mothers with the skills and knowledge they needed to care for themselves and their families. In addition to bringing their children to group meetings, the mothers volunteered at McRae and in after-school tutoring programs for the BBACC kids. They opened a short-lived restaurant across from Selma University and grew their own vegetables on Rose and Hank Sanders's land to the east of Selma.[100] In 1983 MOMS partnered with J. L. Chestnut's uncle, the local black cosmetics entrepreneur Preston Chestnut, to manufacture their own home cleaning product. Sales of "Clean-All" financed MOMS programs while teaching economic literacy and self-sufficiency skills.[101] Three years later, the organization received a $30,000 grant to expand their work.[102]

While Rose Sanders mobilized Selma's children and women around "whatever the need was," Hank Sanders and J. L. Chestnut found themselves running for political office when they weren't filing lawsuits. Even in counties with black majorities, getting out the vote was an uphill battle. Whites still held the power and controlled the election machinery, black people had been conditioned to think that voting was white people's business, and almost everybody, as Chestnut explained, was "more intent on daily, personal survival than a better future for the group."[103] So in 1974 Chestnut decided to enter the race against longtime state senator and segregationist Farm Bureau president Walter Givhan. He wasn't looking to win but to spark black people's excitement for voting and politics. "I promise you I won't sell you out," Chestnut roared to packed backwoods churches across the Black Belt. "I can't do it alone, but together we can do a lot." Unsurprisingly, he lost. When Givhan died two years later, Chestnut ran and lost again—but not by much.[104]

Then, in 1978, Chestnut entered the race for the Alabama House of Representatives. On election night, he was fifteen hundred votes ahead of his opponent, Noopy Crosby. But by the morning, he had lost for a third time, this time because of absentee ballots. The white courthouse crowd had mastered the art of winning elections by absentee ballot in the years after the Voting Rights Act. They would bolster the white vote by visiting nursing homes, talking to those who worked outside the county, and collecting votes from college students. When Chestnut raised the issue with the Department of Justice, they suggested that the time had come for black people to take advantage of the absentee voting system themselves. By the late 1970s, all of the local black organizations had "two or three people in charge of nothing but absentee ballots."[105] This helped elect some of the first black majorities in county government in the Black Belt: in Greene County in 1969, Perry County in 1978, Lowndes County in 1980, and Wilcox and Sumter Counties in 1982. "When black candidates finally produced more votes, black candidates won," Chestnut explained.[106]

In 1982 Hank Sanders challenged Earl Goodwin, the president of Bush Hog, for his seat in the Alabama Senate. It was an efficient and deliberate campaign. Rose Sanders had BBACC teens and MOMS women out knocking on doors, and scores of sample ballots were delivered across the district. On election day, black taxis drove voters to the polls, and volunteers went out looking for people who hadn't voted yet. According to the federal courts, it took a 65 percent black district to guarantee the election of a black person owing to the legacy of discrimination. The Dallas County district was 55 percent black, but Sanders lost by only 490 votes out of 33,500. However, it happened to be the year that the law required the Alabama Legislature to reapportion its districts. After a back-and-forth that involved legal action (some of it filed by Chestnut, Sanders, and Sanders), negotiations, and counternegotiations, the Black Belt was split into one white and one black district. In 1983 Hank Sanders won the newly created majority-black district, while Goodwin won the seat in the white district, and Selmians took to joking about Selma's "separate but equal state senators."[107]

The Election of 1984

The political organizing surrounding Senator Sanders's election led up to an all-out fight for black political power in the election of 1984. While Republicans lined up for another four years of President Reagan, Jesse Jackson, a black SCLC minister, challenged Walter Mondale for the Democratic nomination. Jackson's candidacy "took on more of the character of a movement than a political campaign" in the Alabama Black Belt, recalled Chestnut.[108] For once, a black man was running for president on a civil rights platform, and people were excited. Jackson, a veteran of the voting rights movement of 1965, made Selma one of his regular and repeated campaign stops.

Caught up in the fervor of the Jackson campaign, F. D. Reese decided to challenge Smitherman's twenty-year hold and throw in his hat for mayor. As a longtime city councilman, Reese had become the most important elected protector of black interests and, as Chestnut saw it, "an insider, a part of the administration."[109] One week after Reese announced his candidacy, Jackson stumped through Selma again. In front of a crowd at Selma University, he "preached the gospel of voter registration and black voting power" and threw his support behind Reese. Like at a Sunday offering, Jackson asked every nonregistered person older than eighteen to come to the front of the hall and register with the waiting deputy registrar.[110] From the very beginning, both the municipal and national elections in 1984 promised to be racially charged and contentious.

Jackson's rallying of black voters provoked a backlash from some of Dallas County's white citizens. Less than a week after Jackson's speech, white council member Cecil Williamson kicked off Project SAVE—Selma Area Voter Enlistment—with the express purpose of registering white voters.

"We are trying to do the same thing the blacks are trying to do," he explained, "register all eligible voters." Williamson, a minister at Crescent Hill Presbyterian Church, had taken up the cause of East Selma's white parents during school desegregation back in 1970 and was a vocal supporter of white local control and conservative causes.[111] It was no accident that white southerners' enthusiasm for voting rose as more and more black names were added to the rolls.[112]

In the midst of the fierce registration drive, Mayor Smitherman called a meeting in his office with the two white members of the three-member board of registrars and two white state representatives. There, in the mayor's office, the two registrars voted to cancel the appointments of all ten deputy registrars, citing alleged violations. Marie Foster and Perry Varner—both longtime activists who were especially effective at registering black voters and getting them to the polls—were on that list. Those at the meeting conveniently forgot to inform Edwin Moss, the sole black registrar, or Hank Sanders, the black state representative, of the event. When questioned about their absence, Smitherman explained that Moss was on the campaign staff of Reese, his opponent, and that "Hank is diametrically opposed to me." Both Moss and Sanders decried Smitherman's actions as a racially motivated political move. "We were dismissed simply because we were registering too many blacks," Foster summed up straightforwardly. But she vowed that the change would not stop her. She would just go back to what she'd been doing for twenty-five years and bring people directly to the courthouse to register.[113]

Local voter registration continued at a frenzied pace in the lead-up to the July 10 municipal election. Black activists worked to mobilize black voters, while Williamson and Project SAVE went door to door in Selma's majority-white wards.[114] In only six months, the rolls gained 918 new black and 827 new white voters, growing to a total of 9,909 registered black voters and 11,963 white voters.[115] But when the numbers came in on election night, Smitherman still soundly defeated Reese by some twenty-five hundred votes despite black activists' best efforts.[116] Only a little over half of eligible black voters had gone to the polls that election day; without black votes, black candidates could not win.[117]

Early in the campaign, Hank Sanders and J. L. Chestnut had met with Reese and his campaign manager, a computer consultant named James Perkins Jr. Reese and Perkins wanted to avoid running a "racial" campaign. That meant talking about improving garbage collection and creating jobs instead of racial justice. In doing so, they thought they could win enough of the white vote to make up for low black voter turnout. But Sanders and Chestnut advised against it. "In racially polarized Selma," Chestnut explained, "what it takes to turn out black voters often turns off white voters and vice versa." Turning out black voters required dealing "with racism in a forthright manner," but Reese and Perkins disagreed. On election day, Reese got no more than 2 percent of the white vote, and black voter turnout was poor. It was a lesson that Perkins carried with him.[118]

The pushback against black voter registration efforts and political organizing extended all the way up to the federal government. During the election in 1984, President Reagan's Department of Justice brought charges of voter fraud against a number of black political activists. Partnering with local district attorneys and registrars, it charged movement stalwarts, like Albert Turner in Perry County and John Hulett in Lowndes County, of coercing elderly or illiterate voters into voting for black candidates or changing their absentee ballots. Federal investigators descended on the Black Belt during the fall elections, knocking on black residents' doors and asking pointed questions. None of the charges held up, and many Black Belt residents wondered where the government officials, so eager to investigate black voter fraud, had been twenty years earlier before the Voting Rights Act had been passed.[119]

In a year of disappointing election results and white opposition, Jackie Walker, a devoted member of MOMS, decided to run for Dallas County's tax collector. It was a campaign to ward off defeatism among black voters. With Senator Hank Sanders as her campaign manager, Walker quietly crossed the county, meeting people in their homes and at rural churches, intentionally keeping a low profile. She stressed that the time had come to put a black person in the county courthouse. Her white opponents knew nothing of her behind-the-scenes organizing, and on election day Walker surprised her opponent, Tommy Powell, when she received enough votes to force a run-off election.[120] Then in September 1984—by a margin of forty-eight votes—Walker became the first black woman elected to the Dallas County courthouse.[121] "As a female, I am particularly aware of the effects of public decisions on the total community," she wrote. She credited MOMS and BBACC with helping her understand "some of the crying needs of our community" and pushing her "to serve on a larger scale."[122] But Walker tragically did not get to see her dreams through to fruition. The following February, she died after her car hit an icy patch and ran into a tree.[123]

Local custom dictated that when a county officeholder died, their spouse was appointed in their place. But the all-white county commission ignored black citizens' petitions to appoint Nathaniel Walker or another black person. Instead, they appointed Walker's white opponent, Powell, as the tax collector.[124] Black residents had already resented the all-white county commission, but this was, as many saw it, "spitting on Jackie's grave." Dallas County had spent thousands of tax dollars—much of it paid by black residents—in legal fees to maintain at-large elections and white control. At an all-night meeting at Brown Chapel a few days later, black citizens formed the Committee to Ouster Political Enemies. Long-range plans for registering voters and kicking white incumbents out of office weren't immediate enough. "We feared an explosion could come from almost anywhere and might not be nonviolent," Chestnut recalled. So on Monday morning, Rose Sanders, Dan Rutledge, Hank Sanders, Perry Varner, J. L. Chestnut, and Edwin Moss occupied the county commissioners' seats. When the white commissioners walked in, they found that their black stand-ins had symbolically appointed Nathaniel Walker as tax collector. But the sit-in only forced the white commissioners to hold their meeting elsewhere and nothing more.[125]

On a statewide level, a new black political organization—the Alabama New South Coalition (ANSC)—coalesced out of the heated election in 1984. Many of the connections at the heart of the new organization had been forged during Hank Sanders's senate campaign in the Black Belt in 1982, a "Campaign for a New South." Then, in 1984, when the Alabama Democratic Conference—the major political organization of black Alabamians—endorsed Walter Mondale over Jesse Jackson on the grounds that a black man could not win, its members revolted. Hank Sanders and forty other black leaders held a press conference at Brown Chapel to declare their support for Jackson. After a year of grassroots organizing, twelve hundred black delegates gathered in Birmingham in January 1986 to form the ANSC. People from Dallas County like Samson Crum, Marie Foster, Perry Varner, and F. D. Reese were all there. The ANSC looked not only to political solutions but also to economic development, youth, and education to solve the many issues that faced black Alabamians. "Making a change for the better in our lifetime" was its motto. Unsurprisingly, J. L. Chestnut and Hank and Rose Sanders stood at the ANSC's helm as it became a major political contender in Alabama, home to a more expansive, sustained black political activism.[126]

Local Government, Black Majorities, and the Justice Department

Almost two decades after the passage of the Voting Rights Act, black residents were fed up. None of the county's most important governing bodies— the Selma City Council, the Dallas County Commission, or the city and county school boards—had a black majority. It was partly a problem of at-large election districts diluting black voting power and partly a problem of low black voter turnout. Throughout the 1980s, election district lines were drawn through a process that was repeated over and over again. It went something like this: white city council members would pass a redistricting plan that preserved the council's white majority over the objections of black council members and citizens. The Justice Department then rejected that plan. Council members would then reliably fail to agree on a racially fair alternative, prompting U.S. district judge Brevard Hand in Mobile to intervene. After redrawing the district lines himself, Judge Hand would threaten that the city council had better come up with new lines by the next election or else. In 1984 he actually cut the number of council members from ten to five and gave the swing ward a slight black majority as a symbol of his annoyance. "I guess the judge got tired of having to do the city of Selma's work," Mayor Smitherman admitted.[127]

Depending on the circumstances of the particular battle, the Chestnut, Sanders, and Sanders law firm would file suit against the local governing body on behalf of black citizens. In 1977, for example, Chestnut and Hank Sanders filed a lawsuit challenging the entirely white Dallas County Commission and school board, as well as the constitutionality of at-large elections. For the next decade, disagreements sent the suit volleying back and forth from the county commission to Judge Hand's court to the Eleventh Circuit Court of Appeals.[128] All the while, the white majority continued ruling the county, either unaware or unconcerned that the frustrations of their black neighbors were rising to the boiling point.[129] When asked, thirty years later, whether white political leaders would have willingly increased black representation, Reese laughed. "It would be very unlikely that it would have happened even as soon as it did without federal intervention," he stated.[130] Getting more black representatives required not only the sheer determination of black residents but the might of the U.S. Justice Department.

The fight against the all-white county commission appeared to be over in 1986 when Judge Hand ordered Dallas County to institute district-based elections.[131] But it came as no surprise when the all-white commission chose to resist to its very last breath. Local intransigence, judicial appeals, and Justice Department rejections governed the next two years. Meanwhile, the tax dollars of black residents went to pay the county government's mounting legal costs. Ignoring loud protests, the commissioners pursued their appeal all the way to the Supreme Court. But their efforts failed. In 1988 Dallas County was ordered to hold elections under a Justice Department plan calling for two black-majority districts, two white-majority districts, and one swing district.[132] It was a costly and selfish fight that only further exacerbated the distrust between Dallas County's black and white residents and belied any remnants of good faith.

Twenty-three years after the Voting Right Act, black Dallas Countians finally secured their first majority on a local governing body. In the county commission election in 1988, black representatives won three of the five seats.[133] But the new black-majority commission assumed power after a hard decade of industrial decline and federal abandonment. Craig Air Force Base's closing in 1977 marked the beginning of an era of economic decline for Dallas County. The Black Belt's antiunionism and cheap-labor policy sputtered as industries headed overseas and new companies moved to the expanding cities of the Sunbelt South. All the while, Reagan's deliberate dismantling of federal social programs and funding cuts throughout the 1980s exacerbated the pressing problems, and black families bore the brunt of the federal government's retraction. When Dallas County's first black-majority commission took their seats, they confronted a dire landscape of economic depression and deep poverty, having few resources with which to create solutions.

At the end of 1980s, the battle lines between white and black Selma also had been drawn. As Smitherman maneuvered to preserve his personal power, he became the upholder of white political power for people like Cecil Williamson. Mayor Smitherman, unironically, took to calling his adversaries at the Chestnut, Sanders, and Sanders law firm "the Jeff Davis crowd," as their office was located on Jefferson Davis Avenue. The Sanderses and Chestnut headed up an all-out war against white control in Dallas County, and they fought this battle through the courts, political offices, community organizations, and direct action. The mayor's and the law firm's two visions of Selma had little, if any, overlap, and their bitter ongoing battles did not bring them any closer. As the 1980s closed, the chasm between white and black citizens was wide and deep.

Superintendent Norward Roussell
and School Leveling

Norward Roussell had never been to Selma before he accepted the job as superintendent of the city's schools in 1987. The board of education, in a somewhat surprising move, unanimously voted to hire Roussell, a black associate superintendent from New Orleans, after his predecessor, Martha Barton, stepped down. Roussell had grown up with his twin brother on Magnolia Street in New Orleans. His father, a vegetable dealer who had played baseball in the Negro Leagues, died when his sons were eight, and his mother made sure that her boys got an education. They attended Dillard University after serving a stint in the Korean War, then Fisk University for their master's degrees, and finally Wayne State University for PhDs in educational administration. Roussell was a fourteen-year veteran of the New Orleans schools when he packed his bags for Selma with big dreams. "There was a real opportunity here to show that you can have serious quality education in a town that had been so racially torn in the sixties," he remembered. "The name Selma means something."[1]

Black Selmians had less faith that Roussell's hiring marked the beginning of a new day. Both before and after 1965, white officials had fought tooth and nail to keep black citizens from gaining meaningful power, so some wondered why the white-majority school board chose to hire a black superintendent now. J. L. Chestnut guessed that white administrators were looking for "a black superintendent to hide behind."[2] But when Roussell arrived in Selma, he made it clear that he was nobody's man except his own. Impeccably dressed, dignified, and self-confident to the extent that some called it "swagger," Roussell avoided aligning himself too closely with either the white business and political elite or the Chestnut, Sanders, and Sanders law firm. He became the first black member of the Rotary Club, Selma's most prestigious civic association, but quickly bowed out when rumors spread that he was being considered for membership at the whites-only Selma Country Club. He had not come to Selma "to claw down racial barriers," he told inquiring reporters.[3] Instead, Roussell threw himself into upgrading the education of the district's nearly six thousand students.

Back in 1970—the first year of real school desegregation—the Selma school system had begun grouping students by ability. School officials cited "recent forces and alterations which are taking place and changing the way of life in our society" as the impetus for instituting a tiered curriculum. In theory, classroom performance, achievement and intelligence scores, and teacher recommendations were used to group students in an appropriate level, ranging from honors to remedial. But, in practice, there were no uniform, district-wide criteria for student placement; instead, teacher recommendations and parent advocacy dictated who was placed in which level. Many well-to-do whites stayed in the public school system, and their children plus a handful of black children from better-off families made up level one. Meanwhile, levels three and four (the latter was eventually phased out) were 95 percent black. Not only could students in the bottom levels not take college prep classes, like algebra, biology, or foreign languages, but their grades were worth less than those in higher levels. An A in level one was worth five grade points, but in level three it was worth three.[4]

"Virtually all white people said they didn't see anything racial about learning levels," Chestnut explained, and "virtually all black people saw levelling [as] if not racist, racial." White residents overwhelmingly thought ability levels helped children at all levels learn and achieve more, while the black community felt concerned that children in the lower levels were not being adequately challenged and prepared.[5] Many black parents had experienced firsthand having their children placed in lower levels. Nancy Sewell, the librarian at Selma High School, and her husband, Andrew, the basketball coach, encountered tracking when their daughter, Terri, was

Inter8.1 First graders from Selma's Edgewood Elementary School on a field trip to Good Samaritan Hospital in 1981. Courtesy of Society of Saint Edmund Archives, Saint Michael's College, Colchester, Vermont.

placed in a lower level at Cedar Park Elementary. School administrators refused to move her up to the next level, so Mrs. Sewell waited until Terri entered Westside Middle School and met with the counselors there to ensure she was enrolled in more difficult courses. Likewise, Rose Sanders found out that her daughter had been placed in a lower level only when Malika's teacher mentioned it in passing at another meeting. "I didn't know that they were leveling children in elementary school," Sanders exclaimed later. Black middle-class parents could insist that their children be placed in higher levels, Nancy Sewell recalled, but lower-class parents working in factory jobs did not or could not do the same.[6]

In 1987—the same year Roussell became superintendent—a group of black parents organized the Best Education Support Team (BEST) for the purpose of dismantling the "institutionalized racial tracking system." With Rose Sanders in the lead, BEST petitioned Superintendent Roussell to eliminate leveling within the Selma city schools.[7] But Roussell did things according to his own schedule, and he saw other needs as more pressing. When he arrived, there were ten students to each computer at historically white schools, but that ratio was a hundred to one at historically black schools. "They had old dictionaries, old books, old desks, in the old black schools," Roussell explained. "Some of their maps had only forty-eight states." So he began updating supplies and revamping the math, science, and technology curriculum. Roussell applied for and received a $1.2 million federal grant shortly after his arrival, which helped him install new computer labs in the schools. By the end of his first year, Selmians and the board of education were singing his praises.[8]

It was in his second year as superintendent that Roussell took up an extensive review of the leveling system. He pored over English scores for all students from the two years prior. He found students in levels two and three whose achievement scores were far higher than some of the level-one students'. He discovered that all of the level-one teachers at Selma High were white. "General Math, Business Math, Everyday Math—that kind of foolishness"—that the level-two and level-three students took amounted to nothing more than "education for the cotton fields," Roussell concluded.[9] "He did his research. He wouldn't just take our word," Rose Sanders remembered. "He came back and said y'all are right." At the end of his study, Roussell concluded that leveling in the Selma schools had created "two school systems in one."[10]

In the spring of 1988, rumors flew that Roussell was dismantling leveling. In actuality, he proposed two changes to the system: (1) establish uniform criteria for placing students in different levels and (2) give more students a chance to take advanced and honors courses. "I think parents and children have a right to know, if they are placed in the highest or the lowest level, why they were placed there," he told a crowd of two hundred gathered at a community meeting at Eastside Middle School.[11] Even though his proposal was far from radical, Roussell's meddling made him a target. "When you come in and change the structure that has existed, and transfer and tamper with the mind-set of who is superior and who is inferior," he reflected later, "you're going to have problems."[12]

While Roussell had done good things for Selma's school system in his first year in town, his independence and domineering management style had rubbed people the wrong way. He made some enemies on the school board when he pressured them to hire a black contractor. School districts were big business. The system had always operated on "the good ole boys system," Roussell explained, "and if you were not in that circle, white or black, you didn't get any help."[13] He also transferred some black employees to other schools when they did not think they should be transferred. Meanwhile, Mayor Joe Smitherman resented Roussell, who made more money than he did. According to some, Smitherman actively encouraged the city council to appoint school board members who were against the superintendent. "Roussell had the mistaken view he was in charge," David Hodo, a white Selma psychiatrist, explained. "The board said, 'We hired you, but we're in charge.'"[14]

The superintendent's entry into the leveling debate pushed tensions to new heights in May 1988. Amid criticism, the *Selma Times-Journal* demanded that the city school board either "back him . . . or boot him."[15] Roussell took it on himself to respond. "What Selma has to come to grips with is not Norward Roussell as its superintendent of schools," he wrote, "but whether, the education of its children is important enough to put it above personalities and politics."[16] The school board promptly affirmed its support for Roussell, but the underlying issues, especially that of leveling remained. Sullivan Jackson, the dentist whose house had served as SCLC headquarters during the voting rights movement in 1965, labeled "the uncalled for unilateral criticism of Dr. Roussell" as being "almost a lynching."[17]

Beneath the controversies over Roussell and leveling were the same struggles for power that had defined Selma ever since 1965. Black residents' frustration with the white-controlled school board had grown more acute with each passing year. Even though the courts rejected its self-appointing nature in 1976, board members were still appointed by the white-controlled city council, and they governed a black-majority school district. Black enrollment surpassed white enrollment by over two to one— 4,150 to 1,798—by the 1987–1988 school year.[18] But demographics didn't mean as much as economics to people like Carl Morgan, the city council president. Because Selma's economic base was still vested in white people, he explained, whites were entitled to more representation on the school board. Keeping this balance would, in his estimation, prevent white flight to private schools. Many white citizens agreed that white involvement—not equalizing the criteria of student leveling—was a priority. [19]

At the start of the next school year, Rose Sanders announced that BEST would be willing to accept Roussell's leveling system, which proposed uniform standards and parent participation.[20] In October 1988 a three-tiered student-grouping system went before the school board for approval, and in January they voted five-four in favor. The four dissenting votes came from white members who opposed lower requirements for honors courses.[21] Only a month later, the school board's five white members raised the standards for honors courses over the objections of the four black members.[22]

Disagreements on the school board spilled over into the wider community during the spring of 1989. Superintendent Roussell blamed the fights that broke out between black and white students on adults: "If we express attitudes of racial intolerance, our children will do the same." Black Selmians' frustration grew when a white student was named the valedictorian of Selma High School over black student Kwambi Dover. The white student had received more grade points for honors debate than Dover had for honors band. Meanwhile, businessman and sitting council member Edwin Moss brought the deeper issue to the city council: why, he asked, could blacks never hold a majority on any city board?[23]

By July the controversies surrounding Selma schools had settled on Superintendent Roussell. "If he could just remove the personal pronouns, 'I,' 'me,' 'my' and 'I am boss' from his vocabulary, he might do fairly well," read an editorial in the *Selma Times-Journal*, indicating that more than school levels was at play. At a meeting in late summer, white school board members voted to fire him. They backed down only when one black member threatened to resign and another threatened to call a press conference.[24] When the 1989–1990 school year opened that August, not all was well.

CHAPTER

8

Two Selmas

1989–2000

At the start of each term, the newly elected city council members posed in the council chambers to take an official picture. In the twenty-five years since the voting rights movement, those photos reflected some of the changes that had taken place in Dallas County. People like F. D. Reese, who had once demanded fair treatment as a civil rights protestor, stood tall in numerous photos, having helped make Selma a more equitable city from within. The black city department heads, police officers, and school superintendent highlighted how the vote had given African Americans a fundamental place in running the city. But those who had marched in Selma in 1965 had hoped that the vote would bring more. "People had been told and now believed they could become captains of their own destiny through the ballot," J. L. Chestnut remembered, but three decades later it was clear that wasn't so.[1]

In Dallas County at the end of the twentieth century, racial tensions ran high against a backdrop of widespread poverty, a sagging local economy, and bitter political divisions. The 1990s began with massive protests, boycotts, and lawsuits by black residents who were fed up with leveling—or what was also called tracking—in the schools and white dominance on the city school board. The school tracking protests coincided with the twenty-fifth anniversary of Bloody Sunday, putting Selma in the media spotlight once more. When the dust had settled, Selma's public schools were nearly all-black and faced as many problems as before.

The school protests reflected a long-standing bitterness in Selma. At the heart of these divisions were the unfulfilled promises of the voting rights movement. It was now clear that the vote had not ended poverty in the black community, had not transferred meaningful political power to African Americans.[2] When a black majority finally gained control of Selma's city council in 1993, they inherited problems far beyond the scope of local municipal authority. Crack cocaine had arrived in Dallas County, decimating already-struggling poor neighborhoods. Still in the shadow of the Sunbelt, the Black Belt's economy staggered forward with a smattering of industries and government transfer payments, and the federal government continued its policy of neglect toward the country's poorest residents and regions. So black residents turned inward yet again.

Historical memory became a new political battleground as groups of white and black citizens fought for control of local government. The city's new motto—"From Civil War to Civil Rights"—played out more like civil war versus civil rights. After decades of white resistance, black political activists opened the National Voting Rights Museum and Institute to honor the past while mobilizing for the present. Meanwhile, Mayor Joe Smitherman and his backers made increasingly desperate attempts to maintain his personal power and white political control. This pushed a coalition of black citizens, many connected to the Chestnut, Sanders, and Sanders law firm, to mount increasingly powerful political challenges. Unfortunately, politics was only part of the solution; politics alone could not fix segregated schools, drugs, scarce and inadequate jobs, and state and federal governments uninterested in pursuing policies aimed at economic justice for all residents.

In the fall of 1989, the twenty-fifth anniversary of Bloody Sunday was only six months away. Both movement veterans and white civic leaders hoped, although in different ways, that the commemoration would bring good things to Selma. The unforgettable images of billy clubs and tear gas on the Edmund Pettus Bridge had plagued white residents since 1965, and they were eager to demonstrate their southern hospitality and the city's friendly business climate to the world. Mayor Smitherman and the Chamber of Commerce dreamed of a cooperative commemoration that would bring Selma's factions together. The mayor explained to the *Selma Times-Journal* that a better image could make the city more attractive to industry and tourists, which would benefit the local economy.[3] "We could get $50 million in free publicity," he rather uncouthly told the Chamber of Commerce. Smitherman needed black support to give his plan credibility, and Reese, his sometimes political ally and sometimes nemesis, gave the commemoration plan the backing it needed by agreeing to cochair the committee with white banker Rex Morthland.[4]

Others in Selma's black community rebuffed attempts to use the commemoration for economic gain, especially while the school situation was simmering. "If there is not some honest effort to resolve the many volatile issues surrounding the school board," Chestnut declared, "I'm afraid a racially cooperative effort may not be possible." He and other black activists called a press conference to warn the city that it was heading toward two different commemoration events, one black and one white. "When it becomes a Chamber of Commerce project, count us out," Chestnut avowed. "The mayor had nothing but bad things to say, and all of a sudden he wants to be the grand marshal."[5] Under serious pressure, Reese resigned one month later to join the National Right to Vote Celebration Committee, made up of national civil rights groups and local activists. In the name of community harmony, the mayor and chamber abandoned their plans.[6]

Selma School Crisis

Rising anger toward the city school board that fall made peace between black and white Selmians even more unlikely. Edwin Moss repeatedly appealed to his colleagues on the city council to address the long-standing racial imbalance on the board of education. "You all know I'm no rabble-rouser," Moss declared at a council meeting. "Seldom do I put issues in terms of white and black, but the feeling among blacks is that the board of education situation where we have a white majority is unfair and has been for years." He warned that the issues with the school board and the pending renewal of Superintendent Norward Roussell's contract could lead to boycotts and protests.[7]

Moss put forward plans to equalize black and white representation, but white council members took no action on the proposal. Mayor Smitherman only made matters worse by inserting himself into the controversy. Carl Barker, the white president of the school board, had been planning to resign, but Smitherman convinced him to postpone his resignation indefinitely so as not to create a vacancy on the eleven-member board (with six white and five black members). Meanwhile, Moss urged Barker to step down in favor of racial balance and goodwill. Smitherman then rebuked Moss, accusing him of being influenced by the Chestnut, Sanders, and Sanders law firm, which he described as "seek[ing] to control the superintendent, the school, the city council, and everything else in Selma."[8]

Meanwhile, Superintendent Roussell's three-year contract was set to expire in June 1990, and the school board was obligated to give six months' notice regarding their contract-renewal decision. The superintendent's strong personality had rubbed numerous Selmians—especially white school board members—the wrong way, and tampering with the leveling system further aggravated this dislike. Still, Roussell had advocates in the lead-up to the December renewal vote. White Selmians Martha and David Hodo praised Roussell "for being his own man rather than an instrument of divisive political forces." They argued that he had "aggressively and tenaciously attacked school problems and sought what was best for our children."[9]

On a late December afternoon, four days before Christmas, the six white school board members voted not to renew Roussell's contract, over the opposition of the five black members. All five black members responded by resigning their positions. As they walked out of the meeting, they paused to make clear that their actions were in protest of the failure to renew the superintendent's contract. Twenty-five years after the voting rights movement, the school board's decision marked another breaking point for Selma. "This is not about what's best for our children or our schools. It's about politics, personalities and race," Roussell said to the seventy-five people crowded into the boardroom. "It's a message from one group of people to another. . . . This vote has sent Selma back to the Pettus Bridge."[10]

All of black Selma's frustration and anger about school tracking, white control, ongoing poverty, and everything else poured out in response to the Roussell decision. The next day black protesters braved the below-zero wind chill to form picket lines in front of city hall and two downtown banks with ties to white school board members. They sported signs reading "Smitherman appointed school board must go," and "Education without representation means deprivation."[11] The Best Education Support Team (BEST) quickly assumed leadership of the protests, giving shape to black residents' outrage. Rose Sanders, county commissioner Perry Varner, and others called for parents to keep their children out of Selma's schools until the city met a list of demands. These included an elected board of education, the resignation of the "six elitist school board members" and the reinstatement of the five black members "representing the people," the employment of more black teachers, a prohibition against parents with children in private academies serving on the school board, and a safety clause for those who chose to participate in the school boycott. Nowhere in BEST's demands was the reinstatement of Roussell or any reference to recent leveling debates.[12]

The superintendent opposed the BEST-supported boycott, even though he agreed that race and politics were the root of the problem. "Student and staff absenteeism do not show concern for me or for the education of our students," he wrote. The absentee policy would remain in effect, and "students must not have to give up a year of their effort to move on in school in order to solve adult problems in this community."[13] Regardless of Roussell's stance, fourteen hundred children—almost a quarter of all students—stayed away from school on the first day back from winter break in January.[14] After two days of high absenteeism, BEST announced that it was postponing additional boycotts so that students could prepare for their midyear exams.[15]

Although most students participating in the boycott were black, the controversy did not divide neatly along racial lines. A devoted group of white Selma families supported the public schools and refused to send their children to the all-white private academies. In fact, a battle of bumper stickers played out among white Selma parents: city school supporters sported stickers reading, "MY HEART IS IN THE PUBLIC SCHOOLS AND SO ARE MY CHILDREN," while the cars of Morgan Academy parents proclaimed, "MY CHILDREN ARE IN MY HEART, AND THEY ATTEND MORGAN ACADEMY."[16] White public school supporters were not in favor of the boycotts, but they also disapproved of the school board's short-sighted actions.[17] Behind the scenes, people like white attorney Harry Gamble Jr. (the grandson of the Rev. Edward W. Gamble), black librarian Nancy Sewell, and other community members attempted to persuade the school board to renew Roussell's contract.[18]

But the school crisis solidified Selma's already-existing factions. The mayor did not help matters when he allegedly told a *Newsweek* reporter that Roussell was an "overpaid nigger." In response, BEST called for a boycott on January 17, and an astounding 33 percent of employees and 37 percent of students—a total of 2,209—did not show up for work or school.[19] Sewell recalled that the more average black and white citizens got involved, the harder the positions of the white school board members became.[20] Negotiations stalemated when white board members refused to discuss any proposals without their black colleagues who had walked out in December. Meanwhile, black members refused to negotiate until white members agreed to extend Roussell's contract.[21] Twenty years later, Sewell remembered, "I didn't expect the majority white school board to dig in and take the stance they took and not yield."[22]

On February 2, the six white members of the board of education voted to relieve Roussell immediately of his duties as superintendent in the name of restoring "peace and tranquility."[23] They appointed F. D. Reese, then the principal of Selma High School, as the acting superintendent. Black Selmians did not look lightly on Reese's intrusion into the situation. When he attempted to address a mass meeting at First Baptist Church two days later, boos echoed through the sanctuary.[24] The following day, Rose Sanders, Perry Varner, and attorney Carlos Williams of BEST attempted to force their way into Mayor Smitherman's office, after waiting for hours to meet with him. Police officers arrested the three and bodily dragged them out of the building.[25]

Then, on Tuesday, February 6, all remnants of order broke down. The air crackled with tension that morning as students arrived at Eastside and Westside Middle Schools and Selma High School. Reese ordered all students to remain in their homerooms, and by 9:30 a.m., after consulting with the school board president and the mayor, he ordered Eastside Middle School and Selma High School closed. Westside Middle School remained in session, but a throng of singing and chanting protesters stampeded through the hallways later that morning and brought concerned parents out en masse to pick up their children. Awash in disapproval, Reese tendered his resignation later that day, and the six white members of the school board reinstated Roussell in a desperate attempt to alleviate the mayhem. They then unanimously voted to close the city schools on Wednesday.[26]

The schools did not open again for the next five school days. That weekend, over sixteen hundred black Selmians marched on city hall and formed a human chain around the building and parking lot, singing "We Shall Overcome." Connie Tucker, a BEST organizer, attributed Roussell's dismissal to his efforts to revamp the school leveling system. This was one of the first explicit ties BEST had drawn between the current protests and school tracking. "Why should our children attend schools under the laws of Jim Crow in an era of integration. We are tired of living in the era of Plessy vs. Ferguson," Tucker exclaimed.[27] At Selma High School, nearly two hundred students seized the school's cafeteria on Thursday afternoon in a protest sit-in. They kept up their vigil until the following Monday, when Superintendent Roussell requested that they cease and desist, explaining that he would rather resign than be forced to expel them. Meanwhile, a group of BEST protesters, including Senator Hank Sanders and Perry Varner, occupied city hall and stayed there after a federal judge denied the city's request for a temporary restraining order.[28]

On Tuesday morning, the eleven city schools reopened under the watchful presence of police, state troopers, and members of the National Guard. A crowd of BEST protesters gathered on the edges of the circle of law enforcement officers surrounding Selma High's entrance. The six white members of the board of education had made no concessions to protesters' demands, but Rose Sanders claimed success in garnering national media attention. "Our overall purpose is to educate the people about this tracking issue," she told one reporter. Despite protests, 77 percent of the district's students returned to classes.[29] That number grew to 92 percent on Wednesday, but tensions remained. At Selma High, Roussell suspended eighty-seven students after they ran through the cafeteria chanting, "Ain't gonna take it no more."[30] When the dust began to settle, 278 students—nearly all white—had withdrawn from the city's public schools.[31]

The events of the first few months of 1990 deepened the already-raw divisions between black and white Selmians. While BEST members continued their protests and their occupation of city hall, a group of white parents formed the Public Education Support Team (PEST). The two organizations had common ground in supporting public education, but PEST defended the actions of the Selma school board. "Our elected officials by law have the right and authority to govern and carry out their specific duties," PEST affirmed, arguing that "any unlawful interference should not be tolerated."[32] It was a problem that J. L. Chestnut had identified soon after the movement in 1965. "We constantly were confronted with a white perspective and a black perspective as to what was reasonable progress for black people," he recalled. As BEST and PEST unleashed a torrent of verbal jabs at each other, they kept the rancor raw and fresh.[33]

Meanwhile, a flurry of lawsuits and injunctions flew between the city of Selma, the board of education, and BEST protesters. Roussell added to the legal flood when he sued the board of education for $10 million, charging that the nonrenewal of his contract was racially motivated.[34] By March a circuit court judge from Lauderdale County was brought in to mediate and strong-arm all sides into an agreement.[35] But the group of devoted BEST members refused to halt their ongoing protests, which ranged from pickets to occupations to tents on the lawn outside city hall.[36] Without their participation, settlement attempts stagnated.[37]

Against the backdrop of the school crisis, Selma and the nation marked the twenty-fifth anniversary of Bloody Sunday. Instead of the positive publicity the mayor and the Chamber of Commerce had hoped for, the national media compared the current protests to 1965. "25 Years after March, Selma Still a City Divided by Race," a headline in the *Washington Post* read. The article noted that objections to the tracking system had been one cause of the boycott, but it put more emphasis on Roussell's take on the situation. "This is not a matter of my performance here. This is a matter of who is going to be in control," he had explained. "Whites have final say on everything in this community—including the schools." The article explored the ongoing power struggle between white and black Selmians, highlighting the white majorities on city boards, the reign of Mayor Smitherman, the racially separate Elks Clubs and YMCA branches, and the segregated Selma Country Club.[38] Over thirty-five hundred people came to the city in early March to pay homage. Jesse Jackson, Representative John Lewis, comedian Dick Gregory, Coretta Scott King, and others joined with local movement veterans to honor the people and place that had secured voting rights for all Americans.[39] But with the city more divided than ever, white Selmians stayed away.

The school controversy fizzled out over the next year, but the polarization remained. In early May Roussell resigned as part of a settlement with the board of education. He received an additional $150,000 and in return dropped the discrimination lawsuit he had filed.[40] Negotiations regarding the outstanding lawsuits between the city, the board of education, and BEST continued throughout the summer. When the school year opened in August, BEST demonstrators gathered outside of Selma High and burned Mayor Smitherman in effigy. Flames engulfed a stuffed figure with "Joe T., repression, miseducation must die" emblazoned on its chest.[41] But the black interim superintendent, James Carter, squelched the protests. He signed warrants for the protestors' arrest and forbade them from entering school property.[42] The next week, the eleven-member school board reunited, more or less under the compromise that Edwin Moss had proposed nine months earlier. Five white and five black members would sit on the board, and the nonvoting chairperson would alternate between black and white on a yearly basis.[43] When BEST, the city of Selma, and the board of education agreed to dismiss all lawsuits at the end of August, the immediate crisis came to a close.[44]

But the year of turmoil had widened the already-deep chasm between white and black residents. The 1990–1991 school year opened with six hundred fewer white students than in the previous year. White enrollment dropped from 26.8 percent to 19.9 percent, a trend that accelerated with each passing year. The white parents who had staunchly supported integrated public schools transferred their children to private schools, citing concerns about their safety.[45] Nancy Bennett, the daughter of probate judge Bernard Reynolds, kept her two daughters and her two foster children in Selma High, but when the youngest two graduated, they were practically the only white students in their graduating class. Former superintendent Joe A. Pickard observed later that the school crisis was more about power and politics than about education or Roussell. Whether or not the school board's actions or the protests achieved their goals, the events of the 1989–1990 school year spelled the death of integrated public education in Selma.[46]

After the year of turmoil, the U.S. Commission on Civil Rights conducted a study of local race relations.[47] They interviewed 140 people and held public hearings in December at the George Wallace Community College. Despite the vastly different viewpoints of the fifty-one people who testified, "a surprisingly large number of people" were united on one theme: a struggle for power raged behind the façade of race relations in Selma. The former publisher of the *Selma Times-Journal* summarized it as a battle between "Mayor Joe Smitherman and his loyal band" and the Chestnut, Sanders, and Sanders law firm, a.k.a. "the Jeff Davis crowd."[48] In all likelihood, the majority of black and white Selmians fell into the middle ground, not defined by either faction. But the school controversy left a bitter taste in the mouths of all and fostered a widespread belief that Mayor Smitherman and Rose Sanders were engaged in a bitter ongoing power struggle.

Even though black and white Selmians agreed on the cause of the problem, their solutions couldn't have been more different. County commissioner Perry Varner channeled the feelings of most black Selmians when he stated that race relations would not be solved until equitable sharing of power existed. But Richard Morthland of the People's Bank and Trust Company, the son of Rex Morthland, spoke for many white citizens: economic power was concentrated in the white community, and that was not going to "just shift." In the eyes of white Selmians, wealth entitled the holder to a larger share of governance.[49] The Civil Rights Commission study highlighted the unequal balance of power that both Varner and Morthland spoke of. It found that black city employees overwhelmingly served in low-level, hard-labor jobs and that tight financing and lack of a biracial social and economic network kept African Americans out of business. Public housing sites remained clearly identifiable by race, and black residents felt excluded from equal political representation.[50] "In spite of integration in the schools, housing, and the workplace," the report concluded, "there remain two Selmas: black and white."[51]

Crack and the War on Drugs

While these political battles raged, a new adversary—crack cocaine—put down roots in the Black Belt. The Selma City Council first declared war against street-corner drug dealers at the end of 1985. Within five years, drugs had already laid waste to some of Dallas County's poorest neighborhoods.[52] Crack, a cheaper, crystallized version of cocaine, first hit the nation's streets in 1985 and had made its way to Selma by sometime in 1987. Captain Billy Duke, head of the narcotics division in the Dallas County Sheriff's Department, estimated that cocaine use was up nearly 40 percent in 1987. A gram of powder cocaine cost around a hundred dollars in Selma, but crack, the newcomer in town, ran at fifteen dollars a gram. "People here are just beginning to fool with it," he reported.[53]

By 1988 a mobile home park in Selmont, south of the Alabama River, had gained the nickname "Crack City."[54] "It's just devastating," Rev. Fairro J. Brown, pastor of the Selmont Community Baptist Church, explained. "This thing has touched, directly or indirectly, 75 percent of my congregation."[55] That December, thirty law enforcement officers from four different agencies raided a bar and general store in Selmont, TC's Place. They confiscated $14,000 in cash and nearly $30,000 worth of crack.[56] Selmont's residents did not take their neighborhood's new nickname lightly. Less than three days after the raid, flames engulfed the house of bar owner Tommy Lee Cole in what was deemed a suspected arson. "A lot of people want me out," Cole admitted.[57]

At the same time, harsh new laws added to the damage drugs were causing in poor neighborhoods. President Ronald Reagan declared a war on drugs in late 1982 and initiated a new era of federal intervention into local policing, severe penalties for drug use, and skyrocketing incarceration rates. The president had campaigned on promises to be tough on racially laden issues like crime and welfare. Throughout the 1970s, stricter sentencing laws had gained traction as the way to combat crime. In 1979 Alabama passed the Habitual Felony Offender Act, which automatically increased sentences for anyone with a previous felony conviction. Cracking down on drug users and street crime was a way for Reagan to target black and poor Americans, whom he painted as undeserving. When the war on drugs began, illegal drug use was actually declining, and hardly any Americans thought it was a pressing issue.[58]

In the early 1980s, the federal government pumped billions of dollars into drug enforcement efforts across the nation, funding new units like the narcotics division of the Dallas County Sheriff's Department. At the same time, the Department of Justice began pursuing drug cases with a vengeance. Congress passed two anti–drug abuse acts, one in 1986 and one in 1988, that established severe mandatory minimum sentences for drug possession. If harsher sentences weren't enough, the acts tacked on civil penalties like eviction from public housing and exclusion from other federal benefits. Mandatory add-ons, like for selling within a school zone, took sentences to the extreme.[59] Alabama's drug-free zones extended to a three-mile radius from any school. In Selma this wide reach—most states mandated only a thousand feet—meant that almost any drug conviction within the city fell within a school zone and automatically upped the minimum sentence.[60]

The war on drugs came down hardest on poor black residents, even though rates of drug use and selling were remarkably similar across all Americans. Of the approximately one hundred people arrested for dealing or possessing crack in Dallas County in 1989, ninety-five were black. Policing patterns contributed to the lopsided numbers. Local law enforcement concentrated their street-level drug patrols in poor black neighborhoods, like Crack City. It was not a coincidence that Selmont was nearly entirely black and that its residents brought home an average $4,613 a year—barely half the per capita income of Selmians and well below the poverty threshold of $6,310. Nightly news stories only made matters worse with reports of "crack whores," "crack babies," and "gangbangers," all of whom were black. Meanwhile, drug sentencing laws doled out harsher penalties for crack cocaine, used more widely by black Americans, at a ratio of a hundred to one, compared to powder cocaine, which was used more frequently by white Americans.[61]

Double-digit unemployment rates and drugs went hand in hand in places like Crack City. "Selma still can't find enough jobs to keep all its willing workers working. Many Selmians [seem] to have dropped out of the job market entirely," the *Selma Times-Journal* reported. "Real poverty continues to keep many of our people in rural ghettoes. In this atmosphere, drugs and crime flourish in the streets of Selma." African Americans bore the brunt of job scarcity.[62] In Selmont 27 percent of black residents were unemployed, while a devastating 56 percent lived below the poverty line. The police chief, Randy Lewellen, pointed to money as the primary reason kids and teenagers got involved in drugs. Working eight hours a day for minimum wage, if they could even find a job, "would bring home somewhere around $32 to $35 a day. Some juveniles make $500 a night selling drugs," he explained. With jobs scarce and good jobs scarcer, selling drugs was a way for black residents, left dredging through the muck of Dallas County's economy, to make some needed cash.[63]

President Reagan's war on drugs locked drug users away for years, taking them away from their families and communities. In 1989 Michael Page, a twenty-four-year-old from Selmont, was sentenced to thirty years in prison for robbing two service stations. He had started using crack in the mid-1980s and began stealing from his father and others to support his habit. Page first spent eighteen months in the Dallas County jail for stealing thirty-two gold necklaces from a local jewelry store. For his next offense, he went to Montgomery's Kilby Prison for three decades.[64] Similarly, twenty-five-year-old Joe Hatcher made the mistake of selling crack to an undercover agent. It was his second drug offense. The circuit judge called Hatcher a "threat to the community" before sentencing him to life in prison.[65]

As young black men in Dallas County disappeared into prisons, their neighborhoods felt the impact. Page's seventy-five-year-old father watched dealers in luxurious cars drive down Selmont's streets at all hours of the night. "They sell it on the playgrounds, for goodness sakes," he explained. "It's like a picnic ground in parts of Selmont with people buying and selling drugs." Chain fences and "Beware of Dog" signs now appeared on the houses. Rev. Brown had known Page since he was a baby. He saw Page's promising future wither away when he got involved with drugs. "Now they have no hope of reaching their potential," he said of the young men from the neighborhood, like Page and Hatcher. Locking people up took needed contributors away from already-impoverished communities and broke up families in neighborhoods that needed all the help they could get. "I've seen this place hit rock bottom," Rev. Brown explained. "It's fallen from an upstanding community to Crack City in no time."[66]

Selma City Council and Black Political Control

Behind black parents' struggle to keep their children away from crack and bring home a paycheck big enough to feed their families, the fight for black political representation raged on. Perry Varner, Erskine Minor, and D. L.

Pope, the three black Dallas County commissioners, had a decade of litigation to thank for their seating in 1989 and their majority on the five-person governing body. They appointed Bruce Boynton, the son of S. W. and Amelia Boynton, as the first African American county attorney. He laid out how at-large election districts had kept black citizens voiceless. "You might be able to elect one black who was absolutely powerless," he explained, "and that was the extent of post-1965 political progress for a long time."[67]

No one was surprised when the fight for black representation on Selma's city council played out almost exactly the same way as it had for the Dallas County Commission—white political intransigence, lawsuits, polarization, and the heavy hand of the Justice Department. By 1990 black residents made up 58.5 percent of Selma's population. Yet the city council had four white members, four black members, and a white council president who held the deciding vote. In the twenty-five years since the Voting Rights Act, black citizens' patience had worn thin. "No one should forget the years and public dollars thrown away trying to keep black people off the county commission," Dr. Samuel Lett, an ally of the Chestnut, Sanders, and Sanders law firm, reminded black residents.[68]

In August 1992 county commissioner Perry Varner filed a lawsuit demanding the redrawing of ward lines to give African Americans a majority on the council. District judge Brevard Hand called off the city's scheduled elections in response.[69] Over the next six months, Selma's black and white council members struggled to come up with district lines acceptable to themselves, the community, and the Justice Department. The chances of negotiations going well looked about as good as those of an unsuspecting raccoon facing down an alligator lurking in the Alabama River. As in the past, white council members used their majority to pass plans over the vetoes of black members, and the Justice Department then rejected these plans as unconstitutional.[70] Black council members then castigated the white elected officials for refusing to transfer political control despite the city's black majority.[71] Eventually the Justice Department approved a plan with five black districts, and white council members came back to the negotiating table mainly to avoid a court-ordered political reprimand.[72] In April 1993 a white councilman and the council president, Carl Morgan, broke rank and voted with the four black members to approve the new plan. "In the name of God, in the name of Selma, remember all our history—do not let your anger affect your vote," white moderate Alston Fitts had pleaded.[73]

But Joe Smitherman—with his personal power and continued reign as mayor at risk—wasn't ready to throw in the towel. After the new plan passed, the mayor enlisted council member Rita Franklin to propose a new ordinance that transferred the appointing of certain city officials from the city council to the mayor. This move stopped any future black-majority council from controlling some of the most important positions in municipal government, including those of tax collector, purchasing agent, and city attorney.[74] Next, Smitherman vetoed the recently passed redistricting plan, making a two-thirds council vote necessary to overrule his veto.[75]

Cecil Williamson, a champion of white political control, applauded the mayor's "attempt to save Selma from political terrorists." In a letter to the editor, Williamson asked whether those elected to the council would be black moderates or "the political terrorists who have nearly wrecked the city school system, bankrupted surrounding counties, lied to federal judges, created a Banana Republic atmosphere in the county government, and appear motivated by hate rather than love?"[76] Every reader of the *Selma Times-Journal* knew that Williamson was referring to all those connected with "the Jeff Davis crowd" but especially Rose Sanders. At the next city council meeting, all white members voted both to sustain the mayor's veto and to transfer appointing powers to the mayor over objections from the black minority. The moment of compromise had been fleeting.[77]

Thus, white political intransigence yet again forced intervention by the federal government. In May 1993 the Justice Department filed a voting rights lawsuit against Mayor Smitherman, the city of Selma, and the city council. It charged that discriminatory ward boundaries diluted black voter strength and that the named parties had failed to develop a racially fair plan. Smitherman, in typical fashion, refused to take any of the blame. "I think it's a sad state of affairs," he told a *Selma Times-Journal* reporter, "when the Justice Department gets involved with our tax dollars in a lawsuit brought by a local firm."[78] Meanwhile, Judge Hand submitted the compromise plan over the council's objections, and the Justice Department approved it.[79] J. L. Chestnut, speaking in front of the Selma Rotary Club, assured the nearly all-white audience that his law firm had no interest in taking over city hall. But he questioned Smitherman's desperate attempts to maintain a white-controlled council. "Do you think we'll ever get to a point where we won't have to go through this?," he asked.[80]

The new ward lines guaranteed that the first black majority would sit on the city council after the August elections.[81] In October five black representatives—Selma High librarian Nancy Sewell, attorney Yusuf Salaam, McArthur McWilliams, returning councilman Bill King, and Mark West—took their seats on the council, but black Selmians reacted quietly.

Activist Sam Walker commented on the absence of visible celebration. "People have been living with this administration for 30 years," he explained, referring to Mayor Smitherman. "They don't expect everything to change at once."[82] Meanwhile, Selma City Council's new black majority inherited a host of problems. "Black folk now had the responsibility of running some of the poorest counties in America with a multitude of problems and a scarcity of resources in a racially polarized atmosphere," Chestnut summarized bleakly.[83] He applauded the win but tempered any enthusiasm about what a black majority would be able to accomplish. "What a government can do to create jobs is very limited," he explained.[84]

By 1993 Dallas County had lost nearly 13 percent of its population compared to 1980, a drop that reflected the closing of Craig Air Force Base and the Alabama Black Belt's weak economy. One in eight people in the job market could not find jobs, and unemployment ran at least five points above the national average. Although manufacturing workers were the best paid locally, they still made "considerably less" than comparable workers in the rest of Alabama and the nation. Meanwhile, "poorly educated and untrained workers" made up the majority of the local workforce. An independent report assessing the area's economic health found three factors standing in the way of Dallas County's potential for economic development: first, an unskilled labor force; second, an underfunded and divided education system; and, finally, a history and continuing image of racial tension. The report castigated the county's four separate school systems— two public and two private—for fighting over "scarce resources" when the student population hardly justified two.[85] Most revealing, however, was the frank assessment by the person heading up the study. Admitting that Selma was a nice community to live in with potential for growth, he concluded that nothing would change "as long as those making public policy are more interested in their own personal agendas than in the community's best interests. The message from my point of view is economically, you don't have a lot of time."[86]

Black citizens assumed control of local government at a time when more than thirty-two hundred Dallas County families were receiving some sort of public assistance, nearly 50 percent of the area's children were living in poverty, and the drug war weighed heavily on poor neighborhoods.[87] In December 1994 a deputy sheriff stopped three young black men walking down an alley in a Craig Field neighborhood, allegedly looking for crack cocaine. A scuffle broke out between Robert Walker Jr. and Deputy Jay Dempsey. Although the details remained foggy, it was known that the deputy had fired several shots, and the eighteen-year-old had collapsed, dead.[88] Whether Walker had threatened Dempsey's life or Dempsey had acted recklessly, black residents knew that "a young black man had just been shot and killed by a white cop," explained *Montgomery Advertiser* reporter Al Benn.[89] The Coalition of Alabamians Reforming Education—a statewide organization that had emerged from Selma's school protests—sponsored another march from Selma to Montgomery in the wake of Walker's death. They called it "From the Graveyard to the Schoolyard," tying together violence and Alabama's substandard education system.[90] The schools that Walker had attended were severely underfunded—Dallas County ranked last out of Alabama's 129 school systems in local funding in 1992. But unemployment, drugs, and targeted law enforcement played an equally central role in his death.[91]

Black leaders yet again turned inward in their search for a solution. Councilwoman Sewell organized "Save Our Male Students Day" for Selma High School's young men after Walker's death and a string of other shootings. Over five hundred students spent the day at George Wallace Community College listening to motivational speakers talk about AIDS, juvenile crime laws, and drug abuse. "We want to put them on track, get them focused," Sewell explained.[92] A few days later, the Black Leadership Summit sponsored a community forum to discuss "critical issues," including "black-on-black and youth crime, education, housing, spiritual and moral confusion, economic development, voter apathy and political divisiveness."[93] History had made clear that white business leaders, the state, and the federal government would not be coming to the rescue, so concerned black Selmians worked to do what they could from within, using whatever resources were available.[94]

No Jobs, No Justice, No Welfare

On a national level, President Bill Clinton's campaign promise in 1992 to "end welfare as we know it" ominously pointed to more hard days ahead for Black Belt residents. Since the late 1960s, a conservative backlash had methodically dismantled social programs and the country's safety net for its poor, sick, and elderly residents. Following a decade of Ronald Reagan's and George H. W. Bush's conservative policies, the Democrat Clinton pulled himself into office on a reputation for moderation and pragmatism, offering a new, centrist approach to politics.[95] Conservatives had long accused the nation's welfare system of fostering dependency and failing to encourage poor people to work. In 1994 Republicans mounted a united campaign known as their "Contract with America" and captured control of Congress, with mastermind Newt Gingrich at the helm.[96] The new conservative majority enthusiastically took up Clinton's promise of welfare reform as a chance to dismantle the long-standing system of government assistance to the poor. In 1996 Clinton signed the Personal Responsibility and Work Opportunity Act, instituting work requirements and a five-year time limit on aid for welfare recipients.[97]

The conservative social policies passed in the halls of Congress looked very different on the ground in Dallas County. Craig's closing, Reagan's economic reforms, and globalization had decimated the Alabama Black Belt. The unemployment rate consistently broke double digits. Those numbers included only people who were still looking for work, not those who had dropped out in frustration. A large number of Dallas County residents owed their livelihood to government transfer payments, making the local economy equally dependent.[98] Since 1992 the Department of Human Resources' Job Opportunity for Basic Skills (JOBS) program had been working with a select group of welfare recipients to educate and train them and help them find jobs.[99] Three years later, 341 local JOBS women had found employment.[100] But the changes in 1996 required all participants—not just those best positioned and able—to hold a job after two years of aid. As Dallas County's Department of Human Resources administrators saw it, welfare reform left them with "a tough job that they can't handle alone."[101]

Jamie Wallace, the president of the Chamber of Commerce, laid out the biggest question regarding welfare reform for the *Selma Times-Journal*: "In Alabama counties where you already have double digit unemployment the question is where do you find jobs to put these people to work?" To do so, Dallas County would need to create approximately two thousand additional jobs, and that number did not include jobs for new graduates and others. Wallace criticized Congress's welfare reform legislation for failing to come "to the real world like Dallas County" and talk to those administering local programs. What legislators saw as reform in Washington, D.C., made no sense in the Alabama Black Belt.[102]

The local Department of Human Resources understood that the switch to Temporary Assistance to Needy Families from the old system of Aid to Families with Dependent Children on December 1, 1996, marked the beginning of a race against time. From that date, welfare recipients had sixty months of aid, and no more. "If you're forcing people to go to work—if you're talking about forcing people to meet these work requirements then you have to be looking at providing [jobs]," director James Ware explained. Then, even if there were enough jobs, there were transportation and childcare costs to consider. Ware also warned that some welfare recipients could never become self-sufficient owing to limited abilities or other circumstances. He expressed concern that the reforms would fall hardest on the black residents, who, because of a history of Jim Crow and unequal opportunities, made up the majority of aid recipients.[103]

After the voting rights movement in 1965, many black Dallas County residents had placed their faith in the federal government as a new ally in the long fight for political and economic justice; by the mid-1990s, decades of cuts to social programs had made it clear to African Americans that the federal government would provide little if any support. In 1996 welfare reform balanced the national budget on the backs of the country's neediest citizens. It did this without addressing the underlying structural issues that kept the majority of black Dallas County residents unemployed, undereducated, and impoverished. While the Sunbelt South flourished with defense contracts, military bases, interstate highways, and skilled workforces, the rural Black Belt struggled as globalization sucked up scarce jobs and federal spending came in the form of transfer payments.

Mobilizing the Past

The decades following the voting rights movement had not delivered the "good freedom" that Joanne Bland's grandmother had promised.[104] But for all that Selma was lacking in resources and opportunities, it did have history. The Chamber of Commerce had first attempted to capitalize on Selma's role in the Civil War and civil rights movement after the closing of Craig Air Force Base. By the 1990s historical tourism had taken off as a revenue source. But dredging up jagged, raw pasts brought more than just tourism dollars. As had happened with regard to the twenty-fifth anniversary of Bloody Sunday, historical memory became a potent tool for political mobilization.[105] Fierce, bitter political organizing had deepened the rift between black and white Selma. On one side stood Smitherman and backers like Cecil Williamson, and on the other the Chestnut, Sanders, and Sanders law firm, with Rose Sanders and her many organizations. A number of black and white Selmians fell into the middle, but the heated rivalry between the two extremes drowned out more moderate voices. In the mine-filled political terrain of Selma, remembering the Civil War and the civil rights movement became a matter of white history versus black history, as well as a battle between whites and blacks for political control.

In the early 1990s, Rose Sanders, county commissioner Perry Varner, and activists Marie Foster, Amelia Boynton, Albert Turner, and others decided to start a voting rights museum. They hoped that history could also be a way to mobilize Selma's black community. A museum first needed a physical home, and raising funds proved a prodigious undertaking. Their first attempt to purchase a building fell through, but it turned out that all the group needed was a little luck and some political rivalry. White commissioner Deans Barber owned the building at 1012 Water Avenue—the former headquarters of the local white Citizens' Council. While the museum group was searching for a location, Mayor Smitherman, in his typical blustery fashion, did or said something that infuriated Barber. Choosing the sweetest revenge he could, Barber called up Rose Sanders and the museum committee and offered them the building at the cost of taking over the mortgage. "And that's how we started the museum," Sanders recalled. By November 1991 Selma's new civil rights museum had found a home.[106]

The National Voting Rights Museum and Institute (NVRMI) grew from "a truly grassroots effort," explained Joanne Bland, its first director. Black Belt activists invested their sweat and labor to build a museum from scratch. Marie Foster, Hank Sanders, Perry Varner, and Amelia Boynton curated exhibits that showcased the Selma movement and black history. They relied on the many services of the local Walmart to copy and frame photos and build displays. Through it all, Bland was the glue that held the museum together. She was working as the director of MOMS when the NVRMI first opened its doors in 1992, but she moved her entire operation—a computer, a phone, a desk, and files—into the museum's red-carpeted lobby to unlock the door of 1012 Water Avenue for visitors. "I loved that little museum," she explained.[107] In 1993 she got some help from Sam Walker, a native of Selma who returned home to visit and stayed to become the museum's other biggest advocate.[108]

At the museum's grand opening in March 1993, Rose Sanders announced that "the museum will explore the past and will also focus on how the past can make life better for us all in the future." The NVRMI put forward the stories of the local men and women on the front lines of the voting rights struggle. "Heroes" and "She-roes" were celebrated in living-history exhibits, dedicated to recognizing and recording the memories of movement veterans. Every March, the annual Bridge Crossing Jubilee brought thousands of people from across the country to Selma over a weekend to commemorate the voting rights movement.[109] Meanwhile, the museum became the base for existing groups like BBACC and MOMS and for new organizations like the 21st Century Youth Leadership Movement, the youth wing of the Alabama New South Coalition.[110] It wasn't unusual to find a table set up outside the museum's doors with volunteers helping people register to vote.[111] The NVRMI took up the dual mission of preserving history and organizing for change. Its organizers were even willing to turn down outside funding to ensure that the museum could act in whichever ways it saw fit.[112]

The NVRMI became a hub for black self-help projects. Museum coordinator Sam Walker started the Teens in Crises, Triumphantly Addressing Crime project. Four days a week, the young men in the program worked half a day and studied for the other half, receiving a fifty-dollar paycheck each week. The program helped the teens deal with "problems of low self-esteem, negative peer pressure and miseducation" that hurt them and their communities. "Making the right moves, the right choices, can lead to a victory over crime, apathy and a digressive community," Walker explained.[113] Personal responsibility was a mantra that had gained popularity across black America. In October 1995 sixty black men from Selma joined the Million Man March in Washington, D.C., to promote black unity and self-help.[114] Seven hundred people gathered outside the museum for a local march one month later, pledging to support black businesses, avoid violence, and "improve themselves spiritually, morally, mentally, socially, politically, and economically."[115]

But the NVRMI was not the only organization that turned to history for tourism dollars and political mobilization.[116] In the late 1960s, local white boosters transformed one of Selma's antebellum Greek Revival mansions into a lavish period house they named Sturdivant Hall. By the mid-1970s, Sturdivant had become the centerpiece of the annual Historic Pilgrimage, which sold the magnificence of historic homes and a romanticized version of the Old South to tourists.[117] Then, in 1987, the Black Belt's antebellum history gained a new platform when the Kiwanis Club staged the first reenactment of the Battle of Selma.[118] Throughout the weekend, Nathan Bedford Forrest's Confederate troops faced Yankee soldiers under the direction of James H. Wilson, and costumed guests danced at Sturdivant Hall's "antebellum" ball.[119]

Though not as large as the NVRMI's jubilee celebration, the Battle of Selma reenactment became a staple of the city's tourism calendar.[120] The local chapters of the Sons of Confederate Veterans and the United

Daughters of the Confederacy rallied behind the event. Cecil Williamson, who periodically served as a city councilman, and Patricia Godwin, a white housewife whom the Southern Poverty Law Center later labeled "a hard-line neo-Confederate activist," became outspoken advocates of a romanticized version of Civil War history. "We are foolish indeed in Selma, if we do not emphasize all of our history to get tourist dollars into this city," Williamson explained. As a minister, local official, and later chair of the Dallas County Republicans, Williamson actively mobilized Confederate history to help champion conservative causes.[121]

Each year, the annual reenactments of the Bridge Crossing Jubilee and the Battle of Selma celebrated Selma's past, but they overlapped about as much as a Sunday morning church service did with a juke joint on Saturday night. White Selma residents stayed home when black citizens marched across the Edmund Pettus Bridge with a renewed call for justice. Meanwhile, few if any local black residents came out to the battlefield a month later to watch the cannons and smoke of Confederate and Yankee troops. Here, states' rights and privatization—the children of segregation—drew the most cheers. Elaborately costumed guests at the Sturdivant ball twirled in an antebellum house where the tour mentioned slavery only once and then called enslaved men and women "servants." For the NVRMI and the Sons and Daughters of the Confederacy, remembering the past became another way to organize for political power in the present.[122]

Black Farmers Lawsuit

For all that had gone wrong since the closing of Craig Air Force Base, one bright spot came for black farmers at the very end of the century. Thousands of black farmers had been forced off the land during the agricultural revolution that had begun in the 1930s. Federal agricultural programs that were supposed to aid farmers systematically discriminated against black farmers. A class-action lawsuit filed by black attorneys from across the South—including the Chestnut, Sanders, and Sanders law firm—won some redress. In the *Pigford v. Glickman* decision in 1999, the USDA agreed to a multimillion-dollar settlement with black farmers. The plaintiffs included twenty-eight Dallas County farmers and 152 Alabamians.[123] In November 1998 hundreds of black farmers from across the South gathered in Selma at the black Elks Club to hear the terms of the proposed settlement. All farmers who could verify that they had filed a complaint against the USDA between 1983 and 1997 were eligible for $50,000 or more, plus debt forgiveness.[124]

The settlement came too late for most of the black families who had worked Dallas County's land over the past fifty years. Discrimination and limited capital had forced the majority of black farmers from the land well before 1983.[125] By 1997 black farmers operated only 83 of Dallas County's 435 remaining farms. Their combined 9,439 acres amounted to only 4.8 percent of all farmland in the county.[126] Calvin Strong belonged to one of the lucky farm families in Dallas County that had survived. The Strong uncles, brothers, and cousins grew peas, beans, watermelons, greens, and other vegetables on their three hundred acres of land. After having been denied loans at the local USDA office for farm equipment in the past, the Strong family planned to invest their settlement money in implements and irrigation. "We're hopeful that the opportunities will come to us," said Strong. Thirty-five years after the voting rights movement, African Americans in Dallas County, like Strong, had a long list of things they were still waiting for.[127]

Black citizens finally won control of local governing bodies in the closing decade of the twentieth century, after thirty years of litigation and white resistance. "But economic power? It's still in white hands, and a lot of those white hands are not exactly reaching out to shake the black hands," NVRMI director Joanne Bland explained. It was now clear that the vote on its own was not enough to bring economic justice. "You must understand, Selma is still Selma. We're still chasing the dream, and we're still behind," she summed up.[128] Political rancor made dreams of progress seem very far away. The school crisis had deepened feelings of distrust and bitterness between black and white Selmians, and white civic leaders' continuing efforts to keep power out of the hands of African Americans had only made matters worse. To many in Selma, it seemed that Mayor Smitherman and attorney and activist Rose Sanders, on opposite ends of Selma's political extremes, were in a knock-down, drag-out fight for power. All of this came to a head in a battle over who would be Selma's first mayor of the twenty-first century.

INTERLUDE

Joe Gotta Go

Back in 1964 the young and ambitious Joe T. Smitherman had orches-
trated a contentious overthrow of Selma's old guard when he unseated
Chris Heinz as mayor. For three decades afterward, Mayor Smitherman
masterfully tended and cultivated his position as Selma's political kingpin. As
one reporter put it, he "wound up redefining 'political establishment' in
Selma." Smitherman renounced his segregationist past when black voters
became an increasingly important part of the electorate. He made much
to-do about paving all of the city's streets and appointing African Americans as city department heads. He held barbecues in black neighborhoods
and made regular appearances at the black Elks Club, cultivating relationships.[1] Throughout the years, black candidates had attempted to unseat the
mayor but came up short owing to a combination of Smitherman's politick-
ing and low turnout among black voters.

James Perkins Jr., a businessman and Selma native, emerged as the
mayor's most formidable and determined challenger. Perkins had cut his
teeth in politics as campaign manager for F. D. Reese in the latter's run
for mayor in 1984. Perkins decided to run for the position himself in 1991

under the slogan "Moving Forward, United." He pledged to prioritize economic expansion and "real issues" over "political struggles." It was a similar strategy to the election of 1984, when Reese and Perkins attempted to downplay race to win white votes.[2] That approach failed in 1992 as well when Smitherman won reelection with the help of absentee ballots. But Perkins, undeterred, entered the race again in 1996.[3] Feeling more pressure on this second go-around, the mayor accused Perkins of being in league with Rose Sanders, the political nemesis of white Selma. When twenty-five cans of spray paint were discovered in Hank and Rose Sanders's van after the mayor's campaign signs were vandalized, Smitherman took this as verification "that Rose Sanders is running Perkins's mayoral campaign."[4] Perkins put up a good fight, and only a 371-vote majority returned Smitherman to office at August's election.[5]

The standoff grew more heated over the next four years.[6] Cecil Williamson, a vocal conservative, united with Mayor Smitherman, desperately fighting to keep political control in white hands. Williamson published an editorial in which he told a fable of how the sheep (black citizens) and the cattle (white citizens) lived harmoniously in Selma until "a pack of jackals masquerading as sheep" (Rose and Hank Sanders) came to town. Local historian Alston Fitts accused Williamson of utter absurdity. Although Selmians faced serious problems, Fitts argued that no solution was possible "by demonizing our opponents, whether they be black or white, sheep or cattle."[7] But pleas for reason fell on deaf ears. In a city council meeting soon afterward, the council president, Carl Morgan, tried to silence Rose Sanders by shouting, "Shut up!" She then retaliated by attempting to snatch Morgan's gavel away from him.[8]

Fanning the flames of political rivalry, the mayor then filed a complaint against Senator Hank Sanders with the Alabama Ethics Commission, accusing him of "unethical use of public funds."[9] He charged that the state senator had used his chairmanship of the Senate budget committee to channel excessive amounts of money to his wife's civic projects.[10] But the attorney general deflated Smitherman's crusade. He refused to open an investigation against Sanders, finding no "credible allegation of criminal wrongdoing."[11] The same could not be said for Selma's city officials. Shortly after Sanders's name was cleared, Selma's police chief, city clerk, and assistant building inspector—a nephew of the mayor—resigned or were fired. Allegations of the misuse of hundreds of thousands of dollars of public funds had led to investigations by the Federal Bureau of Investigation, the Internal Revenue Service, and other bodies.[12] One year later, Smitherman himself appeared in front of the Alabama Ethics Commission on charges of inappropriate use of city-owned vehicles. He was fined $4,000.[13] "Imagine the kind and number of stories which would have appeared if I and/or my wife had been anywhere remotely connected to the widespread theft in City Hall," Hank Sanders reservedly commented.[14]

When James Perkins Jr. announced his third attempt at the mayor's office, he returned to the war zone of Selma politics. His "Moving Forward, United," campaign again called for education and economic development, as well as "truth and reconciliation" to build stronger community bonds. "Know this," he told a crowd of supporters at city hall. "No one, I mean no one, controls me. Not my mother, not my father, not city hall, not Chestnut, Sanders and Pettaway Law Firm—no one controls Perkins."[15] Two other black candidates, Yusuf Salaam and Edward Maull, also entered the race for mayor.[16]

During the first summer of the new century, the air hung thick with accusations of voter fraud, vandalism, and everything in between. Cecil Williamson took charge of policing voter registration, something he had perfected back in the election of 1984. He filed complaints against the chairwoman of the board of registrars (Synethia Pettaway, the sister of James Perkins) and Rose Sanders, accusing them of registering to vote at city addresses and not their actual residences in the county.[17] Williamson also represented Mayor Smitherman as a manager of absentee voting, issuing more charges of fraud against black citizens.[18] Alabama's attorney general resolutely avoided the mine-ridden ground of Selma's politics, refusing to send election observers and claiming that his office was not a law enforcement agency.[19]

On August 22, 2000, Selma's citizens went to the polls to make their decision.[20] The vote yet again came down to absentee ballots. Perkins maintained a lead with 3,735 votes to Smitherman's 3,311 in the city ballot boxes until the absentee ballots came in. Then Smitherman vaulted ahead with 4,065 votes, or 46 percent of the vote, over Perkins's 43 percent. A runoff election was scheduled for September 12.[21] The "mayoral campaign will turn ugly fast," a *Selma Times-Journal* reporter predicted. "Smitherman won't take the lead in attacking Perkins; and Perkins won't take the lead in attacking Smitherman," he wrote. "Rather, supporters of both candidates will drop everything they're doing and sling mud in every direction they turn."[22] The forecast proved all too true.

While Perkins publicly maintained his distance from the Sanderses, the "Joe Gotta Go" campaign organized by Rose Sanders, the ANSC, and the NVRMI was vital to his success. To encourage black voters to support the same candidate and avoid splitting the black vote, a cadre of black citizens bombarded Selma's streets with the message that Smitherman's time was up. Joanne Bland, the NVRMI director, remembered grabbing her "Joe Gotta Go" sign at lunchtime and joining the crowd of activists at the foot of the Edmund Pettus Bridge, waving and yelling at the cars driving by.[23] The Joe Gotta Go activity only gave Mayor Smitherman another reason to accuse Perkins of being in the Sanderses's pocket.

Then all hell broke loose at the end of August when a car with a "Joe Gotta Go" sign parked in front of the Chestnut, Sanders, and Sanders law firm was doused with gasoline and set on fire. The resulting whirlwind of fanatical accusations highlighted how the mayoral runoff had become yet another battle in the war between Mayor Smitherman and the Sanderses. The Sanderses blamed the car burning on the mayor and Williamson, calling it a political fear tactic and accusing them of fearmongering to rally white votes. Williamson then suggested that the Sanderses had set the car on fire themselves. "If our political opponents did this, it sure is an expensive publicity stunt," he remarked. Smitherman accused the Joe Gotta Go campaign of creating a hateful atmosphere in the city.[24] A political scientist from the University of Alabama ventured to opine that Selma's mayoral race was about racial politics, not concrete issues.[25] One of Smitherman's campaign posters showed the truth of this assessment: "Joe Gotta Stay! YOU DON'T WANT ROSE RUNNING SELMA!" Nowhere was Perkins, the actual candidate, mentioned.[26]

On September 12, the campaign circus came to an end when Perkins finally defeated Mayor Smitherman. He won by 1,336 votes, giving him 58 percent of the vote, making him Selma's first black mayor.[27] The combined efforts of Perkins's "Moving Forward, United," approach and the Joe Gotta Go campaign secured his victory. Perkins described them as working "separately but in concert."[28] Smitherman agreed, blaming Rose Sanders for his loss. "It's almost like I was running against the whole world," the mayor claimed. "They say Joe gotta go and Joe's gone."[29]

On the first weekend in October, thousands of black Selmians celebrated their victory. After parading through the downtown, the crowd amassed at Memorial Stadium—where the Citizens' Council and Farm Bureau used to host rallies of thousands—to watch the inauguration of the city's first black mayor. The Selma High School choir marked the occasion by singing "Lift Every Voice and Sing," the anthem of black America.[30] The song matched the feelings of Selma's black residents; thirty-five years after the voting rights movement, black Selmians had finally won the political representation they had been fighting for.

Epilogue

Fifty years after the voting rights movement, Barack Obama, the nation's first black president, returned to Selma to pay homage. From a platform in front of the Edmund Pettus Bridge on that warm March weekend, Obama called Selma one of the "places and moments in America where this nation's destiny has been decided." He praised the actions of those, like Amelia Boynton, who made up the movement and compelled President Lyndon Johnson to act. The events that transpired in Selma were the essence of America. "What greater form of patriotism is there than the belief that America is not yet finished," Obama asked, "that each successive generation can look upon our imperfections and decide that it is in our power to remake this nation to more closely align with our highest ideals?" The Voting Rights Act, a product of campaigns like the one in Selma, opened the way for black Americans—and all Americans—to inhabit boardrooms, courtrooms, and political offices.[1]

But celebrating the successes of Selma was not enough. Two years earlier, the Supreme Court had struck down Section 5 of the Voting Rights Act in its *Shelby v. Holder* decision. This section was the legal grounding on which the Chestnut, Sanders, and Sanders law firm had successfully waged war against at-large election districts and other Black Belt schemes to dilute black voting power.[2] "If Selma taught us anything, it's that our work is never done," the president stated. "The American experiment in self-government gives work and purpose to each generation." Obama urged the one hundred members of Congress who were in Selma that day to gather their colleagues back in Washington and restore the Voting Rights Act. Meanwhile, he encouraged Americans to take up the work—from the broken criminal justice system to police brutality, from poverty to unequal wages—and feel "the fierce urgency of now."

The problems confronting Selma, however, exceeded President Obama's narrative of American becoming, his empowering and upbeat message "that America is a constant work in progress."[3] As forty thousand people congregated in Selma that weekend, the poverty rate in Dallas County lingered at 31.3 percent, among the very worst in the state, along with the rest of the Alabama Black Belt. Meanwhile, 49.6 percent of the county's children lived in poverty. Unemployment was at 13.1 percent, and that number didn't include the hundreds of people who had stopped even looking for jobs. With only 14.2 percent of the county's residents holding bachelor's degrees, the skilled jobs that were available remained vacant because no one had the training to fill them.[4] Abandoned, boarded-up houses and terrifying gun violence were the norm in the city's poorest neighborhoods.[5] President Obama had applauded the power of voting rights at the same time as he urged the nation to continue the work of becoming a better, more just America. There in Selma, fifty years later, the work left to be done was tremendous, and the triumphal legacy of voting rights was not so certain.

It was also not clear that doing more could ever be enough for Selma. Black residents had held out hope for the possibilities of political control, but fifteen years of black mayors—first James Perkins and then George Evans—had not begun to repair the economic straits of the Alabama Black Belt at the dawn of the twenty-first century. The legacies of cotton and white supremacy had made poverty endemic in Dallas County, like kudzu vines in a watermelon patch. For one short decade after the passage of the Voting Rights Act, it had seemed as though the vote could dismantle this world of disparity. Then, during the last quarter of the twentieth century, the federal government, followed by industry, all but abandoned the Alabama Black Belt. The closing of Craig Air Force Base took with it millions of dollars, hundreds of people, and dozens of local businesses. Black Belt industries and jobs disappeared overseas just as Reaganomics shredded the social safety net. Selma's first African American mayors took charge of a city plagued by economic problems much bigger than itself.

But Bloody Sunday and the Voting Rights Act of 1965 had cemented Selma and voting rights together in a grand story of American progress and democracy, making Selma into a symbol of the civil rights movement's overarching success. Historian Taylor Branch authored an epic and beautifully told trilogy on the United States during the years of Martin Luther King Jr., best-selling books that historian John Dittmer called "most important" in shaping Americans' understanding of the civil rights movement.[6] In the opening paragraph of his final volume, Branch wrote, "Every ballot is a piece of nonviolence, signifying hard-won consent to raise politics above firepower and bloody conquest." Selma, he goes on, was "the last revolution" to secure this right, the battle that made possible the guarantees of the Fifteenth Amendment.[7] And he was right. The Voting Rights Act did extend the power of the ballot to American citizens regardless of race. Southern voting rolls exploded with newly registered African Americans, and over time black elected officials began showing up to work in city council chambers and county courthouses.

Unfortunately, that was only part of the story. African Americans had never seen the vote as an end in itself. It was the brick and mortar needed to build a community with well-funded schools and qualified teachers, accessible mortgages and loans, good jobs, self-sufficiency, and security. All of these things—political representation, economic opportunity and independence, quality education, and hope for a better life—were part and parcel of what NVRMI director Joanne Bland called the "good freedom."[8] While the vote brought some political power, it did not come with the rest of what African Americans wanted. As SNCC's Courtland Cox had said, the vote was "necessary but not sufficient." Only by overlooking these parallel demands, only by focusing solely on achieving voting rights, did Selma become a triumphant story. It is this voting rights story that is told again and again, now even as a blockbuster movie, simply and appropriately called *Selma*.[9]

The Edmund Pettus Bridge has become a site of pilgrimage, a place where politicians, activists, students, and ministers come to cast themselves within the history and legacy of the fight for voting rights.[10] Obama claimed that legacy of the civil rights movement, situating himself as the inheritor of the struggle to make American democracy truly democratic. But there's a saying in Selma that Selma did more for civil rights than civil rights did for Selma. The triumphal narrative of voting rights is part of that problem.

In all of the iconic images, the blockbuster movies, the presidential homages, there is little mention of the economic objectives that had always been the other half of the local freedom struggle to black residents. Those parallel demands for equity in jobs, loans, and land remained pressing long after African Americans in Dallas County could exercise their right to vote. Missing from the triumphal narrative is the dramatic transformation that fundamentally altered the economic landscape of the Black Belt. In the transitions from cotton to cattle, from industry to unemployment checks, black citizens perpetually found themselves on the losing end of economic change. Many had neither savings nor a high school education to rely on. At the start of the twenty-first century, nearly four decades of federal divestment and globalization had sapped Dallas County of jobs. Now the major presence of the government came in the form of disability checks, housing projects, and SNAP cards. The political rights that black Dallas County citizens had shed their blood for in 1965 could not alone undo this legacy of economic disparity. When African Americans finally secured meaningful political representation in the last decade of the twentieth century, it could not single-handedly fix a resegregated school system, the steady flow of jobs overseas, and the long miles to the nearest interstate. As politicians— even the United States' first black president—come and go, the harsh economic realities of Selma carry on unchanged.

Sitting on the platform with President Obama that March day was Congresswoman Terri Sewell, a Selma native and the representative of Alabama's Seventh Congressional District. Sewell had been the first black valedictorian at Selma High School when she graduated in 1982. She continued on to Princeton, then to Oxford, and finally to Harvard Law School, becoming a hometown star, proof that children from Selma, black or white, could be something. Sewell spoke to the crowds as she introduced John Lewis, her fellow congressman and a veteran of Bloody Sunday. "My Selma was fully integrated," Sewell recalled. "My Selma nurtured me. My Selma led me to believe that a little black girl could achieve any of her dreams."[11]

In the Selma that Sewell grew up, its citizens, black and white, were reckoning with what inclusion meant in the years after the voting rights movement. Her parents, both Black Belt natives, moved to Selma with their daughter in 1966 when Andrew Sewell became the head basketball coach at R. B. Hudson High School. They took up what Nancy Sewell described as the Booker T. Washington approach: "Let your bucket down wherever you are and try to make a difference." When school desegregation came in the 1970s, Nancy Sewell became the assistant librarian and Andrew Sewell the assistant coach to their white counterparts at the new Selma High School. Coach Sewell filed a suit contending that he had been denied promotion because of his race. It took six years, but the courts ruled in his favor. The Sewells eventually became the head coach and head librarian. In Selma's polarized climate, the Sewells tried to build bridges. "They were waiting for somebody to reach out," Nancy Sewell explained with regard to white Selmians.

Terri Sewell and her twin brothers attended Selma's integrated public schools. Terri had been placed in a lower level at Cedar Park Elementary School, but when she moved up to Westside Middle School, Nancy Sewell visited the counselors to make sure her daughter would be placed in the most advanced level. At the award ceremony at the end of ninth grade, Terri and another white student were named the most outstanding students, even though Terri had the highest marks in math, English, and most of the other subjects. Nancy Sewell remembered her daughter crying all night and then swearing that she would put her achievements so far out of reach in high school that there could be no debate over who was the most outstanding. "Sure enough," Nancy Sewell explained, "when she graduated from high school, there was no tying."[12]

Back in 2007 Terri Sewell had been in the pews of Brown Chapel, her home church, when Obama claimed the torch from the civil rights generation. "The questions that I have today, is what's called of us in this Joshua generation?," she heard him ask. "What do we do in order to fulfill that legacy, to fulfill the obligations and the debt that we owe to those who allowed us to be here today?" In that church that she had grown up in, she felt that the question from her former classmate at Harvard was directed at her.[13] Her mother had fought hard to become the first African American councilwoman on Selma's very first black-majority city council in the early 1990s, and Sewell knew the shoulders she stood on. So she entered the race for Congress and, with a combination of Black Belt and Ivy League connections, won.[14]

Terri Sewell addressed her hometown as the first African American congresswoman from Alabama, fifty years after the voting rights movement. The movement had ushered in great changes, and Sewell had benefited from them perhaps as much as any black Selmian could. However, since those days, Selma High School had been resegregated, and the debate team that had started Sewell on her way was gone. "I don't know if my old high school could produce me anymore," she admitted not long afterward.[15] The missing debate team wasn't even the tip of the iceberg; deep poverty, drugs, nonexistent jobs, and welfare were the daily problems that black Selmians faced. A year after the fiftieth anniversary, a reporter from the *Guardian* spent two days with a man dealing drugs in some of Selma's roughest and poorest neighborhoods. The dealer had come to Selma as a teenager in the mid-1990s when his crack-addicted mother brought him to live with his grandmother. "I want to get out of this life, but to do what?," he explained. "Ain't no jobs here. I got no skills and four felonies, who is gonna hire me?"[16]

The causes of and solutions to the Alabama Black Belt's dismal economic realities seemed so elusive, so unsolvable a decade and a half into the twenty-first century. Meanwhile, fierce factions and political rancor continued to hang over Selma, all but consuming municipal politics. As the rival factions thundered louder and louder, many of Selma's residents felt as though their needs and the best interests of the city had gotten lost in the storm.[17] They worried about how their part-time job at Walmart or McDonald's was going to pay for the rent, medical bills, groceries, and school supplies. Parents worried about how safe their children were in the city's streets, where the murder rate was more than ten times the national average.[18] Many questioned how business could grow when bitter arguments—brandished for political purposes, personal power, and grandstanding in the name of justice—echoed in city hall and on radio talk shows. The fighting and fussing drowned out the concerns of those buried under the daily challenges of Dallas County's daunting economic woes.

Figuring out a genuine solution to the Black Belt's deeply rooted troubles was a daunting and elusive task. "The civil rights battles our parents' generation faced," Terri Sewell explained, "have led to the economic battles our generation is facing."[19] And battles they were. On an almost entirely abandoned block in Selma, Council McReynolds lived in one of the two houses that weren't boarded up or falling down. He had lived in the city all fifty-plus years of his life and watched the factories pack up, the jobs disappear, and the drugs and guns move in. "Selma ain't like the movie. There everyone is shown working together and putting the past behind them," he explained. "But the reality is Selma has been left behind, and folks are certainly not working together." Fifty years later, Joanne Bland's good freedom was still a long way off.[20]

NOTES

Introduction

1 Gutterman, "Obama Fought"; Remnick, *Bridge*.

2 Much of the scholarship about the Selma movement focuses on Dr. Martin Luther King Jr. and the nationally oriented goals of the Southern Christian Leadership Conference, which sought to secure voting rights legislation. This body of scholarship tells only an abbreviated version of the black freedom struggle in Selma, one that focuses so intently on the campaign for voting rights that it misses the battle for economic opportunities and indepen-dence that African Americans fought simultaneously. Often climaxing with the victorious passing of the Voting Rights Act, scholarship focusing on Selma "the moment" tells a triumphal story in which Selma becomes a monument to the justice and righteousness of American democracy. See Branch, *At Canaan's Edge*; Branch, *Pillar of Fire*; Eagles, *Outside Agita-tor*; Fager, *Selma, 1965*; Garrow, *Bearing the Cross*; Garrow, *Protest at Selma*; Longnecker, *Selma's Peacemaker*; May, *Bending toward Justice*; Patterson, *Eve of Destruction*; Stanton, *From Selma to Sorrow*; Sheyann Webb, *Selma, Lord, Selma*. The most comprehensive study of Selma from its earliest days through the civil rights movement is Fitts, *Selma*. J. Mills Thornton examines in detail how municipal politics affected the voting rights movement in Selma; see Thornton, *Dividing Lines*.

3 Windham, *She*, 37.

4 The idea of the "long civil rights movement," put forward by historians such as Jacquelyn Dowd Hall and William Chafe, contends that African Americans' struggles for citizenship and justice extended well before and after the traditional civil rights movement and included demands for economic, sexual, and political as well as civil rights. Recent scholarship by Susan Youngblood Ashmore, Cynthia Griggs Fleming, and Hasan Kwame

Jeffries has extended the scope and timeline of the black freedom struggle in the Alabama Black Belt beyond a narrow focus on 1965 and voting rights. See Chafe, "Presidential Address"; Hall, "Long Civil Rights Movement"; Ashmore, *Carry It On*; Fleming, *Shadow of Selma*; Jeffries, *Bloody Lowndes*. Other excellent scholarship in this vein includes Brown, *Upbuilding Black Durham*; Chafe, *Civilities and Civil Rights*; Dittmer, *Local People*; Gilmore, *Defying Dixie*; Korstad, *Civil Rights Unionism*; McGuire, *Dark End of the Street*; Payne, *Light of Freedom*; Ransby, *Ella Baker*; Tyson, *Radio Free Dixie*.

5 The scholarship on urban studies and the Sunbelt South offers an explanation of why voting rights did not bring economic justice for African Americans in the Black Belt, exploring how unequal relations of power are inscribed in the regional and urban geography. See Jackson, *Crabgrass Frontier*; Kruse, *White Flight*; Lassiter, *Silent Majority*; Self, *American Babylon*; Sugrue, *Urban Crisis*. Bruce Schulman expands this framework to the Sunbelt South, examining how the unequal distribution of federal dollars intended to address the region's underdevelopment bolstered majority-white, urban areas while leaving the South's Black Belt in the shadows. Schulman, *Cotton Belt to Sunbelt*. During the 1980s political scientists and economists studied the uneven development taking place in the Sunbelt South. See Beaulieu, *Rural South in Crisis*; Falk and Lyson, *High Tech*; Lyson, *Two Sides*; Rosenfeld, *After the Factories*; Southern Growth Policies Board, *Halfway Home*.

Interlude: The Constitution of 1901

1 Hardy, *Selma*, 16; U.S. House of Representatives, "Haralson, Jeremiah," History, Art, and Archives, http://history.house.gov/people/ (accessed February 2, 2014); Historical Census Browser, University of Virginia, Geospatial and Statistical Data Center, 2004, http://mapserver.lib.virginia.edu /collections/ (accessed February 1, 2014).

2 U.S. House of Representatives, "Haralson, Jeremiah." During the Civil War, Selma had served as an arsenal for the Confederacy, manufacturing ammunition and artillery. The city was attacked by General James H. Wilson's troops on April 2, 1865, and Confederate General Nathan Bedford Forrest could not hold back Union troops. Wilson's troops burned the Confederate and private manufacturing facilities as well as much of the town. Rogers et al., *Alabama*, 195–196, 220–221; Hardy, *Selma*.

3 Douglass, quoted in U.S. House of Representatives, "Haralson, Jeremiah."

4 Schweninger and Fitts, "Haralson, Jeremiah," American National Bibliography Online, http://www.anb.org.proxy.lib.duke.edu/articles/04/04 -00466.html (accessed February 10, 2017).

5 Quote from Schweninger and Fitts, "Haralson, Jeremiah"; newspaper article, quoted in U.S. House of Representatives, "Haralson, Jeremiah." A

less radical amended version of Haralson's bill passed the state senate but failed when the Alabama legislature adjourned before the House of Representatives could vote on the act.

6 Foner, *Freedom's Lawmakers*, 94.

7 Quote from "Alabama," *Chicago Daily Tribune*, October 14, 1878; see also Schweninger and Fitts, "Haralson, Jeremiah," 37–38; Woodward, *New South*.

8 In the Compromise of 1877, Rutherford B. Hayes agreed to remove federal troops from the South in exchange for becoming president in the disputed election of 1876. The political bargain effectively ended Reconstruction. Woodward, *New South*, 20–21, 51.

9 When James Rapier won the Republican nomination in 1876, Haralson entered the race as an independent. A split vote and fraud allowed the white Democrat to win the election. U.S. House of Representatives, "Haralson, Jeremiah."

10 Perman, *Pursuit of Unity*.

11 For more on Populist organizing in Alabama, see Samuel Webb, *Two-Party Politics*; Rogers, *One-Gallused Rebellion*; Flynt, *Alabama*, 6, 11.

12 Hahn, *Nation under Our Feet*, 367.

13 "Large Meeting," *Selma Morning Times* (*SMT*), April 21, 1901.

14 W. Jackson, *Story of Selma*, 429; "Large Vote Polled," *SMT*, April 24, 1901.

15 Part of the power of Black Belt politicians came from the large numbers of black residents who were in practice kept from the polls through intimidation and violence, giving white voters inflated influence. Rogers et al., *Alabama*, 347–348, 412–413.

16 Flynt, *Alabama*, 8–9. For more on nonracial voting requirements adopted by southern states, see Alexander, *New Jim Crow*.

17 Reese, quoted in *Official Proceedings of the Constitutional Convention*, 1465, 3327, 3368.

18 Flynt, *Alabama*, 8–9.

19 "Public Speaking," *SMT*, November 9, 1901.

20 "The Election," *SMT*, November 12, 1901. Booker T. Washington and fourteen others—including Selma's Charles O. Boothe, William Pettiford, and R. B. Hudson—submitted a petition to the convention, asking that the black man, "a taxpayer and a worthy reliable citizen," have "a humble share in choosing those who shall rule over him." Riser, *Defying Disfranchisment*, 8–10; Washington, *Up from Slavery*; "To Members of the Alabama Constitutional Convention," Alabama Secretary of State Constitutional Convention Proceedings, SG 17778, Alabama Department of Archives and History, http://www.archives.alabama.gov/teacher /ccon/lesson3/doc2.html (accessed July 26, 2013); Fallin, *Uplifting the People*, 120.

21 "The Vote Tabulated," *SMT*, November 17, 1901.

22 "The State Canvassing Board . . ." *SMT*, November 22, 1901.

23 In November 1901, 9,871 black men and 2,524 white men were registered to vote on the county rolls. Rogers et al., *Alabama*, 346.

24 "The Blackbelt Counties . . . ," *SMT*, November 15, 1901; "The State Canvassing Board . . . ," *SMT*, November 22, 1901; Rogers et al., *Alabama*, 352–354.

25 "By Proclamation of . . . ," *SMT*, November 27, 1901.

26 "Poll Taxes in Dallas," *SMT*, February 10, 1902.

27 Quote from "Honest Election Methods," *SMT*, December 14, 1901.

28 Quote from "A Suggestion," *SMT*, March 13, 1902; see also "Honest Primaries and Elections," *SMT*, July 30, 1902.

29 "Dallas County People . . . ," *SMT*, May 10, 1901.

30 Haralson, quoted in Foner, *Freedom's Lawmakers*, 94.

Chapter 1: The World That Cotton Made

1 "First Open Boll Sent This Office," *SMT*, August 7, 1903; Historical Census Browser, University of Virginia, Geospatial and Statistical Data Center, 2004, http://mapserver.lib.virginia.edu/collections/.

2 Historical Census Browser, University of Virginia, Geospatial and Statistical Data Center, 2004, http://mapserver.lib.virginia.edu/collections/; "First Open Boll Sent This Office," *SMT*, August 7, 1903. In *Nature's Metropolis* William Cronon examines how economic demands of urban areas shaped the landscape of the surrounding hinterlands.

3 "First Open Boll Sent This Office," *SMT*, August 7, 1903.

4 Clark, *Pills, Petticoats, and Plows*, 28; "Selma, the Gem of All Alabama Cities," *SMT*, May 11, 1905.

5 Sisk, "Alabama Black Belt," 103–105.

6 Sisk, "Alabama Black Belt," 81.

7 Dattel, *Cotton and Race*, 294–297.

8 Few southern banks were operating in the wake of the Civil War, which tightened the availability of credit. Dattel, *Cotton and Race*, 304–310; Sisk, "Alabama Black Belt," 31–36.

9 Sisk, "Alabama Black Belt."

10 "First Open Boll Sent This Office," *SMT*, August 7, 1903.

11 "Brilliant Career of Boy Who Began Life Threading Needles for the Girls Sewing Class," *Selma Times-Journal* (*STJ*), May 1, 1921.

12 "First Open Boll Sent This Office," *SMT*, August 7, 1903; "First Bale to Selma Brings a Fancy Price at Exchange Today," *Selma Journal* (*SJ*), July 30, 1914.

13 Sisk, "Alabama Black Belt," 104.

14 "First Open Boll Sent This Office," *SMT*, August 7, 1903; People's Bank and Trust Company, *Historic Selma*.

15 As railroads grew in importance, R. H. and W. C. Agee and other wholesalers moved to new facilities directly alongside the railroad tracks. "To Move March the First," *SMT*, February 8, 1905.

16 Peck, "The Other 'Peculiar Institution.'"

17 "Mr. Eagle, . . . ," *SMT*, March 24, 1907; "City and Vicinity," *New York Times*, February 8, 1894; June Cohn, interview by the author, November 30, 2011; "75th Anniversary of Local Store Prods Memory," *STJ*, November 15, 1960.

18 "Services for Lee Adler at Four O'Clock," *STJ*, August 20, 1945; "History of Selma Jewry," folder: Jewish Temple Mishkan Israel, Old Depot Museum Archives (ODMA).

19 "The business section of the city . . . ,"*STJ*, September 10, 1934. For more on Jewish life in the South, see Evans, *Provincials*.

20 None of the city's remaining Jewish residents remembered in 2011 and 2012 experiencing discrimination in Selma, and they attended school and were friends with Protestant children. While a few Jewish clubs did exist, most local organizations had both Jewish and Protestant members. Unlike Birmingham or Montgomery, Selma was a small, more isolated town. It's likely that both the city's size and Jewish residents' loyalty to local customs of white supremacy helped support this somewhat atypical interchange among Jewish and Protestant residents.

21 Ellen Rush Sturdivant, "Memories of Old Church Street Church" prior to April 1940, folder: Church Street Methodist, ODMA.

22 "Chamber of Commerce Urges Solons Beat Soldier Bonus Bill," *STJ*, February 15, 1922.

23 Quote from June Cohn, interview by the author, November 30, 2011; see also "Brilliant Career of Boy Who Began Life Threading Needles for Girls Sewing Class," *STJ*, May 1, 1921.

24 Ellen Rush Sturdivant, "Memories of Old Church Street Church" [1940], folder: Church Street Methodist, ODMA; "Reciprocity Meeting Held," *SMT*, April 17, 1907; "Council of Dallas Co. Clubs to Be Organized Saturday," *STJ*, September 20, 1923.

25 "Selma's Financial Institution Solid," *STJ*, November 1, 1907; Moore, *History of Alabama*, 201; "Chamber of Commerce," *SMT*, August 20, 1902; "Buy a Bale Committee Is Well Received," *SJ*, September 18, 1914.

26 Fitts, *Selma: Bicentennial*, 159–161; "Old Court House for Sanitorium," *SJ*, January 13, 1911.

27 W. Jackson, *Story of Selma*, 461–475.

28 "A Disastrous Blaze," *SMT*, May 18, 1901.

29 Quote from Chamber of Commerce, "Selma and Dallas County" [ca. 1910], folder: Selma-General Information, ODMA. For more on cotton's influence in the Black Belt, see Aiken, *Cotton Plantation South*; Daniel, *Breaking the Land*; Dattel, *Cotton and Race*.

30 It's likely that working-class whites made up at most around 20 percent of the adult white population in Dallas County. The census of 1900 lists 1,375 wage earners over the age of sixteen (likely including some black workers) employed in manufacturing. The total white adult population in Dallas County was around 6,162 residents. Historical Census Browser, University

of Virginia, Geospatial and Statistical Data Center, 2004, http://mapserver
.lib.virginia.edu/collections/.

31 Chamber of Commerce, "Selma and Dallas County" [ca. 1910], folder:
Selma-General Information, ODMA.

32 "Machinists Get Raise," SMT, August 21, 1904; "The Southern Railway . . . ,"
SMT, September 20, 1901.

33 Sisk, "Alabama Black Belt," 112–113; Sanborn Fire Insurance Company,
Fire Insurance Maps.

34 M. Mitchell, "California Cotton Mill Memories," 29.

35 Jeff Mansell, "Milltown Minors: The Laboring Youth of Selma, Alabama,
1907–1915." Seminar paper, 1990. ODMA; For more about southern textile
workers, see Hall et al., Like a Family.

36 Quote from "Condition of the Mill District as They Exist Today," SMT,
February 3, 1908; see also M. Mitchell, "California Cotton Mill Memories,"
1–12.

37 Historical Census Browser, University of Virginia, Geospatial and Statistical Data Center, 2004, http://mapserver.lib.virginia.edu/collections/.

38 Hart, Land That Feeds Us, 261–262; Sisk, "Alabama Black Belt," 375.

39 "The Emigration Scheme," SMT, December 24, 1902.

40 Olde Towne Association, Tastes of Olde Selma, 1.

41 Susan Smith to Mallory and McLeod, August 29, 1896, folder: Letters,
1896, July–August, box 12, Washington M. Smith Papers, David M.
Rubenstein Rare Book and Manuscript Library, Duke University, Durham,
NC; John Moseley to Susan Smith, August 27, 1897; Susan Smith to Bill
Smith and Alfred Hunter, August 29, 1897; Mrs. Washington Smith to
B. F. Ellis and Son, September 8, 1897, all in folder: Letters 1897, June–
September, box 13, Washington M. Smith Papers, David M. Rubenstein
Rare Book and Manuscript Library, Duke University, Durham, NC.

42 Mark Schultz calls the unequal day-to-day interactions between black and
white residents that enforced white supremacy in rural areas a "culture
of personalism." See below for how threats of violence were an important
aspect of this system. Schultz, White Supremacy, 2–8, 15, 67, 88, 131.

43 Transcripts of the hearings of the Board of Railroad Wages and Working
Conditions, quoted in Arnesen, Brotherhoods of Color, 12; see also Shoemaker, White Court, 139–142.

44 Raper, Preface to Peasantry, 397–398; Reformed Presbyterian Church,
"Missionary Operations."

45 Historical Census Browser, University of Virginia, Geospatial and Statistical Data Center, 2004, http://mapserver.lib.virginia.edu/collections/.

46 Snyder, "Negro Migration," 26.

47 Robinson, Bridge across Jordan, 53–57; Dattel, Cotton and Race, 302–307.

48 Cobb, quoted in Shaw and Rosengarten, All God's Dangers, 146. For more
details of how sharecropping contracts limited black farmers, see the rest
of Cobb's account in Shaw and Rosengarten's book.

49 W. Edwards, *Twenty-Five Years*, xv.

50 "Emancipator Representative Visits Bullock County," *Emancipator*, December 8, 1917.

51 "The White Man's Ward," *SMT*, August 3, 1902. For a detailed analysis of how white supremacy operated in the rural Black Belt, see Schultz, *White Supremacy*.

52 Sisk, "Alabama Black Belt," 273–274.

53 C. Cobb, *This Nonviolent Stuff*, 6–11.

54 "Deputy Edwards Killed," *SMT*, April 30, 1901.

55 "The Deadly Work of the Mob . . . ," *SMT*, May 3, 1901.

56 "A Terrible Tragedy," *SMT*, May 3, 1901.

57 "Captured," *SMT*, May 4, 1901.

58 "The Deadly Work of the Mob . . . ," *SMT*, May 3, 1901.

59 Sisk, "Alabama Black Belt," 286.

60 Plessy v. Ferguson, 163 U.S. 537 (1896); Sullivan, *Lift Every Voice*, 1–2.

61 Schultz, *White Supremacy*, 2–8.

62 Woodward, *Strange Career of Jim Crow*; Foner, *Forever Free*, 207–208.

63 Quote from "The Laboring Men of Alabama," *SMT*, April 24, 1902.

64 "Shooting Scrape," *SMT*, April 24, 1902.

65 "The Laboring Men of Alabama," *SMT*, April 26, 1902.

66 Harper quoted in W. Jackson, *Story of Selma*, 443. Regulation emerged out of concern for meat quality, largely spawned by Upton Sinclair's exposé on the Chicago meat-packing industry. Sinclair, *Jungle*.

67 The *Selma Morning Times* lists Martin's first name as Miles, while the Selma, Alabama, city directory for 1909–1910 has it as Milas. "Mandamus in Market Case," *SMT*, January 4, 1905; R. L. Polk and Company, *City Directory, 1909–1910*; "He Gets License," *SMT*, July 6, 1905; "L. G. Clark Gets Place," *SMT*, December 21, 1905.

68 "Separate Cars on Union Street," *SMT*, December 8, 1906.

69 Quote from "Selmians to Ask that Races Be Separated in Local Street Cars," *SMT*, February 13, 1908; see also "Citizens Approve Separation of Races in Cars," *SMT*, May 29, 1908.

70 Letter to the editor, *SJ*, April 13, 1911; Sanborn Fire Insurance Company, *Fire Insurance Maps*; Fred Williams, interview by the author, September 18, 2012.

71 "They Must Move Elsewhere," *SMT*, August 11, 1905.

72 "Promiscuous Shooting Came Near Causing the Death of a White Woman Sunday Afternoon," *SMT*, September 24, 1901.

73 "White Boys Assault Negro," *SMT*, May 18, 1902.

74 "A Brutal Murder," *SMT*, May 20, 1902.

75 "Law Reigns Supreme in Dallas County," *SMT*, May 29, 1902.

76 Quote from "Wear Greater Selma Buttons," *SMT*, August 18, 1906. Historian Laura Edwards calls members of this class "best men." Edwards, *Gendered Strife and Confusion*, 230–238.

77 "An Appeal to Democrats," *SMT*, January 24, 1902.

78 "Separate Cars on Union Street," *SMT*, December 8, 1906; "East Selmians Want Electric Line Extended," *SJ*, June 18, 1908; "Dumping Grounds Abandoned," *STJ*, July 10, 1923.

79 Fred Williams, interview by the author, September 18, 2012; R. L. Polk and Company, *City Directory, 1909–1910*.

80 For more on African American institution building and community organizing from Reconstruction to the early years of Jim Crow, see Ayers, *New South*; Gilmore, *Gender and Jim Crow*; Hahn, *Nation under Our Feet*; Ortiz, *Emancipation Betrayed*.

81 Quote from "18th Annual Catalogue of Alabama Colored Baptist University, 1895–1896," Selma University Catalogues (SUC), reel 1; see also "Annual Catalogue of Alabama Colored Baptist University, 1902–1903," SUC, reel 1; Fallin, *Uplifting the People*, 85–89.

82 Knox Academy opened in 1874. U.S. Department of the Interior, National Park Service, "Civil Rights Movement in Selma"; Reformed Presbyterian Church, *Missionary Operations*; "Selma Negroes Observe Day of Emancipation," *STJ*, January 4, 1925.

83 U.S. Department of the Interior, National Park Service, "Civil Rights Movement in Selma."

84 Hamilton, *Beacon Lights*, 376–384.

85 R. L. Polk and Company, *City Directory, 1913–1914*.

86 "Annual Catalogue of Alabama Colored Baptist University, 1905–1906," SUC, reel 1.

87 Fallin, *Uplifting the People*, 148–156.

88 Quoted in Fallin, *Uplifting the People*, 147.

89 Hamilton, *Beacon Lights*, 376–384.

90 Pauline Anderson, interviewed in Vaughan, *Selma Campaign*, 78; Ward, "Black Hospital Movement."

91 "Negro Owns Selma's Richest Cotton Gin," *Jet*, December 23, 1965.

92 U.S. Department of the Interior, National Park Service, "Civil Rights Movement in Selma."

93 Yvonne Hatcher, interview by the author, December 12, 2011.

94 For more about African American aspirations after emancipation, see Hahn, *Nation under Our Feet*.

95 R. L. Polk and Company, *City Directory, 1913–1914*.

96 "Struck for Higher Wages," *SMT*, September 6, 1901; "Many Negroes before Court," *SMT*, June 24, 1910.

97 For more about the history of sexual assault of black women by white men and black women's resistance, see McGuire, *Dark End of the Street*; Schwalm, *Hard Fight*; White, *Ar'n't I a Woman?*

98 Quoted in Sisk, "Alabama Black Belt," 366; see also, "Negro Cooks," *SMT*, February 18, 1902. For more on black women who protected themselves and set the terms of their labor, see Hunter, *To 'Joy My Freedom*.

99   Minute Book, Independent Benevolent Society, No. 28, 1927–1932, box 2, Andrew Arthur Papers, David M. Rubenstein Rare Book and Manuscript Library, Duke University, Durham, North Carolina.

100 For an excellent account of how members of mutual aid societies supported the voting rights movement in the 1960s, see Jeffries, *Bloody Lowndes*, 40–42.

101 Fitts, *Selma*, 73; U.S. Department of the Interior, National Park Service, "Tabernacle Baptist Church."

102 Quote from Chestnut and Cass, *Black in Selma*, 24–25. For more on black women's activism within the church, see Higginbotham, *Righteous Discontent*.

103 Quote from Marie Foster, interviewed in Vaughan, *Selma Campaign*, 69; see also U.S. Department of the Interior, National Park Service, "Civil Rights Movement in Selma"; Fitts, *Selma*, 73; U.S. Department of the Interior, National Park Service, "Tabernacle Baptist Church."

104 "Scientists Predict . . . ," *SMT*, August 25, 1903; "Boll Weevil in Louisiana," *SMT*, June 8, 1906; "Boll Weevil Has Crossed Mississippi," *SMT*, September 22, 1907; "Boll Weevils Invade Clarke," *SJ*, May 6, 1911.

105 Giesen, *Boll Weevil Blues*, 2, 25.

106 Rieff, "'Rousing the People,'" 27–28; T. M. Campbell, *Movable School*, 83.

107 Giesen, *Boll Weevil Blues*, 2, 25.

108 Rieff, "'Rousing the People,'" 42–50.

109 "Will Fight Weevil in Dallas County," *SJ*, February 13, 1910.

110 "Interesting Story of Selmians Trip to Boll Weevil Territory," *SJ*, September 6, 1912.

111 "Weevils Found at Richmond by Demonstrator," *SJ*, July 11, 1913.

112 John Blake, "Report of the Work of the County Agent," 1915, folder: Dallas County, box 111, Alabama Cooperative Extension Service Records, Department of Special Collections and University Archives, Auburn University, Auburn, Alabama (hereafter cited as ACES Records).

113 Tower, "Cotton Change in Alabama," 13.

114 Resolution of a Committee of the Selma, Alabama, Chamber of Commerce, quoted in Moss, *Boll Weevil Problem*, 78–80; see also "Meeting Today at Orrville on Farm Subjects," *SJ*, October 14, 1915.

115 Fitts, *Selma*, 107.

116 William Palmer Moulder "A History of Centre Ridge Dallas County, Alabama." Seminar paper, University of Alabama, 1936. ODMA, 88.

117 Giesen, *Boll Weevil Blues*, 109; Sisk, "Alabama Black Belt," 480; Strickland, "Boll Weevil."

Interlude: World War I and Making the World Safe for Democracy

1   C. J. Adams to NAACP, New York, February 4, 1920, folder: African American Voting and Disenfranchisement, February 1, 1920–July 31, 1920, NAACP Papers, pt. 4, ProQuest History Vault, http://congressional.proquest

.com/histvault (hereafter cited as NAACP Papers); Rubio, *Post Office*, 30–34.

2 Kennedy, *Over Here*, 10–13.

3 Wilson, quoted in Lentz-Smith, *Freedom Struggles*, 37.

4 Kennedy, *Over Here*, 61.

5 McGerr, *Fierce Discontent*, 282–287.

6 Lentz-Smith, *Freedom Struggles*, 41.

7 "The Problem of the Negro Soldier," *Selma Times* (*ST*), August 26, 1917.

8 "2,896 Names in Dallas County on War Rolls," *ST*, June 6, 1917.

9 Quote from "Colored Soldiers at Camp Sheridan Ordered to Newport News," *Emancipator*, December 8, 1917; see also Wilson, *African American Army Officers*, 5.

10 The tradition of using black military service as proof of worthiness for citizenship stretched back to the Civil War. See Du Bois, *Black Reconstruction in America*; Schwalm, *Emancipation's Diaspora*; Lentz-Smith, *Freedom Struggles*, 113–114, 34; "The War Department Is . . . ," *ST*, August 19, 1917; "Selma Negroes in List of Officers," *ST*, October 24, 1917.

11 Alsobrook, "Call to Arms," 91.

12 "Colored Troops Will Leave to Be Cheered," *SJ*, March 28, 1918; "Fine Ovation to Negro Selectmen," *SJ*, March 31, 1918.

13 "Selma Ablaze with Patriotism," *Emancipator*, April 20, 1918.

14 Lentz-Smith, *Freedom Struggles*, 38.

15 Quote from "Justice for the Negro," *Emancipator*, October 6, 1917; see also "Selma News," *Emancipator*, March 30, 1918.

16 Littleton, "Alabama Council of Defense," 152; W. C. Agee to Dallas County Council of Defense, "The Development of Community Councils," May 1, 1918, folder 10, box 1, Alabama State Council of Defense, Administrative Files, 1917–1919, Alabama Department of Archives and History, Montgomery, Alabama (hereafter cited as ASDC); Council of National Defense, "Program for Organization of Negroes by the Southern State Councils," February 23, 1918, folder 6, box 1, ASDC; McGerr, *Fierce Discontent*, 287.

17 "Parade of 700 Colored People," *ST*, July 9, 1917; "Parade of 700 Colored People," *ST*, July 10, 1917.

18 "Prominent Selmians to Address Patriotic Meet of Colored Citizens," *ST*, April 13, 1917.

19 Advertisement, *Emancipator*, October 6, 1917.

20 "Negroes Raise $1530 for War Savings," *SJ*, July 30, 1918.

21 Quote from "Some Work for the N.A.A.C.P.," *Emancipator*, September 7, 1918; see also Lentz-Smith, *Freedom Struggles*, 25–27; Sullivan, *Lift Every Voice*.

22 Membership numbers for the Selma chapter in "Branches Authorized during Year of 1918," folder: annual business meeting, including discrimination in employment and education, December 14, 1915–December 31, 1919, NAACP Papers, pt. 1; "Selma News," *Emancipator*, June 21, 1919.

23 Quote from "News of Selma and Dallas County, Ala.," *Emancipator*, September 21, 1918. Not all prominent black Selmians agreed with the NAACP's dual purpose of patriotism and black uplift. After a December meeting in 1918, Sams asked, "Where are those so called leaders who were very busy a little while back, installing patriotism, selling bonds, and War stamps?" When the NAACP demanded more justice and less cooperation, Sams noted of those leaders, "Ah they are miss," and then spiritedly demanded, "Page all slackers!" "Selma Bureau," *Emancipator*, December 14, 1918.

24 J. A. Martin, Selma, Alabama, "Rural Conditions of Labor," Tenth Anniversary Conference of the NAACP, June 24, 1919, folder: Annual Convention, 1919, Speeches, NAACP Papers, pt. 1.

25 C. J. Adams to NAACP, New York, February 4, 1920, and NAACP secretary to C. J. Adams, February 9, 1920, folder: African American Voting and Disenfranchisement, February 1, 1920–July 31, 1920, NAACP Papers, pt. 4; Chestnut and Cass, *Black in Selma*; Robinson, *Bridge across Jordan*.

Chapter 2: "Our Country First, Then Selma"

1 Quotes from "The New Chamber of Commerce President" and "Cothran Is Elected President of Chamber of Commerce," *SJ*, December 30, 1919, respectively; see also "Do Not Realize Worth of Chamber of Commerce," *SJ*, December 31, 1919.

2 Upbuilding was a concept adopted by both white and black progress-minded citizens. For more on how African Americans understood upbuilding within Jim Crow, see Brown, *Upbuilding Black Durham*, 9–11.

3 Chestnut and Cass, *Black in Selma*, 22–23.

4 Kennedy, *Over Here*, 117–118.

5 Advertisement, *Emancipator*, February 9, 1918.

6 "Campaign for Food Conservation," *Emancipator*, October 13, 1917.

7 "Will the American Farmer Kill the Kaiser's Wolf-Famine," *SJ*, March 8, 1918.

8 W. C. Agee to members of Dallas County Council of Defense, January 10, 1918, folder 10, box 1, ASDC.

9 "County Begins Work of Repairing Damage Done to Roads by Floods," *ST*, July 12, 1916.

10 "Issue Rations to 1000 for a Week," *ST*, July 30, 1916.

11 Quoted in S. Adams, "Changing Organization," 50.

12 "Negroes Leaving the Farm," *ST*, September 19, 1916; "The Exodus of Negro Farm Labor," *ST*, October 3, 1916.

13 "The Labor Crisis," *ST*, November 15, 1917.

14 W. C. Agee to L. M. Hooper, May 13, 1918, folder 10, box 1, ASDC. Lloyd Hooper chaired the Alabama State Council of Defense.

15 "Writes Officials to Exempt Dallas from Labor Drain," *SJ*, April 23, 1918.

16 Wilkerson, *Warmth of Other Suns*, 36–37. For more about black migration from the rural South to northern cities, see Grossman, *Land of Hope*; Marks, *Farewell*.

17 "Race Labor Leaving," *Chicago Defender*, February 5, 1916.

18 Letter from Selma, Alabama, May 19, 1917, reproduced in Scott, "Letters of Negro Migrants," 317.

19 Mr. S. H. Dykstra, address at the NAACP Convention, June 28, 1939, folder: Annual Convention, 1939, February 11–June 28, 1939, NAACP Papers, pt. 1.

20 "Four Men, Suspected of Being Labor Agents, Arrested with Two Girls from Montgomery," *ST*, January 16, 1917.

21 Quote from "Negro Labor Agent Suspect Is Arrested," *ST*, January 21, 1917; see also "Negro Labor Agent Given $50 Fine," *ST*, January 29, 1917; "Negro Labor Agents Suspects Are Arrested," *ST*, February 1, 1917.

22 *Montgomery Advertiser*, January 4, 1921, in Sisk, "Alabama Black Belt," 446.

23 "Will Furnish No More Trains for Negro Exodus," *ST*, June 6, 1917.

24 "Labor Situation in Dallas County Needs Attention," *SJ*, May 15, 1918.

25 W. C. Agee to Lloyd Hooper, August 15, 1918, folder 11, box 1, ASDC.

26 Curtin, *Black Prisoners*, 46.

27 Quote from "Labor Loyalty League Formed in Dallas County," *SJ*, August 28, 1918; see also "To See That Every Man Is Hard at Work: Organization of Self Preservation Loyalty League Is Under Way," *SJ*, September 2, 1918.

28 "Loyalty League Meets Tonight," *SJ*, September 9, 1918.

29 "Vagrancey [sic] Cases," *SJ*, October 3, 1918.

30 "World War Ended—Fighting Ceased," *SJ*, November 11, 1918.

31 Historical Census Browser, University of Virginia, Geospatial and Statistical Data Center, 2004, http://mapserver.lib.virginia.edu/collections/; "Dallas County Shows a Gain," *STJ*, October 6, 1920. While diversification helped expand the production of food crops, cotton remained the staple crop of the Black Belt. John Blake, "Report of Work of the County Agent," 1918, folder: Dallas County, box 113, ACES Records.

32 Mjagkij, *Loyalty*, xix–xxiii.

33 McGerr, *Fierce Discontent*, xiv–xv.

34 The Alabama state legislature's refusal to extend women the vote was an example of this intransigence. Fitts, *Selma*, 98, 113–115; Rogers et al., *Alabama*, 362–363, 383; Saunders, "World War I," 184–185.

35 Saunders, "World War I," 184–198.

36 Quote from "The Committee at Work," *SMT*, August 12, 1905; see also Rogers et al., *Alabama*, 363–365.

37 Col. W. W. Quarles, "Tuberculosis and Servants," *SJ*, June 19, 1908. Only a few weeks after he made these comments against black servants, a black resident pelted Col. Quarles in the knee with a rock as he was walking

down Broad Street. Black bystanders then mocked Quarles. "Col. Quarles Is Target for Rock of Negro," *SJ*, October 9, 1908.

38 "Mill People Needing Help for a While," *STJ*, December 6, 1914.

39 "Machinery of Dallas County Health Unit Ready to Turn for Better Conditions Here," *STJ*, November 13, 1921.

40 "Vaccination of Negroes Planned," *STJ*, January 13, 1922; "Ridding the Town of Mosquitoes," *STJ*, April 6, 1924; "Selma to Be Mosquito-Free," *STJ*, April 16, 1924.

41 "Complaints of Negro Shacks," *SJ*, April 13, 1911.

42 "May Close Ditch near Creamery," *STJ*, May 23, 1922; "Citizens State Grievances to City Council," *STJ*, September 11, 1923.

43 Historical Census Browser, University of Virginia, Geospatial and Statistical Data Center, 2004, http://mapserver.lib.virginia.edu/collections/. The *Selma Times-Journal* reported in 1926 that the average tenant farmer grossed $256 per year and consumed more than they produced. "Tenant Farmers Draw Low Wages," *STJ*, May 7, 1926.

44 Alabama Legislature, House of Representatives, *Journal*, 779. For more on the conditions of black tenant farmers, see Raper, *Preface to Peasantry*; C. Johnson, *Shadow of the Plantation*.

45 Jeffries, *Bloody Lowndes*, 19.

46 Sisk, "Negro Education," 128.

47 Flynt, *Alabama*, 10.

48 Norrell, *Reaping the Whirlwind*, 14–18; Jeffries, *Bloody Lowndes*, 19–22.

49 Washington's philosophy is captured in his Atlanta exposition address in 1895; see Washington, *Up from Slavery*, 127–131. For more on the Tuskegee Institute, see Norrell, *Reaping the Whirlwind*.

50 W. Edwards, *Twenty-Five Years*, 35, 68; see also 39.

51 W. Edwards, *Twenty-Five Years*, 112.

52 Sisk, "Educational Awakening," 194.

53 D. M. Callaway to J. S. Lambert, April 7, 1921, folder: Dallas County, Supt. D. M. Callaway, 1920–1922, box SG15455, Alabama Department of Education, Correspondence of the Rural School Agent, Alabama Department of Archives and History, Montgomery (hereafter cited as ADECRSA).

54 J. S. Lambert to D. M. Callaway, April 9, 1921, folder: Dallas County, Supt. D. M. Callaway, 1920–1922, box SG15455, ADECRSA.

55 D. M. Callaway to J. S. Lambert, November 14, 1921, folder: Dallas County, Supt. D. M. Callaway, 1920–1922, box SG15455, ADECRSA.

56 Rosenwald Fund Card File Database, Fisk University, http://rosenwald .fisk.edu (accessed January 29, 2013).

57 Correspondence from R. T. Pollard, president of Selma University, folder: P 1918, box SG15451, ADECRSA.

58 J. S. Lambert, "Summary of Reports from Jeanes Industrial Teachers and Home Makers Clubs, 1918–1919," folder: Jeanes Fund 1918, box SG15451, ADECRSA.

59 "Summarized Statement of Home Maker's Club Work for the Summer of 1918 in the State of Alabama," folder: Jeanes Fund 1918, box SG15451, ADECRSA.

60 John W. Abercrombie, "Report Concerning Agencies Employed for the Advancement of Negro Education," folder: Dr. John W. Abercrombie, box SG15451, ADECRSA.

61 A. B. Wilson to J. S. Lambert, December 7, 1920, folder: Dallas County, Mrs. A. B. Wilson (J), 1920–1921, box SG15455, ADECRSA.

62 J. S. Lambert to Mrs. Lydia Martin, August 22, 1921, folder: Dallas County, Mrs. A. B. Wilson (J), 1920–1921, box SG15455, ADECRSA.

63 Louretta Wimberly, interview by the author, December 4, 2012.

64 Quote from "'Organization' Watchword of Dallas County Farm Tour," *STJ*, August 1, 1929; see also "Blake Honored for Long Service to Dallas Farmers," *STJ*, July 19, 1931; John Blake, "Report of Work of the County Agent," 1915, folder: Dallas County, box 111, ACES Records.

65 John Blake, "Report of Work of the County Agent," 1919, folder: Dallas County, box 115, ACES Records.

66 T. H. Toodle, "Report of Work of the County Agent," 1916, folder: Dallas County, box 112, ACES Records.

67 W. Edwards, *Twenty-Five Years*, 87–89.

68 "Ellis, Allgood and Hall Speak at Negro Meet," *STJ*, February 13, 1921.

69 "Marion Jct. Endorses Movable School," *STJ*, April 14, 1925.

70 John Blake, "Report of Work of the County Agent," 1918, folder: Dallas County, box 113, ACES Records. For more about the Negro Extension Service, see Hersey, *My Work*; Reid, *Reaping a Greater Harvest*.

71 John Blake, "Report of Work of the County Agent," 1921, folder: Dallas County, box 117, ACES Records.

72 Campbell, *Farm Bureau*, 5–7.

73 Burritt, *County Agent*, 93.

74 "Forty Four New Names of Dallas Farmers Added to Farm Bureau Roll," *STJ*, March 22, 1923.

75 "The Farm Bureau and Its Program," *STJ*, February 20, 1923.

76 "Farm Bureau to Buy Vetch Seeds and Pecan Trees for Members," *STJ*, June 13, 1923.

77 "The Farm Bureau," *STJ*, April 1, 1923.

78 John Blake, "Annual Report of Extension Work in Dallas County, Alabama," 1924, folder: Dallas County, box 121, ACES Records.

79 In 1924 the USDA created the Office of the Cooperative Extension Service and established the home demonstration agent to work with women. Rieff, "'Rousing the People,'" 61.

80 "Demonstration Clubs Formed at All Points," *STJ*, April 18, 1920.

81 Annette S. Tyndall, "Annual Report of Extension Work in Dallas County, Alabama," 1925, folder: Dallas County, box 123, ACES Records.

82 John Blake, "Annual Report of County Extension Workers," 1925, folder: Dallas County, box 123, ACES Records.

83 "Huge Electric Sign Bearing Slogan 'Our Country First, Then Selma,' Planned for Broad Street," *STJ*, August 23, 1922.

84 "Helping the Negro Solve His Problem," *STJ*, January 18, 1925.

85 Quotes from "Inter-racial Meeting Held at Ct. House," *STJ*, January 18, 1925.

86 Gamble also supported women's suffrage in 1918. U.S. Congress, House Committee on Woman Suffrage, *Right of Suffrage*, 268.

87 "Gamble Speaks on Negroes at Rotary Club," *STJ*, February 27, 1925.

88 "Meeting Discusses Negro Problems," *STJ*, March 12, 1925.

89 "Renovated Samaritan Hospital for Negroes and New Annex to Be Open for Public Inspection Sunday July 12," *STJ*, July 5, 1925.

90 J. Cobb, *Selling of the South*, 36; "New Mills in City Tax Exempt for a Ten Year Period," *STJ*, June 12, 1923.

91 "[Frazier] and Raiford to Chicago in Effort to Secure New Plants," *STJ*, March 27, 1927. The *Selma Times-Journal* frequently spelled Harmon Hunt Frazier's name as both "Frasier" and "Frazier."

92 "Commerce Chamber and Paper Praised for Mill Success," *STJ*, June 7, 1928; "Effort to Bring Union Mills Here Proves Failure," *STJ*, April 22, 1929.

93 "Selma—Ideal City for Manufacturers," *STJ*, August 21, 1923.

94 "The Acres Back of Selma," *STJ*, November 12, 1922.

95 "Chamber of Commerce Urges Farmers to Grow Food Stuffs," *STJ*, April 20, 1924.

96 "Farm Bureau Submits Practical Program," *STJ*, January 29, 1925.

97 John Blake, "Annual Report of County Extension Workers," 1925, folder: Dallas County, box 124, ACES Records.

98 "Farm Bureau Submits Practical Program," *STJ*, January 29, 1925.

99 "Mayor Rowell Makes Some Telling Points on the Negro Farmer's Place in the Business Equation at the Selma University Meeting," *STJ*, February 15, 1925.

100 John Blake, "Annual Report of County Extension Workers," 1925, folder: Dallas County, box 124, ACES Records.

101 "Agricultural Movable School Coming to Dallas from Auburn and Tuskegee for the Negro Farmers," *STJ*, March 8, 1925.

102 T. M. Campbell, *Movable School*, 92, 120-125.

103 Quoted in "Report of the Chamber Giving Approval to Farming Plan," *STJ*, February 22, 1925.

104 "Negro Movable School Ends Fine Week with 987 Attending at Night and Day Session on South Side," *STJ*, April 12, 1925; "Marion Jct. Endorses Movable Farm School," *STJ*, April 14, 1925; "Movable Farm School Leaves the County with Fine Record of Good Work Done in a Practical Manner,"

STJ, April 26, 1925; "Movable Farm School This Week at Summerfield and Four Other Points for the Negro Farmers," *STJ*, April 27, 1925.

105 Raiford to Campbell, November 23, 1921, reproduced in T. M. Campbell, *Movable School*, 164.

106 "Program for Negro Farmers by Menafee," *STJ*, September 14, 1925.

107 "Annual Conference Attracts Several Hundred Negro Farmers to Session," *STJ*, February 12, 1926.

108 "Farm Demonstration Agent C. A. Menafee Dies by the Roadside," *STJ*, March 29, 1928.

109 For more on the rebirth of the Ku Klux Klan during the 1920s, see Blee, *Women of the Klan*; Feldman, *Politics, Society, and the Klan*; MacLean, *Mask of Chivalry*.

110 "WANTED One Hundred Percent Americans . . . ," *SJ*, February 6, 1919.

111 "A Statement—in Opposition to a Ku Klux Klan in Selma," *STJ*, May 16, 1923.

112 "Klux Organizer in Selma Trying to Get Up Lodge, Protests Made," *STJ*, May 16, 1923.

113 "A Statement—in Opposition to a Ku Klux Klan in Selma," *STJ*, May 16, 1923; "Ku Klux Klan in Selma Gets the Finishing Blow from City Council," *STJ*, May 29, 1923.

114 Nonexistent records make it impossible to know exactly who filled the ranks of the local Klan. "Knights in Full Regalia Hold Initiation Attended by Huge Assemblage at Swimming Pool," *STJ*, September 14, 1924.

115 S. Jonce, Selma, Alabama, to U.S. district attorney requesting investigation of Ku Klux Klan, December 5, 1924, Department of Justice, RG60, National Archives and Records Administration, http://research.archives .gov/description/6857747.

116 Ku Klux Klan of Selma, Alabama, letter to the editor, *STJ*, April 27, 1925.

117 S. Jonce, Selma, Alabama, to U.S. district attorney, December 5, 1924, Department of Justice, RG60, National Archives and Records Administration, http://research.archives.gov/description/6857747.

118 Rolinson, *Grassroots Garveyism*, 1.

119 Rolinson argues that "race pride, solidarity, nationalism, independence, self-defense, and redemption formed the essence of the ideology for Southern Garveyites." *Grassroots Garveyism*, 17.

120 Rolinson, *Grassroots Garveyism*, 73–88.

Interlude: The Great Depression

1 "Negroes Marooned on Plantations near Cahaba," *STJ*, March 17, 1929.

2 "Gamble Reports on Progress of Relief Work in Flood Area," *STJ*, March 27, 1929.

3 "Singleton Completes Flood Relief in Selma Territory," *STJ*, May 19, 1929.

4 "Local Solution of Employment Problem Urged," *STJ*, December 15, 1929.

5 "Needy Negroes Get Supplies of Coal," *STJ*, December 19, 1929.

6 "Effort Made to Solve Problem of Unemployment," *STJ*, December 27, 1929.

7 "Orrville Bank in State Hands as Doors Close," *STJ*, February 28, 1930.

8 "Mill Here Will Remain Closed during August," *STJ*, August 1, 1930.

9 Schultz, *White Supremacy*, 183.

10 "Unemployment Relief Program Planned Here," *STJ*, October 2, 1930.

11 "Relief Association Hears Many Calls," *STJ*, October 7, 1930.

12 "Plea for Funds to Assist Poor Made by Kayser," *STJ*, October 12, 1930.

13 "Soup Kitchen for Negroes Out of Employment Will Be Opened Monday by Mrs. Joe Rosenberg," *STJ*, November 8, 1930.

14 "Relief Kitchen to Close Doors Here on Sunday," *STJ*, February 1, 1931.

15 "100 Negroes Apply to Gamble for Aid," *STJ*, January 19, 1931.

16 "Negroes Start Drive to Assist Needy in Selma," *STJ*, January 20, 1931.

17 "City Charity Fund Raised This Month," *STJ*, February 10, 1931.

18 "Save Food, Plea Made to County," *STJ*, August 13, 1931.

19 Reproduced in "Bloch Makes Appeal for Relief Fund," *STJ*, September 14, 1931.

20 "Negro Tenants Refused Aid by Red Cross Here," *STJ*, October 20, 1931.

21 "Carter Drug First Host to Customers at New Soda Fount," *STJ*, March 12, 1931.

22 "New Dance Pavilion to Open on September 23," *STJ*, September 13, 1932.

23 "Kress Building Will Be Opened Here on Friday," *STJ*, October 4, 1931; "Tissier to Open New Store Soon," *STJ*, November 12, 1931.

24 June (Eagle) Cohn, interview by the author, November 30, 2011; Miller Childers, interview by the author, January 20, 2012.

25 Hagedorn, quoted in "Jewish Leaders to Start Drive Here This Week," *STJ*, May 15, 1932.

26 "Relief Gas Tax to Take Effect on October 1," *STJ*, September 29, 1931.

27 "More Cash Needed by Relief Workers," *STJ*, January 6, 1932.

28 "Negro Churches of City Held Open for Relief of Homeless," *STJ*, March 10, 1932.

29 "A 5-[Month] School Term Only," *STJ*, May 15, 1932.

30 "Red Cross Work Report Made at Friday Meeting," *STJ*, July 22, 1932.

31 "Selma Will Ask Government Loan for Relief Program," *STJ*, August 23, 1932.

32 "Our Local Charity Problem," *STJ*, September 21, 1932.

33 "Big Budget Cut Asked for City by Committee," *STJ*, October 7, 1932; "Dallas Revenue Board Cuts $25,000 from Annual Budget," *STJ*, October 11, 1932.

34 "Both Bonds and Tax Spurned by Dallas County," *STJ*, November 9, 1932.

35 "Relief for Negroes of County Planned," *STJ*, November 22, 1932.

36 "Negro Relief Fund Refused by Board," *STJ*, December 6, 1932.

37 "Five Thousand Unemployed on List Kept Here," *STJ*, December 8, 1932; "Red Cross to Cease Charity Work beyond Jurisdiction of Police," *STJ*, January 6, 1933.

38 Quote from "County Budget Slash Asked by Judge Vaughan," *STJ*, January 2, 1933.

39 "Dallas County Relief Problem Now Pressing," *STJ*, January 24, 1933.

40 Under the Hoover administration, the RFC did not loan money to municipalities, so Selma's People's Bank was named as the disbursing officer in the application. "Burns to Make Plea for Loan by Government," *STJ*, February 8, 1933; Schlesinger, *Age of Roosevelt*, 425–430.

41 "Scrip Plan Grows in Favor," *STJ*, February 28, 1933.

Chapter 3: Plowing Under

1 Robinson, *Bridge across Jordan*, 33; "Boynton Named as Farm Agent," *STJ*, May 3, 1928; "Negro Home Agent Starts Work Here," *STJ*, April 9, 1929.

2 Sullivan, *Days of Hope*, 22–23.

3 Quote from "Confidence Reigns as Four Banks of Selma Open," *STJ*, March 15, 1933; see also "Special Guards for County and City Dismissed," *STJ*, March 15, 1933.

4 For more on the RFC, see Schlesinger, *Age of Roosevelt*, 425–430.

5 "Weekly Report Made on Relief Program," *STJ*, March 13, 1933.

6 "Red Cross to Divide Trade among Stores," *STJ*, November 6, 1932; "Ten Youths Listed for Forestry Work Pending Next Call," *STJ*, May 8, 1933.

7 "County Plans to Endorse Roosevelt's Program," *STJ*, June 7, 1933.

8 "Plowing under the Cotton Crop," *STJ*, June 18, 1933.

9 Quote from "Poll Shows Dallas in Favor of Farm Aid Plan," *STJ*, June 20, 1933. For more on the operation of the AAA, see Schlesinger, *Age of Roosevelt*, 59–62.

10 "Dallas County Nears Success in Cotton Drive," *STJ*, July 9, 1933.

11 "County to Receive Big Sum on Cotton," *STJ*, July 26, 1933; "Blanket Order for Plowing of Cotton Issued," *STJ*, July 31, 1933.

12 The NRA worked to establish industry-wide codes fostering fair competition and restoring purchasing power. Sullivan, *Days of Hope*, 44. For a more detailed explanation of the NRA, see Schlesinger, *Age of Roosevelt*, 107–118.

13 "Posters Appear as Code Applied Here," *STJ*, August 1, 1933.

14 "Shift Added at Local Industry," *STJ*, August 1, 1933.

15 "Steps Taken by Local Labor to Get Protection," *STJ*, August 11, 1933.

16 "Recover Program Will Be Presented at Churches Sunday," *STJ*, August 17, 1933; "Colored Women Will Gather to Hear NRA Talks," *STJ*, August 23, 1933.

17 "Selma Praised for Support of Recovery Drive," *STJ*, November 9, 1933.

18 "Works Program to Create 1,590 Jobs in County," *STJ*, November 13, 1933.

19 "Dallas Seeks Benefits of Civil Work Program," *STJ*, November 12, 1933.

20 "Jobs for 790 by Tuesday Civil Works Goal Here," *STJ*, November 20, 1933.

21 Quote from "Works Payroll Helps Business," *STJ*, November 26, 1933. For more on the CWA, see Schlesinger, *Age of Roosevelt*, 270–271.

22 Sitkoff, *New Deal for Blacks*, 34–37.

23 "Tenant Farmers Left Out in the Cold," *STJ*, October 19, 1933.

24 "County to Receive Big Sum on Cotton," *STJ*, July 26, 1933; "A Number of Negro Residents . . . ," *STJ*, December 27, 1933.

25 U.S. Department of Commerce, Bureau of the Census, *Census of Agriculture: 1935*.

26 "Bureau Lays Plans for Cotton Relief," *STJ*, October 11, 1933.

27 "Tenant Farmers to Be Dropped," *STJ*, January 8, 1933.

28 "Dallas to Cast Good Ballot on Bankhead Plan," *STJ*, November 30, 1934.

29 Quoted in Sitkoff, *New Deal for Blacks*, 73; see also 74–78.

30 Quotes from "Drive Begun to Seek Solution of NRA Problem," *STJ*, September 27, 1933. Local labor leaders held an emergency meeting at the courthouse to protest the modification of the NRA wage code. "Meeting Called to Protest Code Move by Local Chamber," *STJ*, October 15, 1933.

31 Letter from Ames, reproduced in "Colored Labor Advisory Board Member Again Urged," September 29, 1933, NAACP peonage, labor, and New Deal files: National Recovery Act, June 16–December 29, 1933, folder: 001418-015-0619, NAACP Papers, pt. 10.

32 Reply reproduced in Report of the Secretary, October 5, 1933, Monthly Reports, January 5–December 31, 1933, folder: 001412-005-0636, NAACP Papers, pt. 1.

33 "Minister Run Out of Selma, Ala. for Supporting NRA Code for Race," September 15, 1933, NAACP peonage, labor, and New Deal files: National Recovery Act, June 16–December 29, 1933, folder: 001418-015-0619, NAACP Papers, pt. 10.

34 Report of the Secretary, October 5, 1933, Monthly Reports, January 5–December 31, 1933, folder: 001412-005-0636, NAACP Papers, pt. 1; Robinson, *Bridge across Jordan*, 80–81.

35 Letter from Walter White, reproduced in "NRA Chief Has 'Hands Off' Policy in Selma Outrage," *Chicago Defender*, October 7, 1933; see also "Driving Out Minister Called 'Local Affair' by NRA Heads," September 29, 1933, NAACP peonage, labor, and New Deal files: National Recovery Act, June 16–December 29, 1933, folder: 001418-015-0619, NAACP Papers, pt. 10.

36 "Relief Workers in County in Walkout," *STJ*, July 2, 1934.

37 Maring, quoted in "Selma Leaders Will Strike to Avert Walkout," *STJ*, August 21, 1934; see also "Selma Workers to Heed Order for Textile Strike," *STJ*, August 20, 1934.

38 Clark, "Textile Workers Union of America," 1368; "Labor Hearing Scheduled for City on Friday," *STJ*, July 14, 1937.

39　"Mill Workers Hold Bargaining Ballot," *STJ*, July 22, 1937.

40　"CIO Rule Repudiated at Worker Ballot," *STJ*, July 23, 1937.

41　Sitkoff, *New Deal for Blacks*.

42　"Boynton Named as Farm Agent," *STJ*, May 3, 1928; Robinson, *Bridge across Jordan*, 33, 109.

43　"Negro Home Agent Starts Work Here," *STJ*, April 9, 1929.

44　S. W. Boynton, quoted in Robinson, *Bridge across Jordan*, 52; see also 4–7, 33, 47–49, 51.

45　Quote from Robinson, *Bridge across Jordan*, 56; see also 52, 109.

46　A. I. Platts, "Annual Narrative Report," 1932, folder: Dallas County—Annual Report 1932, box 366, ACES Records.

47　A. I. Platts, "Supplement to the Annual Report," 1930, folder: Dallas 1930 Supplement to Annual Report, box 366, ACES Records.

48　What was known as the Quarles plantation in the 1930s was most likely the Washington Smith plantation. W. W. Quarles married the daughter of Washington Smith and assumed responsibility for the Smith assets.

49　Robinson, *Bridge across Jordan*, 62–69.

50　A. I. Platts, "Supplement to the Annual Report," 1930, folder: Dallas 1930 Supplement to Annual Report, box 366, ACES Records.

51　Quotes from A. I. Platts, "Supplement to the Annual Report," 1930, folder: Dallas 1930 Supplement to Annual Report, box 366, ACES Records; see also Robinson, *Bridge across Jordan*, 62–69.

52　Fleming, *Shadow of Selma*, 77–79, 136–139; Jeffries, *Bloody Lowndes*, 24–25.

53　"Negro Farmers Urged to Plant Own Food Crop," *STJ*, February 1, 1931.

54　E. Mitchell, *Born Colored*, 73–74, 80–81.

55　Chestnut and Cass, *Black in Selma*, 33–34.

56　"Negro Schools to Close during Meet," *STJ*, February 10, 1929; "Five Hundred Hams on Exhibit as Negro Farmers Open Conference," *STJ*, February 15, 1929.

57　"Negroes Stage Ham Show Here," *STJ*, February 7, 1930.

58　A. I. Platts, "Supplement to the Annual Report," 1933, folder: Dallas County, box 367, ACES Records.

59　Dinkins, "Teacher-Training at Selma University," 45.

60　S. W. Boynton, "Annual Report of County Extensions Workers," 1931, folder: Dallas County, box 366, ACES Records.

61　"Negro Farmers Called to Meet," *STJ*, November 25, 1934.

62　"Dallas County's Delegation to . . . ," *STJ*, December 13, 1935.

63　"Negro Farmers Will Hear Wallace Speak," *STJ*, September 8, 1936.

64　"New Leader Selected for Negro Club Work," *STJ*, July 12, 1935.

65　Quote from Robinson, *Bridge across Jordan*, 131; see also 76.

66　Amelia Boynton Robinson, interview by Blackside, Inc., December 6, 1985, in *Eyes on the Prize: America's Civil Rights Years, 1954–1965*, Henry

Hampton Collection, Film and Media Archive, Washington University Libraries.

67 "Negroes to Operate Knox Academy Here," *STJ*, August 5, 1935.

68 Quote from Robinson, *Bridge across Jordan*, 137; see also 136, 138.

69 "City Will Run Knox Academy," *STJ*, June 11, 1937.

70 "Eleventh Grade for Negro School Planned," *STJ*, October 4, 1940.

71 *Southern Farm Leader*, June 1936, box 2, Clyde Johnson Papers, Southern Historical Collection, Wilson Library, University of North Carolina at Chapel Hill (hereafter cited as CJP).

72 Quoted in Shaw and Rosengarten, *All God's Dangers*, 296, 304. Ned Cobb used the alias "Nate Shaw" in the writing of *All God's Dangers*. For more about Communist organizing in the South before World War II, see Gilmore, *Defying Dixie*; Kelley, *Hammer and Hoe*; Korstad, *Civil Rights Unionism*.

73 Kelley, *Hammer and Hoe*, 40–41.

74 Kelley, *Hammer and Hoe*, 54.

75 "The Bosses in Alabama Are Goin' Crazy," *Daily Worker*, July 3, 1935.

76 "Alabama Sheriff Hands Prisoners to Terror Gang," *Daily Worker*, June 4, 1935; "Negro and White Alabama Cotton Choppers Win Strike," *Daily Worker*, June 21, 1935.

77 Robert Wood to Bibb Graves, May 18, 1935, folder: Communism #1 1935, box SG 12165, Alabama Governor (Graves) administrative files, Alabama Department of Archives and History, Montgomery (hereafter cited as AGG); "The Bosses in Alabama Are Goin' Crazy," *Daily Worker*, July 3, 1935.

78 Robert Wood to Bibb Graves, May 24, 1935, folder: Communism #1 1935, box SG 12165, AGG Files.

79 "Missed Negro Feared Victim of Vigilantes," *Daily Worker*, June 12, 1935.

80 "Body of Willie Foster, Missing Negro, Believed Buried by Cops Who Handed Him to Vigilantes," *Daily Worker*, July 2, 1935.

81 Robert Wood to Bibb Graves, May 21, 1935, folder: Communism #1 1935, box SG 12165, AGG Files.

82 Historian Glenn Feldman has argued that the vigilante violence surrounding the SCU strikes during the 1930s is a sign that Dallas County had an active Klan chapter. All references to the Klan in relevant sources, however, are written by people who use *Klan* as a general descriptor for white vigilantes. The *Selma Times-Journal* makes no mention of a local Klan chapter during the 1930s as it did during the 1920s. While the vigilante violence of white sheriffs and landlords might have been identical to that carried out by the Klan, that in itself is not concrete evidence of an active Klan chapter. "Negro and White Alabama Cotton Choppers Win Strike," *Daily Worker*, June 21, 1935; Feldman, *Politics, Society, and the Klan*, 259–268.

83 "The Bosses in Alabama Are Goin' Crazy," *Daily Worker*, July 3, 1935.

84 During the entire summer of violence against the scu, the *Selma Times-Journal* made no reference to the strike or the arrests. Only the *Daily Worker* reported the violence taking place against the strikers.

85 Quoted in "The Bosses in Alabama Are Goin' Crazy," *Daily Worker*, July 3, 1935.

86 *Southern Farm Leader*, July 1936, box 2, cjp.

87 "Defend Your Right to Organize and Strike," *Southern Farm Leader*, August 1936, box 2, cjp.

88 "Defense," *Southern Farm Leader*, September 1936, box 2, cjp.

89 "Women Are Entitled to Free Medical Aid" and "Poll Tax Keeps Poor Farmers from Voting," *Southern Farm Leader*, August 1936, box 2, cjp; "a.a.a. Hurts Small Farmers," *Southern Farm Leader*, September 1936, box 2, cjp.

90 "Life and Liberty," *Southern Farm Leader*, February 1937, box 2, cjp; 1930 U.S. Census, Dallas County, Alabama, population schedule, Lexington, p. 16B, available via Ancestry.com, http://ancestry.com (accessed February 5, 2014); *Birmingham, Alabama, City Directory*, 1937, available via Ancestry.com, http://ancestry.com (accessed February 5, 2014).

91 "Life and Liberty," *Southern Farm Leader*, February 1937, box 2, cjp.

92 Sitkoff, *New Deal for Blacks*, 73.

93 Sullivan, *Days of Hope*, 42.

94 Sitkoff, *New Deal for Blacks*, 44–45.

95 Leighninger, *Long-Range Public Investment*, 9, 38–41.

96 Leighninger, *Long-Range Public Investment*, 38–41.

97 Sitkoff, *New Deal for Blacks*, 50–51.

98 "Negroes after Project Funds," *stj*, January 22, 1936; "Much Interest Shown in Community House Campaign of Negroes," *stj*, February 2, 1936; "Good Progress Made on Community House," *stj*, February 16, 1936; "Local Project Meets with Temporary Delay," *stj*, May 3, 1936.

99 "The Building for Negroes," *stj*, July 15, 1936.

100 "Negro Project Plans Changed after Protests," *stj*, August 11, 1936.

101 Quote from Robinson, *Bridge across Jordan*, 142; see also "Site for Negro Community House Purchased by City Heads Today," *stj*, January 21, 1938.

102 Quote from Robinson, *Bridge across Jordan*, 142–143; see also W. Jackson, *Story of Selma*, 503; "Tragedy Strikes Twice at Selma City Council," *stj*, December 28, 1937.

103 "Site for Negro Community House Purchased by City Heads Today," *stj*, January 21, 1938; "300 Negroes Attend Outlook Conference," *stj*, February 11, 1940.

104 "Selmians Seek Building Funds at Washington," *stj*, October 20, 1936.

105 "pwa Grant Funds for City Building Project," *stj*, October 22, 1936.

106 W. Jackson, *Story of Selma*, 502–504.

107 "Grant Assures Speedy Action on New School," *STJ*, August 7, 1938.

108 "New High School Will Open Here Monday," *STJ*, December 3, 1939.

109 W. Jackson, *Story of Selma*, 506–508.

110 Quote from Robinson, *Bridge across Jordan*, 97. The New Deal changed the federal government's relationship with its citizens across the entire country. For an in-depth analysis of this in Chicago, see Cohen, *Making a New Deal*.

111 "Allen Resigns Position with AAA in Dallas," *STJ*, May 7, 1941.

112 "Black-Connery Bill Threat to Farmer," *STJ*, July 8, 1937.

113 Fleck, "Democratic Opposition."

114 "Revision Has Not Mitigated Labor Legislation Threat," *STJ*, July 11, 1937.

115 Quote from "Labor Measure Condemned by Dallas Bureau," *STJ*, July 25, 1937; see also "Black-Connery Bill Attacked at Club Lunch," *STJ*, July 21, 1937.

116 "WPA Plans for Boosting Farm Incomes Bared," *STJ*, August 25, 1938.

117 "Dallas County Opinion Varies about WPA Aid," *STJ*, August 28, 1938.

118 "Merchants to Ask for Farm Family Funds," *STJ*, August 31, 1938.

119 Roosevelt, quoted in Sullivan, *Days of Hope*, 65.

120 "And Now Comes the Harvest," *STJ*, February 23, 1940.

121 "What the Farmer Needs," *STJ*, May 3, 1940.

122 Luella C. Hanna, "Annual Narrative Report of the Home Demostration Work Among Negro Women and Girls in Alabama," 1935, folder: Annual Report, Negro Women 1935, box 356, ACES Records.

Interlude: Craig Air Force Base

1 "Hobbs Seeking Plane Factory for This City," *STJ*, May 26, 1940.

2 "City Gets Air Training School," *STJ*, June 21, 1940.

3 "Air School Site Lease Conferences Held Here," *STJ*, June 26, 1940.

4 "Airfield Leases' Details Almost Complete Here," *STJ*, June 30, 1940.

5 "Air School Gets Housing Unit," *STJ*, June 23, 1940.

6 Katznelson, *Fear Itself*, 38–41, 277–281, 305–307.

7 "Selma's Greatest Development," *STJ*, June 23, 1940.

8 "Selma Gets Full Benefits of Air School," *STJ*, June 27, 1940.

9 "Construction Air School to Begin Shortly," *STJ*, July 2, 1940.

10 "Air Field Work to Begin Soon," *STJ*, July 14, 1940.

11 "Trades Classes Scheduled for Local Workers," *STJ*, July 24, 1940.

12 "Labor Classes Registration Opens Monday," *STJ*, July 28, 1940.

13 "More Jobs at Aerial School," *STJ*, April 18, 1941.

14 "Welfare Lists of County Reduced by Defense Program," *STJ*, April 27, 1941.

15 "Bus Line Will Serve Airport," *STJ*, December 14, 1940.

16 "New Bus Added to Serve City Lines," *STJ*, March 9, 1941.

17 "Grist Elected as Recreation Unit Director," *STJ*, July 15, 1941.

18 "Housewives Invited to Keep Cookie Jar Full for Soldiers," *STJ*, September 2, 1941.

19 Jean Martin, interview by the author, December 6, 2011; June Cohn, interview by the author, November 30, 2011.

20 "Flying Cadets Receive Wings at Rite Here," *STJ*, May 30, 1941.

21 "More Soldiers to Camp Here Tonight," *STJ*, June 3, 1940.

22 Katznelson, *Fear Itself*, 312–313; "Young Americans March to Registration Booths," *STJ*, October 16, 1940.

23 "Total of 224 Dallas Counties Called by First 1,500 Drawings," *STJ*, October 30, 1940; "Eleven Negro Draftees Get Call to Duty," *STJ*, January 19, 1940; "Fifty Negroes Leave Monday to Join Army," *STJ*, April 14, 1941.

24 "Defense Council of County Is Complete," *STJ*, May 30, 1941.

25 "Hooper Named Defense Head," *STJ*, June 5, 1941.

26 Chafe, *Unfinished Journey*, 7–11.

Chapter 4: Becoming White-Faced Cows

1 Quote from Chestnut and Cass, *Black in Selma*, 28; see also 26, 27, 29.

2 "Where Selma Stands," *STJ*, August 3, 1941; Chestnut and Cass, *Black in Selma*, 30–37.

3 Chestnut and Cass, *Black in Selma*, 47–51, 67.

4 "Twenty Volunteers from County Offer Service for Army," *STJ*, October 6, 1940.

5 "County Draft System Gets Final Touches," *STJ*, October 14, 1940.

6 "Fifty Negroes Leave Monday to Join Army," *STJ*, April 14, 1941.

7 "Forty Four Negroes Leave for Service," *STJ*, June 23, 1941; "Twenty Negroes Off for Service in the Army," *STJ*, September 17, 1941.

8 Flynt, *Alabama*, 401.

9 "Thousands of Posts Open to Negroes in United States Navy," *STJ*, October 15, 1941.

10 Sullivan, *Lift Every Voice*, 253.

11 Franklin Delano Roosevelt, "Annual Address to Congress 1941," Franklin Delano Roosevelt Presidential Library and Museum, https://fdrlibrary.org/four-freedoms.

12 Gilmore, *Defying Dixie*, 358–360. For more about the Double V campaign and African Americans' push for full citizenship during the war, see James, *Double V*.

13 Dixon, quoted in "A Champion Arises," *STJ*, July 26, 1942; see also "Governor Guest at Barbecue Here," *STJ*, August 2, 1942.

14 Witkowski, "Poster Campaigns," 73.

15 "Aluminum Depository Established at Store," *STJ*, July 6, 1941.

16 Robinson, *Bridge across Jordan*, 138; "Recreation Building for Negro Soldiers," *STJ*, February 1, 1942.

17 "Yule Program for Colored Soldiers," *STJ*, December 24, 1942.

18 "Recreation Center for Negro Soldiers," *STJ*, January 17, 1943; "Formal Opening of Colored USO Here," *STJ*, May 9, 1943; Robinson, *Bridge across Jordan*, 143.

19 Robinson, *Bridge across Jordan*, 87.

20 Adams, quoted in "Negroes Plan Bond Rally," *STJ*, January 21, 1943.

21 "Dallas Will Help to Feed the World," *STJ*, November 11, 1941.

22 "What Can I Do?," *STJ*, June 20, 1943; "Negroes Urged to Attend Town Meet," *STJ*, September 22, 1943.

23 Forty-Eight in series of Negro Extension Service monthly program, August 25, 1944, folder: Radio Transcripts 1943–44, box 392, ACES Records.

24 "Need of Food Discussed at County Meets," *STJ*, November 13, 1941.

25 For more on black extension agents' involvement in the war effort, see Reid, *Reaping a Greater Harvest*, 178–209.

26 "Negroes Will Hold Defense Conference Here on Wednesday," *STJ*, January 13, 1941.

27 S. W. Boynton, "Supplement to the Annual Report," 1944, folder: Dallas County Negro Reports 1943–1944," box 367, ACES Records; see also Lucy M. Upshaw, "Supplement to the Annual Report," 1944, folder: Dallas County Negro Reports 1943–1944," box 367, ACES Records.

28 Luella C. Hanna, "Home Demonstration Leader (Negro) Annual Report," 1944, folder: Annual Report, Negro Work 1944, box 357, ACES Records.

29 S. W. Boynton, "Supplement to the Annual Report" folder: Dallas, Annual Report 1945, box 368, ACES Records.

30 S. W. Boynton, "Supplement to the Annual Report," 1944, folder: Dallas County Negro Reports 1943–1944, box 367, ACES Records.

31 Lucy M. Upshaw, "Supplement to the Annual Report," 1944, folder: Dallas County Negro Reports 1943–1944, box 367, ACES Records.

32 Sixth in a weekly series of Negro Extension Service programs, November 17, 1945, folder: Radio Scripts 1942–43, box 392, ACES Records; S. W. Boynton, "Supplement to the Annual Report," 1944, folder: Dallas County Negro Reports 1943–1944, box 367, ACES Records; Members of 4-H also played an active role in local war bond drives. In their clubs, schools, and communities, 4-H boys and girls sold war bonds and stamps as well as purchasing them themselves.

33 Quote from Robinson, *Bridge across Jordan*, 146; see also 143–148. Many of the rural people who were pivotal in the purchase of the recreational area were the same ones who chaired patriotic undertakings. J. A. Williams from Beloit, B. J. Rountree of Burnsville, R. W. Harrison and Arthur Sanders from Orrville, David Peasant of Minter, Rev. A. T. Carson of Bogue Chitto, Jeff Thomas in Summerfield, and Emma Johnson in Marion Junction all served on Joyland's central committee as well as organizing bond drives in their communities. "Negro Recreational Program Perfected," *STJ*, June 26, 1941; "Negro 4-H Event to Attract Huge Crowd," *STJ*, August 20, 1944; "Negroes Seek $125,000 Goal in Bond Drive," *STJ*, June 14, 1944.

34 Quotes from S. W. Boynton, "Supplement to the Annual Report," 1944, folder: Dallas County Negro Reports 1943–1944, box 367, ACES Records; see also "Negro Rural Camp Fund Growing Here," *STJ*, September 22, 1942.

35 Quote from Lucy M. Upshaw, "Supplement to the Annual Report," 1944, folder: Dallas County Negro Reports 1943–1944, box 367, ACES Records; see also "Negroes Will Burn 4-H Club Mortgage," *STJ*, August 9, 1944; "Negro 4-H Event to Attract Huge Crowd," *STJ*, August 20, 1944; Robinson, *Bridge across Jordan*, 143–148.

36 Brown and Boynton, quoted in Twentieth in series of Negro Extension Service monthly reports, November 3, 1942, folder: Radio Scripts, 1942–43, box 392, ACES Records.

37 "A New Problem for Farmers," *STJ*, April 16, 1941.

38 U.S. Department of Commerce, Bureau of the Census, *Census of Agriculture: 1945*. The emergency farm labor assistant for Dallas County estimated that a quarter of them had gotten jobs at I. Lewis Cigar Manufacturing Company and the Zeigler meat processing plant in Selma. Hereford, "Study of Selma," 47.

39 "A New Problem for Farmers," *STJ*, April 16, 1941.

40 "Farmers Look to WPA for Laborers," *STJ*, August 27, 1941.

41 Burns, quoted in "Vagrancy Law to Be Invoked Here Shortly," *STJ*, May 12, 1942.

42 "There Is No Place for Drones in War," *STJ*, February 22, 1943.

43 "Farmers Classified under New System," *STJ*, December 7, 1942.

44 "Local Draft Boards Will Follow Policy of Army Preference," *STJ*, March 17, 1944.

45 "No War Prisoners Sought for Dallas," *STJ*, September 2, 1943.

46 Stickney, "Conversion from Cotton," 41, 157.

47 J. R. Otis, state leader of Negro work, "Changes in the Characteristics of the Type of Farming Areas in Alabama, 1880–1940" (unpublished thesis, 1949), box 383, ACES Records.

48 Historical Census Browser, University of Virginia, Geospatial and Statistical Data Center, 2004, http://mapserver.lib.virginia.edu/collections/; U.S. Department of Commerce, Bureau of the Census, *Census of Agriculture: 1950*.

49 Stickney, "Conversion from Cotton," 2.

50 "John Blake Closes an Era," *STJ*, October 10, 1940.

51 Blevins, *Cattle*, 70.

52 Alsobrook, quoted in Hart, *Land That Feeds Us*, 260; see also Stickney, "Conversion from Cotton," 159.

53 Stickney, "Conversion from Cotton," 158, 209, 227–228.

54 "There Was a Time," *STJ*, July 13, 1942.

55 Quote from Stickney, "Conversion from Cotton," 188; see also 187–191.

56 Two of the earliest purebred cattle operations in Dallas County, started after World War I, were Bon Aire Farm in Safford, operated by Cecil Shuptrine, and West Dallas Farms near Orrville, owned by J. E. Dunaway,

who also ran a mercantile company and the Orrville Bank and Trust Company. He operated his six thousand acres together with Kentucky-born cattle buyer Joe Lambert, raising both cattle and cotton. *Jersey Bulletin and Dairy World*, Indianpolis, IN, 1 (1920): 150, http://books.google.com/books?id=i5U5AQAAMAAJ&source=gbs_navlinks_s; Blevins, *Cattle*, 67; Stickney, "Conversion from Cotton," 201–206.

57 Tenth in Series of Negro Extension Service Programs, April 26, 1941, folder: Radio Scripts, 1940–1941, box 391, ACES Records.

58 104th in a Weekly Series of Negro Extension Service Programs, folder: Radio Scripts 1947–8, box 392, ACES Records.

59 Chestnut and Cass, *Black in Selma*, 26–27.

60 104th in a Weekly Series of Negro Extension Service Programs, folder: Radio Scripts 1947–8, box 392, ACES Records.

61 Chestnut and Cass, *Black in Selma*, 29.

62 Chestnut and Cass, *Black in Selma*, 58–59.

63 U.S. Department of Commerce, Bureau of the Census, *Census of Agriculture: 1935* and *Census of Agriculture: 1950*.

64 Heinicke and Grove, "'Machinery Has Taken Over,'" 69.

65 "Farm Facts for the Farm Family," *STJ*, November 29, 1943.

66 J. R. Otis, "Changes in the Characteristics of the Type of Farming Areas in Alabama, 1880–1940," box 383, ACES Records.

67 Heinicke and Grove, "'Machinery Has Taken Over,'" 70.

68 U.S. Department of Commerce, Bureau of the Census, *Census of Agriculture: 1945*.

69 S. W. Boynton, "Narrative Report of County Extension Agents," folder: Dallas, Annual Report 1946, box 369, ACES Records.

70 J. C. Ford, "Annual Report of the Coordination of Negro Work, Alabama Extension Service," folder: Annual Report—Negro Work 1940, box 356, ACES Records.

71 Robinson, *Bridge across Jordan*, 159.

72 Chestnut and Cass, *Black in Selma*, 74.

73 Stickney, "Conversion from Cotton," 154. For more about the rural transformation taking place across the South after the war, see Kirby, *Rural Worlds Lost*.

74 Roosevelt, quoted in Sullivan, *Days of Hope*, 65.

75 Sullivan, *Days of Hope*, 42, 64–67.

76 Hobbs, quoted in Ward, "A War for States' Rights," 135; see also Sullivan, *Days of Hope*, 106–107.

77 Smith v. Allwright, 321 U.S. 649 (1944); Ward, "War for States' Rights," 139.

78 Foster, "'Boswellianism,'" 26–27.

79 "The Boswell Amendment," *STJ*, September 24, 1946.

80 "County Votes Strongly for Boswell Plan," *STJ*, November 6, 1946; Foster, "'Boswellianism,'" 35–36.

81 Marshall, quoted in Sullivan, *Lift Every Voice*, 299; see also 298.

82 Morgan v. Virginia, 328 U.S. 373 (1946); Shelley v. Kraemer, 334 U.S. 1 (1948); Brown v. Board of Education of Topeka, 347 U.S. 483 (1954); NAACP, "NAACP Legal History," http://www.naacp.org/pages/naacp-legal-history (accessed February 23, 2013). For an extensive study of the NAACP school desegregation campaign, see Kluger, *Simple Justice*.

83 Kluger, *Simple Justice*, 256–284.

84 Quote from Chestnut and Cass, *Black in Selma*, 47; see also 48–51; "Eleventh Grade for Negro School Planned," STJ, October 4, 1940.

85 "Session of Negro Schools Extended," STJ, April 25, 1943.

86 "Negro School Funds Sought," STJ, February 20, 1944.

87 "Negro High School Is Federal Project," STJ, June 14, 1944.

88 "Negro School Work Started," STJ, April 14, 1948.

89 "Negro Education in Dallas County," STJ, December 14, 1948.

90 "County Board Let Contract on Two Negro High Schools," STJ, December 12, 1948.

91 "Hundreds See Negro School Building Here," STJ, May 9, 1949.

92 Quotes from "Proof of Good Intention," STJ, May 8, 1949; see also Wofford, "Status of the Negro," 27. For more on white southerners' defense of white supremacy, see K. Johnson, *Reforming Jim Crow*; J. Ward, *Defending White Democracy*.

93 Chestnut and Cass, *Black in Selma*, 47.

94 Quote from Chestnut and Cass, *Black in Selma*, 50; see also 46–51.

95 Louretta Wimberly, interview by the author, December 4, 2012.

96 Charles Bonner and Bettie Mae Fikes, interview by Bruce Hartford, 2005, Civil Rights Movement Veterans (CRMVET) website, http://www.crmvet.org/nars/chuckbet.htm.

97 Quote from Anderson, "'Sound Mind,'" 55; see also 52–58.

98 Etta Smith Perkins, interview by the author, December 14, 2011.

99 Moss, quoted in "Moss: Voting Is Key," STJ, September 6, 1981; see also "Third Credit Union Listed for Selma," STJ, October 17, 1960; Norrell, *Reaping the Whirlwind*, 38–39.

100 Sullivan, *Days of Hope*, 228, 245.

101 Perman, *Pursuit of Unity*, 261–265.

102 "Political Perfidy," STJ, February 4, 1948.

103 Perman, *Pursuit of Unity*, 266–269. For more on the Dixiecrats' reaction against Truman and the Democratic Party, see Barnard, *Dixiecrats and Democrats*; Frederickson, *Dixiecrat Revolt*.

104 "The Choice Is Made," STJ, August 9, 1948.

105 "Senator Givhan Lands Six Committee Seats in State Legislature," STJ, January 12, 1955. For more about the Farm Bureau's growing political influence in the 1950s, see Berger, *Dollar Harvest*.

106 Givhan, quoted in "Givhan Defies Elector Club," STJ, October 8, 1948.

107 Wright, quoted in "South Urged to Stand Solid in Talk by Wright," *STJ*, October 19, 1948.

108 J. Cobb, *Selling of the South*, 85–98.

109 Rubin, *Plantation County*, 85.

110 "Cigar Factory Benefits for City Stressed," *STJ*, October 19, 1941.

111 M. Mitchell, "California Cotton Mill Memories," 12.

112 "Okra Cut for Processing at Cannery Here," *STJ*, August 3, 1944.

113 "An Ideal Acquisition," *STJ*, August 6, 1944.

114 "Selma's Progress Program," *STJ*, March 6, 1949.

115 "Selma Gets Large Industry," *STJ*, October 15, 1950; "Congratulations," *STJ*, November 15, 1950.

116 During the 1940s and earlier, the South's racial conservatives, concerned with the maintenance of segregation, had made common cause with the region's economic conservatives seeking to prevent federal interference in their private businesses. Federal wage standards, protection for labor unions, and the creation of the Fair Employment Practices Committee challenged the racially stratified labor practices that southern industries used to keep wages low and unions out. At the same time, the realignment of the Democratic Party toward civil rights posed a new threat to southern segregation. By uniting against both racial and labor challenges, white southern businessmen, landowners, and civic leaders could resist federal economic policies that also challenged the South's racial order. Feldman, "Southern Disillusionment," 201–207; Perman, *Pursuit of Unity*, 260.

117 "A Challenge to Every Selmian," *STJ*, April 14, 1945.

118 Walter Givhan, "Farm Success Based on Freedom," *STJ*, March 18, 1951.

119 Quote from Chestnut and Cass, *Black in Selma*, 51; see also 47–50, 67–68, 86.

Interlude: "I Like Ike"

1 "Opportunity Knocks," *STJ*, October 9, 1951.

2 "Where Morgan and Pettus Rest," *Alabama Journal* editorial, published in *STJ*, October 29, 1951. For more on the political careers of Morgan and Pettus, see Fry, *John Tyler Morgan*.

3 Gilmore, *Defying Dixie*, 3.

4 "States Righters May Form Plans for Battle Here," *STJ*, October 12, 1951; "Half-Dozen Governors Expected for Talk by Senator Byrd Here," *STJ*, October 14, 1951.

5 Byrd, quoted in "Byrd Calls for Political Virility in South," *STJ*, November 1, 1951.

6 "Barbecue Spectacle," *STJ*, November 1, 1951.

7 "State Democratic Group Formed at Session Here," *STJ*, November 2, 1951.

8 "Open Letter to General Eisenhower," *STJ*, October 16, 1951.

9 "It Looks Like Ike for Us," *STJ*, January 8, 1952.

10 "South's Last Candidate Hope Lost," *STJ*, May 7, 1952.

11 "Ike Delivers the Goods," *STJ*, June 6, 1952.

12 "Truman Will Not Run for Re-election," *STJ*, March 30, 1952.

13 "More Than 300 Former Democrats Sign Dallas County Pledge to Support Ike," *STJ*, July 6, 1952.

14 "Eisenhower Banner Raised," *STJ*, August 31, 1952.

15 "Ike Supporters Open Local Headquarter," *STJ*, September 28, 1952.

16 "Still Like Ike," *STJ*, November 5, 1952.

17 "Why Thousands of Life-Long *Democrats* Have Become Democrats for Eisenhower," *STJ*, October 28, 1952.

18 "How to Vote a Split Ticket," *STJ*, November 2, 1952.

19 Quotes from "Ironic Political Twist," *STJ*, November 14, 1952; "Eisenhower Elected by Landslide Ballot: Dallas County Joins in Procession to Ike," *STJ*, November 5, 1952.

20 Dwight D. Eisenhower, letter to the editor, *STJ*, December 7, 1952.

Chapter 5: Segregation's Last Stand

1 Wofford, "Status of the Negro," 1–2.

2 Brown v. Board of Education of Topeka, 347 U.S. 483 (1954).

3 "Several Held in Rape Probe," *STJ*, March 22, 1953.

4 Chestnut and Cass, *Black in Selma*, 72.

5 "Attack Foiled by Young Mother in Bout with Negro," *STJ*, April 26, 1953.

6 Myrdal, *American Dilemma*, 587.

7 Tyson, *Radio Free Dixie*, 93–94.

8 "Prowler Escapes after Effort to Enter Residence," *STJ*, May 10, 1953.

9 Chestnut and Cass, *Black in Selma*, 72–73.

10 "Negro Confesses to Prowl Attacks Here," *STJ*, May 19, 1953.

11 "Negro Held at Prison Confesses Rape Guilt and Other Raids Here," *STJ*, May 24, 1953.

12 Chestnut and Cass, *Black in Selma*, 73.

13 Three psychiatrists from Tuskegee gave expert testimony that Fikes was schizophrenic. "Life Term Given Negro by Jurors at Rape Hearing," *STJ*, June 25, 1953; Thornton, *Dividing Lines*, 388.

14 Quote from Robinson, *Bridge across Jordan*, 178; see also 163, 176–182; Chestnut and Cass, *Black in Selma*, 132, 74.

15 Quote from Chestnut and Cass, *Black in Selma*, 53; see also "Notary Public Gets Sentence to Prison," *STJ*, April 29, 1949.

16 Ransby, *Ella Baker*, 105–131.

17 "Report of the Secretary for the Month of April 1953," Board of Directors Meeting, [April] 11, 1953, folder: Secretary's Reports, NAACP Papers, pt. 1; Chestnut and Cass, *Black in Selma*, 74.

18 "Fikes Attorneys File Motion for Insanity Probes," *STJ*, September 23, 1953.

19 Quote from Chestnut and Cass, *Black in Selma*, 75; see also 74.

20 "Court Hears Motions by Fikes Defense Lawyers," *STJ*, October 1, 1953; "Hearing on Motions Forces Delay of Fikes Trial," *STJ*, October 4, 1953.

21 The Supreme Court reversed the decision in January 1957. However, the earlier ninety-nine-year prison sentence still stood, and Fikes served twenty-one years before Chestnut convinced a federal district judge to overturn it. Thornton, *Dividing Lines*, 388–389.

22 Chestnut and Cass, *Black in Selma*, 78.

23 J. Ward, *Defending White Democracy*, 124.

24 Walter Givhan to Governor Gordon Persons, Reprinted in *STJ*, January 10, 1953

25 Brady, *Black Monday*; Dittmer, *Local People*, 45–46; "Serious Concern Created Here by Segregation Ban," *STJ*, May 18, 1954.

26 J. Ward, *Defending White Democracy*, 160.

27 Five months after the *Brown* decision, NAACP representatives met in Selma for the Alabama state conference. Executive secretary Walter White, Constance B. Motley, and Thurgood Marshall attended the event, where delegates resolved to wipe out segregation from all areas of Alabama. "NAACP Will Hold Sessions in City," *STJ*, November 11, 1954; "Segregation Ban Sought by NAACP," *STJ*, November 14, 1954; "NAACP Promises Legal Fight to 'Open' Alabama," *STJ*, November 15, 1954.

28 "Group Reveal Plan of Defense for Segregation," *STJ*, November 28, 1954.

29 "Large Crowd Present as Council Organizes to Defend Segregation," *STJ*, November 30, 1954.

30 Bartley, *Rise of Massive Resistance*, 88.

31 Thornton, *Dividing Lines*, 399–400.

32 Smitherman, quoted in Chestnut and Cass, *Black in Selma*, 84; see also "Candidates Back Council Policies by Poll Answers," *STJ*, April 24, 1958.

33 Keith, quoted in "Citizens Council Head Hits Charge of Editor Carter," *STJ*, March 8, 1955; see also "Patterson Warns of Mongrel Race before WCC Here," *STJ*, February 1, 1955.

34 "Large Crowd Cheers as Speakers Appeal for Racial Defense," *STJ*, June 23, 1955.

35 Author's field notes, conversation with Joseph Knight, March 12, 2013.

36 On Blalock's move to desegregate the Selma Public Library, see Graham, *Right to Read*.

37 Windham, quoted in Chestnut and Cass, *Black in Selma*, 84. For examples of other white moderates in Selma, see Longnecker, *Selma's Peacemaker*.

38 Reproduced in "Petition from Negroes Calls for Elimination of School Segregation," *STJ*, August 30, 1955.

39 Hunter and Keith, quoted in "Schools Petition Signers Reduced by Withdrawals," *STJ*, September 8, 1955; see also "Now That We Know," *STJ*, October 11, 1955.

40 Doyle, quoted in Chestnut and Cass, *Black in Selma*, 85.

41 Chestnut and Cass, *Black in Selma*, 85.

42 Thornton, *Dividing Lines*, 396–397; Dittmer, *Local People*, 55–58; "Kidnaping, Arson Cases on Docket of County Panel," *STJ*, November 13, 1955.

43 "Smitherman Boycotted Out of Selma Has New Life in Detroit," *Jet*, April 1, 1965.

44 Two Selma police officers were among those arrested and charged in the incidents, one for setting fire to the house and firing shots and the other for kidnapping. The officer charged with arson committed suicide shortly thereafter. "Two Officers of Force Here Face Serious Charges," *STJ*, October 22, 1955; "Indictments Voted by Grand Jurors on Kidnap, Arson Counts," *STJ*, November 15, 1955.

45 "Smitherman Boycotted Out of Selma Has New Life in Detroit," *Jet*, April 1, 1965.

46 Historical Census Browser, University of Virginia, Geospatial and Statistical Data Center, 2004, http://mapserver.lib.virginia.edu/collections/; U.S. Department of Commerce, Bureau of the Census, *Census of Agriculture: 1935*, *Census of Agriculture: 1959*, and *Census of Agriculture: 1964*.

47 Davis, *Cotton Kingdom in Alabama*, 38.

48 Historical Census Browser, University of Virginia, Geospatial and Statistical Data Center, 2004, http://mapserver.lib.virginia.edu/collections/.

49 "Public Given Facts in School Survey," *STJ*, February 28, 1954.

50 U.S. Department of Commerce, Bureau of the Census, *Census of Manufacturers: 1947* and *Census of Population: 1960*; "Increase of More Than Thousand Units Shown by Selma Housing in Ten Years," *STJ*, October 22, 1950; "Public Given Facts of School Survey," *STJ*, February 28, 1954; U.S. Department of Commerce, Bureau of the Census, *Census of Housing: 1950*.

51 "Slum Clearance Housing Okeyed," *STJ*, October 6, 1949.

52 "Rapid Progress Made on Housing Project Site Clearance," *STJ*, February 4, 1951; "Housing Area Cleared," *STJ*, July 15, 1951.

53 "Hearing Postponed on Condemnation of Housing Units Site," *STJ*, April 30, 1951.

54 "Why? Ask Colored Home Owners," *STJ*, August 20, 1950.

55 The Selma Housing Authority claimed it had made every effort to establish fair prices, while stressing the "sub-standard character" of the neighborhood. Letter to editor, Selma Housing Authority Board of Commissioners, "Housing Project Methods Explained," *STJ*, August 24, 1950.

56 "Citizen School Survey Studies City Extension," *STJ*, January 13, 1954; J. Cobb, *Selling of the South*, 2.

57 Quote from Selma City Council Minutes, April 24, 1950, County Clerk Office, City Hall, Selma, AL. The Cater Act of 1949 allowed for the creation of industrial development corporations, and the Wallace Act of 1951 allowed

cities to issue public bonds for the construction of plants for private industry. J. Cobb, *Selling of the South*, 36.

58 J. Cobb, *Selling of the South*, 2–15; Industrial Committee, Selma and Dallas County Chamber of Commerce, "An Economic Report on the Selma and Dallas County Area," 1961, folder 135, box 7, Judge James Hare Papers, Vaughan-Smitherman Museum, Selma, AL (hereafter cited as JJHP).

59 "Phone Employees Here Join Southwide Strike," *STJ*, March 14, 1955; "Two Rail Services Here Put Out of Operation by Strike Workers," *STJ*, March 17, 1955.

60 "Strike Violence Averted as Off-Duty Service Men Leave Phone Posts Here," *STJ*, April 5, 1955.

61 "Walkouts Forced to Choke Unions, Charge of Labor," *STJ*, April 21, 1955.

62 "An Open Letter to the Employees of Independent Lock Company of Alabama: Which Is the Better Way?," *STJ*, October 6, 1953.

63 The *Selma Times-Journal* did not report the results of the union vote, likely in an attempt to not draw attention to the new union. However, references to the union at ILCO appear in later articles, suggesting that the union vote was successful.

64 "Lock Plant Operations Sharply Curtailed by Strike," *STJ*, September 21, 1955.

65 "Half of Workers Back on Job at Lock Plant Here," *STJ*, September 22, 1955.

66 "The Community Has a Stake," *STJ*, September 25, 1955.

67 "Strike Ended at Lock Plant Here after Injunction," *STJ*, September 28, 1955. Judge Hare would use the same strategy in July 1964 to squelch civil rights protests in the wake of the passage of the Civil Rights Act of 1964.

68 "Union Beaten in Cigar Plant Vote by Large Margin," *STJ*, September 5, 1957; "Challenged Ballots to Decide Outcomes of Union Test Here," *STJ*, September 13, 1957; Industrial Committee, Selma and Dallas County Chamber of Commerce, "An Economic Report on the Selma and Dallas County Area," 1961, folder 135, box 7, JJHP.

69 Ellwanger, interview, December 9, 1964, from Ralph Smeltzer Papers, folder: Selma, Main (6 of 7), box 120, Taylor Branch Papers, Southern Historical Collection, Wilson Library, University of North Carolina at Chapel Hill (hereafter cited as TBP); Korstad, *Civil Rights Unionism*, 97.

70 Assistant secretary of the Chamber of Commerce, quoted in Wofford, "Status of the Negro," 44.

71 Selma City Council Minutes, January 23, 1956.

72 "We Will Not Surrender," *STJ*, September 26, 1957.

73 "Cross Burn to Mark Resurgence of Klan in Area," *STJ*, November 15, 1957.

74 "Unwelcome Visitors," *STJ*, December 2, 1957.

75 Baker later clarified his appearance at the Klan rally, claiming that he was not a member of the Klan but appeared to demonstrate his support

of segregation. "Klan Rally Here Draws Big Crowd," *STJ*, March 16, 1958; "Paper Corrects Error Concerning KKK Rally," *STJ*, March 17, 1958.

76 Wofford, "Status of the Negro," 19.

77 "Robed Klansmen of Four Counties in Local Parade," *STJ*, August 27, 1958.

78 "Klan Welcome Signs Erected at Hiway Entrances," *STJ*, July 17, 1959.

79 "Attack on Negro Deplored by Bar," *STJ*, January 25, 1959.

80 "Strong Hint of Formation of Black Belt Congress District with Selden as Representative," *STJ*, October 15, 1958.

81 "County Credited with Leadership in Council Move," *STJ*, February 12, 1956; Bartley, *Rise of Massive Resistance.*

82 "Selma Chosen as Headquarters of Citizens' Council," *STJ*, June 18, 1958; "Sen. Givhan Elected Permanent Chairman of Citizens Council," *STJ*, March 6, 1959.

83 Quote from "Blackwell Will Head CC Membership Drive," *STJ*, October 27, 1959; see also "Eastland Favors Ad Fund to Tell South Viewpoint," *STJ*, October 22, 1959.

84 "Dallas Added to Roster of Counties Instructed to Produce Voting Lists," *STJ*, December 3, 1958.

85 "New Carpetbagger Invasion," *STJ*, December 4, 1958.

86 "Patterson Welcomes Test of Rights Probe Defiance," *STJ*, December 10, 1958.

87 "Wilcox Jury Expected to Follow Pattern Set on Vote Records Here," *STJ*, March 13, 1959.

88 "List of Qualified Voters in Dallas County, Alabama," *STJ*, March 9, 1960.

89 S. W. and Amelia Boynton, Sullivan Jackson, Jennie Anderson, Ruth Lindsey, and Frank Gordon testified about the economic pressure, widespread fear, and blatant racial discrimination that kept African Americans from voting. "Patterson Welcomes Test of Rights Probe Defiance," *STJ*, December 10, 1958.

90 Testimony of Sullivan Jackson, Selma, Dallas County, Alabama, Tuesday morning session, December 9, 1958, Civil Rights Commission hearing at U.S. Circuit Court of Appeals, Montgomery, Alabama, TBP.

91 Mrs. Sullivan [Jean] Jackson, interview by Taylor Branch, May 27, 1990, Audiocassette C-5047/118, TBP.

92 "Sheriff Clark Charged with Collusion," *STJ*, January 18, 1959; "Sheriff Clark Issues Countercharges," *STJ*, January 19, 1959; "Bullets Riddle Auto of Ex-Deputies," *STJ*, January 25, 1959; "A Responsibility of the People," *STJ*, January 26, 1959.

93 "James Clark Selected by Governor to Serve as Sheriff of County," *STJ*, November 8, 1955; "The Cause of the County People and Jim Clark Rests with the People of Selma," *STJ*, June 2, 1958.

94 "Vigil Maintained at Zeigler Plant," *STJ*, October 10, 1958.

95 "Beyond Toleration," *STJ*, October 8, 1958.

96 McLeod, quoted in "Three Hundred Aides Enlisted by Sheriff," *STJ*, March 13, 1960.

97 "Mounted Posse Parades Downtown Streets Here in Training Session," *STJ*, March 14, 1960.

98 "Preparedness Precludes Action," *STJ*, March 15, 1960.

99 "Magnesium Plant Ground-Breaking Set for Fall," *STJ*, July 20, 1956.

100 Marring, quoted in "Selma Gets Big Industry," *STJ*, July 19, 1956.

101 Quotes from A. E. Peterman, Alabama Metallurgical Corporation, Selma, Alabama, to Alamet Employees (ca. 1960), folder 137, box 7, JJHP; see also "Magnesium Plant Ground-Breaking Set for Fall," *STJ*, July 20, 1956.

102 Jack Miles, general manager of the Chamber of Commerce, to all members, March 25, 1960, folder 137, box 7, JJHP.

103 "Alamet Employees Turn Down Union," *STJ*, October 22, 1961.

104 Quoted in "Production Halted at Lock Factory by Labor Balk," *STJ*, October 18, 1961; see also "Production Stays near Standstill at Lock Plant," *STJ*, October 19, 1961.

105 "Our Only Consideration," *STJ*, October 20, 1961.

106 "An Emergency Statement to the Employees of Independent Lock Company," *STJ*, October 22, 1961.

107 "Lock Plant Meets Critical Need," *STJ*, October 24, 1961; "Government Takes Hand as Strike Ends at Plant," *STJ*, October 26, 1961.

108 Zetwick, quoted in "Union Calls for Chamber to Aid Worker Return," *STJ*, October 30, 1961.

109 Zetwick, "LOCKED OUT," *STJ*, November 1, 1961.

110 Four months later, in nearly a three-to-one vote, ILCO workers voted against union representation. The 142 ballots cast by the workers that ILCO refused to rehire were not counted. "ILCO Given Boost for Operation Lifetime Here," *STJ*, November 15, 1961; "Lock Plant Votes to Reject Union by Big Margin," *STJ*, February 18, 1962.

111 For more on SNCC's organizing and its differences from SCLC, see C. Cobb, *This Nonviolent Stuff*; Hogan, *Many Minds, One Heart*; Holsaert et al., *Freedom Plow*.

112 Mrs. Sullivan [Jean] Jackson, interview by Taylor Branch, May 27, 1990, Audiocassette C-5047/118, TBP; Chestnut and Cass, *Black in Selma*; R. Jackson, *House*; Robinson, *Bridge across Jordan*.

113 Bernard Lafayette, interview by James Findlay, 2002–2003, Bernard LaFayette Oral History Project, Mss. Gr. 123, University of Rhode Island Special Collections, http://web.uri.edu/specialcollections/oralhist_list2/; Pt. C. "The Beginnings of the Voter Registration Movement, 1961–1963," 1988, from "We Shall Not Be Moved: Videos of a 1988 Conference on the Student Non-violent Coordinating Committee," Trinity College Digital Repository, http://digitalrepository.trincoll.edu/sncc/4.

114 Quote from Bernard Lafayette, Walk in History Workshop, National Voting Rights Museum and Institute (NVRMI), June 2005; Bernard Lafayette, interview by James Findlay, 2002–2003, Bernard LaFayette Oral History Project, Mss. Gr. 123, University of Rhode Island Special Collections,

http://web.uri.edu/specialcollections/oralhist_list2/; Bernard Lafayette, "SNCC Field Report from Selma, Alabama, February 11–15, 1963," CRMVET, http://www.crmvet.org/lets/630215_sncc_selma-r.pdf.

115 Quote from Chestnut and Cass, *Black in Selma*, 137; see also 134–136; Marie Foster, "The Selma Movement: One of America's Most Successful Non-violent Movements," Chronology, May 1989, folder: Selma Background, box 120, TBP; Marie Foster, interview by Taylor Branch, August 8, 1990, audiocassette C-5047/105, TBP.

116 Mrs. A. P. Boynton Robinson, interview by Taylor Branch, August 9, 1990, folder: Selma Main (3 of 7), box 120, TBP.

117 In January or February 1963, local SNCC recruit James Austin reported that there were 230 registered black voters in Dallas County. Lafayette and Johnson, *In Peace and Freedom*, 7; James Austin, "SNCC Report from Selma, Alabama" [February 1963], CRMVET, http://www.crmvet.org/lets /6302_sncc_selma_austin.pdf.

118 Chestnut and Cass, *Black in Selma*, 156.

119 Colia Liddell Lafayette, "SNCC Field Report, Dallas County," April 6, 1963, CRMVET, http://www.crmvet.org/lets/630406_sncc_selma_colia-r.pdf; Charles Bonner, Walk in History Workshop, NVRMI, June 2005; Lafayette and Johnson, *In Peace and Freedom*, 39; Bettie Mae Fikes, "Singing for Freedom," in *Freedom Plow*, 465–467.

120 Colia Liddell Lafayette, "SNCC Field Report from Selma, Alabama," February 11–15, 1963, CRMVET, http://www.crmvet.org/lets/630215_sncc_selma -r.pdf; Rev. S. W. Powell, "Report," July 16, 1963, Orrville, Alabama, SNCC Papers, reel 17, University of North Carolina at Chapel Hill.

121 C. D. Scott and G. C. Brooks, "Narrative Report of Negro County and Assistant Agents," folder: Dallas County Negro Annual Reports, 1955, box 377, ACES Records.

122 C. D. Scott, G. C. Brooks, and E. S. Harrison, "Narrative Report of Negro County and Assistant Agents," folder: Dallas Annual Report 1957, box 379, ACES Records; C. D. Scott and Ernest S. Harrison, "Narrative Report of Negro County and Assistant Agents," folder: Dallas Negro Reports 1958, box 381, ACES Records.

123 Amelia P. Boynton Robinson, interview by Taylor Branch, August 9, 1990, folder: Selma (main) 3 of 7, box 121, TBP.

124 Bernard Lafayette, Walk in History Workshop, NVRMI, June 2005.

125 Tabernacle's Rev. L. L. Anderson opened the church for the occasion after threatening his cautious deacons with public embarrassment. "Voter Registration Rally Concluded Quietly Here," STJ, May 15, 1963; Bernard Lafayette, interview by Taylor Branch, May 29, 1990, Audiocassette C-5047/134-136, TBP.

126 Forman, quoted in Lafayette and Johnson, *In Peace and Freedom*, 57; quote from Bernard Lafayette, Walk in History Workshop, NVRMI, June 2005. For more about the role of self-defense in the black freedom

struggle, see C. Cobb, *This Nonviolent Stuff*; Dittmer, *Local People*; Payne, *Light of Freedom*; Tyson, *Radio Free Dixie*; Wendt, *Spirit and Shotgun*.

127 "Negroes Urged to Push Quest for Right to Vote," *STJ*, June 25, 1963; "Prayer Services Urged as Means to Win Ballot," *STJ*, July 2, 1963.

128 Dallas County Citizens' Council, advertisement, *STJ*, June 9, 1963.

129 Bernard Lafayette, Walk in History Workshop, NVRMI, June 2005; Lafayette, *In Peace and Freedom*, 75.

130 "Integration Acceptance Flouted by Governor before Large Crowd," *STJ*, August 30, 1963.

131 Quote from "Negro Committee Airs Grievances, Urges Harmony," *STJ*, August 11, 1963; see also Longnecker, *Selma's Peacemaker*, 43–44.

132 DCIA, Edwin L. Moss, chairman, to Selma Retail Merchants Association, August 29, 1963, folder 137, box 7, JJHP.

133 Minutes, "Special Emergency Meeting of the Board of Directors, Selma Chamber of Commerce," September 3, 1963, folder 137, box 7, JJHP.

134 "A Declaration of Rights and Principles," Chamber of Commerce Board of Directors, September 20, 1963, folder 137, box 7, JJHP.

135 "Field Report: From Bruce Gordon," November 9, 1963, SNCC Papers, reel 37.

136 Charles Bonner and Bettie Mae Fikes, interview by Bruce Hartford, 2005, CRMVET, http://www.crmvet.org/nars/chuckbet.htm; Charles Bonner, Walk in History Workshop, NVRMI, June 2005.

137 Quote from "Field Report: From Bruce Gordon," November 9, 1963, SNCC Papers, reel 37; see also "Five Arrested in Sit-In Attempts during Morning in Downtown Demonstrations," *STJ*, September 16, 1963; Zinn, *SNCC*, 149. For more on SNCC's early campaign in Selma, see Branch, *Pillar of Fire*; Garrow, *Bearing the Cross*; Lafayette and Johnson, *In Peace and Freedom*.

138 Quote from Zinn, *SNCC*, 154; see also 147–166.

139 "Selma: Town in a Reign of Terror," *Student Voice*, July 22, 1964.

140 A. P. Boynton to James Forman, November 30, 1963, SNCC Papers, reel 6.

141 For an impressively detailed account of municipal politics in Selma during the 1950s, see Thornton, *Dividing Lines*, 380–386.

142 Quotes from Chestnut and Cass, *Black in Selma*, 127, 196; see also 127, 195; Flynt, *Alabama*, 98–100; Longnecker, *Selma's Peacemaker*, 41.

143 Thornton, *Dividing Lines*, 431.

144 "New City Image Committee Goal," *STJ*, October 28, 1962.

145 Rubin, *Plantation County*, 79–80.

146 Adam, quoted in Thornton, *Dividing Lines*, 431.

147 "Nominees of Chamber Elected Directors in Unique Ballot Here," *STJ*, December 6, 1962.

148 Thornton, *Dividing Lines*, 431–432.

149 1940 U.S. Census, Dallas County, Alabama, population schedule, Selma, p. 3A, Ancestry.com, http://ancestry.com (accessed February 5, 2014); "He

Has Worn Many Labels," *STJ*, July 29, 1979; "The Smitherman Story," *STJ*, July 29, 1979.

150 "Experience Back of New Concern," *STJ*, February 15, 1955.

151 "Only One Runoff Required by Outcome of Primary Here," *STJ*, March 23, 1960; author's field notes, conversation with Joseph Knight, March 10, 2013; "Foes of Renewal Plans Here Win Major Victory," *STJ*, May 14, 1963; "Smitherman in Race for Mayor Post in March," *STJ*, January 7, 1964.

152 Author's field notes, conversation with Joseph Knight, March 10, 2013.

153 "Joe Smitherman for Mayor," *STJ*, March 6, 1964.

154 Quote from Chestnut and Cass, *Black in Selma*, 195–196; see also "Joe Smitherman for Mayor," *STJ*, March 6, 1964.

155 "Joe Smitherman Elected Mayor as Record 4,530 Cast Votes," *STJ*, March 18, 1964.

Interlude: 1965

1 Varela, "Time to Get Ready," in Holsaert et al., *Freedom Plow*, 557–559; Pt. H. "Alabama Bound: Selma, and the Lowndes County Black Panther Party, 1964–1966," 1988, from "We Shall Not Be Moved: Videos of a 1988 Conference on the Student Non-violent Coordinating Committee," Trinity College Digital Repository, http://digitalrepository.trincoll.edu/sncc/9.

2 "Total Segregation: Black Belt, Alabama," *Commonwealth*, August 7, 1964, 536–539; "Violence Threat Quelled at Movie" and "Missiles Thrown," *STJ*, July 5, 1964; United States v. Clark, 249 F. Supp. 720 (S.D. Ala. 1965).

3 "Full Scale Test Set for Sunday in Civil Rights," *STJ*, July 8, 1964; Thornton, *Dividing Lines*, 462.

4 Chafe, *Unfinished Journey*, 214–217; Branch, *Pillar of Fire*, 387–388.

5 "Mass Registration Here Occupies Monday Calm," *STJ*, July 6, 1964; "Judge Hare Bars Meetings For or Against Civil Rights Laws," *STJ*, July 10, 1964.

6 Thornton, *Dividing Lines*, 463.

7 Bernard Lafayette, Walk in History Workshop, NVRMI, June 2005.

8 Garrow, *Bearing the Cross*, 359.

9 Young, quoted in "Selma, 1965," in Hampton, ed., *Voices of Freedom*, 214.

10 Vivian, quoted in Garrow, *Bearing the Cross*, 360. For more on SNCC's voting rights organizing and the Mississippi Freedom Democratic Party, see Dittmer, *Local People*; Payne, *Light of Freedom*.

11 Walter Stafford, "Selma Workshop Report," December 13–16, 1963, SNCC Papers, reel 9.

12 For more on SCLC's strategy in regard to violent law enforcement officials and the media, see Garrow, *Bearing the Cross*, 360, 390–391.

13 King, quoted in Garrow, *Bearing the Cross*, 372; King, quoted in May, *Bending Toward Justice*, 54. Public safety director Wilson Baker had informed SCLC before the meeting that he did not plan to arrest those in attendance. Garrow, *Bearing the Cross*, 371; Fager, *Selma, 1965*, 9–10.

14 "Freedom Days Being Monday-18th at the Dallas County Courthouse,"
   [1965], SNCC Papers, reel 36; Powell, "Playtime Is Over," in Holsaert et al.,
   Freedom Plow, 477.

15 Garrow, *Bearing the Cross*, 377–379.

16 "Alabama Sheriff Turns Back Negro Teachers," *Los Angeles Times*, January 23, 1965; "Negro Teachers Protest in Selma," *New York Times*, January 23, 1965.

17 Quoted in Garrow, *Bearing the Cross*, 391.

18 "A Matter of Satisfaction," *STJ*, January 6, 1965.

19 In February local officials introduced an "appearance book" at the courthouse where potential registrants could sign their names and then be served in a first-come, first-served manner instead of waiting in line. This caused a split between SCLC and DCVL, with SCLC viewing the "appearance book" as a delaying tactic and DCVL seeing it as mediocre progress. Garrow, *Bearing the Cross*, 386–387.

20 Garrow, *Bearing the Cross*, 391.

21 "Wounded Negro Dies in Alabama," *New York Times*, February 27, 1965.

22 Quote from Hall, "Bloody Selma," in Holsaert et al., *Freedom Plow*, 470–472; see also Fager, *Selma, 1965*, 93–97.

23 "Dr. King Announces Plan for New Walk and Assails Attack," *New York Times*, March 8, 1965; "Disgust, Shock Felt in Capital over Clubbings," *Los Angeles Times*, March 9, 1965; "Thousands across U.S. Protest Racial Violence," *Los Angeles Times*, March 10, 1965.

24 Garrow, *Bearing the Cross*, 403; Lawson, "Selma Movement," 539–545.

25 "Death Feared Near for Beaten Minister," *Los Angeles Times*, March 11, 1965.

26 Johnson, quoted in Garrow, *Bearing the Cross*, 408.

27 R. Jackson, *House*, 123.

28 Fager, *Selma, 1965*, 146.

29 "Freedom March Begins in Selma," *New York Times*, March 22, 1965.

30 "25,000 Go to Alabama's Capitol," *New York Times*, March 26, 1965.

31 May, *Informant*.

32 "President Signs Voting Rights Bill into Law," *Los Angeles Times*, August 7, 1965.

Chapter 6: Making the "Good Freedom"

1 Joanne Bland, "Growing Up in the Segregated South," Presentation at Winona Senior High School, February 2011, *Culture Clique*, KQAL, Winona State University, http://www.prx.org/pieces/59935.

2 Chestnut and Cass, *Black in Selma*, 225.

3 Quote from Chestnut and Cass, *Black in Selma*, 226; Smitherman, quoted in "Cooperation of Negro Leaders Is Requested," *STJ*, May 8, 1965; see also Fager, *Selma, 1965*, 166–178, 188–191; "What the Negroes of Selma and Dallas County Want," *STJ*, May 2, 1965.

4 Fager, *Selma, 1965,* 166–178, 188–191.

5 F. D. Reese, interview by Andrew M. Manis, August 8, 1981, Andrew M. Manis Oral History Interviews, Birmingham Public Library, AL; Chestnut and Cass, *Black in Selma,* 134–135, 226–228.

6 Ashmore, *Carry It On,* 170–172; Fager, *Selma, 1965,* 190–191.

7 Doug and Tina Harris and Janet Jemmott, "Over 200 at East Selma People's Convention," SNCC Papers, reel 36.

8 "East Selma People Are Getting Together for Some Bar-B-Q, Some Movies, Some Talk," SNCC Papers, reel 17.

9 Doug and Tina Harris and Janet Jemmott, "Over 200 at East Selma People's Convention" SNCC Papers, reel 36.

10 Fuller, quoted in "Selma Coke Workers Vote on Union Aug. 18," *Southern Courier (SC),* July 30, 1965.

11 Quoted in "Coke Union Loses Again," *SC,* August 28, 1965.

12 Joseph Smitherman, interview by Blackside, Inc., December 5, 1985, in *Eyes on the Prize: America's Civil Rights Years, 1954–1965,* Henry Hampton Collection, Film and Media Archive, Washington University Libraries.

13 Black workers at Henry Brick Yard, Lovoy's, and Stewart King and McKenzie Grocers also attempted to form unions. Meeting Men from Coca Cola, June 21, 1965, SNCC Papers, reel 17.; Memo: To Silas, Staff; From: Doug, Tina, Janet, SNCC Papers, reel 17.

14 The formal census poverty line was not established until 1963–1964. U.S. Department of Commerce, Bureau of the Census, *Census of Population: 1960* and *Census of Housing: 1960*; "Results Given on Housing Survey," *STJ,* March 20, 1962; Ashmore, *Carry It On,* 164.

15 Cox, quoted in remarks by Judy Richardson, "In the Mississippi River: Heroes and Sheroes: A Tribute to Those Murdered and Martyred in Mississippi," Freedom Summer 50 Conference, Jackson, MS, June 27, 2014, CRMVET, http://www.crmvet.org/comm/judyr14.htm.

16 Ashmore, *Carry It On,* 58–59.

17 Ashmore, *Carry It On,* 164–165.

18 Clarence Williams and Joe Johnson, interview by Hardy Frye, 1972, Hardy Frye Oral History Collection, Auburn University.

19 Quote from Noonan, "Captured by the Movement," in Holsaert et al., *Freedom Plow,* 497.

20 "Sanction Sought by Local Group on Anti-poverty," *STJ,* October 27, 1965.

21 Edward Rudd, "Race Complicates Black Belt's Anti-poverty Plans," *SC,* October 16, 1965.

22 Smitherman, quoted in "City Will Apply for Anti-poverty Funds," *STJ,* October 29, 1965.

23 Ashmore, *Carry It On,* 169.

24 "Mayor Asks for Broad Base Plan in Anti-poverty," *STJ,* November 5, 1965.

25 "Poverty Dispute in Selma," *SC,* November 13, 1965.

26 "Poverty Parley Punctuated by Spirited Debate," *STJ,* November 10, 1965.

27 Quote from Francis X. Walter, interview by Stanley Smith, August 1968, Ralph J. Bunche Oral History Collection, Moorland-Spingarn Research Center, Howard University, Washington, DC (hereafter cited as RJBOHC), 26–27; see also "Poverty Dispute in Selma," *SC*, November 13, 1965.

28 Hunter, quoted in "Selma Negroes Wonder, What Did Mayor Mean?" *SC*, February 2, 1966.

29 Quote from Shirley Mesher, interview by Stanley Smith, 1968, RJBOHC, 44; see also Ashmore, *Carry It On*, 174–175.

30 Jeffries, *Bloody Lowndes*, 144–145.

31 "Two Old Foes Battle in Selma," *SC*, March 19, 1966.

32 Quote from Dallas County Independent Free Voters Information [1966], SNCC Papers, reel 17; see also Ashmore, *Carry It On*, 174.

33 Reese, quoted in "Dallas County Voters Start Third Party," *SC*, March 19, 1966; quote from Chestnut and Cass, *Black in Selma*, 228.

34 "How Did Your County Vote," *SC*, May 7, 1966.

35 "Sheriff's Fight Enters Federal Court," *STJ*, May 6, 1966; "Re-tabulation Set on Disputed Boxes," *STJ*, May 26, 1966.

36 Advertisement, Jim Clark for sheriff, *STJ*, October 23, 1966.

37 "Baker Edges Clark in Sheriff's Race," *STJ*, November 9, 1966.

38 Williams, quoted in "Dallas: DCIFVO Head Not Discouraged," *SC*, November 12, 1966.

39 J. Cobb, *The South and America*, 101.

40 "Hammermill to Construct $30 Million Plant Here," *STJ*, February 3, 1965; J. Cobb, *The South and America*, 104–105.

41 J. Cobb, *The South and America*, 105; "Hammermill Takes Realistic Stand," *STJ*, May 14, 1965.

42 Smitherman, quoted in Chestnut and Cass, *Black in Selma*, 224; see also 223; "City Council in Agreement Here on Declaration," *STJ*, April 16, 1965; "Chamber Reverses Stand on Advertisement Issue," *STJ*, April 18, 1965.

43 "New Type of Farmer Emerging," *STJ*, March 30, 1969.

44 U.S. Department of Commerce, Bureau of the Census, *Census of Agriculture: 1969*.

45 "A Welcome to Dan River Mills," *STJ*, August 25, 1966; "Marchers Ride to Laura for Demonstration Here," *STJ*, September 11, 1967.

46 U.S. Department of Commerce, Bureau of the Census, *Census of Manufacturers: 1972*.

47 "'Illegal Strike' Called Alleges Spokesman for Laura Industries," *STJ*, August 3, 1967.

48 "Plea Issued for Workers Return Here," *STJ*, August 6, 1967.

49 "Strikers in Selma Ask Recognition of Union," *SC*, September 2, 1967.

50 Douglas Levins, quoted in "Marchers Ride to Laura for Demonstration Here," *STJ*, September 11, 1967.

51 "Action Asked in Support of Local Dispute," *SC*, September 6, 1967.

52 "Marchers Ride to Laura for Demonstration Here," *STJ*, September 11, 1967.

53 Nunn, quoted in "Strikers in Selma Plan Next Move," *SC*, September 9, 1967.

54 "Alert Force Unneeded at Laura Site," *STJ*, September 14, 1967.

55 "Laura Industries Has Closed," *STJ*, June 17, 1969.

56 Mesher, interview by Stanley Smith, 1968, RJBOHC, 11, 343–346.

57 "Law Doesn't Provide for Working Mothers," *STJ*, May 13, 1974; "She's Always Been a Maid—Now What?," *STJ*, May 14, 1974.

58 Mesher, interview by Stanley Smith, 1968, RJBOHC, 61–62.

59 Solinger, "First Welfare Case," 19. For more on how black women protested their treatment in welfare offices, see Orleck, *Storming Caesars Palace*; White, *Too Heavy a Load*.

60 Smith, quoted in Solinger, "First Welfare Case," 20; see also 18–21.

61 Quoted in "Warren's Last Ruling," *SC*, June 29, 1968.

62 "County Board Bows to Pressure, Seeks Surplus Food Aid," *STJ*, June 23, 1965.

63 Harville, quoted in "People Criticize New Stamp Plan," *SC*, March 18, 1967.

64 "Summer Project Funds Approved," *STJ*, June 16, 1966; "150 Working on Project Drain-O and Forty More Workers Needed," *STJ*, October 6, 1966; "Project Center Funding Sought," *STJ*, May 18, 1967.

65 "Operation Mainstream Gives Opportunity to Job Seekers," *STJ*, November 30, 1969.

66 "Carver Neighborhood Center Here Prepares Children for School," *STJ*, February 22, 1970.

67 Joseph Knight, interview by the author, October 31, 2012.

68 "Joe Knight Resigns Position with OEO," *STJ*, September 14, 1970.

69 Ashmore, *Carry It On*, 7–16.

70 Mesher, interview by Stanley Smith, 1968, RJBOHC, 42–43.

71 Quoted in Ashmore, "Going Back to Selma," 326; Anderson, quoted in Ashmore, *Carry It On*, 226.

72 "Noisy Meeting Extends Selma's Poverty Fight," *SC*, December 23, 1967; "Head Start Centers Open despite Denial," *STJ*, June 11, 1967.

73 Knight, quoted in "Proposed Session on Head Start Ended Abruptly," *STJ*, June 20, 1967.

74 "The Kids from SHAPE," *SC*, February 24, 1968.

75 "Head Start Has Been Refunded," *STJ*, May 5, 1972.

76 Johnson, quoted in "Farmers Joining New Cooperative," *SC*, February 18, 1967; see also Ashmore, *Carry It On*, 208–211.

77 "Mayor Protests Award to OEO," *STJ*, May 11, 1967.

78 Johnson, quoted in "Fighting to Stay on the Land," *SC*, February 18–19, 1967; Johnson, quoted in "Ala. Negroes Operate Co-op to Help Poor Families," *Jet*, June 1, 1967.

79 1965 Civil Rights Commission Report, *Equal Opportunity in Farm Programs*, quoted in U.S. Commission on Civil Rights and Good, *Cycle to Nowhere*, 17.

80 Johnson, quoted in "Ala. Negroes Operate Co-op to Help Poor Families," *Jet*, June 1, 1967; see also Ashmore, *Carry It On*, 224–226.

81 Turner, quoted in Ashmore, *Carry It On*, 200; see also Mesher, interview by Stanley Smith, 1968, RJBOHC, 86; "SWAFCA Leaders Answer White Officials' Charges," SC, May 20–21, 1967. For more about discrimination against African Americans by USDA employees and programs, see Daniel, *Dispossession*.

82 "Resistance to Collective Is Being Organized Here," STJ, March 31, 1967.

83 "Protest Hearing Presentation Is Held Excellent," STJ, April 5, 1967.

84 Ashmore, *Carry It On*, 216–229; Mesher, interview by Stanley Smith, 1968, RJBOHC, 211–225.

85 Mesher, interview by Stanley Smith, 1968, RJBOHC, 63.

86 "SWAFCA Fund Plea Gets Nod," STJ, February 3, 1974.

87 "Schools Desegregation Plan Here Is Approved," STJ, May 17, 1965.

88 "Schools Integrate Quietly in Selma," STJ, September 3, 1965.

89 M. Alston Keith to James Hare, June 16, 1965, folder 134, box 7, JJHP.

90 M. Alston Keith to MacDonald Gallion, November 13, 1963, folder 134, box 7, JJHP.

91 "Articles and Certificate of Incorporation to the _____ School," to the Honorable B. A. Reynolds, judge of probate of Dallas County, Alabama [1959?], folder 134, box 7, JJHP.

92 The Selma Baptist Association had attempted to open an all-white private school in 1959 but had abandoned the effort when only one child registered for classes. "Private School Purchases Land," STJ, July 24, 1966.

93 John T. Morgan Academy, *Yearbook*.

94 Joanne Bland, interview by Thomas Dent, August 22, 1991, Southern Journey Oral History Collection, Tulane University Digital Library, New Orleans, Louisiana.

95 Pickard, quoted in "Plan Submitted for Schools Here," STJ, January 11, 1970; see also "Board Meets to Plan School Opening Here," STJ, June 19, 1970.

96 "In Support of Public Education," STJ, June 28, 1970.

97 Father, quoted in "Parents' Meet Is Set Tonight for Ball Park," STJ, August 11, 1970; Williamson, quoted in "Allen Tells Parents School Segregation 'Thing of Past'; Urges Pressure for 'Freedom of Choice,'" STJ, August 12, 1970; see also "Massive Defiance Urged for 'Concerned Parents' at Public Meeting Here," STJ, August 5, 1970; "Concerned Parents and Politics," STJ, August 9, 1970; "Three New School Board Members," STJ, July 24, 1970; "New School Board Members," STJ, July 26, 1970; "'Concerned Parents' Offered Cut-Rate Tuition Proposal by Meadowview Private School," STJ, August 19, 1970.

98   Quote from "Things Went Quite Well," *STJ*, September 6, 1970; see also Advertisement for John T. Morgan Academy, *STJ*, April 8, 1970.

99   "Heavy Balloting Expected Tomorrow," *STJ*, March 4, 1968.

100 "Incumbents Lead in Primary Ballot," *STJ*, March 6, 1968; "Reflections on City Politics," *STJ*, March 10, 1968.

101 Moss, quoted in Chestnut and Cass, *Black in Selma*, 259.

102 "Vote Draws Quick Response, Challenge," *STJ*, January 25, 1971.

103 Selma City Council Minutes, October 2, 1972.

104 "Former Alabama Leader, Carl C. Morgan, Jr., Dies," *STJ*, May 6, 2006.

105 Smitherman, quoted in Selma City Council Minutes, October 9, 1972.

106 J. Cobb, *The South and America*, 107.

107 Quote from Chestnut and Cass, *Black in Selma*, 260; see also 261–262.

108 Hank Sanders, "How Did You Come to Live in Selma?," Senate Sketches #1295, April 3, 2012, Facebook, https://www.facebook.com /hanktherocksanders.

109 Quote from Chestnut and Cass, *Black in Selma*, 252; see also 249–253.

110 "Suit Charges Selma and Dallas County with Hiring Bias," *STJ*, August 18, 1972; "Suit Requests Court Ordered Redistricting in County," *STJ*, December 21, 1972.

111 "Mayor Critical of Pressure," *STJ*, February 11, 1972.

112 Chestnut and Cass, *Black in Selma*, 257.

113 Quote from Chestnut and Cass, *Black in Selma*, 252–253; see also 254–258.

114 Smitherman, quoted in Chestnut and Cass, *Black in Selma*, 266; see also 267–268. The city received a $3 million grant from the Department of Housing and Urban Development to rebuild a black slum area. But when the Clarke School project (which misspelled the name of Clark School) began in 1972, the city's plans concentrated housing projects in already poor and black areas, reclassified valuable residential property occupied by blacks as industrial zones, and included virtually no black input in the planning. The NAACP Legal Defense Fund intervened, suing Housing and Urban Development and the city for perpetuating residential segregation with federal funds. After much negotiation, all parties involved signed the Selma Accord, agreeing to locate low-income housing outside of majority-black areas, to hire a black urban-renewal director, and to appoint a fifty-fifty racially split advisory board. "Renewal Project Will Turn Area into Model," *STJ*, November 19, 1972; Chestnut and Cass, *Black in Selma*, 266–268.

115 "East Selma's 'Big Ditch' Now Well Underway," *STJ*, August 9, 1970; "Anti-poverty Agency Lists Where Money Went," *STJ*, April 25, 1971.

116 Chafe, *Unfinished Journey*, 374–378, 413.

117 "Cut Feared Mainstream Is Threatened," *STJ*, April 22, 1973; "City Loses Mainstream Reins," *STJ*, November 4, 1973.

118 Donal Cunningham, quoted in "Anti-poverty Agency Lists Where Money Went, Plans," *STJ*, April 25, 1971.

119 "Youth Work," *STJ*, July 11, 1973; "City-County Troubleshooter Now on the Job Fulltime," *STJ*, July 15, 1973.

120 "Selma Transit System," *STJ*, February 27, 1977; "EOB Seeks Funds," *STJ*, May 5, 1977.

121 Smitherman, quoted in "Mayor Has $2 Million Worth of Good News," *STJ*, October 7, 1974.

122 Ashmore, "Going Back to Selma," 325.

123 Meyer and the Alabama-Tombigbee Regional Commission, *Downtown Selma Plan*, 11.

124 "Sears Opening Set at Mall," *STJ*, July 11, 1971.

125 "Though Broad Street Hurting, Businessmen Remain Optimistic," *STJ*, December 31, 1972.

126 "Municipal Complex within Reach," *STJ*, June 14, 1972.

127 "After 88 Years Eagles Is Closing," *STJ*, May 20, 1973; "Rothschild's Here Is Closing Doors," *STJ*, December 31, 1974; "'Mr. Sam' Closes the Doors of Barton's," *STJ*, February 29, 1976.

128 Quote from Wallace, "Economic History;" see also "At Peak Power Plant May Employ 2,875; Weekly Payroll $750,000," *STJ*, April 28, 1972; "Fighting for Farmland," *STJ*, March 1, 1981.

129 "180 All-Lock Layoffs Told," *STJ*, November 13, 1974; "Hammermill Plans Shut Down," *STJ*, January 14, 1975; "Dan River at Benton Plans Week Shutdown," *STJ*, February 18, 1975.

130 Meyer and the Alabama-Tombigbee Regional Commission, *Downtown Selma Plan*, 9; "Unemployment: State Watches Problem Closely, Sends 'Rate Watcher' to Selma," *STJ*, July 2, 1975.

131 Nancy Sewell, interview by the author, December 6, 2012; Chestnut and Cass, *Black in Selma*, 268; "Suit Filed against City School Board," *STJ*, April 30, 1975.

132 Letter to the editor from "Black Parents," *STJ*, May 7, 1975.

133 Chestnut and Cass, *Black in Selma*, 287–290.

134 "Closed-Door Session Continues," *STJ*, August 22, 1975.

135 "Westbrook Resigns Post," *STJ*, August 24, 1975.

136 "School Picket Plan Revealed," *STJ*, October 12, 1975.

137 Smitherman, quoted in "Mayor to Enforce Pickets," *STJ*, October 13, 1975; Sanders, quoted in "LDF Airs List of Grievances," *STJ*, October 25, 1975; see also "Mayor Asks Meeting between Board, LDF," *STJ*, October 18, 1975; "Selma Businessman Appointed to Selma City School Board," *STJ*, November 14, 1975.

138 Chestnut and Cass, *Black in Selma*, 268.

Interlude: Closing Craig Air Force Base

1 Quote from "Craig Investment May Be Best Money Selma People Ever Spent," *STJ*, August 8, 1965; see also Golembe Associates, "Impact of Closure," v.

2 "City Schools Get 95,682 Payment," *STJ*, April 21, 1970.

3 Heinz, quoted in "Local Delegation Expresses Optimism for Retention of Craig AFB," *STJ*, April 22, 1962; see also "Personnel of 2,000 Expected at Craig," *STJ*, October 18, 1945; "Craig Given Back," *STJ*, April 20, 1971.

4 "The Problem of Air Pollution," *STJ*, September 17, 1970.

5 Berkey, "Closing," 6; Campagna, *Economy*, 12.

6 "Craig Closing Seen," *STJ*, January 21, 1976.

7 Robinson, quoted in "Black Leader Here Urges Some 'Soul Negotiation' for Craig," *STJ*, January 22, 1976.

8 "Alabama May Lose U.S. Air Force Base," *Jet*, April 15, 1976; "Air Force Explains Craig Decision," *STJ*, March 11, 1976; Golembe Associates, "Impact of Closure," table III-2.

9 Berkey, "Closing," 3.

10 Davis and Army Engineers Study Center, "Army Base Realignment Methodology," F-2-3.

11 Berkey, "Closing," 16–18.

12 Davis and Army Engineers Study Center, "Army Base Realignment Methodology," F-2-1.

13 Berkey, "Closing," 18–24.

14 Quote from Golembe Associates, "Impact of Closure," 9; see also vii–x.

15 Quote from Golembe Associates, "Impact of Closure," 59; see also 63–64.

16 Morthland, quoted in "Craig: Input from Public Sought," *STJ*, September 25, 1976.

17 "Top o' the Day," *STJ*, November 14, 1976.

18 "Sylvan Street Unchanged," *STJ*, May 11, 1976; "Top o' the Day," *STJ*, June 15, 1976.

19 Selma City Council Minutes, May 10, 1976.

20 "Council Rejects Renaming," *STJ*, July 13, 1976; "Sylvan Street Remains Unchanged," *STJ*, October 11, 1976.

21 Reese, quoted in "White Councilmen OK Sylvan Change," *STJ*, November 15, 1976.

22 Berkey, "Closing," 35–36.

23 Robinson, quoted in "Economics: Speakers Paint Bleak Picture," *STJ*, November 16, 1976.

24 Berkey, "Closing," 40–41.

25 "Armed with Troy Study, Team Attacks Pentagon," *STJ*, November 29, 1976.

26 Berkey, "Closing," 40–44.

27 "Group Off to D.C. to Plan Craig Strategy," *STJ*, March 1, 1977; "Carter to Keep Eye on Craig Situation," *STJ*, March 3, 1977.

28 "Officials Tour Base," *STJ*, March 16, 1977.

29 "Decision Made to Close Craig," *STJ*, March 30, 1977.

30 "Last Class Finishes at Craig AFB," *STJ*, August 13, 1977.

31 "Low-Key Ceremony Marks 'Closing Date,'" *STJ*, October 2, 1977.

32 President's Economic Adjustment Committee, "Economic Adjustment Program, Selma/Dallas County, Alabama, Federal Team Visit Report," January 1978, Office of Economic Adjustment, Office of the Assistant Secretary of Defense, Pentagon, Washington, DC, January 1978, ODMA.

Chapter 7: "Last One Out of Selma, Turn Off the Lights"

1 June Cohn, interview by the author, November 30, 2011; U.S. Department of Commerce, Bureau of the Census, *U.S. Census of Retail Trade: 1977* and *Census of Retail Trade: 1982*.

2 Quoted in Trend and Auburn Technical Assistance Center, *What Happens to Workers*, 130; see also 128–129; University of Alabama, Office of Economic and Community Affairs, *Economic Development Planning Report*, 10–11.

3 University of Alabama, Office of Economic and Community Affairs, *Economic Development Planning Report*, 16.

4 The Economic Adjustment Committee helped coordinate the federal resources available to assist communities left behind after a base's closing. Berkey, "Closing," 33–34.

5 Smitherman, quoted in "Senator Incurs Mayor's Wrath," *STJ*, April 2, 1977; see also "Selma Starts on Road Block," *STJ*, April 1, 1977.

6 "One Group to Handle Craig Development," *STJ*, April 14, 1977.

7 "Craig Field: Five Men Prepare to Handle Redevelopment," *STJ*, May 22, 1977.

8 "Redevelopment Takes a Team Effort," *STJ*, April 27, 1977.

9 "Systematic Search On for Industries," *STJ*, July 20, 1977; "Industrial Development Reps Came, Saw, Were Impressed," *STJ*, August 9, 1977.

10 Morgan, quoted in "Authority Searches for Best Industries to Come to Craig," *STJ*, August 30, 1977.

11 "Industry: What Kind to Attract," *STJ*, September 8, 1977.

12 "Strikers Picketing at Bush Hog," *STJ*, January 10, 1977.

13 "Cars Turned Over; 7 Strikers Arrested," *STJ*, January 19, 1977; "Industry Offers Strike Meeting," *STJ*, January 21, 1977.

14 "Steel Workers Set Up Police Station Pickets," *STJ*, February 24, 1977.

15 "Explosion Rips Hole in Wall of Bush Hog Plant," *STJ*, March 20, 1977; "Bush Hog to Meet with Union Officials," *STJ*, March 22, 1977.

16 "Meeting of Union, Firm Important," *STJ*, March 23, 1977.

17 "Deadlock Halt Bush Hog Negotiations," *STJ*, March 26, 1977.

18 "Strikers Are Hoping for End to Picket," *STJ*, June 29, 1977; "Settlement Seen as Defeat for Local Union," *STJ*, July 8, 1977.

19 Jones, quoted in "Strikers Bitter about 'Weak' Workers," *STJ*, July 8, 1977.

20 Wright, quoted in "Wright Believes Unions Can Help," *STJ*, November 21, 1977. The union locals were concentrated in only nine of the area's seventy manufacturing firms. "Union in County Viewed Suspiciously," *STJ*, November 20, 1977.

21 For more on how the idea of the "Sunbelt" developed, see Nickerson and Dochuk, *Sunbelt Rising*, 4–13.

22 Falk and Lyson, *High Tech*, 45; Schulman, *Cotton Belt to Sunbelt*, 176–179.

23 Southern Growth Policies Board, *Halfway Home*, 11.

24 Bradley, quoted in "Leaders Plan Future of Area," *STJ*, September 24, 1977.

25 "Craig Envoys Return Here," *STJ*, November 12, 1977.

26 "Lockheed Turned Craig Site Down," *STJ*, November 17, 1977.

27 "No One Specific Thing Swayed Lockheed to Webb," *STJ*, November 17, 1977.

28 "Lifetime Industries Secures Lease," *STJ*, January 30, 1978; "New Industry Picks Craig," *STJ*, November 16, 1978; "Welcome Beechcraft," *STJ*, December 24, 1978.

29 President's Economic Adjustment Committee, "Economic Adjustment Program, Selma/Dallas County, Alabama, Federal Team Visit Report," January 1978, Office of Economic Adjustment, Office of the Assistant Secretary of Defense, Pentagon, Washington, DC, ODMA.

30 Chafe, *Unfinished Journey*, 447–450; Troy, *Morning in America*, 27–31. For more on automation and the elimination of industrial jobs, see Sugrue, *Urban Crisis*.

31 "Recession Arrives, but 'Things Could Be Lots Worse,'" *STJ*, May 7, 1980.

32 "Dallas County's Jobless Rate Increases," *STJ*, July 13, 1980; "Unemployment Dips to 8.9 Percent," *STJ*, July 13, 1990.

33 Ronald Reagan, Neshoba County Fair speech, Mississippi, August 3, 1980, transcript of speech, *Neshoba Democrat*, November 15, 2007, http://neshobademocrat.com/Content/NEWS/News/Article/Transcript -of-Ronald-Reagan-s-1980-Neshoba-County-Fair-speech/2/297/15599 (accessed January 27, 2017).

34 Reagan, quoted in Troy, *Morning in America*, 57; see also 68.

35 U.S. Department of Commerce, Bureau of the Census, *Census of Population: 1980*.

36 Smitherman, quoted in "Smitherman's Rhetoric: Fast and Breezy," *STJ*, February 6, 1981.

37 "Dallas Could Hurt; Budget Impact Left to Congress," *STJ*, February 15, 1981.

38 Mrs. Jewel Kynard, letter to the editor, *STJ*, August 9, 1981.

39 Campagna, *Economy*, 40.

40 "Reagan Cuts Pinch Dallas Slow but Sure," *STJ*, October 4, 1981.

41 Both quotes are from "People Look Elsewhere," *STJ*, February 21, 1982.

42 "Selma Is a Home Buyer's Market," *STJ*, October 4, 1981.

43 Troy, *Morning in America*, 209–211.

44 Campagna, *Economy*, 90.

45 "Economy Forces Closing, Industry Cutbacks in Area," *STJ*, February 24, 1982.

46 "Bush Hog Lays Off 100 Workers," *STJ*, March 5, 1982; "Bush Hog to Shut Down in July," *STJ*, April 13, 1982.

47 "Economy Blamed as 376 Workers Out," *STJ*, April 18, 1982.

48 "140 Apply for Police Vacancies," *STJ*, March 17, 1982; "More Than 400 Apply for 40 Temporary Jobs," *STJ*, January 26, 1983.

49 "Jobless Rate Keeps Jumping," *STJ*, January 4, 1983.

50 Henderson, quoted in "His Farm to the Highest Bidder," *STJ*, July 10, 1983.

51 "Forced Sales: 15 Fewer Farmers Will Be Tilling Dallas County Soil," *STJ*, March 6, 1983.

52 "Farm Auctions Prevalent," *STJ*, March 16, 1983.

53 Campagna, *Economy*, 79–82.

54 Campagna, *Economy*, 90.

55 Rosenfeld, "Tale of Two Souths," 51–53.

56 Schulman, *Cotton Belt to Sunbelt*, 178–179.

57 Lichter, "Race and Unemployment," 184. For a detailed example of one company's efforts to secure cheap labor, see Cowie, *Capital Moves*.

58 Trend and Auburn Technical Assistance Center, *What Happens to Workers*, 1–5, 89.

59 Rev. David Pettaway, quoted in Trend and Auburn Technical Assistance Center, *What Happens to Workers*, 195; see also 194–197, 228.

60 "Dallas County Unemployment Rate Jumps to 17.6," *STJ*, September 9, 1985; Trend and Auburn Technical Assistance Center, *What Happens to Workers*, 2.

61 Quoted in Trend and Auburn Technical Assistance Center, *What Happens to Workers*, 242.

62 Quoted in Trend and Auburn Technical Assistance Center, *What Happens to Workers*, 256.

63 "Beech Closing Expected to Hit Hard," *STJ*, March 7, 1986.

64 Quoted in Trend and Auburn Technical Assistance Center, *What Happens to Workers*, 118; see also 116–117.

65 Quoted in Trend and Auburn Technical Assistance Center, *What Happens to Workers*, 130; see also 121, 129.

66 University of Alabama, Office of Economic and Community Affairs, *Economic Development Planning Report*, 11.

67 Quoted in Trend and Auburn Technical Assistance Center, *What Happens to Workers*, 229; see also 228, 230.

68 "Growth," *STJ*, January 4, 1987.

69 Campagna, *Economy*, 129.

70 "Sound Planning," *STJ*, December 24, 1985.

71 "Gramm-Rudman, Local Officials Expect Cuts to Dig Deeper," *STJ*, February 2, 1986.

72 "Proposed City Budget: Raise Taxes and Squeeze," *STJ*, September 7, 1986.

73 "Reagan Cut Cost Alabama $1.9 Bill," *STJ*, September 30, 1986.

74 Troy, *Morning in America*, 4, 11–16, 215–218.

75 U.S. Department of Commerce, Bureau of the Census, *Census of Population: 1980*.

76 Clarence Williams and Joe Johnson, interview by Hardy Frye, 1972, Hardy Frye Oral History Collection.

77 The international and economic uncertainty of the late 1970s, as well as political gains by African Americans, helped sparked the revival of white vigilante organizations like the Ku Klux Klan all across the country. "Klan Help Not Needed," *STJ*, April 1, 1979; Musgrove, *Racial Politics*, 114.

78 Joseph Knight, interview by the author, October 31, 2012.

79 Selma City Council Minutes, March 26, 1979, and June 25, 1979; "Klan Marches in Selma Saturday," *STJ*, April 15, 1979; "City Pools Are Closed," *STJ*, June 17, 1979; "Selma Police to 'Beef Up' Patrols Following Klan Appearance at Pools," *STJ*, June 19, 1979.

80 J. L. Chestnut Jr., "Perspective," *STJ*, April 1, 1979.

81 A history of police brutality had also taught black Selma residents to be wary. In 1970 the black community had staged a week of protests after a police officer killed a black man, Lloyd Bizzell, while taking him into custody; just one year later, however, the police officer had been acquitted and reinstated. "Group Asks Suspension of Officer," *STJ*, January 2, 1970; "Chambers Held Not Guilty by Jury Here," *STJ*, April 1, 1971.

82 "Blacks Want End to Violence," *STJ*, April 3, 1979.

83 "Board Selection Ends," *STJ*, March 6, 1977.

84 Selma City Council Minutes, September 10, 1979; "School Board Vacancies Filled," *STJ*, September 25, 1979.

85 Reese, quoted in Selma City Council Minutes, July 12, 1982.

86 President's Economic Adjustment Committee "Economic Adjustment Program, Selma/Dallas County, Alabama, Federal Team Visit Report," January 1978, Office of Economic Adjustment, Office of the Assistant Secretary of Defense, Pentagon, Washington, DC, ODMA; "Attorney Charges Access Denied," *STJ*, June 23, 1978; "Control Delayed," *STJ*, July 13, 1978; "Suit for Craig Housing Filed," *STJ*, November 7, 1978.

87 "Craig Property Suit Is Filed," *STJ*, May 27, 1979.

88 "Craig Attorneys Told 'Settle or Go to Trial,'" *STJ*, January 22, 1980.

89 "Craig Families Take a Chance," *STJ*, January 31, 1980.

90 Ebbinghouse, quoted in "Craig 'Truce' Is Declared," *STJ*, February 1, 1980.

91 In *In Search of Another Country*, historian Joseph Crespino argues that white politicians practiced calculated compliance with civil rights laws or "strategic accommodation" to preserve their political power. *In Search*, 11–12.

92 J. L. Chestnut, "Perspective," *STJ*, February 3, 1980.

93 "'Treaty Room' Conference Resumes," *STJ*, February 14, 1980; "Overtime Effort Seals Craig Deal," *STJ*, March 5, 1981; "Craig's Section 8: On Wrong Side of Road?," *STJ*, August 31, 1988.

94 These plays were typically written by Rose Sanders. Faya Rose (Sanders) Toure, interview by the author, August 17, 2013.

95 "African Extravaganza Planned for July 1," *STJ*, June 23, 1974; "Selma Churches Salute King," *STJ*, January 16, 1980; "BlackFest," *STJ*, November 19, 1981.

96 Faya Rose (Sanders) Toure, interview by the author, August 17, 2013; "Teacher, 74, 'Retiring' for Second Time," *STJ*, May 29, 1977; "McRae Learning Center Opens Decade Celebration," *STJ*, October 21, 1987.

97 Forty percent of children paid McRae's full fee of $120 per month; the Department of Pensions and Securities helped fund the rest. "Learning Center Established," *STJ*, June 25, 1978; "'Building Today for Tomorrow' at McRae Learning Center," *STJ*, April 6, 1986.

98 Roy Edwards, quoted in "Hearts to Hands at McRae," *STJ*, April 13, 1986; "McRae Center Not Closing," *STJ*, January 12, 1987.

99 Faya Rose (Sanders) Toure, interview by the author, August 17, 2013.

100 "MOMs Sponsors Mother's Skills Conference Here," *STJ*, May 20, 1983.

101 "It's Economics," *STJ*, May 29, 1983.

102 "$30,000 Grant Awarded Here," *STJ*, January 9, 1986.

103 Quote from Faya Rose (Sanders) Toure, interview by the author, August 17, 2013; quote from Chestnut and Cass, *Black in Selma*, 311.

104 Quote from Chestnut and Cass, *Black in Selma*, 315–316; see also 311–314. Many black candidates entered in the late 1960s and early 1970s as candidates for the National Democratic Party of Alabama, which had grown out of the third-party efforts across the Black Belt following the passage of the Voting Rights Act. The party supported the national Democrats but backed black candidates in local elections. For more, see Frye, *Black Parties*.

105 Quote from Chestnut and Cass, *Black in Selma*, 322; see also 321, 323; Musgrove, *Racial Politics*, 153–159.

106 Quote from Chestnut and Cass, *Black in Selma*, 324.

107 Quote from Chestnut and Cass, *Black in Selma*, 344; see also 339–343; "Lawsuit Seeks to Halt Reed Remap Plan," *STJ*, January 12, 1983; Musgrove, *Racial Politics*, 149.

108 Quote from Chestnut and Cass, *Black in Selma*, 363; see also 359–362.

109 Quote from Chestnut and Cass, *Black in Selma*, 262; see also 363.

110 Quote from "Jackson 'Preaches' Voter Registration," *STJ*, February 8, 1984; see also Chestnut and Cass, *Black in Selma*, 359–363; Faya Rose (Sanders) Toure, interview by the author, August 17, 2013; Frederick D. Reese, interview by the author, October 17, 2012.

111 Williamson, quoted in "Williamson Heads Up Voter Drive," *STJ*, February 12, 1984.

112   Cobb, *The South and America*, 120–121.

113   Smitherman quoted in "Smitherman Denies Charges by Sanders," *STJ*, February 15, 1984; Foster, quoted in "Marie Foster to Continue to Help," *STJ*, March 2, 1984; see also J. L. Chestnut Jr., "Enough of This Shame," Perspective, *STJ*, February 19, 1984.

114   "Registration Race Gets 'Frantic,'" *STJ*, June 13, 1984.

115   "Rolls Show Whites Have Vote Majority," *STJ*, June 21, 1984.

116   "Smitherman Wins, Reese Vows Support," *STJ*, July 11, 1984.

117   J. L. Chestnut Jr., "Had Blacks 'Stooped,' They Would Have Won," Perspective, *STJ*, July 15, 1984.

118   Quote from Chestnut and Cass, *Black in Selma*, 366; see also 365, 367.

119   "Smitherman Denies Charges by Sanders," *STJ*, February 15, 1984; Musgrove, *Racial Politics*, 153–159.

120   Chestnut and Cass, *Black in Selma*, 367–369.

121   "Voters Elect First Black Courthouse Official in a Century," *STJ*, September 26, 1984.

122   Jackie Walker, "Letting the 'First' Speak for Herself," Perspective, *STJ*, September 30, 1984.

123   "Friends Hope Jackie Walker's Legacy Won't Die," *STJ*, February 3, 1985.

124   "Blacks Meet on Collector Decision," *STJ*, May 12, 1985.

125   Quotes from Chestnut and Cass, *Black in Selma*, 369; see also 371; "Blacks Eye Seats on Commission," *STJ*, May 13, 1985; "Group Takes over County Board Seats," *STJ*, May 14, 1985.

126   Michael Figures quoted in Tullos, *Alabama Getaway*, 204–208; see also Alabama New South Coalition, "History of ANSC," http://alnewsouthcoalition.org/history/ (accessed October 22, 2013); "Jackson Blackbelt's Choice?," *STJ*, December 14, 1983; "Hayden Fears Coalition Will Have Divisive Effect," *STJ*, January 26, 1986.

127   Versions of this scenario happened in 1980 and 1984 with the city council. Smitherman, quoted in "Decision Stuns City Officials," *STJ*, May 18, 1984; see also "Racially Split Vote Okays Ward Lines," *STJ*, January 11, 1983; Selma City Council Minutes, January 10, 1983, and April 23, 1984; "New Districts Pass Muster," *STJ*, February 9, 1988; "Mayor Calls August Election," *STJ*, June 23, 1988; "Council Plan Approved," *STJ*, June 28, 1988; "Blacks Reassess," *STJ*, August 1, 1984.

128   Chestnut and Cass, *Black in Selma*, 409.

129   In the midst of the lawsuit controversy, the commissioners appointed white landowner James Wilkinson to fill a vacancy, instead of a black citizen. "James Wilkinson appointed . . . ," *STJ*, March 20, 1987.

130   Frederick D. Reese, interview by the author, October 17, 2012.

131   "Political Leaders Predict District Judgment Should Put 2–3 Blacks on Board," *STJ*, March 2, 1986.

132   "Court Slaps Down Hand Plan," *STJ*, July 14, 1988.

133   "Blacks, Whites Vow to Govern Together," *STJ*, December 28, 1988.

Interlude: Superintendent Norward Roussell and School Leveling

1 Roussell, quoted in Dent, *Southern Journey*, 303; see also 305; "School Superintendent Hired," *STJ*, January 27, 1987.

2 Chestnut, quoted in Talese, *Writer's Life*, 201.

3 Roussell, quoted in Talese, *Writer's Life*, 203; see also 202; Dent, *Southern Journey*, 321–322.

4 Quote from Alabama Advisory Committee to the U.S. Commission on Civil Rights, *Crisis and Opportunity*, 33; see also 34; "LDF Airs List of Grievances," *STJ*, October 25, 1975; "Honor Promises, Blacks Ask Board," *STJ*, August 14, 1981; Dent, *Southern Journey*, 306–307.

5 Chestnut, quoted in Dent, *Southern Journey*, 309; see also Alabama Advisory Committee to the U.S. Commission on Civil Rights, *Crisis and Opportunity*, 34–35.

6 Quote from Faya Rose (Sanders) Toure, interview by the author, August 17, 2013. Terri Sewell became the valedictorian of Selma High before attending Princeton University. She then received a master's from Oxford University and a law degree from Harvard University. In 2011 she was elected as Alabama's Seventh Congressional District's representative to the U.S. House of Representatives. Nancy Sewell, interview by the author, December 6, 2012. West Side and Eastside Junior High Schools were interchangeably referred to as Westside and Eastside Middle School. By the end of the 1980s, West Side was often written as one word instead of two.

7 Quote from Alabama Advisory Committee to the U.S. Commission on Civil Rights, *Crisis and Opportunity*, 32; see also 4, 33; "Parents Meet to Challenge Leveling," *STJ*, September 14, 1988.

8 Roussell, quoted in Dent, *Southern Journey*, 306; see also Nancy Sewell, interview by the author, December 6, 2012; Talese, *Writer's Life*, 205.

9 Roussell, quoted in Dent, *Southern Journey*, 307.

10 Quote from Faya Rose (Sanders) Toure, interview by the author, August 17, 2013; Roussell, quoted in Alabama Advisory Committee to the U.S. Commission on Civil Rights, *Crisis and Opportunity*, 35.

11 Roussell, quoted in "Parents Respond to Level Changes," *STJ*, May 8, 1988; see also "School Leveling under Scrutiny," *STJ*, April 24, 1988.

12 Roussell, quoted in Dent, *Southern Journey*, 311; see also "School Leveling under Scrutiny," *STJ*, April 24, 1988.

13 Roussell, quoted in Dent, *Southern Journey*, 305–306.

14 Hodo, quoted in Dent, *Southern Journey*, 321–322.

15 "Back Him . . . or Boot Him," *STJ*, May 20, 1988; Talese, *Writer's Life*, 205.

16 Norward Roussell, letter to the editor, *STJ*, May 22, 1988.

17 Jackson, quoted in "Group Rallies around Roussell," *STJ*, May 29, 1988; see also "School Board Backs Roussell,"*STJ*, May 29, 1988.

18 Chestnut and Cass, *Black in Selma*, 291; Alabama Advisory Committee to the U.S. Commission on Civil Rights, *Crisis and Opportunity*, 18.

19 Alabama Advisory Committee to the U.S. Commission on Civil Rights, *Crisis and Opportunity*, 4, 14–16, 35; J.L. Chestnut, "Papering Over the Problem," *STJ*, September 18, 1988.

20 "Parents Meet to Challenge Leveling," *STJ*, September 14, 1988.

21 "3-Tiered Leveling Proposed," *STJ*, October 14, 1988; "Schools Pass 3-Tiered Plan," *STJ*, January 13, 1989.

22 "City BOE Stiffens Honors Standards," *STJ*, February 10, 1989.

23 Quote from Norward Roussell "Passing on Adult Problems," *STJ*, May 4, 1989. Fights between black and white students broke out inside and outside of Selma High after cars flying Confederate flags parked nearby. "Heightened Tension at Selma High," *STJ*, May 3, 1989; Rufus Lee Ford, letter to the editor, *STJ*, June 1, 1989; Edwin Moss, letter to the editor, *STJ*, June 22, 1989.

24 Edward Maull, letter to the editor, *STJ*, August 1, 1989; "Whispers and Rumors," *STJ*, July 23, 1989.

Chapter 8: Two Selmas

1 Chestnut and Cass, *Black in Selma*, 234.

2 Alabama Advisory Committee to the U.S. Commission on Civil Rights, *Crisis and Opportunity*, 3.

3 "Leaders Talk as Anniversary Nears," *STJ*, September 19, 1989.

4 Smitherman, quoted in "Right Men for the Job," *STJ*, September 21, 1989.

5 Chestnut, quoted in "Leaders Talk as Anniversary Nears," *STJ*, September 19, 1989; Chestnut, quoted in "Some Blacks Predict Dual Celebrations," *STJ*, September 22, 1989.

6 "Reese Resigns Local March Post," *STJ*, October 24, 1989; "Celebration Group 'Off and Running,'" *STJ*, November 10, 1989; "City-Backed Committee Disbands," *STJ*, November 19, 1989.

7 Moss, quoted in "White Majority on City BOE Questioned," *STJ*, October 12, 1989.

8 Smitherman, quoted in "Council to Meet with BOE," *STJ*, December 3, 1989; see also "Moss Asks for Barker's Resignation," *STJ*, November 24, 1989; "Mayor Replies to Moss' Letter," *STJ*, December 1, 1989.

9 Martha and David Hodo, letter to the editor, *STJ*, December 13, 1989.

10 Roussell, quoted in "Roussell's Contract Not Renewed," *STJ*, December 22, 1989.

11 "Roussell Firing Brings Pickets," *STJ*, December 24, 1989.

12 "Group Urges Class Boycott," *STJ*, December 28, 1989.

13 Roussell "An Appeal for Our Children to Stay in School," *STJ*, December 31, 1989.

14 "On Boycott's First Day, 1,400 Absent," *STJ*, January 4, 1990.

15 "School Boycott Suspended," *STJ*, January 5, 1990.

16 Applebome, *Dixie Rising*, 72.

17 Martha J. Hodo, letter to the editor, *STJ*, January 4, 1990.

18 Nancy Sewell, interview by the author, December 6, 2012.

19 "Roussell: Report of Slur Could Spark Tension" and "Boycott Cut to One Day," *STJ*, January 16, 1990; "Students' Feelings on Boycott Mixed," *STJ*, January 18, 1990.

20 Nancy Sewell, interview by the author, December 6, 2012.

21 "Roussell Outvoted on School Closing," *STJ*, January 25, 1990.

22 Nancy Sewell, interview by the author, December 6, 2012.

23 "BOE Ousts Roussell Early," *STJ*, February 4, 1990.

24 "Group Calls for Boycott," *STJ*, February 5, 1990.

25 "Sanders, Varner, Two More Arrested in City Hall Melee," *STJ*, February 6, 1990.

26 "Reese Resigns, Roussell Back In" and "City Schools Close," *STJ*, February 7, 1990.

27 Tucker, quoted in "Selma, Ala. in Uproar over School Controversy," *Norfolk Journal and Guide*, February 14, 1990.

28 "Schools Open, Court Order Denied," *STJ*, February 13, 1990.

29 Sanders, quoted in "Selma's Schools Reopen Following Racial Dispute," *Washington Post*, February 14, 1990.

30 "Trouble Spurs 87 Suspensions," *STJ*, February 15, 1990.

31 "Judge Won't Intervene in BOE Dispute," *STJ*, February 21, 1990.

32 Advertisement, "Join in Support of Public Education Support Team," *STJ*, February 18, 1990.

33 Chestnut and Cass, *Black in Selma*, 281; "BEST Spars with PEST," *STJ*, February 25, 1990; "BOE Draws Another Crowd," *STJ*, March 16, 1990.

34 "Roussell Sues City BOE for $10 Million," *STJ*, February 18, 1990; "City Files Suit against BEST," *STJ*, February 22, 1990.

35 "Judge Works Out Terms for City, BEST," *STJ*, March 18, 1990.

36 "Judge: Move the Tents Now," *STJ*, March 26, 1990.

37 "Judge Restricts Protests to Sidewalks," *STJ*, April 11, 1990.

38 Roussell, quoted in "25 Years after March, Selma Still a City Divided by Race," *Washington Post*, February 20, 1990.

39 "Marchers Retrace Civil Rights Path," *STJ*, March 5, 1990; "Visitors Boost Local Economy," *STJ*, March 6, 1990.

40 "Roussell Tenders Resignation," *STJ*, May 8, 1990.

41 "Group Torches Effigy of Mayor," *STJ*, August 16, 1990.

42 "Sanders, 17 Protesters Arrested," *STJ*, August 19, 1990.

43 "Agreement Brings BOE Back Together," *STJ*, August 28, 1990.

44 "Compromise Makes It Past 11th Hour Scare," *STJ*, August 28, 1990.

45 Alabama Advisory Committee to the U.S. Commission on Civil Rights, *Crisis and Opportunity*, 17; Applebome, *Dixie Rising*, 74.

46 Alabama Advisory Committee to the U.S. Commission on Civil Rights, *Crisis and Opportunity*.

47 "Civil Rights Study Set for Second Stage," *STJ*, November 21, 1990.

48 Shelton Prince, quoted in Alabama Advisory Committee to the U.S. Commission on Civil Rights, *Crisis and Opportunity*, 13.

49 Morthland, quoted in Alabama Advisory Committee to the U.S. Commission on Civil Rights, *Crisis and Opportunity*, 15; see also 12–16.

50 Alabama Advisory Committee to the U.S. Commission on Civil Rights, *Crisis and Opportunity*, 61–65.

51 Quote from Alabama Advisory Committee to the U.S. Commission on Civil Rights, *Crisis and Opportunity*, ii; see also "Civil Rights Observers Head Back to Town," *STJ*, December 7, 1990.

52 "City Declares War on Corner Drug Dealers," *STJ*, November 14, 1985.

53 Duke, quoted in "Cocaine Cracks Selma," *STJ*, August 16, 1987. For more on federal funding for the creation of local drug units, see Alexander, *New Jim Crow*, 72–73.

54 "Police Move In on Crack City," *STJ*, October 12, 1988.

55 Brown, quoted in "Crack Trade Is Selma's New Struggle," *Washington Post*, November 21, 1989.

56 "Law Raids Selma Coke House," *STJ*, December 18, 1988.

57 Cole, quoted in "Trailer Fire Follows Crack City Bust," *STJ*, December 20, 1988.

58 Alexander, *New Jim Crow*, 6, 48–49; Equal Justice Initiative of Alabama, *Criminal Justice Reform*, 15–24.

59 Bourne, "'Just Say No,'" 48; Alexander, *New Jim Crow*, 52. For more on the war on drugs and the rise of prisons, see Perkinson, *Texas Tough*.

60 Clear, *Imprisoning Communities*, 52.

61 U.S. Department of Commerce, Bureau of the Census, *Census of Population: 1990*; "Crack Trade Is Selma's New Struggle," *Washington Post*, November 21, 1989; Alexander, *New Jim Crow*, 7, 51.

62 Quote from "Still with Us in 1989," *STJ*, January 2, 1989; see also "Crack Trade Is Selma's New Struggle," *Washington Post*, November 21, 1989.

63 Lewellen, quoted in "Crack Changes Face of Crime in Selma Area," *STJ*, October 4, 1991; see also U.S. Department of Commerce, Bureau of the Census, *Census of Population: 1990*.

64 "Crack City's Devastating Burden," *STJ*, May 19, 1989.

65 J. C. Norton, quoted in "Man Sentenced to Life Here for Crack Conviction," *STJ*, May 10, 1991.

66 Quotes from "Crack City's Devastating Burden," *STJ*, May 19, 1989; see also Bourne, "'Just Say No,'" 46; Clear, *Imprisoning Communities*, 5.

67 Boynton, quoted in Dent, *Southern Journey*, 280.

68 Quote from Dr. Samuel Lett, letter to the editor, *STJ*, June 17, 1990; see also U.S. Department of Commerce, Bureau of the Census, *Census of Population: 1990*; "Justice Rejects City Council's Districting Plan," *STJ*, November 15, 1992. When a vacancy opened in ward 4 in January 1992, the black council members urged their white colleagues to appoint a black

person. A racially deadlocked vote forced the vacancy to be decided by special election and led to another white council member being elected in April. "Council Fails to Fill Vacant Ward 4 Seat," *STJ*, January 28, 1992; "Special Election Set for Ward 4," *STJ*, February 4, 1992; "Ward 4 Hopefuls in Runoff," *STJ*, April 29, 1992.

69 "Council Elections Called Off," *STJ*, August 5, 1992.

70 "Justice Rejects City Council's Districting Plan," *STJ*, November 15, 1992; "Judge to City: Submit Varner's Plan," *STJ*, December 3, 1992; "Whites on Council Approve Another Redistricting Plan," *STJ*, December 29, 1992.

71 "Black Councilmen Want OK of Varner Plan," *STJ*, December 29, 1992.

72 "Justice Rejects City Ward Plan," *STJ*, March 16, 1993; "Council Agrees on Redistricting Plan," *STJ*, March 31, 1993.

73 Fitts, quoted in "Split Council Passes Districting Plan," *STJ*, April 6, 1993.

74 "Proposal Would Shift Power to Mayor," *STJ*, April 13, 1993.

75 "Mayor Vetoes Districting Plan," *STJ*, April 16, 1993.

76 Cecil Williamson, letter to the editor, *STJ*, April 25, 1993.

77 "Council Upholds Mayor's Veto," *STJ*, April 27, 1993.

78 Smitherman, quoted in "Justice Department Sues Mayor, Council," *STJ*, May 20, 1993.

79 "Hand Sending 'Citizen Plan' for Justice OK," *STJ*, May 21, 1993; "Justice Oks District Plan for City," *STJ*, June 15, 1993.

80 Chestnut, quoted in "Chestnut Lays It Out in Black and White," *STJ*, May 25, 1993.

81 "Black Majority, Three Women to Govern City," *STJ*, August 25, 1993.

82 Walker, quoted in "Selma Reacts Quietly to City Hall Power Shift from Whites to Blacks," *STJ*, September 6, 1993; see also "Three of Five Council Members Re-elected," *STJ*, August 28, 1996.

83 Chestnut and Cass, *Black in Selma*, 325.

84 Chestnut, quoted in "Blacks, Whites Vow to Govern Together," *STJ*, December 28, 1988.

85 Report, reproduced in "Selma-Dallas County Economic Development Competitiveness Summary," *STJ*, June 15, 1993.

86 Ross Boyle, quoted in "Survey: Leaders' Attitudes a Drawback," *STJ*, May 23, 1993.

87 "Half of County Children in Poverty," *STJ*, August 13, 1992.

88 Benn, *Reporter*, 176–177; "Man Killed by Officer's Bullets," *STJ*, December 8, 1994.

89 Benn, *Reporter*, 176–177.

90 "Black Leadership Council Initiates Plan to Learn More of Shooting," *STJ*, December 11, 1994; "CARE [Coalition of Alabamians Reforming Education] Plans Walk to Curb Violence," *STJ*, December 21, 1994; "Selmians March to Help End Violence through Education," *STJ*, January 1, 1995.

91 The underfunding of public schools in Alabama in general and Dallas County in particular stemmed from the tax limitations in the constitution of 1901. In the Alabama Black Belt, this was compounded by the "current-use" tax structure that allowed for timber and cropland to be assessed at a much lower tax rate. Tullos, *Alabama Getaway*, 198–199; "Dallas County School Funding Lowest in State," *STJ*, January 1, 1992.

92 Sewell, quoted in "Selma High Boys Get Away for Day of Timely Topics," *STJ*, January 27, 1995; "Latest Death Prompts Action to Stem Violence," *STJ*, December 23, 1994.

93 "Black Leadership Summit Brings HOPE," *STJ*, February 6, 1995.

94 "Project Helps Boys Make Right Choices," *STJ*, June 19, 1994.

95 O'Connor, *American Welfare System*, 185–187.

96 O'Connor, *American Welfare System*, 209.

97 O'Connor, *American Welfare System*, 223.

98 "Selma-Dallas County Economic Development Competitiveness Summary," *STJ*, June 15, 1993.

99 "JOBS Moves Adults from Welfare Rolls into Work Force," *STJ*, November 17, 1992.

100 "State's JOBS Program Ranks No. 2 in Nation," *STJ*, September 7, 1995.

101 "JOBS Fair Friday at Library," *STJ*, November 21, 1996.

102 Wallace, quoted in "Welfare Reform Expected to Impact Economy," *STJ*, January 13, 1997.

103 Ware, quoted in "Welfare Reform Expected to Impact Economy," *STJ*, January 13, 1997.

104 Joanne Bland, "Growing Up in the Segregated South," Presentation at Winona Senior High School, February 2011, *Culture Clique*, KQAL, Winona State University, http://www.prx.org/pieces/59935.

105 Jamie Wallace, interview by the author, March 13, 2013.

106 Quote from Faya Rose (Sanders) Toure, interview by the author, August 17, 2013; see also "Rights Museum Planned," *STJ*, November 3, 1991; Eskew, "Selling," 170.

107 Quote from Joanne Bland, interview by Teri Tenseth, February 2011, *Culture Clique*, KQAL, Winona State University, PRX, http://www.prx.org/pieces/59934.

108 Sam Walker, interview by the author, August 12, 2013.

109 Rose Sanders, "National Voting Rights Museum Growing with Community Support," *STJ*, March 3, 1993.

110 "Voting Rights Museum to Pay Tribute to Pope," *STJ*, November 27, 1992; "Resource Center, MOMS Teach Drug-Free Life," *STJ*, September 29, 1988.

111 Faya Rose (Sanders) Toure, interview by the author, August 17, 2013; "Museum Hosting Voter Registration," *STJ*, July 21, 1993.

112 Eskew, "Selling," 168–170.

113 Walker, quoted in "Project Helps Boys Make Right Choices," *STJ*, June 19, 1994.

114 "D.C. March Offers Positive Experience for Many Selmians," *STJ*, October 18, 1995.

115 "Speakers Urge Men to Improve Selves in Black Belt Version of Million Man March," *STJ*, November 26, 1995.

116 Selma and Dallas County Chamber of Commerce, "Progress Report 1977," Vertical Files, Selma Public Library.

117 Eskew, "Selling," 166.

118 "Blacks Worried Weekend Battle May Reflect Racist Point of View," *STJ*, April 19, 1987.

119 Eskew, "Selling," 166.

120 "Visitors Boost Local Economy," *STJ*, March 6, 1990.

121 Quote from "An Interview with Selma City Council President Cecil Williamson," uploaded on February 16, 2012 by Selma's Truth, https://youtu.be/fKi22kx-EpM; see also "In Alabama, a 'Wizardess' Disputes Her Title," *Intelligence Report*, July 27, 2005; Cecil Williamson, "Activists Confront Hate in Selma, Ala.," *Intelligence Report*, November 29, 2008.

122 "Honoring the Confederate Dead," *STJ*, April 25, 2006; Eskew, "Selling," 160.

123 Pigford v. Glickman, 185 F.R.D. 82 (D.D.C. 1999); "Black Farmers Eye Settlement in National Suit," *STJ*, November 17, 1998.

124 "US to Black Farmers: We're Ready to Pay Up," *STJ*, November 9, 1998. For a detailed account of racial discrimination within the USDA and the *Pigford v. Glickman* decision, see Daniel, *Dispossession*; Grim, "Forty Acres," 271–298.

125 Daniel, "African American Farmers," 3.

126 U.S. Department of Commerce, Bureau of the Census, *Census of Agriculture: 1997*.

127 Strong, quoted in "Break New Ground," *STJ*, January 10, 1999.

128 Bland, quoted in "Activists Confront Hate in Selma, Ala.," *Intelligence Report*, November 29, 2008.

Interlude: Joe Gotta Go

1 Quote from Benn, *Reporter*, 373; see also "Old Southern Strategy Faces Test in Selma Vote," *New York Times*, September 10, 2000; Chestnut and Cass, *Black in Selma*, 240.

2 Perkins, quoted in "Perkins Begins Bid for Mayor," *STJ*, September 17, 1991; see also Chestnut and Cass, *Black in Selma*, 365–366; Perkins' Election Contest Claim Goes Back to Courtroom," *STJ*, September 6, 1993.

3 Thornton, *Dividing Lines*, 558.

4   Smitherman, quoted in "Smitherman: Racial Posters Are Hate Crimes,"
    STJ, August 11, 1996.
5   "'Joe T.' Takes Photo Finish," *STJ*, August 28, 1996.
6   "Critics Don't Mention Civic Deeds," *STJ*, December 22, 1996.
7   Alston Fitts, letter to the editor, *STJ*, January 27, 1997.
8   "Adults Prove Poor Examples of City Leadership," *STJ*, January 29, 1997.
9   "Mayor to File Ethics Charges," *STJ*, April 18, 1997.
10 "Sanders Triples Funding to Wife's Private Projects," *STJ*, April 22, 1997.
11 Bill Pryor, quoted in "Sanders Not under AG Investigation," *STJ*, May 2, 1997.
12 "Ethics Probe Clears Sanders," *STJ*, October 22, 1997; "City Council Oks
    Investigation," *STJ*, November 7, 1997; "Investigation Still Taking Place,"
    STJ, November 16, 1997.
13 "Commission Says Smitherman Violated Ethics Law," *STJ*, May 7, 1998;
    "Ethics Fines Mayor $4,000," *STJ*, June 5, 1998.
14 Hank Sanders, letter to the editor, *STJ*, October 20, 1998.
15 Perkins, quoted in "Perkins, Is Third Time a Charm?," *STJ*, December 29,
    1999. By the 1990s, the Chestnut, Sanders, and Sanders law firm had taken
    in more partners. The name of the law firm eventually became Chestnut,
    Sanders, Sanders, Pettaway, and Campbell, LLC.
16 "Mayoral Candidate Complains of Wrong-Doing," *STJ*, January 31, 2000;
    "Smitherman Goes for 40," *STJ*, April 6, 2000; "Maull Wants No Part of
    Mayoral Endorsements," *STJ*, June 1, 2000.
17 "Registrar under Fire for Voting Practices," *STJ*, July 30, 2000; "Sanders'
    Voting Practice Disputed," *STJ*, August 2, 2000.
18 "City Voting Scandal Surfaces," *STJ*, August 18, 2000.
19 "Selmians to Decide City's Future," *STJ*, August 22, 2000.
20 "Smitherman Leaves Others in Fiscal Dust," *STJ*, August 22, 2000.
21 "Run-Off: Perkins and Smitherman Go at It for Fourth Time," *STJ*, August 23, 2000.
22 "Campaign Is Going to Get Ugly," *STJ*, August 23, 2000.
23 Linda Stewart, letter to the editor, *STJ*, August 16, 2000; author's field
    notes, conversation with Joanne Bland, May 2005.
24 Williamson, quoted in "Car Set Ablaze at Sanders' Firm," *STJ*, August 29, 2000.
25 "Expert: Organization, Not Issues, Key to Election," *STJ*, September 6, 2000.
26 "Judgement Day," *STJ*, September 12, 2000.
27 "JOE GOES: Perkins Finally Unseats Smitherman," *STJ*, September 13, 2000.
28 Perkins, quoted in "Winning a Victory for Selma—and a Strong Black
    Woman," *New Pittsburgh Courier*, October 7, 2000.
29 Smitherman, quoted in "JOE GOES: Perkins Finally Unseats Smitherman,"
    STJ, September 13, 2000.
30 "Selma Gets Perk-ed," *STJ*, October 1, 2000.

Epilogue

1   Barack Obama, "Remarks by the President at the 50th Anniversary of the Selma to Montgomery Marches," March 7, 2015, the White House Office of the Press Secretary, https://www.whitehouse.gov/the-press-office/2015/03 /07/remarks-president-50th-anniversary-selma-montgomery-marches.

2   For a detailed history of the dismantling of the Voting Rights Act, see Berman, *Give Us the Ballot*; Shelby v. Holder, 570 US __ (2013).

3   Barack Obama, "Remarks by the President at the 50th Anniversary of the Selma to Montgomery Marches," March 7, 2015, the White House Office of the Press Secretary, https://www.whitehouse.gov/the-press-office/2015/03 /07/remarks-president-50th-anniversary-selma-montgomery-marches.

4   Alabama Possible, "Alabama Poverty Data Sheet," 2015, http://alabama possible.org/datasheet/.

5   "'Still a City of Slaves'—Selma, in the Words of Those Who Live There," *Guardian*, February 4, 2016.

6   Branch, *Parting the Waters*; Branch, *Pillar of Fire*; Branch, *At Canaan's Edge*; Dittmer, "Taylor Branch's America," 791.

7   Quotes from Branch, *At Canaan's Edge*, vii, x; see also xi–3.

8   Joanne Bland, "Growing Up in the Segregated South," Presentation at Winona Senior High School, February 2011, *Culture Clique*, KQUAL, Winona State University, http://www.prx.org/pieces/59935; Hasan Kwame Jeffries has called these diverse but interlocking demands "freedom rights." *Bloody Lowndes*, 4.

9   Cox, quoted in remarks by Judy Richardson, "In the Mississippi River: Heroes and Sheroes: A Tribute to Those Murdered and Martyred in Mississippi," Freedom Summer 50 Conference, Jackson, MS, June 27, 2014, CRMVET, http://www.crmvet.org/comm/judyr14.htm; Duvernay, *Selma*.

10 Tullos, *Alabama Getaway*, 256.

11 "Rep Sewell Introduces John Lewis in Selma on the 50th Anniversary of Bloody Sunday," Congresswoman Terri Sewell's website, March 7, 2015, https://sewell.house.gov/media-center/videos/rep-sewell-introduces-john -lewis-selma-50th-anniversary-bloody-sunday.

12 Nancy Sewell, interview by the author, December 6, 2012.

13 Obama, quoted in "Rep. Terri Sewell, a Daughter of Selma, Rues Her City's Lost Promise," *Washington Post*, March 1, 2015.

14 "Homecoming," *Princeton Alumni Weekly*, December 8, 2010.

15 "Q&A: Rep. Terri Sewell '86 on the Legacy of Selma," *Princeton Alumni Weekly*, March 18, 2015.

16 Quoted in "'Still a City of Slaves'—Selma, in the Words of Those Who Live There," *Guardian*, February 4, 2016.

17 For only a few examples of the many ongoing, vituperative political exchanges, see "Stop Antics at Meetings," *STJ*, August 17, 2006; "Council Debates Work Sessions," *STJ*, January 22, 2007; Cecil Williamson, "Who

Is Really in Control of Mayor?," *STJ*, May 6, 2007; "Much Ado about City Ballyhoo," *STJ*, March 5, 2008.

18 "'Still a City of Slaves'—Selma, in the Words of Those Who Live There," *Guardian*, February 4, 2016.

19 Sewell, quoted in "Homecoming," *Princeton Alumni Weekly*, December 8, 2010.

20 McReynolds, quoted in "'Still a City of Slaves'—Selma, in the Words of Those Who Live There," *Guardian*, February 4, 2016.

BIBLIOGRAPHY

Archival Sources

Alabama Cooperative Extension Service (ACES). Records. Department of Special Collections and Archives, Auburn University, Auburn, AL.

Alabama Department of Education. Correspondence of the Rural School Agent (ADECRSA). Alabama Department of Archives and History, Montgomery.

Alabama Governor (1935–1939: Graves) (AGG). Administrative Files. Alabama Department of Archives and History, Montgomery.

Alabama State Council of Defense (ASCD). Administrative Files, 1917–1919. Alabama Department of Archives and History, Montgomery.

Branch, Taylor. Papers (TBP). Southern Historical Collection. Wilson Library, University of North Carolina at Chapel Hill.

Bunche, Ralph J., Oral History Collection (RJBOHC). Moorland-Spingarn Research Center, Howard University, Washington, DC.

Edmundite Southern Missions Collection. Society of Saint Edmund Archives. Saint Michael's College. Colchester, VT.

Eyes on the Prize: America's Civil Rights Years, 1954–1965. Henry Hampton Collection. Film and Media Archive, Washington University Libraries, St. Louis, MO. http://digital.wustl.edu/eyesontheprize/.

Hare, Judge James A. Papers (JJHP). Vaughan-Smitherman Museum, Selma, AL.

Johnson, Clyde. Papers (CJP). Southern Historical Collection. Wilson Library, University of North Carolina at Chapel Hill.

LaFayette, Bernard. Oral History Project. Mss. Gr. 123. University of Rhode Island Special Collections, Kingston. http://webarchives.apps.uri.edu/xml /Guide%20to%20the%20Bernard%20LaFayette%20Oral%20History%20 Project.xml

Minute Book, Independent Benevolent Society, No. 28, 1927–1932. Andrew
    Arthur Papers. David M. Rubenstein Rare Book and Manuscript Library,
    Duke University, Durham, NC.
Minutes of Selma City Council. County Clerk Office, City Hall, Selma, AL.
NAACP. Papers. ProQuest History Vault. http://congressional.proquest.com
    /histvault.
New York Public Library. Digital Collections. New York, NY. https://digital
    collections.nypl.org/.
Old Depot Museum Archives (ODMA), Selma, AL.
Peppler, Jim. Southern Courier Photograph Collection. Alabama Department of
    Archives and History, Montgomery.
Roosevelt, Franklin Delano. "Annual Address to Congress 1941." Franklin
    Delano Roosevelt Presidential Library and Museum. https://fdrlibrary.org
    /four-freedoms.
Rosenberg, Billy. Photograph Collection. Temple Mishkan Israel, Selma, AL.
Rosenwald Fund Card File Database. Fisk University. http://rosenwald.fisk
    .edu.
Sanborn Fire Insurance Company Maps. Selma, Alabama, 1903. Selma Public
    Library, Selma, AL.
Selma Public Library. Vertical Files. Selma, AL.
Selma University Catalogues and the Minutes of the Alabama Colored Baptist
    Convention. Microfilm Collection. Auburn University, Auburn, AL.
Smith, Washington M., Papers. David M. Rubenstein Rare Book and
    Manuscript Library, Duke University, Durham, NC.
Southern Journey Oral History Collection. Tulane University Digital Library,
    New Orleans, LA. https://digitallibrary.tulane.edu/islandora/object
    /tulane:dent.
Student Nonviolent Coordinating Committee (SNCC). Papers. Microfilm. Davis
    Library, University of North Carolina at Chapel Hill.
Walk in History Workshop. 2005. National Voting Rights Museum and
    Institute (NVRMI), Selma, AL.
"We Shall Not Be Moved: Videos of a 1988 Conference on the Student Non-
    violent Coordinating Committee" (WSNBM). Trinity College Digital
    Repository, Hartford, CT. http://digitalrepository.trincoll.edu/sncc/.
Williams, Clarence, and Joe Johnson. Interview by Hardy Frye, 1972. Hardy
    Frye Oral History Collection, Department of Special Collections and
    Archives, Auburn University, Auburn, AL.

Websites

Alabama New South Coalition (ANSC). http://alnewsouthcoalition.org.
Ancestry.com. http://ancestry.com.
Civil Rights Movement Veterans (CRMVET). http://www.crmvet.org.

Historical Census Browser. University of Virginia, Geospatial and Statistical Data Center, 2004. http://mapserver.lib.virginia.edu/collections/. [discontinued]
History, Art and Archives. U.S. House of Representatives. http://history.house .gov.
NAACP. http://www.naacp.org.

Unpublished Interviews

Childers, Miller. Interview by the author, January 20, 2012.
Cohn, June (Eagle). Interview by the author, November 30, 2011.
Hatcher, Yvonne. Interview by the author, December 12, 2011.
Knight, Joseph. Interview by the author, October 31, 2012.
Martin, Jean. Interview by the author, December 6, 2011.
Perkins, Etta Smith. Interview by the author, December 14, 2011.
Reese, Frederick D. Interview by the author, October 17, 2012.
Sewell, Nancy. Interview by the author, December 6, 2012.
Toure, Faya Rose (Sanders). Interview by the author, August 17, 2013.
Walker, Sam. Interview by the author, August 12, 2013.
Wallace, Jamie. Interview by the author, March 13, 2013.
Williams, Fred. Interview by the author, September 18, 2012.
Wimberly, Louretta. Interview by the author, December 4, 2012.

Newspapers and Periodicals

Alabama Journal
Chicago Defender
Chicago Tribune
Commonwealth
Daily Worker (Communist Party)
Emancipator (Montgomery, AL)
Guardian
Intelligence Report (Southern Poverty Law Center)
Jersey Bulletin
Jet
Los Angeles Times
Negro World
New Pittsburgh Courier
New York Times
Norfolk Journal and Guide
Princeton Alumni Weekly
Selma Journal (SJ)
Selma Morning Times (SMT)

Selma Times (*ST*)

Selma Times-Journal (*STJ*)

Southern Courier (*SC*)

Southern Farm Leader (Sharecroppers Union)

Student Voice (Student Nonviolent Coordinating Committee)

Washington Post

Books, Articles, Pamphlets, and Unpublished Sources

Adams, Samuel C., Jr. "The Changing Organization of a Rural Negro Community and Its Implications for Race Accommodation." PhD diss., University of Chicago, 1953.

Aiken, Charles S. *The Cotton Plantation South since the Civil War*. Baltimore: Johns Hopkins University Press, 1988.

Alabama Advisory Committee to the U.S. Commission on Civil Rights. *Crisis and Opportunity: Race Relations in Selma*. Washington, DC: U.S. Commission on Civil Rights, 1991.

Alabama Legislature, House of Representatives. *Journal of the House of Representatives*. Montgomery, AL: The Brown Printing Company, State Printers and Binders, 1920.

Alexander, Michelle. *The New Jim Crow: Mass Incarceration in the Age of Colorblindness*. New York: New Press, 2010.

Alsobrook, David. "A Call to Arms for African Americans during the Age of Jim Crow: Black Alabamians' Response to the U.S. Declaration of War in 1917." In *The Great War in the Heart of Dixie: Alabama during World War I*, edited by Martin T. Olliff, 81–100. Tuscaloosa: University of Alabama Press, 2008.

Anderson, R. Bentley. "'A Sound Mind and a Sound Body': The Don Bosco Boys Club of Selma, Alabama, 1947–1964." *Journal of Ethnic History* 22 (winter 2003): 50–75.

Applebome, Peter. *Dixie Rising: How the South Is Shaping American Values, Politics, and Culture*. New York: Times Books, 1996.

Arnesen, Eric. *Brotherhoods of Color: Black Railroad Workers and the Struggle for Equality*. Cambridge, MA: Harvard University Press, 2001.

Ashmore, Susan Youngblood. *Carry It On: The War on Poverty and the Civil Rights Movement in Alabama, 1964–1972*. Athens: University of Georgia Press, 2008.

——. "Going Back to Selma: Organizing for Change in Dallas County after the March to Montgomery." In *War on Poverty: A New Grassroots History, 1964–1980*, edited by Annelise Orleck and Lisa Gayle Hazirjian, 308–332. Athens: University of Georgia Press, 2011.

Ayers, Edward. *The Promise of the New South: Life after Reconstruction*. New York: Oxford University Press, 1992.

Barnard, William D. *Dixiecrats and Democrats: Alabama Politics, 1942–1950*. Tuscaloosa: University of Alabama Press, 1974.

Bartley, Numan. *The Rise of Massive Resistance: Race and Politics in the South during the 1950s.* Baton Rouge: Louisiana State University Press, 1999.

Beaulieu, Lionel J. *The Rural South in Crisis: Challenges for the Future.* Boulder, CO: Westview, 1988.

Benn, Alvin. *Reporter: Covering Civil Rights . . . and Wrongs in Dixie.* Bloomington, IN: AuthorHouse, 2006.

Berger, Samuel. *Dollar Harvest: The Story of the Farm Bureau.* Lexington, MA: Heath Lexington Books, 1971.

Berkey, Thomas. "The Closing of Craig Air Force Base." Master's thesis, University of Virginia, 1980.

Berman, Ari. *Give Us the Ballot: The Modern Struggle for Voting Rights in America.* New York: Farrar, Straus and Giroux, 2015.

Bland, Joanne. "Growing Up in the Segregated South: Selma Voting Rights Movement." Presentation at Winona Senior High School. February 2011. *Culture Clique,* KQAL, Winona State University. PRX. http://www.prx.org/pieces/59935.

———. Interview by Teri Tenseth, February 2011. *Culture Clique,* KQAL, Winona State University. http://www.prx.org/pieces/59934.

Blee, Kathleen M. *Women of the Klan: Racism and Gender in the 1920s.* Berkeley: University of California Press, 1991.

Blevins, Brooks. *Cattle in the Cotton Fields: A History of Cattle Raising in Alabama.* Tuscaloosa: University of Alabama Press, 1998.

Bourne, Peter. "'Just Say No': Drug Abuse Policy in the Reagan Administration." In *Ronald Reagan and the 1980s: Perceptions, Policies, Legacies,* edited by Cheryl Hudson and Gareth Davies, 41–56. New York: Palgrave Macmillan, 2008.

Brady, Thomas P. *Black Monday.* Winona, MS: Association of Citizens' Councils, 1955.

Branch, Taylor. *At Canaan's Edge: America in the King Years, 1965–68.* New York: Simon and Schuster, 2006.

———. *Parting the Waters: America in the King Years, 1954–63.* New York: Simon and Schuster, 1988.

———. *Pillar of Fire: America in the King Years, 1963–65.* New York: Simon and Schuster, 1998.

Brown, Leslie. *Upbuilding Black Durham: Gender, Class, and Black Community Development in the Jim Crow South.* Chapel Hill: University of North Carolina Press, 2008.

Burritt, Maurice Chase. *The County Agent and the Farm Bureau.* New York: Harcourt, Brace, 1922.

Campagna, Anthony S. *The Economy in the Reagan Years: The Economic Consequences of the Reagan Administration.* Newport, CT: Greenwood, 1994.

Campbell, Christina McFadyen. *The Farm Bureau and the New Deal: A Study of the Making of National Farm Policy, 1933–40.* Urbana: University of Illinois Press, 1962.

Campbell, T. M. *The Movable School Goes to the Negro Farmer*. Tuskegee Institute, AL: Tuskegee Institute Press, 1936.

Chafe, William. *Civilities and Civil Rights: Greensboro, North Carolina, and the Black Struggle for Freedom*. New York: Oxford University Press, 1980.

———. "Presidential Address: 'The Gods Bring Threads to Webs Begun.'" *Journal of American History* 86 (March 2000): 1531–1551.

———. *The Unfinished Journey: America since World War II*. 4th ed. New York: Oxford University Press, 1999.

Chestnut, J. L., and Julia Cass. *Black in Selma: The Uncommon Life of J. L. Chestnut, Jr*. New York: Farrar, Straus and Giroux, 1990.

Clark, Daniel. "Textile Workers Union of America." In *Encyclopedia of U.S. Labor and Working Class History*, edited by Eric Arnesen, Vol. 3:1368–1370 New York: Routledge, 2007.

Clark, Thomas Dionysius. *Pills, Petticoats, and Plows: The Southern Country Store*. Norman: University of Oklahoma Press, 1944.

Clear, Todd R. *Imprisoning Communities: How Mass Incarceration Makes Disadvantaged Neighborhoods Worse*. New York: Oxford University Press, 2007.

Cobb, Charles E., Jr. *This Nonviolent Stuff'll Get You Killed: How Guns Made the Civil Rights Movement Possible*. New York: Basic Books, 2014.

Cobb, James. *The Selling of the South: The Southern Crusade for Industrial Development, 1936–1990*. Urbana: University of Illinois Press, 1993.

———. *The South and America since World War II*. New York: Oxford University Press, 2011.

Cohen, Lizabeth. *Making a New Deal: Industrial Workers in Chicago, 1919–1939*. Cambridge: Cambridge University Press, 1990.

Cowie, Jefferson. *Capital Moves: RCA's Seventy-Year Quest for Cheap Labor*. Ithaca, NY: Cornell University Press, 1999.

Crespino, Joseph. *In Search of Another Country: Mississippi and the Conservative Counterrevolution*. Princeton, NJ: Princeton University Press, 2007.

Cronon, William. *Nature's Metropolis: Chicago and the Great West*. New York: W. W. Norton, 1991.

Curtin, Mary Ellen. *Black Prisoners and their World, Alabama, 1865–1900*. Charlottesville: University Press of Virginia, 2000.

Daniel, Pete. "African American Farmers and Civil Rights." *Journal of Southern History* 73 (February 2007): 3–38.

———. *Breaking the Land: The Transformation of Cotton, Tobacco, and Rice since 1880*. Urbana: University of Illinois Press, 1985.

———. *Dispossession: Discrimination against African American Farmers in the Age of Civil Rights*. Chapel Hill: University of North Carolina Press, 2013.

Dattel, Eugene. *Cotton and Race in the Making of America: The Human Costs of Economic Power*. Chicago: Ivan R. Dee, 2009.

Davidson, James West, Brian DeLay, Christine Leigh Heyrman, Mark Lytle, and Michael Stoff. *Nation of Nations: A Narrative History of the American Republic*. 6th ed. New York: McGraw-Hill Higher Education, 2008.

Davis, Charles S. *The Cotton Kingdom in Alabama*. Montgomery: Alabama Department of Archives and History, 1939.

Davis, Jill M. Wright, and Army Engineers Study Center, Fort Belvoir, VA. *Army Base Realignment Methodology*. Vol. 2. Fort Belvoir, VA: Fort Belvoir Defense Technical Information Center, 1981.

Dent, Thomas C. *Southern Journey: A Return to the Civil Rights Movement*. New York: W. Morrow, 1997.

Dinkins, William Hovey. "Implications of Economics and of Religion in the Development of Teacher-Training at Selma University." Master's thesis, Columbia University, 1931.

Dittmer, John. *Local People: The Struggle for Civil Rights in Mississippi*. Urbana: University of Illinois Press, 1994.

———. "Taylor Branch's America." *Reviews in American History* 26 (December 1998): 786–792.

Du Bois, W. E. B. *Black Reconstruction in America*. New York: Harcourt, Brace, 1935.

DuVernay, Ava, dir. *Selma*. DVD. Los Angeles, CA: Paramount Pictures, 2015.

Eagles, Charles W. *Outside Agitator: Jon Daniels and the Civil Rights Movement in Alabama*. Chapel Hill: University of North Carolina Press, 1993.

Edwards, Laura. *Gendered Strife and Confusion: The Political Culture of Reconstruction*. Urbana: University of Illinois Press, 1997.

Edwards, William James. *Twenty-Five Years in the Black Belt*. Boston: Cornhill, 1918.

Equal Justice Initiative of Alabama. *Criminal Justice Reform in Alabama: A Report and Analysis of Criminal Justice Issues in Alabama*. Montgomery, AL: Equal Justice Initiative of Alabama, 2005.

Eskew, Glen. "Selling the Civil Rights Movement in Selma, Alabama." In *Destination Dixie: Tourism and Southern History*, edited by Karen L. Cox, 160–184. Gainesville: University Press of Florida, 2012.

Evans, Eli. *The Provincials: A Personal History of Jews in the South*. Chapel Hill: University of North Carolina Press, 2005.

Fager, Charles E. *Selma, 1965*. New York: Charles Scribner's Sons, 1974.

Falk, William, and Thomas Lyson. *High Tech, Low Tech, No Tech: Recent Industrial and Occupational Change in the South*. Albany: State University of New York Press, 1988.

Fallin, Wilson. *Uplifting the People: Three Centuries of Black Baptists in Alabama*. Tuscaloosa: University of Alabama Press, 2007.

Feldman, Glenn. *Politics, Society, and the Klan in Alabama, 1915–1949*. Tuscaloosa: University of Alabama Press, 1999.

———. "Southern Disillusionment with the Democratic Party: Cultural Conformity and 'the Great Melding' of Racial and Economic Conservatism in Alabama during World War II." *Journal of American Studies* 43 (2009): 199–230.

Fikes, Bettie Mae. "Singing for Freedom." In *Hands on the Freedom Plow: Personal Accounts by Women in SNCC*, edited by Faith Holsaert, Martha Prescod Norman Noonan, Judy Richardson, Betty Garman Robinson, Jean Smith Young, and Dorothy M. Zellner, 460–470. Urbana: University of Illinois Press, 2010.

Fitts, Alston, III. *Selma: A Bicentennial History*. Tuscaloosa: University of Alabama Press, 2017.

——. *Selma: Queen City of the Blackbelt*. Selma, AL: Clairmont, 1989.

Fleck, Robert K. "Democratic Opposition to the Fair Labor Standards Act of 1938." *Journal of Economic History* 62 (March 2002): 25–54.

Fleming, Cynthia Griggs. *In the Shadow of Selma: The Continuing Struggle for Civil Rights in the Rural South*. Lanham, MD: Rowman and Littlefield, 2004.

Flynt, Wayne. *Alabama in the Twentieth Century*. Tuscaloosa: University of Alabama Press, 2004.

Foner, Eric. *Forever Free: The Story of Emancipation and Reconstruction*. New York: Alfred A. Knopf, 2005.

——. *Freedom's Lawmakers: A Directory of Black Officeholders during Reconstruction*. Baton Rouge: Louisiana State University Press, 1996.

Foster, Vera Chandler. "'Boswellianism': A Technique in the Restriction of Negro Voting." *Phylon* 10 (1949): 26–37.

Frederickson, Kari. *The Dixiecrat Revolt and the End of the Solid South, 1932–1968*. Chapel Hill: University of North Carolina Press, 2001.

Fry, Joseph A. *John Tyler Morgan and the Search for Southern Autonomy*. Knoxville: University of Tennessee Press, 1992.

Frye, Hardy T. *Black Parties and Political Power: A Case Study*. Boston, MA: G. K. Hall, 1980.

Garrow, David. *Bearing the Cross: Martin Luther King, Jr. and the Southern Christian Leadership Conference*. New York: Perennial Classics, 1986.

——. *Protest at Selma: Martin Luther King, Jr., and the Voting Rights Act of 1965*. New Haven, CT: Yale University Press, 1978.

Giesen, James. *Boll Weevil Blues: Cotton, Myth, and Power in the American South*. Chicago: University of Chicago Press, 2011.

Gilmore, Glenda. *Defying Dixie: The Radical Roots of Civil Rights, 1919–1950*. New York: W. W. Norton, 2008.

Golembe Associates, Inc. *Impact of Closure of Craig Air Force Base on the Dallas County Economy, and Comparison with the Effects of Closure of Other Undergraduate Pilot Training Bases*. Washington, DC: Golembe Associates, 1976.

Graham, Patterson Toby. *A Right to Read: Segregation and Civil Rights in Alabama's Public Libraries, 1900–1965*. Tuscaloosa: University of Alabama Press, 2002.

Grim, Valerie. "Between Forty Acres and a Class Action Lawsuit: Black Farmers, Civil Rights, and Protest against the U.S. Department of Agriculture, 1997–2010." In *Beyond Forty Acres and a Mule: African American Landowning Families since Reconstruction*, edited by Debra A. Reid and Evan P. Bennett, 271–298. Gainesville: University Press of Florida, 2012.

Grossman, James R. *Land of Hope: Chicago, Black Southerners and the Great Migration*. Chicago: University of Chicago Press, 1989.

Gutterman, David S. "Obama Fought the Battle of Jericho—and His Story Came Tumbling Down." *Theory and Event* 16 (2013).

Hahn, Steven. *A Nation under Our Feet: Black Politics in the Rural South from Slavery through the Great Migration*. Cambridge, MA: Belknap Press of Harvard University Press, 2003.

Hall, Jacquelyn Dowd. "The Long Civil Rights Movement and the Political Uses of the Past." *Journal of American History* 91 (March 2005): 1233–1263.

Hall, Jacquelyn Dowd, Mary Murphy, James Leloudis, Robert Korstand, Lu Ann Jones, and Christopher B. Daly. *Like a Family: The Making of a Southern Cotton Mill World*. Chapel Hill: University of North Carolina Press, 1987.

Hall, Prathia. "Bloody Sunday." In *Hands on the Freedom Plow: Personal Accounts by Women in SNCC*, edited by Faith Holsaert, Martha Prescod Norman Noonan, Judy Richardson, Betty Garman Robinson, Jean Smith Young, and Dorothy M. Zellner, 470–472. Urbana: University of Illinois Press, 2010.

Hamilton, G. P. *Beacon Lights of the Race*. Memphis, TN: F. H. Clarke and Brother, 1911.

Hampton, Henry, ed. *Voices of Freedom: An Oral History of the Civil Rights Movement from the 1950s through the 1980s*. New York: Bantam Books, 1990.

Hardy, John. *Selma: Her Institutions, and Her Men*. Selma, AL: Times Book and Job Office, 1879.

Hart, John Fraser. *The Land That Feeds Us*. New York: W. W. Norton, 1991.

Heinicke, Craig, and Wayne A. Grove. "'Machinery Has Completely Taken Over': The Diffusion of the Mechanical Cotton Picker, 1949–1964." *Journal of Interdisciplinary History* 39 (Summer 2008): 65–96.

Hereford, Robert Scott. "A Study of Selma and Dallas County, Alabama, 1930–1970." Master's thesis, University of Georgia, 1992.

Hersey, Mark D. *My Work Is That of Conservation: An Environmental Biography of George Washington Carver*. Athens: University of Georgia Press, 2011.

Higginbotham, Evelyn Brooks. *Righteous Discontent: The Women's Movement in the Black Baptist Church, 1880–1920*. Cambridge, MA: Harvard University Press, 1993.

Hogan, Wesley. *Many Minds, One Heart: SNCC's Dream for a New America*. Chapel Hill: University of North Carolina Press, 2007.

Holsaert, Faith S., Martha Prescod, Norman Noonan, Judy Richardson, Betty Garman Robinson, Jean Smith Young, and Dorothy M. Zellner, eds. *Hands on the Freedom Plow: Personal Accounts by Women in SNCC*. Urbana: University of Illinois Press, 2009.

Hunter, Tera. *To 'Joy My Freedom: Southern Black Women's Lives and Labors after the Civil War*. Cambridge, MA: Harvard University Press, 1997.

Jackson, Richie Jean Sherrod. *House by the Side of the Road: The Selma Civil Rights Movement*. Tuscaloosa: University of Alabama Press, 2011.

Jackson, Kenneth T. *Crabgrass Frontier: The Suburbanization of the United States*. New York: Oxford University Press, 1985.

Jackson, Walter M. *The Story of Selma*. Birmingham, AL: Birmingham Printing Co., 1954.

James, Rawn. *The Double V: How Wars, Protest, and Harry Truman Desegregated America's Military*. New York: Bloomsbury, 2013.

Jeffries, Hasan Kwame. *Bloody Lowndes: Civil Rights and Black Power in Alabama's Black Belt*. New York: New York University Press, 2009.

John T. Morgan Academy. Yearbook, 1969. Selma Public Library, Selma, Alabama.

Johnson, Charles S. *Shadow of the Plantation*. Chicago: University of Chicago Press, 1934.

Johnson, Kimberley S. *Reforming Jim Crow: Southern Politics and State in the Age before Brown*. New York: Oxford University Press, 2010.

Jonce, S., letter to U.S. district attorney requesting investigation of Ku Klux Klan, December 5, 1924. Department of Justice, RG 60, National Archives and Records Administration. http://research.archives.gov/description /6857747.

Katznelson, Ira. *Fear Itself: The New Deal and the Origins of Our Time*. New York: Liveright, 2013.

Kelley, Robin D. G. *Hammer and Hoe: Alabama Communists during the Great Depression*. Chapel Hill: University of North Carolina Press, 1982.

Kennedy, David. *Over Here: The First World War and American Society*. Oxford: Oxford University Press, 2004.

Kirby, Jack Temple. *Rural Worlds Lost: The American South, 1920–1960*. Baton Rouge: Louisiana State University Press, 1987.

Kluger, Richard. *Simple Justice: The History of Brown v. Board of Education and Black America's Struggle for Equality*. New York: Vintage Books, 1975.

Korstad, Robert Rodgers. *Civil Rights Unionism: Tobacco Workers and the Struggle for Democracy in the Mid-Twentieth-Century South*. Chapel Hill: University of North Carolina Press, 2003.

Kruse, Kevin M. *White Flight: Atlanta and the Making of Modern Conservatism*. Princeton, NJ: Princeton University Press, 2005.

Kruse, Kevin M., and Stephen Tuck, eds. *Fog of War: The Second World War and the Civil Rights Movement*. New York: Oxford University Press, 2012.

Lafayette, Bernard, Jr., and Kathryn Johnson. *In Peace and Freedom: My Journey in Selma*. Lexington: University Press of Kentucky, 2013.

Lassiter, Matthew D. *The Silent Majority: Suburban Politics in the Sunbelt South*. Princeton, NJ: Princeton University Press, 2006.

Lawson, Steven F. "The Selma Movement and the Voting Rights Act of 1965." In *Civil Rights since 1787: A Reader on the Civil Rights Struggle*, edited by Jonathan Birnbaum and Clarence Taylor, 539–545. New York: New York University Press, 2000.

Leighninger, Robert D. *Long-Range Public Investment: The Forgotten Legacy of the New Deal*. Columbia: University of South Carolina Press, 2007.

Lentz-Smith, Adriane. *Freedom Struggles: African Americans and World War I*. Cambridge, MA: Harvard University Press, 2009.

Lichter, Daniel T. "Race and Unemployment: Black Employment Hardship in the Rural South." In *The Rural South in Crisis: Challenges for the Future*, edited by Lionel Beaulieu, 181–197. Boulder, CO: Westview, 1988.

Littleton, Dowe. "The Alabama Council of Defense, 1917–1918." In *The Great War in the Heart of Dixie: Alabama during World War I*, edited by Martin T. Olliff, 152–168. Tuscaloosa: University of Alabama Press, 2008.

Longnecker, Stephen. *Selma's Peacemaker: Ralph Smeltzer and Civil Rights Mediation*. Philadelphia: Temple University Press, 1987.

Lyson, Thomas A. *Two Sides to the Sunbelt: The Growing Divergence between the Rural and Urban South*. New York: Praeger, 1989.

MacLean, Nancy. *Behind the Mask of Chivalry: The Making of the Second Ku Klux Klan*. New York: Oxford University Press, 1994.

Manis, Andrew. *A Fire You Can't Put Out: The Civil Rights Life of Birmingham's Reverend Fred Shuttlesworth*. Tuscaloosa: University of Alabama Press, 1999.

Marks, Carole. *Farewell, We're Good and Gone: The Great Black Migration*. Bloomington: Indiana University Press, 1989.

May, Gary. *Bending toward Justice: The Voting Rights Act and the Transformation of American Democracy*. New York: Basic Books, 2013.

———. *The Informant: The FBI, the Ku Klux Klan, and the Murder of Viola Liuzzo*. New Haven, CT: Yale University Press, 2005.

McGerr, Michael. *A Fierce Discontent: The Rise and Fall of the Progressive Movement in America, 1870–1920*. New York: Free Press, 2003.

McGuire, Danielle L. *At the Dark End of the Street: Black Women, Rape, and Resistance—a New History of the Civil Rights Movement from Rosa Parks to the Rise of Black Power*. New York: Alfred A. Knopf, 2010.

Meyer, Darrel C., and the Alabama-Tombigbee Regional Commission. *Downtown Selma Plan*. Camden, AL: Alabama-Tombigbee Regional Commission, 1976.

Mitchell, Erin Goseer. *Born Colored: Life before Bloody Sunday*. Chicago: Ampersand, 2006.

Mitchell, Mildred. "California Cotton Mill Memories and Selma Historical Highlights." Unpublished paper, 1990.

Mjagkij, Nina. *Loyalty in Time of Trial: The African American Experience in World War I.* Lanham, MD: Rowman and Littlefield, 2011.

Moore, Albert Burton. *History of Alabama and Her People.* Chicago: The American Historical Society, 1927.

Moss, Benjamin Lawrence. *The Boll Weevil Problem: An Analysis of Its Significance to the Southern Farmer and Business Man.* Birmingham, AL: Progressive Farmer, 1914.

Musgrove, George Derek. *Rumor, Repression, and Racial Politics: How the Harassment of Black Elected Officials Shaped Post-Civil Rights America.* Athens: University of Georgia Press, 2012.

Myrdal, Gunnar. *An American Dilemma: The Negro Problem and Modern Democracy.* New York: Harper and Brothers, 1944.

Nickerson, Michelle, and Darren Dochuk, eds. *Sunbelt Rising: The Politics of Place, Space, and Region.* Philadelphia: University of Pennsylvania Press, 2011.

Norrell, Robert J. *Reaping the Whirlwind: The Civil Rights Movement in Tuskegee.* Chapel Hill: University of North Carolina Press, 1998.

Noonan, Martha Prescod Norman. "Captured by the Movement." In *Hands on the Freedom Plow: Personal Accounts by Women in SNCC,* edited by Faith Holsaert, Martha Prescod Norman Noonan, Judy Richardson, Betty Garman Robinson, Jean Smith Young, and Dorothy M. Zellner, 483–503. Urbana: University of Illinois Press, 2010.

O'Connor, Brendon. *A Political History of the American Welfare System: When Ideas Have Consequences.* Lanham, MD: Rowman and Littlefield, 2004.

Official Proceedings of the Constitutional Convention of the State of Alabama, May 21st–September 3rd, 1901. Wetumpka, AL: Wetumpka Printing Co., 1940. http://www.legislature.state.al.us/aliswww/history/constitutions/1901/proceedings/1901_proceedings_vol1/cover.html.

Olde Towne Association. *Tastes of Olde Selma.* Selma, AL: Olde Towne Association, 2003.

Orleck, Annelise. *Storming Caesars Palace: How Black Mothers Fought Their Own War on Poverty.* Boston: Beacon, 2005.

Ortiz, Paul. *Emancipation Betrayed: The Hidden History of Black Organizing and White Violence in Florida from Reconstruction to the Bloody Election of 1920.* Berkeley: University of California Press, 2005.

Patterson, James T. *The Eve of Destruction: How 1965 Transformed America.* New York: Basic Books, 2012.

Payne, Charles. *I've Got the Light of Freedom: The Organizing Tradition and the Mississippi Freedom Struggle.* Berkeley: University of California Press, 1995.

Peck, Abraham J. "The Other 'Peculiar Institution': Jews and Judaism in the Nineteenth Century South." *Modern Judaism* 7 (February 1987): 99–114.

People's Bank and Trust Company. *Historic Selma and Dallas County*. Selma, AL: People's Bank and Trust Company, 1976.

Perkinson, Robert. *Texas Tough: The Rise of America's Prison Empire*. New York: Metropolitan Books, 2010.

Perman, Michael. *Pursuit of Unity: A Political History of the American South*. Chapel Hill: University of North Carolina Press, 2009.

Powell, Fay Bellamy. "Playtime Is Over." In *Hands on the Freedom Plow: Personal Accounts by Women in SNCC*, edited by Faith Holsaert, Martha Prescod Norman Noonan, Judy Richardson, Betty Garman Robinson, Jean Smith Young, and Dorothy M. Zellner, 473–483. Urbana: University of Illinois Press, 2010.

Ransby, Barbara. *Ella Baker and the Black Freedom Movement: A Radical Democratic Vision*. Chapel Hill: University of North Carolina Press, 2003.

Raper, Arthur. *Preface to Peasantry: A Tale of Two Black Belt Counties*. Chapel Hill: University of North Carolina Press, 1936.

Reagan, Ronald. Neshoba County Fair speech, Mississippi, August 3, 1980. Transcript of speech, *Neshoba Democrat*, November 15, 2007, http://neshobademocrat.com/Content/NEWS/News/Article/Transcript-of-Ronald-Reagan-s-1980-Neshoba-County-Fair-speech/2/297/15599.

Reese, Frederick D. Interview by Andrew M. Manis, August 8, 1981. Andrew M. Manis Oral History Interviews. Birmingham Public Library, AL.

Reformed Presbyterian Church. "Glimpses of the Missionary Operations of the Reformed Presbyterian Church to the Freedmen in Selma, Alabama and the Vicinity." Selma, AL: Knox Academy, 1911.

Reid, Debra Ann. *Reaping a Greater Harvest: African Americans, the Extension Service, and Rural Reform in Jim Crow Texas*. College Station: Texas A&M University Press, 2007.

Reid, Debra Ann, and Evan Bennett, eds. *Beyond Forty Acres and a Mule: African American Landowning Families since Reconstruction*. Gainesville: University Press of Florida, 2012.

Remnick, David. *The Bridge: The Life and Rise of Barack Obama*. New York: Alfred A. Knopf, 2010.

Rieff, Lynne Anderson. "'Rousing the People of the Land': Home Demonstration Work in the Deep South, 1914–1950." PhD diss., Auburn University, 1995.

Riser, R. Volney. *Defying Disfranchisement: Black Voting Rights Activism in the Jim Crow South, 1890–1908*. Baton Rouge: Louisiana State University Press, 2010.

R. L. Polk and Company. *Selma, Alabama, City Directory, 1909–1910*. Birmingham, AL: R. L. Polk and Company.

———. *Selma, Alabama, City Directory, 1913–1914*. Birmingham, AL: R. L. Polk and Company.

Robinson, Amelia Boynton. *Bridge across Jordan*. Washington, DC: Schiller Institute, 1991.

Rogers, William Warren. *The One-Gallused Rebellion: Agrarianism in Alabama, 1865–1896*. Baton Rouge: Louisiana State University Press, 1970.

Rogers, William Warren, Leah Rawls Atkins, Robert David Ward, and Wayne Flynt. *Alabama: The History of a Deep South State*. Tuscaloosa: University of Alabama Press, 1994.

Rolinson, Mary. *Grassroots Garveyism: The Universal Negro Improvement Association in the Rural South, 1920–1927*. Chapel Hill: University of North Carolina, 2007.

Rosenfeld, Stuart A. *After the Factories: Changing Employment Patterns in the Rural South*. Research Triangle Park, NC: Southern Growth Policies Board, 1985.

———. "The Tale of Two Souths." In *The Rural South in Crisis: Challenges for the Future*, edited by Lionel Beaulieu, 51–71. Boulder, CO: Westview, 1988.

Rubin, Morton. *Plantation County*. New Haven, CT: College and University Press, 1951.

Rubio, Philip F. *There's Always Work at the Post Office: African American Postal Workers and the Fight for Jobs, Justice, and Equality*. Chapel Hill: University of North Carolina Press, 2010.

Saunders, Robert, Jr. "World War I: Catalyst for Social Change in Alabama." In *The Great War in the Heart of Dixie: Alabama during World War I*, edited by Martin T. Olliff, 185–200. Tuscaloosa: University of Alabama Press, 2008.

Schlesinger, Arthur M., Jr. *The Coming of the New Deal, 1933–1935*. Cambridge, MA: Riverside, 1958.

Schulman, Bruce. *From Cotton Belt to Sunbelt: Federal Policy, Economic Development, and the Transformation of the South, 1938–1980*. New York: Oxford University Press, 1991.

Schultz, Mark. *The Rural Face of White Supremacy: Beyond Jim Crow*. Urbana: University of Illinois Press, 2005.

Schwalm, Leslie. *Emancipation's Diaspora: Race and Reconstruction in the Upper Midwest*. Chapel Hill: University of North Carolina Press, 2009.

———. *A Hard Fight for We: Women's Transition from Slavery to Freedom in South Carolina*. Urbana: University of Illinois Press, 1997.

Schweninger, Loren, and Alston Fitts III. "Haralson, Jeremiah." In *American National Biography Online*, February 2000. http://www.anb.org.proxy.lib.duke.edu/articles/04/04-00466.html.

Scott, Emmett T. "Letters of Negro Migrants of 1916–1918." *Journal of Negro History* 4 (July 1919): 290–340.

Self, Robert O. *American Babylon: Race and the Struggle for Postwar Oakland*. Princeton, NJ: Princeton University Press, 2003.

Shaw, Nate, and Theodore Rosengarten. *All God's Dangers: The Life of Nate Shaw*. Chicago: University of Chicago Press, 1974.

Shoemaker, Rebecca S. *The White Court: Justices, Rulings, and Legacy*. Santa Barbara, CA: ABC-CLIO, 2004.

Sinclair, Upton. *The Jungle*. New York: The Viking Press, 1946.

Sisk, Glenn N. "Alabama Black Belt: A Social History, 1875–1917." PhD diss., Duke University, 1951.

———. "The Educational Awakening, and Its Effects upon the Black Belt, 1900–1917." *Journal of Negro Education* 25 (spring 1956): 191–196.

———. "Negro Education in the Black Belt, 1875–1900." *Journal of Negro Education* 22 (spring 1953): 126–135.

Sitkoff, Harvard. *A New Deal for Blacks: The Emergence of Civil Rights as a National Issue: the Depression Decade*. New York: Oxford University Press, 1981.

Snyder, Howard. "Negro Migration and the Cotton Crop." *North American Review* 219 (January 1924): 21–29.

Solinger, Rickie. "The First Welfare Case: Money, Sex, Marriage, and White Supremacy in Selma, 1966. A Reproductive Justice Analysis." *Journal of Women's History* 22 (fall 2010): 13–38.

Southern Growth Policies Board. *Halfway Home and a Long Way to Go: The Report of the 1986 Commission on the Future of the South, Southern Growth Policies Board*. Research Triangle Park, NC: Southern Growth Policies Board, 1988.

Stanton, Mary. *From Selma to Sorrow: The Life and Death of Viola Liuzzo*. Athens: University of Georgia Press, 1998.

Stickney, Hazel Latendress. "The Conversion from Cotton to Cattle Economy in the Alabama Black Belt, 1930–1960." PhD diss., Clark University, 1961.

Strickland, Arvarh E. "The Strange Affair of the Boll Weevil: The Pest as Liberator." *Agricultural History* 68 (spring 1994): 157–168.

Sugrue, Thomas. *The Origins of the Urban Crisis: Race and Inequality in Postwar Detroit*. Princeton, NJ: Princeton University Press, 1996.

Sullivan, Patricia. *Days of Hope: Race and Democracy in the New Deal Era*. Chapel Hill: University of North Carolina Press, 1996.

———. *Lift Every Voice: The NAACP and the Making of the Civil Rights Movement*. New York: New Press, 2009.

Talese, Gay. *A Writer's Life*. New York: Alfred A. Knopf, 2006.

Thornton, J. Mills. *Dividing Lines: Municipal Politics and the Struggle for Civil Rights in Montgomery, Birmingham, and Selma*. Tuscaloosa: University of Alabama Press, 2002.

Tower, J. Allen. "Cotton Change in Alabama, 1879–1946." *Economic Geography* 26 (January 1950): 6–28.

Trend, M. G. Hudson, and Auburn Technical Assistance Center. *What Happens to Workers after the Plant Closes: Project Report*. Auburn, AL: Auburn Technical Assistance Center, Auburn University, 1987.

Troy, Gil. *Morning in America: How Ronald Reagan Invented the 1980s*. Princeton, NJ: Princeton University Press, 2005.

Tullos, Allen. *Alabama Getaway: The Political Imaginary and the Heart of Dixie*. Athens: University of Georgia Press, 2011.

Tyson, Timothy B. *Radio Free Dixie: Robert F. Williams and the Roots of Black Power*. Chapel Hill: University of North Carolina Press, 1999.

University of Alabama, Office of Economic and Community Affairs. *Selma/Dallas County Economic Development Planning Report*. Tuscaloosa: University of Alabama, 1986.

U.S. Commission on Civil Rights, and Paul Good. *Cycle to Nowhere*. Washington: U.S. Commission on Civil Rights, 1968.

U.S. Congress, House Committee on Woman Suffrage. *Extending the Right of Suffrage to Women: Hearings before the Committee on Woman Suffrage*. House of Representatives, Sixty-fifth Congress, Second Session on H. J. Res 200. January 3, 4, 5, and 7, 1918. Washington, DC: U.S. Government Printing Office, 1918.

U.S. Department of Commerce, Bureau of the Census. *U.S. Census of Agriculture: 1935. Vol. 1, pt. 21, Statistics for Counties, Alabama*. Washington DC: U.S. Government Printing Office, 1936.

——. *U.S. Census of Agriculture: 1945. Vol. 1, pt. 21, Statistics for Counties, Alabama*. Washington, DC: U.S. Government Printing Office, 1948.

——. *U.S. Census of Agriculture: 1950. Vol. 1, pt. 21, Counties and State Economic Areas, Alabama*. Washington, DC: U.S. Government Printing Office, 1952.

——. *U.S. Census of Agriculture: 1959. Vol. 1, pt. 32, Counties and State Economic Areas, Alabama*. Washington, DC: U.S. Government Printing Office, 1960.

——. *U.S. Census of Agriculture: 1964. Vol. 1, pt. 32, Statistics for the State and Counties, Alabama*. Washington, DC: U.S. Government Printing Office, 1968.

——. *U.S. Census of Agriculture: 1969. Vol. 1, pt. 32, Area Reports, Alabama*. Washington, DC: U.S. Government Printing Office, 1972.

——. *U.S. Census of Agriculture: 1997. Vol. 1, pt. 1, Geographic Area Series, Alabama State and County Data*. Washington, DC: U.S. Government Printing Office, 1999.

——. *U.S. Census of Housing: 1950. Vol. 1, pt. 2, General Characteristics, Alabama*. Washington, DC: U.S. Government Printing Office, 1953.

——. *U.S. Census of Housing: 1960. Vol. 1, pt. 2, States and Small Areas, Alabama—Connecticut*. Washington, DC: U.S. Government Printing Office, 1963.

——. *U.S. Census of Manufacturers: 1947. Vol. 3, Statistics by State, Alabama*. Washington, DC: U.S. Government Printing Office, 1950.

——. *U.S. Census of Manufacturers: 1972. Vol. 3, pt. 1, Area Statistics, Alabama—Montana*. Washington, DC: U.S. Government Printing Office, 1976.

——. *U.S. Census of Population: 1960. Vol. 1, pt. 2, Characteristics of the Population, Alabama*. Washington, DC: U.S. Government Printing Office, 1963.

———. *U.S. Census of Population: 1980. Vol. 1, pt. 2, Characteristics of the Population, General Social and Economic Characteristics, Alabama.* Washington, DC: U.S. Government Printing Office, 1983.

———. *U.S. Census of Population: 1990, Social and Economic Characteristics, Alabama.* Washington, DC: U.S. Government Printing Office, 1994.

———. *U.S. Census of Retail Trade: 1977. Vol. 2, pt. 1, Geographic Area Statistics, Alabama—Indiana.* Washington, DC: U.S. Government Printing Office, 1978.

———. *U.S. Census of Retail Trade: 1982. Geographic Area Series, Alabama.* Washington, DC: U.S. Government Printing Office, 1984.

U.S. Department of the Interior, National Park Service. "The Civil Rights Movement in Selma, Alabama, 1865–1972." National Register of Historic Places multiple property documentation form, May 10, 2013. http://www .nps.gov/history/nr/feature/places/pdfs/64501182.pdf.

———. "Tabernacle Baptist Church," National Register of Historic Places registration form, May 24, 2013. http://www.nps.gov/history/nr/feature /places/pdfs/13000469.pdf.

Varela, Maria. "Time to Get Ready." In *Hands on the Freedom Plow: Personal Accounts by Women in SNCC*, edited by Faith Holsaert, Martha Prescod Norman Noonan, Judy Richardson, Betty Garman Robinson, Jean Smith Young, and Dorothy M. Zellner, 552–572. Urbana: University of Illinois Press, 2010.

Vaughan, Wally G. and Mattie Campbell Davis, eds. *The Selma Campaign, 1963–1965: The Decisive Battle of the Civil Rights Movement.* Dover, MA: Majority Press, 2006.

Wallace, Jamie. "Economic History of Dallas County." Unpublished paper, 2013. In author's possession.

Ward, Jason Morgan. "A War for States' Rights": The White Supremacist Vision of Double Victory." In *Fog of War: The Second World War and the Civil Rights Movement*, edited by Kevin M. Kruse and Stephen Tuck, 126–144. New York: Oxford University Press, 2012.

———. *Defending White Democracy: The Making of a Segregationist Movement and the Remaking of Racial Politics, 1936–1965.* Chapel Hill: University of North Carolina Press, 2011.

Ward, Thomas J., Jr. "Black Hospital Movement in Alabama." In *Encyclopedia of Alabama.* Last updated July 24, 2013. http://encyclopediaofalabama.org /face/Article.jsp?id=h-2410.

Washington, Booker T. *Up from Slavery: An Autobiography.* New York: Doubleday, Page, 1901.

Webb, Samuel L. *Two-Party Politics in the One Party South: Alabama's Hill Country, 1874–1920.* Tuscaloosa: University of Alabama Press, 1997.

Webb, Sheyann. *Selma, Lord, Selma: Girlhood Memories of the Civil Rights Days.* Tuscaloosa: University of Alabama Press, 1980.

Wendt, Simon. *The Spirit and the Shotgun: Armed Resistance and the Struggle for Civil Rights.* Gainesville: University Press of Florida, 2007.

White, Deborah Gray. *Ar'n't I a Woman? Female Slaves in the Plantation South*. New York: W. W. Norton, 1985.

———. *Too Heavy a Load: Black Women in Defense of Themselves, 1894–1994*. New York: W. W. Norton, 1999.

Wilkerson, Isabel. *The Warmth of Other Suns: The Epic Story of America's Great Migration*. New York: Random House, 2010.

Williamson, Cecil. "An Interview with Selma City Council President Cecil Williamson.". YouTube video, [10:06 min], uploaded on February 16, 2012 by Selma's Truth. https://youtu.be/fKi22kx-EpM.

Wilson, Adam P. *African American Army Officers of World War I: A Vanguard of Equality in War and Beyond*. Jefferson, NC: McFarland, 2015.

Windham, Kathryn Tucker. *She: The Old Woman Who Took over My Life*. Montgomery, AL: New South Books, 2011.

Witkowski, Terrence H. "World War II Poster Campaigns: Preaching Frugality to American Consumers." *Journal of Advertising* 32 (spring 2003): 69–82.

Wofford, Harris. "A Preliminary Report on the Status of the Negro in Dallas County, Alabama." Seminar paper, Yale Law School, 1953.

Woodward, C. Vann. *Origins of the New South, 1877–1913*. Baton Rouge: Louisiana State University Press, 1951.

———. *The Strange Career of Jim Crow*. New York: Oxford University Press, 1955.

Zinn, Howard. *SNCC: The New Abolitionists*. Boston: Beacon, 1964.

INDEX

Ware, James, 238–39
War Industries Board, 35
war on drugs, 231–33
War on Poverty, 158, 162–63, 174, 176, 182–83
War Production Board, 98
Washington, Booker T., 28, 46, 251–52
Washington Post (newspaper), 229
welfare reform, 237–39
West, Mark, 235
Western Railway, 17
white supremacy: black accommodations to, 25–26; black churches, role of, 31; black labor and, 49, 134, 139–40; challenges to, 54, 119, 125, 141, 142, 156, 207; Democratic Party and, 165; Dixiecrat movement on, 119, 120–21; economic independence of blacks and, 27, 29, 40, 46–47, 59, 79; Eisenhower on, 136; fascism and, 99; Jewish residents of Selma on, 259n20; legal protection of, 10, 12, 45, 110, 118; NAACP vs., 37; New Deal on, 68, 72, 75, 85, 88, 90, 109–10; segregation and, 113, 118; violence of, 59; voting rights and, 4, 7–9, 157, 249
Wilby Theatre, 184
Wilcox County, AL, 46, 117
Williams, Carlos, 227
Williams, Clarence, 168, 174, 203
Williams, Hosea, 154
Williams, John Henry, 27

Williamson, Cecil, 178, 210–11, 235, 242, 245, 246
Wilson, B. Frank, 148
Wilson, George, 87
Wilson, Woodrow, 34–35
Wimberly, Louretta, 113
Windham, Kathryn, 130
Wise, Phillip, 198–99
Wofford, Harris, 124, 135–36
Wood, Milton, 87
Wood, Robert, 93
Works Progress Administration (WPA), 81, 85, 88, 89–90, 102–3, 111
World War I (1914–1918), 34–38; African Americans soldiers, 35–36, 98–99; black migration during, 41–44; food production for, 39–42, 44; patriotism, 36–37, 41
World War II (1939–1945), food production for, 99–100, 105; mobilization, 96–99, 119; patriotism, 99
WPA. *See* Works Progress Administration
Wright, Jack, 195

Yelder, Joe, 91, 184–85
YMCA, 131, 229
Young, Andrew, 151

Zetwick, Robert, 141
Ziegler Packing Company, 105, 139
Ziter, Nelson, 113